The Granta Book of Reportage

Granta Books

London

Granta Publications, 2/3 Hanover Yard, London N1 8BE

First published in Great Britain by Granta Books 1993
This edition published by Granta Books 1998

A CIP catalogue record for this book is
available from the British Library.

1 3 5 7 9 10 8 6 4 2

Printed and bound in Great Britain by Mackays of Chatham PLC

Introduction

It may say something about the place accorded to journalism in British culture that the title of this collection has had to borrow a French word, and a French word spoken in the French way. Reportage is not pronounced like garbage and verbiage (though it can be both those things) but as *reppawrtahj*, the Frenchness giving it a dignity and literary acceptability denied it by the English *reporting*. This is annoying. The countries that speak and write in the English language have done more for the craft of reporting/reportage than any others and many of its finest exemplars are British or North American, or from those parts of the world which have been particularly influenced by the newspapers and magazines of London and New York rather than Paris or Rome. Why this should be is an interesting question, with answers that range from the former lavishness (and still unique competitiveness) of British national newspapers, to the nature of the English language itself, which is such an ally of everyday curiosity with its preference for the concrete over the abstract, the specific over the general, and (apart from the lines clearly labelled as poetry) the prosaic over the poetic. But, whatever the reason, I don't think we can doubt that it is so. If we accept that good reporting/reportage means to describe a situation with honesty, exactness and clarity, to delve into the questions *who*, *what*, *when*, *why* and *how* without losing sight of the narrative, then it's neither ethno- nor lingua-centric to assert that, with certain famous exceptions, reporting is an English-language specialism, something we're peculiarly good at. During the Falklands War, in 1982, I spent a few weeks in Uruguay, trying (unsuccessfully) from there to add to my newspaper's knowledge about the state of play among the enemy in Argentina, which was just across the River Plate. Every morning that day's newspapers would arrive from Buenos Aires and we would get them translated from the Spanish. The reports were long by the standards of British newspapers and it seemed impossible that they could not contain interesting information. This was, however, hard to come by. The translator would give up half-way through. 'It's just the usual,' he'd say. 'Metaphors, and more metaphors.'

So why not play to local strengths and call it the *Granta Book of*

Reporting? There are some good reasons for the French alternative, and some which reflect poorly on British journalism and the way we now think of it. 'Reporting' seems too narrow a word, suggesting writing which comes exclusively from 'reporters'; in this way the *Granta Book of Reporting* could be mistaken for a professional manual ('Always get the main point of the story in your first paragraph') rather than a collection of eye-witness accounts and investigations, which come in this book from other sorts of writers – poets, novelists – as well as from people who have made their living from writing them. 'Reportage' has that nice sense of the thing seen, the event observed (which may be because its original use in English was confined to documentary photography, a French specialism). 'Reporting', on the other hand, suggests a too well-lunched man or woman with a notebook taking down the more relevant points of what he or she is hearing at a public meeting or on the telephone to a soap star. But there, in that last sentence, you can already detect signs of the British problem: distaste.

Reporting never did have much in the way of social status in Britain, where deference and privacy were valued more than 'people poking their noses in', where a dutiful journalist from the local weekly had the same public standing as a gumshoe. Over the past twenty years, however, the esteem of reporters has slithered even further down the scale – from 'hacks' to 'reptiles'. Newspapers and news organizations are now part of the 'media industry' and a subdivision of showbusiness; the old distinctions between the serious and the frivolous – tabloid, middle-market, broadsheet – have largely broken down; 'stories' are important because they sell newspapers – therefore they will be bought, stolen, distorted, spun (as in 'Let's give it a bit more top-spin'), sentimentalized, over-dramatized and – should all else fail – invented, to woo a public which has ten national dailies to choose from, and another nine on a Sunday. When Rupert Murdoch decided in 1994 that newspapers should have an 'inconsequential' price to the customer, one of the results in the price war that ensued was that newspapers became less . . . consequential. On the one hand, some of them were cheaper. On the other, it seemed to matter less if you read one or not. Perhaps the public had never taken newspapers quite so seriously as we who worked for them might have wanted. Now it began to see them (or some of them) more plainly as crap, and sometimes poisonous crap. This had no obvious effect on their circulations, but when the Princess of Wales died in 1997 there came an unprecedented moment of public opposition and hostility, which, in its excitable unreason (newspapers were blamed for killing the Princess; they didn't), owed a lot to the media which an angry public affected to despise.

Meanwhile, the craft of what the late Martha Gellhorn called 'serious, careful, honest journalism' has entered its own small crisis. Newspapers cutting their costs to meet reductions in cover-price revenue could afford fewer reporters, especially those based abroad with their overheads of house-rents and air fares. Executives did sums. Foreign staffs were the obvious target, but then the exercise would move closer to home. A reasonably productive staff reporter on a weekly might write, say, 2,000 words a week for, say, 45 weeks of the year (six weeks for holiday and one for 'flu); a total of, say, 90,000 words, many of which might never appear in the newspaper because they were judged to be unimportant or uninteresting, or, space being a problem, less important and less interesting than words written by somebody else that week. The cost of these words would only start with the reporter's salary, say, £40,000. There would be expenses for stays in hotels, train fares, car hire, taxis to meet 'contacts', lunches with 'contacts', the company's National Insurance and pension contributions, the reporter's share of general office overheads in terms of heat, light, telephones, computer terminals, desks and desk space, the generous maternity leave, the subsidized canteen. What were we looking at here? Perhaps a total annual cost to the company of £60,000 for perhaps 80,000 published words. More than a dollar a word! Why, you might get Gore Vidal at that rate.

The crudest of sums, this business of words per sterling unit; a guide to cost not value. The less visible benefits of the staff reporter are availability, commitment, persistence, skill, an expertise and authority in such subjects as schools, religion, science or China. These were often discounted. After all, how many actual or potential readers cared about China? Or religion? What did the market research show? It showed that many readers barely glanced at a foreign news page (and that more people would read a story with the word 'Diana' in the headline than with the word 'Janet'). Furthermore, you could contract a freelance reporter or, better still, a freelance columnist (cheaper; columnists stay home) and fill the same space for two thirds of the cost or less. The old C.P. Scott dictum on the *Manchester Guardian* had been: 'Comment is free, but facts are sacred.' Now there was a paraphrase: 'Comment is cheap, but facts are rather expensive.'

That, in rough outline, was the economic case against reporting as I remember it during my last months as editor of the *Independent on Sunday* in 1995 (a case, I must admit, that I often made in my own head when faced with a shrinking budget[1]). But reporting, the serious end of it, is also in trouble more generally. Something in the climate mitigates against those Gellhorn words 'honest', 'careful', 'thoughtful'. Today a spectre haunts the editorial floor – the spectre of the reader's boredom, the viewer's lassitude. If customers are to stay with the product, they need, or are thought to need, a diet of surprise, pace, cuts-to-the-chase, playfulness, provocation, drama, 'human interest'. Britain's popular press has had a shrewd sense of its mass audience since the days of Lord Northcliffe, but that sense now infects every newspaper and television bulletin; in an unforgiving market, all of them perceive the need to be more popular and therefore more dramatic, playful and 'human'. With the possible exception of the *Financial Times*, no British newspaper now has the chill authority of the *New York Times*. All of them are more intimate with their audience. A sort of warmth has been achieved at the expense of credibility and trust.

One effect has been to demote 'straight' reporting – the kind of reporting which relies on accurate information for its value and interest. Another effect – less noticed – has been to encase traditional broadsheet journalism within the borrowed tricks of tabloid presentation. This is not just a case of larger headline type.[2] Something more complicated has occurred: editors and their sub-editors have freed themselves from the reticence and rigidity of the old formula: a headline (with a verb) followed by a byline and the story's first paragraph. Other introductory matter now often comes between stories and headlines, allowing headlines to *sell* the story rather than simply to tell a highly compressed version of it. The result, often, is a thickened layer of editorial artifice and judgement. The writer has another voice added to his or her own, a voice which can say ho-ho, tut-tut or why-oh-why, and suggest to the reader how he should feel about what he is about to read, before he has actually read it. In terms of neutrality, it turns out that the verb was important. When in 1996 a gunman walked into a school classroom in Dunblane, Scotland, and shot dead 16 children and their teacher, the *Financial Times* was alone among British newspapers in using a strictly factual headline: DUNBLANE IN GRIEF AFTER GUNMAN KILLS 17 AT SCHOOL. Every other broadsheet carried a variant of MASSACRE OF THE INNOCENTS, and in this way articulated our sadness and outrage for us, before we could feel it.

In this case, it could be argued, the facts of the story had been made famous by television and radio since lunchtime the previous day; and neither the words 'massacre' nor 'innocents' could really be disputed. But newspapers with claims to be serious in most other countries – the USA, France, Germany, India – would not have presented the story in that way. Britain has developed a singular sort of media culture which places a high premium on excitement, controversy and sentimentality, in which information takes second place to the opinions it arouses. It was much easier, in April 1998, to know what the political factions of Northern Ireland thought of Northern Ireland's peace agreement (pages 1, 2 and 3) than to discover what the agreement itself contained (eventually arriving on page 4).

Nobody can really estimate the social consequences. Though quasi-sociological phrases such as 'dumbing-down' and 'the sentimentalization of Britain' have become common, it is never easy to disentangle the audience's effect on the product from the product's effect on the audience; which had the greater influence on the other? One of the striking features in the week leading up to the funeral of Diana, Princess of Wales was how the media and the public seemed to reinforce one another; the media would report large crowds outside London's royal palaces and in consequence the crowds the next day would be even larger, cause and effect, effect and cause, like a fuel-less machine driven by perpetual motion. There was, as several reports remarked, the feel of a new religion about these crowds. When I saw them on television I thought of something I'd read ten years before, in Professor John Carey's excellent introduction to the *Faber Book of Reportage* (1987). The advent of mass communication in the 19th century, Carey wrote, represented, arguably, 'the greatest change in human consciousness that has taken place in human history'. Once the 'permanent backdrop' to humankind's existence had been religion. Now, Carey wrote, it was reportage:

> Reportage supplies modern man with a constant and reassuring sense of events going on beyond his immediate horizon (reassuring even, or particularly, when the events themselves are terrible, since they then contrast more comfortingly with the reader's supposed safety). Reportage provides modern man, too, with a release from his trivial routines, and a habitual daily illusion of communication with a reality greater than himself . . . When we view reportage as the natural successor to religion, it helps us to understand why it should be so profoundly taken up with the subject of death, in its various forms of murder, massacre, accident, natural catastrophe and warfare.

The Princess of Wales fits the bill perfectly here: religions need saints to celebrate, and the princess also supplied three other religious ingredients that Carey forgot to mention, those of beauty, wonder and ultimate mystery (for who, apart from the prince, can really know the princess?). But if reportage is a religious substitute, are reporters the new priests?

Some are, in this sense: that they believe they know 'the truth' and have a duty to tell it in the belief that it will change the situation, often one of human suffering, that they describe. Sometimes their reports do achieve this; their directness and compassion (in what Martin Bell, the Member of Parliament and former BBC correspondent, has called 'the journalism of attachment') are rewarded by corrections to government policy or plane-loads of food directed to areas of famine. The danger, however, is that dripping sympathy and a certain weary anger with the injustices of the world become part and parcel of the reporter's kit and reputation. It is easy for a reporter to imply that something must be done – who wants to see children die? – but much harder for the reporter's audience to know what *can* be done, or how they are to do it, the world being a complicated place. Also, the impression may grow that this is only a particular reporter's *modus operandi*, a professional strategy to show him as a very decent guy, a route to the celebrity which in the end is the enemy of good reporting; the messenger has become more important than the message. He seems pious and rather full of himself. The viewer searches for the rubber brick to aim at the television set.

These days such people are hardly a fashion in British print journalism – mainly they crop up on TV – and I mention them mainly because their style is often said to be 'reporting at its best' by people who lament the passing of some Golden Age of passionate commitment. When was this? Some say the *Sunday Times* under the editorship of Harold Evans in the 1970s, or the *Daily Mirror* around the same time. The name of James Cameron is often mentioned, and that of Martha Gellhorn. But all these institutions and people were different from each other. The best journalism in the *Sunday Times* of that epoch did not expect strong men to weep in the street, as the *Daily Mirror*'s did. It may have pursued justice in its campaigns, but the stories themselves were carefully constructed and rather dispassionate. James Cameron, a wonderful reporter in his day, in the end grew tiresome in his world-weary omniscience. Gellhorn, who was a reporter for more than 50 years, never became like that. She wrote in 1987 when she was late in her seventies:

A writer publishes to be read; then hopes the readers are affected by the words, hopes that their opinions are changed or strengthened or enlarged, or that readers are pushed to notice something they had not stopped to notice before. All my reporting life, I have thrown small pebbles into a very large pond, and have no way of knowing whether any pebble caused the slightest ripple. I don't need to worry about that. My responsibility was the effort.

I hope that the pieces in this book exemplify Gellhorn's conviction that honourable reporting should be serious, careful and honest (I can only hope that they do, because one of them is my own). But many of them are also more than those things. They are witty, vivid, surprising, sometimes angry. All appeared in *Granta* magazine between 1983 and 1992, the last decade of the Cold War, which has a direct or indirect bearing on most of them. Very few could have been published in a newspaper – length alone would have ruled that out, and some were written several years after the events they describe.

Are they to be described as 'writing' in the sense of literature, or as 'journalism'? I have never quite known where one begins and the other ends and, as Professor Carey pointed out in 1987, the question is neither interesting nor meaningful – literature not being an 'objectively ascertainable category to which certain works naturally belong' but more or less what 'culture-controlling groups' decide it is. Carey went on:

> The question worth asking therefore is not whether reportage is literature, but why intellectuals and literary institutions have generally been so keen to deny it that status. Resentment of the masses, who are regarded as reportage's audience, is plainly a factor in the development of this prejudice . . . But the disparagement of reportage also reflects a wish to promote the imaginary above the real. Works of imagination are, it is maintained, inherently superior, and have a spiritual value absent from 'journalism'. The creative artist is in touch with truths higher than the actual, which give him exclusive entry into the soul of man. Such convictions seem to represent a residue of magical thinking.

Since that was written, the 'culture-controlling groups' have become more catholic, and allowed certain kinds of non-fictional writing – travel, memoir, books of non-fiction posing as fiction and vice versa – into the fold. But I guess reportage still stands at the gates. Perhaps it should stay there; perhaps the word literature would taint it, diminish its purpose. Reportage tends to come, after all, from a different kind of personality; the kind that gives the initial process of *finding out* an equal, or even a greater, priority to the later process of shaping the information discovered – the scene witnessed, the words spoken – into sentences fit for a page.

Seven of the 13 contributors to this anthology were or are reporters. In newsrooms throughout Britain many excellent ones remain, sometimes wondering about their shrinking number, the continuing torrent of columnists ('Yesterday I woke up and thought . . .'), the increase in other job titles (senior writer, assistant policy editor, chief interviewer), and the strange, sad fact that so few people seem willing to call themselves a reporter any more. This book is dedicated to them, and to the idea that the proper scrutiny of society depends on their work.

Ian Jack, April 1998

---

1 In 1993, more than 380 people worked in the editorial departments of the *Independent* and the *Independent on Sunday*. By 1998, the number had shrunk by one third.

2 Though that case can certainly be made; for example, the size of the tabloid *Daily Mirror*'s headline type to announce the sinking of the *Titanic*, in 1912, is half the size of the broadsheet *Guardian*'s headline type to announce the possibility of a small reshuffle of the British Cabinet, in 1998.

CONTENTS

Ryszard Kapuściński

The Soccer War

Luis Suarez said there was going to be a war, and I believed whatever Luis said. We were staying together in Mexico. Luis was giving me a lesson in Latin America: what it is and how to understand it. He could foresee many events. In his time he had predicted the fall of Goulart in Brazil, the fall of Bosch in the Dominican Republic and of Jimenez in Venezuela. Long before the return of Perón he believed that the old *caudillo* would again become president of Argentina; he foretold the sudden death of the Haitian dictator François Duvalier at a time when everybody said Papa Doc had many years left. Luis knew how to pick his way through Latin politics, in which amateurs like me got bogged down and blundered helplessly with each step.

This time Luis announced his belief that there would be a war after putting down the newspaper in which he had read a report on the soccer match between the Honduran and Salvadoran national teams. The two countries were playing for the right to take part in the 1970 World Cup in Mexico.

The first match was held on Sunday 8 June 1969, in the Honduran capital, Tegucigalpa.

Nobody in the world paid any attention.

The Salvadoran team arrived in Tegucigalpa on Saturday and spent a sleepless night in their hotel. The team could not sleep because it was the target of psychological warfare waged by the Honduran fans. A swarm of people encircled the hotel. The crowd threw stones at the windows and beat sheets of tin and empty barrels with sticks. They set off one string of firecrackers after another. They leaned on the horns of cars parked in front of the hotel. The fans whistled, screamed and sent up hostile chants. This went on all night. The idea was that a sleepy, edgy, exhausted team would be bound to lose. In Latin America these are common practices.

The next day Honduras defeated the sleepless El Salvador squad one-nil.

Eighteen-year-old Amelia Bolanios was sitting in front of the television in El Salvador when the Honduran striker Roberto Cardona scored the winning goal in the final minute. She got up and ran to the desk which contained her father's pistol in a drawer. She then shot herself in the heart. 'The young girl could

3

not bear to see her fatherland brought to its knees,' wrote the Salvadoran newspaper *El Nacional* the next day. The whole capital took part in the televised funeral of Amelia Bolanios. An army honour guard marched with a flag at the head of the procession. The president of the republic and his ministers walked behind the flag-draped coffin. Behind the government came the Salvadoran soccer eleven who, booed, laughed at, and spat on at the Tegucigalpa airport, had returned to El Salvador on a special flight that morning.

But the return match of the series took place in San Salvador, the beautifully named Flor Blanca stadium, a week later. This time it was the Honduran team that spent a sleepless night. The screaming crowd of fans broke all the windows in the hotel and threw rotten eggs, dead rats and stinking rags inside. The players were taken to the match in armoured cars of the First Salvadoran Mechanized Division—which saved them from revenge and bloodshed at the hands of the mob that lined the route, holding up portraits of the national heroine Amelia Bolanios.

The army surrounded the ground. On the pitch stood a cordon of soldiers from a crack regiment of the *Guardia Nacional*, armed with sub-machine-guns. During the playing of the Honduran national anthem the crowd roared and whistled. Next, instead of the Honduran flag—which had been burnt before the eyes of the spectators, driving them mad with joy—the hosts ran a dirty, tattered dishrag up the flag-pole. Under such conditions the players from Tegucigalpa did not, understandably, have their minds on the game. They had their minds on getting out alive. 'We're awfully lucky that we lost,' said the visiting coach, Mario Griffin, with relief.

El Salvador prevailed, three-nil.

The same armoured cars carried the Honduran team straight from the playing field to the airport. A worse fate awaited the visiting fans. Kicked and beaten, they fled towards the border. Two of them died. Scores landed in hospital. One hundred and fifty of the visitors' cars were burned. The border between the two states was closed a few hours later.

Luis read about all of this in the newspaper and said that there was going to be a war. He had been a reporter for a long time and he knew his beat.

In Latin America, he said, the border between soccer and politics is vague. There is a long list of governments that have fallen or been overthrown after the defeat of the national team. Players on the losing team are denounced in the press as traitors. When Brazil won the World Cup in Mexico, an exiled Brazilian colleague of mine was heartbroken: 'The military right wing,' he said, 'can be assured of at least five more years of peaceful rule.' On the way to the title, Brazil beat England. In an article with the headline 'Jesus Defends Brazil', the Rio de Janeiro paper *Jornal dos Sportes* explained the victory thus: 'Whenever the ball flew towards our goal and a score seemed inevitable, Jesus reached his foot out of the clouds and cleared the ball.' Drawings accompanied the article, illustrating the supernatural intervention.

Anyone at the stadium can lose his life. Take the match that Mexico lost to Peru, two-one. An embittered Mexican fan shouted in an ironic tone, '*Viva* Mexico!' A moment later he was dead, massacred by the crowd. But sometimes the heightened emotions find an outlet in other ways. After Mexico beat Belgium one-nil, Augusto Mariaga, the warden of a maximum-security prison in Chilpancingo (Guerrero State, Mexico), became delirious with joy and ran around firing a pistol into the air and shouting, '*Viva* Mexico!' He opened all the cells, releasing 142 dangerous hardened criminals. A court acquitted him later, as, according to the verdict, he had 'acted in patriotic exaltation.'

'Do you think it's worth going to Honduras?' I asked Luis, who was then editing the serious and influential weekly *Siempre*.

'I think it's worth it,' he answered. 'Something's bound to happen.'

I was in Tegucigalpa the next morning.

At dusk a plane flew over Tegucigalpa and dropped a bomb. Everybody heard it. The nearby mountains echoed its violent blast so that some said later that a whole series of bombs had been dropped. Panic swept the city. People fled home; merchants closed their shops. Cars were abandoned in the middle of the street. A woman ran along the pavement, crying, 'My child! My child!' Then silence fell and everything became still. It was as if the city had died. The lights went out and Tegucigalpa sank into darkness.

I hurried to the hotel, burst into my room, fed a piece of paper into the typewriter and tried to write a dispatch to Warsaw. I was trying to move fast because I knew that at that moment I was the only foreign correspondent there and that I could be the first to inform the world about the outbreak of the war in Central America. But it was pitch dark in the room and I couldn't see anything. I felt my way downstairs to the reception desk, where I was lent a candle. I went back upstairs, lit the candle and turned on my transistor radio. The announcer was reading a communiqué from the Honduran government about the commencement of hostilities with El Salvador. Then came the news that the Salvadoran army was attacking Honduras all along the front line.

I began to write:

TEGUCIGALPA (HONDURAS) PAP JULY 14 VIA TROPICAL RADIO RCA TODAY AT 6 PM WAR BEGAN BETWEEN EL SALVADOR AND HONDURAS SALVADORAN AIR FORCE BOMBARDED FOUR HONDURAN CITIES STOP AT SAME TIME SALVADORAN ARMY CROSSED HONDURAN BORDER ATTEMPTING TO PENETRATE DEEP INTO COUNTRY STOP IN RESPONSE TO AGGRESSION HONDURAN AIR FORCE BOMBARDED IMPORTANT SALVADORAN INDUSTRIAL AND STRATEGIC TARGETS AND GROUND FORCES BEGAN DEFENSIVE ACTION

At this moment someone in the street started shouting '*Apaga la luz!*' ('Turn off the light!') over and over, more and more loudly with increasing agitation. I blew out the candle. I went on typing blind, by touch, striking a match over the keys every now and then.

RADIO REPORTS FIGHTING UNDERWAY ALONG FULL LENGTH OF FRONT AND THAT HONDURAN ARMY IS INFLICTING HEAVY LOSSES ON SALVADORAN ARMY STOP GOVERNMENT HAS CALLED WHOLE POPULATION TO DEFENCE OF ENDANGERED NATION AND APPEALED TO UN FOR CONDEMNATION OF ATTACK

I carried the dispatch downstairs, found the owner of the hotel and began asking him to find someone to lead me to the post office. It was my first day there and I did not know Tegucigalpa at all. It is not a big city—a quarter of a million people—but it lies among hills and has a maze of crabbed streets. The owner wanted to help but he had no one to send with me and I was in a hurry. In the end he called the police. Nobody at the police station had time. So he called the fire department. Three firemen arrived in full gear, wearing helmets and carrying axes. We greeted each other in the dark; I could not see their faces. I begged them to lead me to the post office. I know Honduras well, I lied, and know that its people are renowned for their hospitality. I was sure they would not refuse me. It was very important that the world find out the truth about who started the war, who shot first and I could assure them that I had written the honest truth. The main thing now was time, and we had to hurry.

We left the hotel. It was a dark night. I could see only the outlines of the street. I do not know why we spoke in whispers. I tried to remember the way and counted my steps. I was close to a thousand when the firemen stopped and one of them knocked on a door. A voice from inside asked what we wanted. Then the door opened, but only for an instant so that the light wouldn't be seen. I was inside. They ordered me to wait: there is only one telex machine in Honduras, and the president was using it. He was engaged in an exchange with his ambassador in Washington, who would be applying to the American government for military assistance. This went on for a long time, since the president and the ambassador were using uncommonly flowery language and, besides, the connection kept breaking every so often.

After midnight I finally made contact with Warsaw. The machine typed out the number TL 813480 PAP VARSOVIA. I leapt up joyfully. The operator asked, 'Is Varsovia some country?'

'It's not a country. It's a city. The country is called *Polonia*.'

'*Polonia, Polonia*,' he repeated, but I could see that the name didn't actually interest him.

He asked Warsaw, 'HOW RECEIVED MSG BIBI?'

And Warsaw answered, 'RECEIVED OK OK GREE FOR RYSIEK TKS TKS!'

I put my arms around the operator, told him I hoped he got through the war in one piece and started back to the hotel. Barely had I set foot in the street when I realized I was lost. I found myself in terrible darkness—thick and clotted and impenetrable, as if a heavy black grease had been smeared over my eyes, and I could see nothing, not even, literally, my hands when I stretched them out in front of me. The sky must have clouded over, because the stars had disappeared and there was no light anywhere. I was alone in an unfamiliar city that, as I couldn't see it, might well have disappeared into the earth. The silence was piercing—not a voice anywhere, not a sound. I moved forward like a blind man, feeling the walls, the drainpipes and the mesh shutters over the shop windows. When I realized that my footsteps were sounding like drumbeats I went up on tiptoe. Suddenly the wall at my fingertips ended; I would have to turn into a side street. Or was it the beginning of a plaza? Or was I on a high escarpment with a long drop in front of me? I tested the ground ahead with my feet. Asphalt! I was in the middle of the street. I moved sideways and bumped into another wall. I no longer knew where the post office could be, let alone the hotel; I was floundering, but I kept going. Suddenly there was a powerful boom! I was losing my footing and was being thrown to the pavement.

I had upset a tin garbage can.

The street must have been on a slope, because the garbage can rolled away with a frightful din. In an instant I heard windows snapping open on all sides above me and hysterical, terrified whispers: '*Silencio! Silencio!*' A city that wanted the world to forget it for one night, that wanted to be alone in silence and darkness, was defending itself against being given away. As the empty garbage can clattered down the hill, more and more windows kept opening as it passed with plaintive, insistent whispers: '*Silencio! Silencio!*' But there was no way to stop the metal monster, it was like something possessed, banging against the cobblestones, smashing into lamp-posts, thundering and booming. I lay on the pavement, hugging it, frightened, sweating. I was afraid that someone would open fire in my direction. I had committed an act of treason: the enemy, unable to find the city in this darkness and silence, could now locate it by the racket of the garbage can. I had to make tracks and run. I got to my feet and found that my head was throbbing—I had struck it on the pavement when I fell—and I sprinted like a madman until I stumbled over something and fell on my face, the taste of blood in my mouth. I picked myself up and leaned against a wall. The wall arched above my head and I had to stand hunched over, feeling more and more imprisoned by a city I could not see. I watched for the light of a lantern: somebody must be looking for me, this intruder who had violated the military order not to go out at night. But there was nothing, only sepulchral silence and unviolated darkness. I crept along with my hands stretched out in front of me, bruised now and bleeding and bloody in a tattered shirt, lost in this labyrinth of walls. Centuries could have passed; I might have reached the end of the world. Suddenly a violent tropical deluge broke. Lightning illuminated the nightmare city for an instant. Standing among unknown streets I glimpsed a decrepit townhouse, a wooden shed, a street-lamp, cobble-stones. It vanished in a second. I could hear only the gush of rain and, from time to time, the whistle of wind. I was freezing, soaked, shivering all over. I felt the recess of a doorway and took cover from the downpour. Jammed between the wall and the door I tried to sleep, but without success.

An army patrol found me at dawn.

'Silly man,' a sleepy sergeant said. 'Where were you strolling on a wartime evening?' He looked me over suspiciously and wanted to take me to city headquarters. Fortunately I was carrying my papers and managed to explain what had happened. They led me to my hotel and on the way mentioned that the battle at the front had gone on all night, but that it was so far away that you couldn't hear the shooting in Tegucigalpa.

Since early morning people had been digging trenches, erecting barricades—preparing for a siege. Women were stocking up supplies and criss-crossing their windows with masking tape. People rushed through the streets directionless; an atmosphere of panic reigned. Student brigades were painting outsized slogans on walls and fences. A bubble full of graffiti had burst over Tegucigalpa, covering the walls with thousands of verses.

Ryszard Kapuściński

ONLY AN IMBECILE WORRIES
NOBODY BEATS HONDURAS

or:

PICK UP YOUR GUNS AND LET'S GO GUYS
CUT THOSE SALVADORANS DOWN TO SIZE

WE SHALL AVENGE THREE-NIL
PORFIRIO RAMOS SHOULD BE ASHAMED OF HIMSELF FOR
LIVING WITH A SALVADORAN WOMAN

ANYONE SEEING RAIMUNDO GRANADOS CALL THE POLICE
HE'S A SALVADORAN SPY

Latins are obsessed with spies, intelligence conspiracies and plots. In war, everyone is a fifth-columnist. I was not in a particularly comfortable situation: official propaganda on both sides blamed communists for every misfortune, and I was the only correspondent in the region from a socialist country. Even so, I wanted to see the war through to the end.

I went to the post office and asked the telex operator to join me for a beer. He was terrified, because, although he had a Honduran father, his mother was a citizen of El Salvador. He was a mixed national and thus among the suspects. He did not know what would happen next. All morning the police had been herding Salvadorans into provisional camps, most often set up in stadiums. Throughout Latin America, stadiums play a double role: in peacetime they are sports venues; in war they turn into concentration camps.

His name was José Malaga, and we had a drink in a restaurant near the post office. Our uncertain status had made brothers of us. Every so often José phoned his mother, who was sitting locked in her house, and said, 'Mama, everything's OK. They haven't come for me; I'm still working.'

By the afternoon the other correspondents arrived from Mexico, forty of them, my colleagues. They had flown into Guatemala and then hired a bus, because the airport in Tegucigalpa was closed. They all wanted to drive to the front. We went to the Presidential Palace, an ugly, bright blue turn-of-the-century building in the centre of the town, to arrange permission. There

10

were machine-gun nests and sandbags around the palace, and anti-aircraft guns in the courtyard. In the corridors inside, soldiers were dozing or lolling around in full battledress.

People have been making war for thousands of years, but each time it is as if it is the first war ever waged, as if everyone has started from scratch.

A captain appeared and said he was the army press spokesman. He was asked to describe the situation and he stated that they were winning all along the front and that the enemy was suffering heavy casualties.

'OK,' said the AP correspondent. 'Let's see the front.'

The Americans, the captain explained, were already there. They always go first because of their influence—and because they commanded obedience and could arrange all sorts of things. The captain said we could go the next day, and that everyone should bring two photographs.

We drove to a place where two artillery pieces stood under some trees. Cannons were firing and stacks of ord-nance were lying around. Ahead of us we could see the road that led to El Salvador. Swamp stretched along both sides of the road, and dense green bush began past the belt of swamp.

The sweaty, unshaven major charged with holding the road said we could go no further. Beyond this point both armies were in action, and it was hard to tell who was who or what belonged to which side. The bush was too thick to see anything. Two opposing units often noticed each other only at the last moment, when, wandering through the overgrowth, they met face to face. In addition, since both armies wore the same uniforms, carried the same equipment, and spoke the same language, it was difficult to distinguish friend from foe.

The major advised us to return to Tegucigalpa, because advancing might mean getting killed without even knowing who had done it. (As if that mattered, I thought.) But the television cameramen said they had to push forward, to the front line, to film soldiers in action, firing, dying. Gregor Straub of NBC said he had to have a close-up of a soldier's face dripping sweat. Rodolfo Carillo of CBS said he had to catch a despondent commander sitting under a bush and weeping because he had lost his whole unit. A French cameraman wanted a panorama shot with a Salvadoran unit charging a Honduran unit from one side, or vice versa. Somebody else wanted to capture the image of a soldier carrying his dead comrade. The radio reporters sided with the cameramen. One wanted to record the cries of a casualty summoning help, growing weaker and weaker, until he breathed his last breath. Charles Meadows of Radio Canada wanted the voice of a soldier cursing war amid a hellish racket of gunfire. Naotake Mochida of Radio Japan wanted the bark of an officer shouting to his commander over the roar of artillery—using a Japanese field telephone.

Many others also decided to go forward. Competition is a powerful incentive. Since American television was going, the American wire services had to go as well. Since the Americans were going, Reuters had to go. Excited by patriotic ambition, I decided, as the only Pole on the scene, to attach myself to the group that intended to make the desperate march. Those who said they had bad hearts, or professed to be uninterested in particulars since they were writing general commentaries, we left behind, under a tree.

There might have been twenty of us who set out along an empty road bathed in intense sunlight. The risk, or even the madness, of the march lay in the fact that the road ran along the top of an embankment: we were perfectly visible to both of the armies hiding in the bush that began about a hundred yards away. One good burst of machine-gun fire in our direction would be enough.

At the beginning everything went well. We heard intense gunfire and the detonation of artillery shells but it was a mile or so away. To keep our spirits up we were all talking (nervously and without necessarily making sense). But soon fear began to take its toll. It is, indeed, a rather unpleasant feeling to walk with the awareness that at any moment a bullet can find you. No one, however, acknowledged fear openly. First, somebody simply proposed we take a rest. So we sat down and caught our breath. Then, when we started again, two began lagging behind—apparently immersed in conversation. Then somebody spotted an especially interesting group of trees that deserved long, careful inspection. Then two others announced that they had to go back because they had forgotten the filters they needed for their cameras. We took another rest. We rested more and more often, and the pauses grew longer. There were ten of us left.

In the meantime, nothing was happening in our vicinity. We were walking along an empty road in the direction of El Salvador. The air was wonderful. The sun was setting. That very sun helped us extricate ourselves. The television men suddenly pulled out their light metres and declared that it was already too dark to film. Nothing could be done—not long shots, or close-ups, or action-shots, or stills. And it was a long way to the front line yet. By the time we got there it would be night.

The whole group started back. The ones who had heart trouble, who were going to write general commentaries, who had turned back earlier because they had been talking or had forgotten their filters, were waiting for us under the tree beside the two artillery pieces.

The sweaty, unshaven major had organized an army truck to carry us to our billets for the night, at a village behind the line called Nacaome. There we held a conference and decided that the Americans would phone the president immediately to request an order for us to see the whole front, to have us transported into the very midst of the fighting, into the hell of gunfire, on to ground soaked with blood.

In the morning an airplane arrived to take us to the far end of the front, where heavy fighting was in progress. Overnight rain had turned the grass airstrip at Nacaome into a quagmire, and the dilapidated old DC-3, black with exhaust smoke, stuck up out of the water like a hydroplane. It had been shot up the day before by a Salvadoran fighter; the holes in its fuselage were patched with rough boards. The sight of these ordinary, simple boards of wood frightened those who said they had bad hearts. They stayed behind and returned later to Tegucigalpa.

We were to fly to Santa Rosa de Copán at the other extreme of the front. As it was taking off the plane trailed as much smoke and flame as a rocket starting for the moon. In the air it screeched and groaned and reeled like a drunk swept along in an autumn gale. It plunged maniacally earthwards and then clambered desperately for altitude. Never level, never in a straight line. The cabin—the plane usually carried freight—contained no seats or benches of any kind. We gripped curved metal handholds to avoid being thrown against the walls. The wind blowing in through the gaping holes was enough to tear our heads off. The two pilots, carefree youngsters, grinned at us the whole time in the cockpit mirror as if they enjoyed some private joke.

'The main thing,' Antonio Rodriguez of the Spanish news agency EFE hollered to me over the roar of the propellors and the wind, 'is for the motors to hold out. Mama mia, let the motors hold out!'

In Santa Rosa de Copán, a sleepy hamlet filled then only with soldiers, a truck carried us through muddy streets to the barracks, which stood in the old Spanish fort, surrounded by a grey wall swollen from the damp. Once inside we heard three wounded prisoners in the courtyard.

'Talk!' the interrogating officer was shouting at them. 'Tell me everything!'

The prisoners mumbled. They were stripped to the waist and weak from loss of blood—the first with a belly wound, the second with one to his shoulder, the third with part of his hand shot away. The one with the belly wound didn't last long. He groaned, turned as if it were a step in a dance and fell to the ground. The remaining two went silent and looked at their colleague with the flat gaze of landed fish.

An officer led us to the garrison commander who, pale and tired, did not know what to do with us. He ordered that military shirts be given to us. He ordered his aide to bring coffee. The commander was worried that Salvadoran units might arrive any moment. Santa Rosa lay along the enemy's main line of attack—that is, along the road that connected the Atlantic and the Pacific. El Salvador, lying on the Pacific, dreamed of conquering Honduras, lying on the Atlantic. In this way little El Salvador would become a two-ocean power. The shortest path from El Salvador to the Atlantic ran right where we were—through Ocotepeque, Santa Rosa de Copán, San Pedro Sula, to Puerto Cortés. Advancing

14

Salvadoran tanks had already penetrated deep into Honduran territory. The Salvadorans were moving to order: push through to the Atlantic, then to Europe and then the world!

Their radio repeated: 'A little shouting and noise and that's the end of Honduras.'

Weaker and poorer, Honduras was defending itself fiercely. Through the open barracks window we could see the higher-ranking officers preparing their units for the front. Young conscripts stood in scraggly ranks. They were small dark boys, Indians all, with tense faces, terrified—but ready to fight. The officers said something and pointed at the distant horizon. Afterwards a priest appeared and sprinkled holy water on platoons going out towards death.

In the afternoon we left for the front in an open truck. The first forty kilometres passed without incident. The road led through higher and higher country, among green heights covered with thick tropical bush. Empty clay huts, some of them burnt out, clung to the mountain slopes. In one place we passed the inhabitants of an entire village straggling along the edge of the road, carrying bundles. Later, as we drove past, a crowd of peasants in white shirts and sombreros flourished their machetes and shotguns. Artillery fire could be heard far, far away.

Suddenly there was a commotion in the road. We had reached a triangular clearing in the forest where the casualties had been brought. Some were lying on stretchers, and others right on the grass. A few soldiers and two orderlies moved among them. There was no doctor. Four soldiers were digging a hole nearby. The wounded lay there calmly, patiently, and the most amazing thing was patience, the unimaginable superhuman endurance of pain. No one was crying out, no one was calling for help. The soldiers brought them water and the orderlies applied primitive dressings as well as they could. What I saw there staggered me. One of the orderlies, with a lancet in his hand, was going from one casualty to another and digging the bullets out of them, as if he were paring the core out of an apple. The other orderly poured iodine on the wounds and then pressed on the bandage.

A wounded boy arrived in a truck. A Salvadoran. He had taken a bullet in the knee. He was ordered to lie down on the grass. The boy was barefoot, pale, spattered with blood. The orderly poked around in his knee, looking for the bullet. The boy moaned.

'Quiet, you poor bastard,' the orderly said. 'You're distracting me.'

He used his fingers to pull out the bullet. Then he poured iodine into the wound and wrapped it in a bandage.

'Stand up and go to the truck,' said a soldier from the escort.

The boy picked himself up off the the grass and hobbled to the vehicle. He didn't say a word, didn't make a sound.

'Climb in,' the soldier commanded. We rushed to give the boy a hand, but the soldier waved us away with his rifle. Something was bothering the soldier; he'd been at the front; his nerves were jangly. The boy rested himself on the high tailgate and dragged himself in. His body hit the bed of the truck with a thud. I thought he was finished. But a moment later his grey, naive, quizzical face appeared, waiting humbly for the next stroke of destiny.

'How about a smoke?' he asked us in a quiet, hoarse voice. We tossed whatever cigarettes we had into the truck. The vehicle moved off, and the boy was grinning at having enough cigarettes to share with his whole village.

The orderlies were giving glucose intravenously to a dying soldier, who had drawn many interested onlookers. Some were sitting around the stretcher where he was lying, and others were leaning on their rifles. He might have been, say, twenty. He had taken eleven rounds. An older, weaker man hit by those eleven rounds would have been dead long ago. But the bullets had ripped into a young body, strong and powerfully built, and death was meeting resistance. The wounded man lay unconscious, already on the other side of existence, but some remnant of life was putting up a last desperate fight. The soldier was stripped to the waist, and everyone could see his muscles contracting and the sweat beading up on his sallow skin. The tense muscles and streams of sweat showed the ferocity of battle, when life goes against death. Everybody was interested in it because everybody wanted to know how much strength there was in life and how much there was in death. Everybody wanted to see how long life could hold off death and whether a young life that's still there and doesn't want to give up would be able to outlast death.

'Maybe he'll make it,' one of the soldiers ventured.

'No way,' the orderly replied, holding the bottle of glucose at arm's length above the casualty.

There was a gloomy silence. The casualty inhaled violently, as if he had just finished a long hard run.

'Doesn't anybody know him?' one of the soldiers asked eventually.

The wounded man's heart was working at maximum effort; we felt its feverish thumping.

'Nobody,' another soldier answered.

A truck was climbing the road, its motor complaining. Four soldiers were digging a hole down in the woods.

'Is he ours or theirs?' a soldier sitting by the stretcher asked.

'Nobody knows,' said the orderly after a moment's quiet.

'He's his mother's,' a soldier standing nearby said.

'He's God's now,' added another after a pause. He took off his cap and hung it on the barrel of the rifle.

The casualty shivered, and his muscles pulsed under his glossy yellowish skin.

'Life is so strong,' a soldier leaning on his rifle said in astonishment. 'It's still there, still there.'

Everyone was absorbed, silent, concentrating on the sight of the wounded man. He was drawing breath more slowly now, and his head had tilted back. The soldiers sitting near him grasped their hands around their knees and hunched up, as if the fire was burning low and the cold creeping in. In the end—it was a while yet—somebody said: 'He's gone. All he was is gone.'

They stayed there for some time, looking fearfully at the dead man and afterwards, when they saw that nothing else would happen, they began walking away.

We drove on. The road snaked through forested moun-tains, past the village of San Francisco. A series of curves began, one after another, and suddenly around one curve we ran into the maw of the war. Soldiers were running and firing, bullets whizzed overhead, long bursts of machine-gun fire ripped along both sides of the road. The driver braked suddenly and at that instant a shell exploded in front of us. Sweet Jesus, I thought, this is it. What felt like the wing of a typhoon swept through the truck. Everybody dived for it, one on top of another, just to make it to the ground, to hit the ditch, to vanish. Out of the corner of my eye, on the run, I could see the fat French TV cameraman scrambling along the road looking for his equipment. Somebody shouted, 'Take cover!' and when he heard that order—grenades going off and the bark of automatic rifles hadn't fazed him—he hugged the road like a dead man.

I lunged in the direction that seemed to be the most quiet, threw myself into the bushes, down, down, as far as I could get from the curve where the shell had hit us, downhill, along bare ground, skating across slick clay, and then into the bush, deep into the bush, but I didn't run far because suddenly there was shooting right in front of me—bullets flying around, branches fluttering, a machine-gun roaring. I fell and crouched on the ground.

When I opened my eyes I saw a piece of soil and ants crawling over it.

They were walking along their paths, one after another, in various directions. It wasn't the time for observing ants, but the very sight of them marching along, the sight of another world, another reality, brought me back to consciousness. An idea came into my head: if I could control my fear enough to stop my ears for a moment and look only at these insects, I could begin to think with some sort of sense. I lay among the thick bushes plugging my ears with all my might, nose in the dirt and I watched the ants.

I don't know how long this went on. When I raised my head, I was looking into the eyes of a soldier.

I froze. Falling into the hands of the Salvadorans was what I feared most, because then the only thing to look forward to was certain death. They were a brutal army, blind with fury, shooting whomever they got hold of in the madness of the war. In any case, this was what I thought, having been fed Honduran propaganda. An American or an Englishman might have a chance, although not necessarily. In Nacaome the day before we had been shown an American missionary killed by the Salvadorans. And El Salvador did not even maintain diplomatic relations with Poland, so I would count for nothing.

The soldier was taken by surprise, too. Crawling through the bush, he hadn't noticed me until the last moment. He adjusted his helmet, which was adorned with grass and leaves. He had a dark, skinny, furrowed face. In his hands there was an old Mauser.

'Who are you?' he asked.

'And what army are you from?'

'Honduras,' he said, because he could tell right off that I was a foreigner, neither his nor theirs.

'Honduras! Dear brother!' I rejoiced and pulled the piece of paper out of my pocket. It was the document from the Honduran high command, from Colonel Ramirez Ortega, to the units at the front permitting me to enter the region of military activity. Each of us had been given the same document in Tegucigalpa before leaving for the front.

I told the soldier that I had to get to Santa Rosa and then to Tegucigalpa so that I could send a dispatch to Warsaw. The soldier was happy because he was already calculating that with an order from the general staff (the documents commanded all subordinates to assist me) he could withdraw to the rear along with me.

'We will go together, *señor*,' the soldier said. '*Señor* will say that he has commanded me to accompany him.'

He was a recruit, a dirt farmer; he had been called up a week ago, he didn't know the army; the war meant nothing to him. He was trying to figure out how to survive it.

Shells were slamming around us. Far, far away we could hear shooting. Cannons were firing. The smell of powder and smoke was in the air. There were machine-guns behind us and on both sides.

His company had been crawling forward among the bushes, up this hill, when our truck came around the corner and drove into the turmoil of war and was abandoned. From where we lay pressing against the ground we could see the thick-ribbed gum soles of his company, only their soles, as the men crawled through the grass. Then the soles of their boots stopped, then they moved ahead, one-two, one-two, a few metres forward, and then they stopped again.

The soldier nudged me: '*Señor, mire cuantos zapatos!*' ('Look at all those shoes!')

He kept looking at the shoes of the other members of his company as they crawled forward. He blinked, weighed something in his mind and at last said hopelessly, '*Toda mi familia anda descalzada.*' ('My whole family goes barefoot.')

We started crawling through the forest.

The shooting let up for a moment and the soldier, fatigued, stopped. In a hushed voice he told me to wait where I was because he was going back to where his company had been fighting. He said that the living had certainly moved forward—their orders were to pursue the enemy to the very border—but the dead would remain on the battlefield and, for them, their boots were now superfluous. He would strip a few of the dead of their boots, hide them under a bush and mark the place. When the war was over, he would return and have enough boots for his whole family. He had already calculated that he could trade one pair of army boots for three pairs of children's shoes, and there were nine little ones back home.

It crossed my mind that he was going mad, so I told him that I was putting him under my orders and that we should keep crawling. But the soldier did not want to listen. He was driven by thoughts of footwear and he would throw himself into the front line in order to secure the property lying there in the grass, rather than let it be buried with the dead. Now the war had meaning for him, a point of reference and a goal. He knew what he wanted and what he had to do. I was certain that if he left me we would be separated and never meet again. The last thing I wanted was to be left alone in that forest: I did not know who controlled it or which army was where or which direction I should set off in. There is nothing worse than finding yourself alone in somebody else's country during somebody else's war. So I crawled after the soldier towards the battlefield. We crept to where the forest stopped and a new scene of combat could be observed through the stumps and bushes. The front had moved off laterally now: shells were bursting behind an elevation that rose up to the left of us, and somewhere to the right—underground, it seemed, but it must have been in a ravine—machine-guns were muttering. An abandoned mortar stood in front of us, and in the grass lay dead soldiers.

I told my companion that I was going no further. He could do what he had to do, as long as he didn't get lost and returned quickly. He left his rifle with me and bolted ahead. I was so worried that someone would catch us there or pop up from behind the bushes or throw a grenade that I couldn't watch him. I felt sick lying there with my head on the wet dirt, smelling of rot and smoke. If only we don't get encircled, I thought, if only we can crawl closer to a peaceful world. This soldier of mine, I thought, is satisfied now. The clouds have parted above his head and the heavens are raining manna—he will return to the village, dump a sackful of boots on the floor and watch his children jump for joy.

The soldier came back dragging his conquest and hid it in the bushes. He wiped the sweat off his face and looked around to fix the spot in his mind. We moved back into the depth of the forest. It was drizzling and fog lay in the clearing. We walked in no specific direction but kept as far as possible from the commotion of the war. Somewhere, not far from there, must have been Guatemala. And further, Mexico. And further still, the United States. But for us at that moment, all those countries were on another planet. The inhabitants there had their own lives and thought about entirely different problems. Perhaps they did not know that we had a war here. No war can be conveyed over a distance. Somebody sits eating dinner and watching television: pillars of earth blown into the air; *cut*—the tracks of a charging tank; *cut*—soldiers falling and writhing in pain;—and the man watching television gets angry and curses because while he was gaping at the screen he oversalted his soup. War becomes a spectacle, a show, when it is seen from a distance and expertly re-shaped in the cutting room. In reality a soldier sees no further than his own nose, has his eyes full of sand or sweat, shoots at random and clings to the ground like a mole. Above all, he is frightened. The front line soldier says little: if questioned he might not answer at all, or might respond only by shrugging his shoulders. As a rule he walks around hungry and sleepy, not knowing what the next order will be or what will become of him in an hour. War makes for a constant familiarity with death and the experience of it sinks deep into the memory. Afterwards, in old age, a man reaches back more and more to his war memories, as if recollections of the front expand with time, as if he had spent his whole life in a foxhole.

Stealing through the forest, I asked the soldier why they were fighting with El Salvador. He replied that he did not know, that it was a government affair. I asked him how he could fight when he did not know why he was spilling blood. He answered that when you live in a village it's better not to ask questions because questions arouse the suspicions of the village mayor, and then the mayor would volunteer him for the road gang, and, on the road gang, he would have to neglect his farm and his family, and then the hunger waiting for him on his return would be even greater. And isn't the everyday poverty enough as it is? A man has to live in such a way that his name never reaches the ears of authorities. If it does, they write it down immediately and then that man is in for a lot of trouble later. Government matters are not fit for the mind of a village farmer, because the government understands such things but nobody's going to let a dirt farmer do anything.

Walking through the woods at sunset and straightening our backs because it was getting quieter all the time, we hit a small village plastered together out of clay and straw: Santa Teresa. An infantry battalion, decimated in the all-day battle, was billeted there. Exhausted and stunned by the experience of the front line, soldiers wandered among the huts. It was drizzling continuously and everybody was dirty, smeared with clay.

The people at the guardpost led us to the battalion commander. I showed him my documents and asked for transportation to Tegucigalpa. That worthy man offered me a car but ordered me to stay put until morning because the roads were soaked and mountainous and ran along the edges of cliffs, and at night, without lights, would be impassable. The commander sat in an abandoned hut listening to the radio. The announcer was reading a string of communiqués from the front. Next we heard that a wide range of governments, the countries of Latin America, along with many from Europe and Asia, wanted to bring the war between Honduras and El Salvador to an end, and had already issued statements about it. The African countries were expected to take a stand presently. Communiqués from Australia and Oceania were also expected. China was silent, which was provoking interest, and so, too, was

Canada. The Canadian reticence could be explained by the fact that a Canadian correspondent, Charles Meadows, was at the front and his situation might be complicated or made more dangerous by a statement now.

The presenter then read that the Apollo 11 rocket had been launched from Cape Kennedy. Three astronauts, Armstrong, Aldrin and Collins, were flying to the moon. Man was drawing closer to the stars, opening new worlds, soaring into the infinite galaxies. Congratulations were pouring into Houston from all corners of the world, the presenter informed us, and all humanity was rejoicing at the triumph of reason and precise thinking.

My soldier was dozing in a corner. At dawn I woke him up and said we were leaving. An exhausted battalion driver, still half-asleep, took us to Tegucigalpa in a jeep. To save time, we drove straight to the post office, where, on a borrowed typewriter, I wrote the dispatch that was later printed in the newspapers at home. José Malaga let the dispatch go out before all the others waiting to be sent and released it without the approval of the military censors (it was, after all, written in Polish).

My colleagues were returning from the front. They arrived one by one, because everyone had got lost after we drove into the artillery fire at that turning in the road. Enrique Amado had run into a Salvadoran patrol, three members of the *Guardia Rural*, the private *gendarmerie* maintained by the Salvadoran *latifundistas* and recruited from among the criminal element. Very dangerous types. They ordered Enrique to stand up to be executed. He played for time, praying at great length and then asking to be allowed to relieve himself. The *guardistas* obviously loved the sight of a man in terror. In the end they ordered him to make his final preparations and were taking aim when a series of shots rang out from the bushes. One of the patrol fell, hit, and the other two were taken prisoner.

The soccer war lasted one hundred hours. Its victims: 6,000 dead, more than 12,000 wounded. Fifty thousand people lost their homes and fields. Many villages were destroyed.

The two countries ceased military action because Latin American states intervened, but to this day there are exchanges of gunfire along the Honduras–El Salvador border, and people die, and villages are burned.

These are the real reasons for the war: El Salvador, the smallest country in Central America, has the greatest population density in the western hemisphere (over 160 people per square kilometre). Things are crowded, and all the more so because most of the land is in the hands of fourteen great landowning clans. People even say that El Salvador is the property of fourteen families. A thousand *latifundistas* own exactly ten times as much land as their hundred thousand peasants. Two thirds of the village population owns no land. For years a part of the landless poor has been emigrating to Honduras, where there are large tracts of unimproved land. Honduras (12,000 square kilometres) is almost six times as large as El Salvador, but has about half as many people (2,500,000). This was illegal emigration but was kept hushed-up, tolerated by the Honduran government for years.

Salvadoran peasants settled in Honduras, established villages, and grew accustomed to a better life than the one they had left behind. They numbered about 300,000.

In the 1960s, unrest began among the Honduran peasantry, which was demanding land, and the Honduras government passed a decree on agricultural reform. But since this was an oligarchical government, dependent on the United States, the decree did not break up the land of either the oligarchy or the large banana plantations belonging to the United Fruit Company. The government wanted to re-distribute the land occupied by the Salvadoran squatters, meaning that the 300,000 Salvadorans would have to return to their own country, where they had nothing, and where, in any event, they would be refused by the Salvadoran government, fearing a peasant revolution.

Relations between the two countries were tense. News-papers on both sides waged a campaign of hate, slander and abuse, calling each other Nazis, dwarfs, drunkards, sadists, spiders, aggressors and thieves. There were pogroms. Shops were burned.

In these circumstances the match between Honduras and El Salvador had taken place.

The war ended in a stalemate. The border remained the same. It is a border established by sight in the bush, in mountainous terrain that both sides claim. Some of the émigrés returned to El Salvador and some of them are still living in Honduras. And both governments are satisfied: for several days Honduras and El Salvador occupied the front pages of the world press and were the object of interest and concern. The only chance small countries from the Third World have of evoking a lively international interest is when they decide to shed blood. This is a sad truth, but so it is.

The deciding game of the best-of-three series was held on neutral ground, in Mexico (El Salvador won, three-two). The Honduran fans were placed on one side of the stadium, the Salvadoran fans on the other side, and down the middle sat 5,000 Mexican police armed with thick clubs.

CAROLYN FORCHÉ

EL SALVADOR:
AN AIDE-MÉMOIRE

The year Franco died, I spent several months on Mallorca translating the poetry of Claribel Alegría, a Salvadoran in voluntary exile. During those months the almond trees bloomed and lost flower, the olives and lemons ripened, and we hauled baskets of apricots from Claribel's small *finca*. There was bathing in the *calla*, fresh squid under the palm thatch, drunk Australian sailors to dance with at night. It was my first time in Europe and there was no better place at that time than Spain. I was there when Franco's anniversary passed for the first time in forty years without notice—and the lack of public celebration was a collective hush of relief. I travelled with Claribel's daughter, Maya Flakoll, for ten days through Andalusia by train, visiting poetry shrines. The *gitanos* had finally pounded a cross into the earth to mark the grave of Federico García Lorca, not where it had been presumed to be all this time, not beneath an olive tree, but in a bowl of land rimmed by pines. We hiked the eleven kilometres through the Sierra Nevada foothills to La Fuente Grande and held a book of poems open over the silenced poet.

On Mallorca I lost interest in the *calla* sunbathing, the parties that carried on into the morning, the staggering home wine-drunk up the goat paths. I did not hike to the peak of the Teix with baskets of *entremesas* nor, despite well-intentioned urgings, could I surrender myself to the island's diversionary summer mystique.

I was busy with Claribel's poems, and with the horrific accounts of the survivors of repressive Latin American régimes. Claribel's home was frequented by these wounded: writers who had been tortured and imprisoned, who had lost husbands, wives, and closest friends. In the afternoon, more than once I joined Claribel in her silent vigil near the window until the mail came, her 'difficult time of day', alone in a chair in the perfect light of thick-walled Mallorquín windows. These were her afternoons of despair, and they haunted me. In those hours I first learned of El Salvador, not from the springs of her nostalgia for 'the fraternity of dipping a tortilla into a common pot of beans and meat', but from the source of its pervasive brutality. My understanding of Latin American realities was confined then to the romantic devotion to Vietnam-era revolutionary pieties, the sainthood of Ernesto Che rather than the debilitating effects of the cult of personality that arose in the collective memory of Guevara. I worked into the late hours on my poems and on translations, drinking '101' brandy and chain-smoking Un-X-Dos. When Cuban writer Mario Benedetti visited, I questioned him about what 'an American' could do in the struggle against repression.

'As a *North* American, you might try working to influence a profound change in your country's foreign policy.'

Over coffee in the mornings I studied reports from Amnesty International, London, and learned of a plague on Latin exiles who had sought refuge in Spain following Franco's death: a right-wing death squad known as the 'AAA'—Anti-Communista Apostólica, founded in Argentina and exported to assassinate influential exiles from the southern cone.

I returned to the United States and in the autumn of 1977 was invited to El Salvador by people who knew Claribel. 'How much do you know about Latin America?' I was asked. Then: 'Good. At least you know that you know nothing.' A young writer, politically unaffiliated, ideologically vague, I was to be blessed with the rarity of a moral and political education—what, at times, would seem an unbearable immersion; what eventually would become a focused obsession. It would change my life and work, propel me towards engagement, test my endurance and find it wanting, and prevent me from ever viewing myself or my country again through precisely the same fog of unwitting connivance.

I was sent for a briefing to Dr Thomas P. Anderson, author of *Matanza,* the definitive scholarly history of Salvador's revolution of 1932, and to Ignacio Lozano, a Californian newspaper editor and former ambassador (under Gerald Ford) to El Salvador. It was suggested that I visit Salvador as a journalist, a role that would of necessity become real.

In January 1978 I landed at Ilopango, the dingy centre-city airport which is now Salvador's largest military base. Arriving before me were the members of a human rights investigation team, headed by then Congressman John Drinan, S.J. (Democrat of Massachusetts). I had been told that a black North American, Ronald James Richardson, had been killed while in the custody of the Salvadoran government and that a North American organization known as the American Institute for Free Labour Development (AIFLD, an organ of the AFL-CIO and an intelligence front) was manipulating the Salvadoran agricultural workers. Investigation of the 'Richardson Case' exposed me to the *sub rosa* activities of the Salvadoran military, whose highest-ranking officers and government officials were engaged in cocaine smuggling, kidnapping, extortion, and terrorism; through studying AIFLD's work, I would learn of the spurious intentions of an organization destined to become the architect of the present agrarian reform. I was delivered the promised exposure to the stratified life of Salvador, and was welcomed to 'Vietnam, circa 1959'. The 'Golden Triangle' had moved to the isthmus of the Americas, 'rural pacification' was in embryo, the seeds of rebellion had taken root in destitution and hunger.

Later my companion and guide, 'Ricardo', changed his description from 'Vietnam' to 'a Nazi forced labour camp'.

'It is not hyperbole,' he said quietly. 'You will come to see that.'

In those first twenty days I was taken to clinics and hospitals, to villages, farms, prisons, coffee mansions and processing plants, to cane mills and the elegant homes of American foreign service bureaucrats, nudged into the hillsides overlooking the capital, where I was offered cocktails and platters of ocean shrimps; it was not yet known what I would write of my impressions or where I would print them. Fortuitously, I had published nationally in my own country, and in Salvador 'only poetry' did not carry the pejorative connotation I might have ascribed to it then. I knew nothing of political journalism but was willing to learn—it seemed, at the time, an acceptable way for a poet to make a living.

I lay on my belly in the *campo* and was handed a pair of field glasses. The lenses sharpened on a plastic tarpaulin tacked to four maize stalks several hundred yards away, beneath which a woman sat on the ground. She was gazing through the plastic roof of her 'house' and hugging three naked, emaciated children. There was an aqua plastic dog-food bowl at her feet.

'She's watching for the plane,' my friend said. 'We have to get out of here now or we're going to get it, too.'

I trained the lenses on the woman's eyes, gelled with disease and open to a swarm of gnats. We climbed back in the truck and rolled the windows up just as the duster plane swept back across the field, dumping a yellow cloud of pesticide over the woman and her children, to protect the cotton crop around them.

At the time I was unaware of the pedagogical theories of Paulo Freire (*Pedagogy of the Oppressed*), but found myself learning *in situ* the politics of cultural immersion. It was by Ricardo's later admission 'risky business', but it was thought important that a few North Americans, particularly writers, be sensitized to Salvador prior to any military conflict. The lessons were simple and critical, the methods somewhat more difficult to detect.

I was given a white lab jacket and, posing as a North American physician, was asked to work in a rural hospital at the side of a Salvadoran doctor who was paid two hundred dollars a month by her government to care for 100,000 *campesinos*. She had no lab, no X-ray, no whole blood plasma, or antibiotics, no anaesthetics or medicines, no autoclave for sterilizing surgical equipment. Her forceps were rusted, the walls of her operating room were studded with flies; beside her hospital, a coffee-processing plant's refuse heaps incubated the maggots, and she paid a *campesina* to swish the flies away with a newspaper while she delivered the newborn. She was forced to do Caesarean sections at times without enough local anaesthetic. Without supplies, she worked with only her hands and a cheap ophthalmoscope. In her clinic I held children in my arms who died hours later for want of a manual suction device to remove the fluid from their lungs. Their peculiar skin rashes spread to my hands, arms, and belly. I dug maggots from a child's open wound with a teaspoon. I contracted four strains of dysentery and was treated by stomach antiseptics, effective yet damaging enough to be banned by our own Food and Drug Administration. This doctor had worked in the *campo* for years, a lifetime of delivering the offspring of thirteen-year-old mothers who thought the navel marked the birth-canal opening. She had worked long enough to feel that it was acceptable to ignore her own cervical cancer, and hard enough, in Salvador, to view her inevitable death as the least of her concerns.

I was taken to the homes of landowners, with their pools set like aquamarines in the clipped grass, to the afternoon games of canasta over quaint local *pupusas* and tea, where parrots hung by their feet among the bougainvillea and nearly everything was imported, if only from Miami or New Orleans. One evening I dined with a military officer who toasted America, private enterprise, Las Vegas, and the 'fatherland', until his wife excused herself, and in a drape of cigar smoke the events of 'The Colonel' were told, almost a *poème trouvé*. I had only to pare down the memory and render it whole, unlined, and as precise as recollection would have it. I did not wish to endanger myself by the act of poeticizing such a necessary reportage. It became, when I wrote it, the second insistence of El Salvador to infiltrate what I so ridiculously preserved as my work's allegiance to Art. No more than in any earlier poems did I choose my subject.

The following day I was let into Ahuachapán prison (now an army *cuartel*). We had been driving back from a meeting with Salvadoran feminists when Ricardo swung the truck into a climb through a tube of dust towards the run-down fortification. I was thirsty, infested with intestinal parasites, fatigued from twenty days of ricocheting between extremes of poverty and wealth. I was horrified, impatient, suspicious of almost everyone, paralyzed by sympathy and revulsion. I kept thinking of the kindly, silver-haired American political officer who informed me that in Salvador, 'there were always five versions of the truth.' From this, I was presumably to conclude that the truth could not therefore be known. Ricardo seemed by turns the Braggioni of Porter's 'Flowering Judas' and a pedagogical genius of considerable vision and patience. As we walked towards the gate, he palmed the air to slow our pace.

'This is a criminal penitentiary. You will have thirty minutes inside. Realize, please, at all times where you are, and whatever you see here, understand that for political prisoners it is always much worse. OK?'

We shook hands with the chief guard and a few subordinates, clean-shaven youths armed with G-3s. There was first the stench: rotting blood, excrement, buckets of urine, and corn slop. A man in his thirties came towards us, dragging a swollen green leg, his pants ripped to the thigh to accommodate the swelling. He was introduced as 'Miguel' and I as a 'friend'. The two men shook hands a long time, standing together in the filth, a firm knot of warmth between them. Miguel was asked to give me a 'tour', and he agreed, first taking a coin from his pocket and slipping it into the guard station soda machine. He handed me an orange Nehi, urging me somewhat insistently to take it, and we began a slow walk into the first hall. The prison was four-square with an open court in the centre. There were bunk rooms where the cots were stacked three deep and some were hung with newsprint 'for privacy'. The men squatted on the ground or along the walls, some stirring small coal fires, others ducking under urine-soaked tents of newspaper. It was suppertime, and they were cooking their dry tortillas. I used the soda as a relief from the stench, like a hose of oxygen. There were maybe four hundred men packed into Ahuachapán, and it was an odd sight, an American woman, but there was no heckling.

'Did you hear the shots when we first pulled up?' Ricardo asked. 'Those were warnings. A visitor—behave.'

Miguel showed me through the workrooms and latrines, finishing his sentences with his eyes: a necessary skill under repressive régimes, highly developed in Salvador. With the guards' attention diverted, he gestured towards a black open doorway and suggested that I might wander through it, stay a few moments, and come back out 'as if I had seen nothing.'

I did as he asked, my eyes adjusting to the darkness of that shit-smeared room with its single chink of light in the concrete. There were wooden boxes stacked against one wall, each a metre by a metre, with barred openings the size of a book, and within them there was breathing, raspy and half-conscious. It was a few moments before I realized that men were kept in those cages, their movement so cramped that they could neither sit, stand, nor lie down. I recall only magnified fragments of my few minutes in that room. I was rooted to the clay floor, unable to move either towards or away from the cages. I turned from the room towards Miguel, who pivoted on his crutch and with his eyes on the ground said in a low voice, *'La oscura'*, the dark place. 'Sometimes a man is kept in there a year, and cannot move when he comes out.'

We caught up with Ricardo, who leaned towards me and whispered, 'Tie your sweater sleeves around your neck. You are covered with hives.'

In the cab of the truck I braced my feet against the dashboard and through the half-cracked window shook hands with the young soldiers, smiling and nodding. A hundred metres from the prison I lifted Ricardo's spare shirt in my hands and vomited. We were late for yet another meeting, the sun had dropped behind the volcanoes, my eyes ached. When I was empty the dry heaves began, and, after the sobbing, a convulsive shudder. Miguel was serving his third consecu-

34

tive sentence, this time for organizing a hunger strike against prison conditions. In that moment I saw him turn back to his supper, his crutch stamping circles of piss and mud beside him as he walked. I heard the screams of a woman giving birth by Caesarean without anaesthetic in Ana's hospital. I saw the flies fastened to the walls in the operating room, the gnats on the eyes of the starving woman, the reflection of flies on Ana's eyes in the hospital kitchen window. The shit, I imagined, was inside my nostrils and I would smell it the rest of my life, as it is for a man who in battle tastes a piece of flesh or gets the blood under his fingernails. The smell never comes out; it was something Ricardo explained once as he was falling asleep.

'Feel this,' he said, manoeuvring the truck down the hill road. 'This is what oppression feels like. Now you have begun to learn something. When you get back to the States, what you do with this is up to you.'

Between 1978 and 1981 I travelled between the United States and Salvador, writing reports on the war waiting to happen, drawing blueprints of prisons from memory, naming the dead. I filled soup bowls with cigarette butts, grocery boxes with files on American involvement in the rural labour movement, and each week I took a stool sample to the parasite clinic. A priest I knew was gang-raped by soldiers; another was hauled off and beaten nearly to death. On one trip a woman friend and I were chased by the death squad for five minutes on the narrow back roads that circle the city; her evasive driving and considerable luck saved us. One night a year ago I was interviewing a defecting member of the Christian Democratic Party. As we started out of the drive to go back to my hotel, we encountered three plainclothesmen hunched over the roof of a taxicab, their machine guns pointed at our windshield. We escaped through a grove of avocado trees. The bodies of friends have turned up disembowelled and decapitated, their teeth punched into broken points, their faces sliced off with machetes. On the final trip to the airport we swerved to avoid a corpse, a man spread-eagled, his stomach hacked open, his entrails stretched from one side of the road to the other. We drove over them like a garden hose. My friend looked at me. *Just another dead man,* he said. And by then it had become true for me as well: the unthinkable, the sense of death within life before death.

Carolyn Forché

II

'I see an injustice,' wrote Czeslaw Milosz in *Native Realm*. 'A Parisian does not have to bring his city out of nothingness every time he wants to describe it.' So it was with Wilno, that Lithuanian/Polish/Byelorussian city of the poet's childhood, and so it has been with the task of writing about Salvador in the United States. The country called by Gabriela Mistral 'the Tom Thumb of the Americas' would necessarily be described to North Americans as 'about the size of Massachusetts'. As writers we could begin with its location on the Pacific south of Guatemala and west of Honduras and with Ariadne's thread of statistics: 4.5 million people, 400 per square kilometre (a country without silence or privacy), a population growth rate of 3.5 percent (such a population would double in two decades). But what does 'ninety percent malnutrition' mean? Or that 'eighty percent of the population has no running water, electricity, or sanitary services?' I watched women push faeces aside with a stick, lower their pails to the water, and carry it home to wash their clothes, their spoons and plates, themselves, their infant children. The chief cause of death has been amoebic dysentery. One out of four children dies before the age of five; the average human life span is forty-six years. What does it mean when a man says, 'It is better to die quickly fighting than slowly of starvation?' And that such a man suffers towards that decision in what is now being called 'North America's backyard'? How is the language used to draw battle lines, to identify the enemy? What are the current euphemisms for empire, public defence of private wealth, extermination of human beings? If the lethal weapon is the soldier, what is meant by 'nonlethal military aid'? And what determined the shift to helicopter gunships, M-16s, M-79 grenade launchers? The State Department's white paper entitled, *Communist Interference in El Salvador,* argues that it is a 'case of indirect armed aggression against a small Third World country by Communist powers acting through Cuba'. James Petras in *The Nation* (March 28 1981) has argued that the report's evidence 'is flimsy, circumstantial or nonexistent; the reasoning and logic is slipshod and internally inconsistent; it assumes what needs to be proven; and finally, what facts are presented refute the very case the State Department is attempting to demonstrate.' On the basis of this report, the popular press sounded an alarm over the 'flow of arms'. But from where have arms 'flowed', and to whom and for what? In terms of language, we could begin by asking why North American arms are weighed in dollar value and those reaching the opposition measured in tonnage. Or we could point out the nature of the international arms market, a complex global network in which it is possible to buy almost anything for the right price, no matter the country of origin or destination. The State Department conveniently ignores its own intelligence on arms flow to the civilian right, its own escalation of military assistance to the right-wing military, and even the discrepancies in its final analysis. But what does all this tell us about who is fighting whom for what? Americans have been told that there is a 'fundamental difference' between 'advisers' and military 'trainers'. Could it simply be that the euphemism for American military personnel must be changed so as not to serve as a mnemonic device for the longest war in our failing public memory? A year ago I asked the American military attaché in Salvador what would happen if one of these already proposed advisers returned to the US in a flag-draped coffin. He did not argue semantics.

'That,' he said, smiling, 'would be up to the American press, wouldn't it?'

Most of that press had held with striking fidelity to the State Department text: a vulnerable and worthy 'centrist' government besieged by left- and right-wing extremists, the former characterized by their unacceptable political ideology, the latter rendered non-ideologically unacceptable, that is, only in their extremity. The familiar ring of this portrayal has not escaped US apologists, who must explain why El Salvador is not 'another Vietnam'. Their argument hinges, it seems, on the rapidity with which the US could assist the Salvadoran military in the task of 'defeating the enemy'. Tactically, this means sealing the country off, warning all other nations to 'cease and desist' supplying arms, using violations of that warning as a pretext for blockades and interventions, but excepting ourselves in our continual armament of what we are calling the 'government' of El Salvador. Ignoring the institutional self-interest of the Salvadoran army, we blame the presumably 'civilian' right for the murder of thousands of *campesinos,* students, doctors, teachers, journalists, nuns, priests, and children. This requires that we ignore

37

the deposed and retired military men who command the activities of the death squads with impunity, and that the security forces responsible for the killings are under the command of the army, which is under the command of the so-called centrist government and is in fact the government itself.

There are other differences between the conflicts of El Salvador and Vietnam. There is no People's Republic of China to the north to arm and ally itself with a people engaged in a protracted war. The guerrillas are not second-generation Vietminh, but young people who armed themselves after exhaustive and failed attempts at non-violent resistance and peaceful change. The popular organizations they defend were formed in the early seventies by *campesinos* who became socially conscious through the efforts of grass-roots clergymen teaching the Medellín doctrines of social justice; the precursors of these organizations were prayer and Bible study groups, rural labour organizations and urban trade unions. As the military government grew increasingly repressive, the opposition widened to include all other political parties, the Catholic majority, the university and professional communities, and the small-business sector.

Critics of US policy accurately recognize parallels between the two conflicts in terms of involvement, escalation, and justification. The latter demands a vigilant 'euphemology' undertaken to protect language from distortions of military expedience and political convenience. Noam Chomsky has argued that 'among the many symbols used to frighten and manipulate the populace of the democratic states, few have been more important than terror and terrorism. These terms have generally been confined to the use of violence by individual and marginal groups. Official violence, which is far more extensive in both scale and destructiveness, is placed in a different category altogether. This usage has nothing to do with justice, causal sequence, or numbers abused.' He goes on to say that 'the question of proper usage is settled not merely by the official or unofficial status of the perpetrators of violence but also by their political affiliations.' State violence is excused as 'reactive', and the 'turmoil' or 'conflict' is viewed ahistorically.

It is true that there have been voices of peaceful change and social reform in El Salvador—the so-called centrists—but the US has never supported them. The US backed one fraudulently-elected military régime after another, giving them what they wanted and still want: a steady infusion of massive economic aid with which high-ranking officers can insure their personal futures and the loyalty of their subordinates. In return we expect them to guarantee stability, which means holding power by whatever means necessary for the promotion of a favourable investment climate, even if it requires us to exterminate the population, as it has come to mean in Salvador.

The military, who always admired 'Generalissimo Franco', and are encouraged in their anti-Communist crusade, grow paranoid and genocidal. Near the Sampul River last summer, soldiers tossed babies into the air for target practice, during the cattle-prod roundup and massacre of six hundred peasants. Whole families have been gunned down or hacked to pieces with machetes, including the elderly and the newborn. Now that the massacre and the struggle against it have become the occasion to 'test American resolve', the Salvadoran military is all too aware of the security of its position and the impunity with which it may operate. Why would a peasant, aware of the odds, of the significance of American backing, continue to take up arms on the side of the opposition? How is it that such opposition endures, when daily men and women are doused with gasoline and burned alive in the streets as a lesson to others; when even death is not enough, and the corpses are mutilated beyond recognition? The answer to that question in El Salvador answers the same for Vietnam.

III

We were waved past the military guard station and started down the highway, swinging into the oncoming lane to pass slow sugar-cane trucks and army transports. Every few kilometres, patrols trekked the gravel roadside. It was a warm night, dry but close to the rainy season. Juan palmed the column shift, chain-smoked, and motioned with his hot-boxed cigarette in the direction of San Marcos. Bonfires lit by the opposition were chewing away at the dark hillside. As we neared San Salvador, passing through the slums of Candelaria, I saw that the roads were barricaded. More than once Juan attempted a short cut, but upon spotting military checkpoints, changed his mind. To relieve the tension, he dug a handful of change from his pocket and showed me

Carolyn Forché

his collection of deutsche marks, Belgian francs, Swedish öre and kronor, holding each to the dashboard light and naming the journalist who had given it to him, the country, the paper. His prize was a coin from the Danish reporter whose cameras had been shot away as he crouched on a roof top to photograph an army attack on protest marchers. That was a month before, on January 22 1980, when some hundreds lost their lives; it was the beginning of a savage year of extermination. Juan rose from his seat and slipped the worthless coins back into his pocket.

Later that spring, Rene Tamsen of WHUR radio, Washington, DC, would be forced by a death squad into an unmarked car in downtown San Salvador. A Salvadoran photographer, Cesar Najarro, and his *Crónica del Pueblo* editor would be seized during a coffee break. When their mutilated bodies were discovered, it would be evident that they had been disembowelled before death. A Mexican photo-journalist, Ignacio Rodriguez, would fall in August to a military bullet. After Christmas an American freelancer, John Sullivan, would vanish from his downtown hotel room. Censorship of the press. In January 1981, Ian Mates, South African TV cameraman, would hit a land mine and would bleed to death. In a year, no one would want the Salvador assignment. In a year, journalists would appear before cameras trembling and incredulous, unable to reconcile their perceptions with those of Washington, and even established media would begin to reflect this dichotomy. Carter policy had been to play down El Salvador in the press while providing 'quiet' aid to the repressive forces.

Between 1978 and 1980, investigative articles sent to national magazines mysteriously disappeared from publication mail rooms, were oddly delayed in reaching editors, or were rejected after lengthy deliberations, most often because of El Salvador's 'low news value'. The American interreligious network and human rights community began to receive evidence of a conscious and concerted censorship effort in the United States. During interviews in 1978 with members of the Salvadoran right-wing business community, I was twice offered large sums of money to portray their government favourably in the American press. By early 1981, desk editors knew where El Salvador was and the play-down policy had been replaced by the Reagan administration's propaganda effort. The right-wing military co-operated in El Salvador by serving death threats on prominent journalists, while torturing and murdering others. American writers critical of US policy were described by the Department of State as 'the witting and unwitting dupes' of Communist propagandists. Those who have continued coverage of Salvador have found that the military monitors the wire services and all telecommunications, that pseudonyms often provide no security, that no one active in the documentation of the war of extermination can afford to be traceable in the country; effectiveness becomes self-limiting. It became apparent that my education in El Salvador had prepared me to work only until March 16 1980, when, after several close calls, I was urged to leave the country. Monsignor Romero met with me, asking that I return to the US and 'tell the American people what is happening.'

'Do you have any messages for certain exiled friends?'

'Yes. Tell them to come back.'

'But wouldn't they be killed?'

'We are all going to be killed—you and me, all of us,' he said quietly. A week later he was shot while saying mass in the chapel of a hospital for the incurable.

In those days I kept my work as a poet and journalist separate, of two distinct *mentalidades*, but I could not keep El Salvador from my poems because it had become so much a part of my life. I was cautioned to avoid mixing art and politics, that one damages the other, and it was some time before I realized that 'political poetry' often means the poetry of protest, accused of polemical didacticism, and not the poetry which implicitly celebrates politically acceptable values. I suspect that underlying this discomfort is a naive assumption: that to locate a poem in an area associated with political trouble automatically renders it political.

All poetry is both pure and engaged, in the sense that it is made of language, but it is also art. Any theory that takes one half of the social-aesthetic dynamic and accentuates it too much results in a breakdown. Stress of purity generates a feeble aestheticism which fails, in its beauty, to communicate. On the other hand, propagandistic hack work has no independent life as poetry. What matters is not whether a poem is political, but the quality of its engagement.

In *The Consciousness Industry,* Hans Magnus Enzensberger has argued the futility of locating the political aspect of poetry outside poetry itself, and that:

> Such obtuseness plays into the hands of the bourgeois aesthetic which would like to deny poetry any social aspect. Too often the champions of inwardness and sensibility are reactionaries. They consider politics a special subject best left to professionals, and wish to detach it completely from all other human activity. They advise poetry to stick to such models as they have devised for it, in other words, to high aspirations and eternal values. The promised reward for this continence is timeless validity. Behind these high-sounding proclamations lurks a contempt for poetry no less profound than that of vulgar Marxism. For a political quarantine placed on poetry in the name of eternal values itself serves political ends.

All language, then, is political; vision is always ideologically charged; perceptions are shaped *a priori* by our assumptions, and sensibility is formed by a consciousness at once social, historical, and aesthetic. There is no such thing as non-political poetry. The time, however, to determine what those politics will be is not the moment of taking pen to paper, but during the whole of one's life. We are responsible for the quality of our vision; we have the say in the shaping of our sensibility. In the many thousand daily choices we make, we create ourselves and the voice with which we speak and work.

From our tradition we inherit a poetic, a sense of appropriate subjects, styles, forms, and levels of diction; that poetic might insist that we be attuned to the individual in isolation, to particular sensitivity in the face of 'nature', to special ingenuity in inventing metaphor. It might encourage a self-regarding, inward-looking poetry. Since Romanticism, didactic poetry has been presumed dead, and narrative poetry has had at best a half-life. Demonstration is inimical to a poetry of lyric confession and self-examination, therefore didactic poetry is seen as crude and unpoetic. To suggest a return to the formal didactic mode of Virgil's *Georgics* or Lucretius's *De Rerum Natura* would be to deny history, but what has survived of that poetic is the belief that a poet's voice must be inwardly authentic and compelling of our attention; the poet's voice must have authority.

I have been told that a poet should be of his or her time. It is my feeling that the twentieth-century human condition demands a poetry of witness. This is not accomplished without certain difficulties; the inherited poetic limits the range of our work and determines the boundaries of what might be said. There is the problem of metaphor, which moved Neruda to write: 'The blood of the children/flowed out onto the streets/like...like the blood of the children.' There is the problem of poeticizing horror, which resembles the problem of the photographic image that might render starvation visually appealing. There are problems of reduction and over-simplification; of our need to see the world as complex beyond our comprehension, difficult beyond our capacities for solution. If I did not wish to make poetry of what I had seen, what is it I thought poetry was?

At some point the two *mentalidades* converged, and the impulse to witness confronted the prevailing poetic; at the same time it seemed clear that eulogy and censure were no longer possible and that Enzensberger is correct in stating: 'The poem expresses in exemplary fashion that it is not at the disposal of politics. That is its political content.' I decided to follow my impulse to write narratives of witness and confrontation, to disallow obscurity and conventions, which might prettify that which I wished to document. As for that wish, the poems will speak for themselves, obstinate as always. I wish also to thank my friends and *compañeros* in El Salvador for persuading me during a period of doubt that poetry could be enough.

THE COLONEL

What you have heard is true. I was in his house. His wife carried a tray of coffee and sugar. His daughter filed her nails, his son went out for the night. There were daily papers, pet dogs, a pistol on the cushion beside him. The moon swung bare on its black cord over the house. On the television was a cop show. It was in English. Broken bottles were embedded in the walls around the house to scoop the kneecaps from a man's legs or cut his hands to lace. On the windows there were gratings like those in liquor stores. We

43

had dinner, rack of lamb, good wine, a gold bell was on the table for calling the maid. The maid brought green mangoes, salt, a type of bread. I was asked how I enjoyed the country. There was a brief commercial in Spanish. His wife took everything away. There was some talk then of how difficult it had become to govern. The parrot said hello on the terrace. The colonel told it to shut up, and pushed himself from the table. My friend said to me with his eyes: say nothing. The colonel returned with a sack used to bring groceries home. He spilled many human ears on the table. They were like dried peach halves. There is no other way to say this. He took one of them in his hands, shook it in our faces, dropped it into a water glass. It came alive there. I am tired of fooling around he said. As for the rights of anyone, tell your people they can go fuck themselves. He swept the ears to the floor with his arm and held the last of his wine in the air. Something for your poetry, no? he said. Some of the ears on the floor caught this scrap of his voice. Some of the ears on the floor were pressed to the ground.

James Fenton

The Fall of Saigon

In the summer of 1973 I had a dream in which, to my great distress, I died. I was alone in a friend's house at the time and, not knowing what to do, I hid the body in her deep freeze. When everyone returned, I explained to them what had taken place: 'Something terrible happened when you were out. I—I died.'

My friends were very sympathetic. 'But what did you do with the body?' they asked.

I was ashamed to tell them. 'I don't know where it is,' I said, and we all set out to search the house for my corpse. Upstairs and downstairs we looked, until finally, unable to bear the deception any longer, I took my hostess aside and confessed. 'There wasn't anything else in the compartment,' I said, 'and I just didn't know what to do.' We went to the deep freeze and opened it. As the curled and frozen shape was revealed, I woke up.

I was glad to be going off on a journey. I had been awarded a bursary for the purpose of travelling and writing poetry; I intended to stay out of England a long time. Looking at what the world had to offer, I thought either Africa or Indochina would be the place to go. I chose Indochina partly on a whim, and partly because, after the Paris Peace Agreement in February of that same year, it looked as if it was in for some very big changes. The essence of the agreement was that it removed American military personnel from Indochina and stopped the B-52 bombing raids. The question was how long could the American-backed regime last without that accustomed support. I wanted to see Vietnam for myself. I wanted to see a war, and I wanted to see a communist victory, which I presumed to be inevitable. I wanted to see the fall of a city.

I wanted to see a communist victory because, in common with many people, I believed that the Americans had not the slightest justification for their interference in Indochina. I admired the Vietcong and, by extension, the Khmer Rouge, but I subscribed to a philosophy that prided itself on taking a cool, critical look at the liberation movements of the Third World. I, and many others like me, supported these movements against the ambitions of American foreign policy. We supported them as nationalist movements. We did not support their political character, which we perceived as Stalinist in the case of the Vietnamese, and in the case of the Cambodians . . . I don't know. The theory was, and is, that when a genuine movement of national liberation was fighting against imperialism it received our unconditional support. When such a movement had won, then it might well take its place among the governments we execrated—those who ruled by sophisticated tyranny in the name of socialism.

There was also an argument that Stalinism was not a simple equivalent of Fascism, that it contained what was called a partial negation of capitalism. Further, under certain conditions it might even lay down the foundations of a socialist organization of society. In the Third World, Stalinism might do the job which the bourgeois revolutions had done in Europe. Even Stalinism had its progressive features.

Our attitudes may have looked cynical in the extreme. In fact they were the formulation of a dilemma. After all, we had not invented the Indochina War, and it was not for us to conjure out of thin air a movement that would match up to our own aspirations for Britain. To remain neutral over Vietnam was to support the Americans. To argue for an end to all US involvement, and leave the matter at that, was to ignore the consequences of one's own argument. If there was a conflict on which one had to choose sides, then it was only right to choose sides honestly, and say: 'Stalinists they may be, but we support them.' The slogans of the Vietnam movement were crude stuff indeed—'One side right, one side wrong, victory to . . . Vi-et-cong!'—but the justice of the cause was deeply felt.

This feeling was shared by many people who were not socialists or communists by any stretch of the imagination, and who did not have any other political axe to grind. Such people had merely to look at what was being done to Vietnam in the name of the Free World to know that the Free World was in the wrong. The broadest support for the anti-war movement was engendered by a disgust at what the Americans were doing. In Britain, the Communist Party made precious few gains in this period. The tradition to which the students looked was broadly or narrowly Trotskyist, a fact that no doubt intrigued the Vietnamese communists, who had taken care to bump off their own Trotskyists a long time before. But the Trotskyist emphasis, like the general emphasis, was again on opposition to American imperialism. Very few people idolized the

Vietcong, or the North Vietnamese, or Uncle Ho, in quite the same way that, for instance, the French Left did. Indeed, it might be fairly said that the Left in Britain was not terribly curious about or enamoured of the Vietnamese movement it was supporting.

By the time I was about to go to Indochina, the issue had fallen from prominence. When the Indochina Solidarity Conference was held in London that year, my own group, the International Socialists, did not bother to send a delegation. There were other, more important campaigns: against the Tories, against the Industrial Relations Act, against racism. Our movement had grown up: it was to be working class in character; it had graduated from what it thought of as student issues. It had not abandoned Vietnam, but it had other fish to fry. At the conference itself, I remember two speeches of interest. One was by I. F. Stone, who was hissed by the audience (which included an unusually large number of Maoists) when he attacked Chairman Mao for shaking hands with a murderer like Nixon. The other was by Noam Chomsky, who warned against the assumption that the war was over, and that direct US intervention in Vietnam would cease. Chomsky argued that the Left were wrong to dismiss the 'Domino Theory' out of hand. As stated by the Cold Warriors it might not measure up to the facts, but there was another formulaton which did indeed make sense; it was US foreign policy, rather than Russian expansionism, which knocked over the dominoes: countries might be forced into positions where the only alternative to accepting American domination was to go over to the opposite camp and would thus be drawn into the power struggle whether they liked it or not.

I mention such arguments because I do not wish to give the impression that I was completely wide-eyed about the Vietnamese communists when I set out. I considered myself a revolutionary socialist, of the kind who believes in no Fatherland of the Revolution, and has no cult hero. My political beliefs were fairly broadly based and instinctively grasped, but they were not, I hope, religiously held.

49

But I wanted very much to see a communist victory. Although I had a few journalist commissions, I was not going primarily as a journalist. I wanted to see a war and the fall of a city because— because I wanted to see what such things were like. I had once seen a man dying, from natural causes, and my first reaction, as I realized what was taking place, was that I was glad to be *there*. This is what happens, I thought, so watch it carefully, don't miss a detail. The first time I saw a surgical operation (it was in Cambodia) I experienced the same sensation, and no doubt when I see a child born it will be even more powerful. The point is simply in being there and seeing it. The experience has no essential value beyond itself.

I spent a long time on my preparations and, as my dream of dying might indicate, I had developed some fairly morbid apprehensions. The journey itself was to be utterly selfish. I was going to do exactly as I pleased. As far as political beliefs were concerned, they were going to remain 'on the table'. Everything was negotiable. But the fear of death, which had begun for the first time to enter my calculations, followed me on my journey. As I went through the passport check at Heathrow, I glanced at the Sunday papers and saw that the poet I most admired, W. H. Auden, had just died in Vienna. People were talking about him in the passenger lounge, or rather they weren't talking about him, they were talking about his face.

I kept seeing the face, on the plane, in the transit lounges, on the empty seat next to mine, and I kept remembering Auden. From the start he had willed himself into old age, and it was not surprising that he had not lived longer. He had courted death, cultivated first eccentricity and then what looked to the world very much like senility. It was not senility, but it was a useful cover for his despair of living, the deep unhappiness which he kept concealed. He had held the world very much at arm's length, and had paid a heavy price for doing so.

Between sleeping and reading, I found myself passing through a depression compounded of one part loneliness, one part uneager anticipation, one part fright and two parts obscure self-pity. In Bombay the depression began to lift: I slept all morning at the Sea Palace Hotel, then, surrendering to the good offices of a driver and guide, set off to see the sights. The evening light was first a muddy yellow; next it turned green. On the Malabar Hill, I paid my respects to the spectacular view, the vultures picking the bones on the Parsee tower, the lights along the waterfront ('Queen Victoria's Necklace') and the couples sitting on the lawns of the Hanging Gardens, in attitudes reminiscent of a Mogul miniature. The most impressive sight was a vast open-air laundry, a yard full of boiling vats between which, through the dark and steam, one could scarcely make out the moving figures of the workers. There was a steamy warmth everywhere, which I liked immediately. Waking the next morning, I looked down on a wide meandering river, either the Salween or the Irrewaddy, whose muddy waters spread out for miles into the sea. Seen from the plane, the landscape of the Far East was dazzling, silver and blue. You could tell you had arrived in Indochina when you saw the rows and rows of yellow circles, where muddy water had filled the bomb craters.

Fear of Madness: November 1973

'I know not whether others share my feelings on this point,' wrote De Quincey, 'but I have often thought that if I were compelled to forego England, and to live in China, and among Chinese manners and modes of life and scenery, I should go mad.' I read this sentence the other day, for the first time, and as I came to the last clause I was struck once again with the full nausea of my first trip to Vietnam. 'The causes of my horror lie deep,' De Quincey went on. But he set them forth beautifully:

> No man can pretend that the wild, barbarous, and capricious superstitions of Africa, or of savage tribes elsewhere, affect him in the way that he is affected by the ancient, monumental, cruel, and elaborate religions of Indostan, etc. The mere antiquity of Asiatic things, of their institutions, histories, modes of faith, etc is so impressive, that to me the vast age of the race and name overpowers the sense of youth in the individual. A young Chinese seems to me an antediluvian renewed .... Man is a weed in those regions.

I was impressed, overawed, by the scale and age of the subject: a war that had been going on for longer than I had been alive, a people about whose history and traditions I knew so little. I had read some books in preparation, but the effect of doing so was only to make the country recede further. So much had been written about Vietnam. I hadn't even had the application to finish Frances Fitzgerald's *The Fire in the Lake*. The purpose of the book seemed to be to warn you off the subject.

I could well have believed that somebody was trying to tell me something when I came out of my room on the first morning in Saigon and stepped over the decapitated corpse of a rat. I was staying, as most British journalists did, in the Hotel Royale, but even there I felt something of an intruder. I had to find work, I had to sell some stories, but I was afraid of trespassing on somebody else's patch. There was an epidemic of infectious neurosis at the time: as soon as one journalist had shaken it off, another would succumb. It would attack without warning—in the middle of an otherwise amiable meal, in the bars, in your room. And it could be recurrent, like malaria.

The reason for the neurosis was not far to seek; indeed it sought you out, and pursued you throughout the day: Saigon was an addicted city, and we were the drug; the corruption of children, the mutilation of young men, the prostitution of women, the humiliation of the old, the division of the family, the division of the country—it had all been done in our name. People looked back to the French Saigon with a sentimental warmth, as if the problem had begun with the Americans. But the French city, the Saigon of the Piastre as Lucien Bodard called it, had represented the opium stage of the addiction. With the Americans had begun the heroin phase, and what I was seeing now was the first symptoms of withdrawal. There was a desperate edge to life. It was impossible to relax for a moment. The last of the American troops had left at the end of March, six months before I arrived, and what I saw now was what they left behind: a vast service industry clamouring for the attention of a dwindling number of customers: Hey you! American! Change money, buy *Time* magazine, give me back *Time* magazine I sell you yesterday, buy *Stars and Stripes,* give me back *Stars and Stripes,* you number one, you number ten, you number ten thousand Yankee, you want number one fuck, you want *Quiet American,* you want *Ugly American,* you give me money I shine shoes; number one, no sweat . . . on and on, the passionate pursuit of money.

The bar at the Royale was half open to the street. The coffee at breakfast tasted of diarrhoea. You washed it down with Bireley's orangeade ('Refreshing . . . and no carbonation!'). Through the windows peered the shoe-shine boys—Hey! You! It was starting up again. One morning I was ignoring a particularly revolting specimen when he picked up a handful of sand which he pretended to eat: 'You! You no give me money, you want I eat shit!' His expression, as he brought the dirt to his mouth, was most horrible. It was impossible to imagine how a boy of that age had acquired such features: he was about ten, but his face contained at least thirty years of degeneration and misery. A few days later I did give him my boots to clean. He sat down in the corner of the bar and set to work, first with a matchstick and a little water, meticulously removing all the mud and dust from the welt, then with the polish. The whole process took about half an hour, and the barman and I watched him throughout, in fascination. He was determined to show his superiority to all other contestants in the trade. I was amused, and gave him a large sum. He was furious; it wasn't nearly enough. We haggled for a while, but I finally gave in. I gave him about a pound. The next day, at the same time, he came into the bar; his eyes were rolling back in their sockets and he staggered helplessly around the tables and chairs. I do not know what he had taken, but I knew how he had bought it.

Of all the ingenious and desperate forms of raising money, the practice of drugging your baby and laying the thing on the pavement in front of the visitor seemed to me the most repulsive. It did not take long to see that none of these children was ever awake during the day, or that, if asleep, something was amiss. Among the foreigners, stories circulated about the same baby being seen in the arms of five different mothers in one week, but the beggar who regularly sat outside the Royale always had the same child, a girl of eighteen months or so. I never gave any money either to the girl and her 'mother', or to any of the other teams.

One day, however, I was returning from a good lunch when I saw that a crowd had formed around the old woman, who was wailing and gesticulating. The child was more than usually grey, and there were traces of vomit around her face. People were turning her over, slapping her, trying to force her eyes open. At one point she and the old woman were bundled into a taxi. Then they were taken out again and the slapping was repeated. I went into the hotel and told the girl at reception to call a doctor.

'No,' she replied.

'But the child is sick.'

'If baby go to hospital or doctor'—and here she imitated an injection—'then baby die.'

'No,' I replied, 'if baby *don't* go to hospital maybe baby die.'

'No.'

I took the girl out into the street, where the scene had become grotesque. All the beggars I had ever seen in Saigon seemed to have gathered, and from their filthy garments they were producing pins and sticking them under the child's toenails. 'You see,' I said to the girl, 'no good, number ten. Baby need number one hospital.'

'No, my grandmother had same-same thing. She need this—number one.' And the receptionist produced a small phial of eucalyptus oil.

'That's not number one,' I said, 'that's number ten. Number ten thousand,' I added for emphasis. But it was no good insisting or appealing to other members of the crowd. Everybody was adamant that if the child was taken to hospital, the doctor would kill it with an injection. While I correspondingly became convinced that a moment's delay would cost the child's life.

Finally, after a long eucalyptus massage and repeated pricking of the fingers and toes had produced no visible results, I seemed to win. If I would pay for taxi and hospital, the woman would come. I pushed my way through the crowd and dragged her towards the taxi—a battered old Renault tied together with string. The baby was wrapped in tarpaulin and her face covered with a red handkerchief. Every time I tried to remove the handkerchief, from which came the most ominous dry gaspings, the woman replaced it. I directed the taxi-man to take us to number one hospital and we set off.

From the start everything went wrong. Within a hundred yards we had to stop for petrol. Then a van stalled in front of us, trapping the taxi. Next, to my amazement, we came to what must have been, I thought, the only level-crossing in Saigon, where as it happened a train was expected in the near future. And around here we were hit by the side-effects of Typhoon Sarah, which at the time was causing havoc in the northern provinces. We also split a tyre, though this was not noticed till later. Driving on through the cloudburst, the taxi-man seemed strangely unwilling to hurry. So I sat in the back seat keeping one hand on the horn and with the other attempting to ease the baby's breathing by loosening the tarpaulin around her neck. I also recall from time to time producing a third arm with which to comfort the old woman, and I remember that her shoulder, when my hand rested on it, was very small and very hard. Everything, I said, was going to be number one, okay: number one hospital, number one doctor, babysan okay. We were travelling through Cholon, the Chinese quarter, on an errand of Western mercy.

All things considered, it took a long time for it to dawn on me that we were not going to a hospital at all. We even passed a first-aid post without the taxi-man giving it a glance. In my mind there was an image of the sort of thing required: a large cool building dating from French times, recently refurbished by American aid and charity, with some of the best equipment in the East. I could even imagine the sententious plaques on the walls. Perhaps there would be a ward named after the former US Ambassador. It would be called the Bunker Ward.

It was when the old woman began giving directions that I saw I had been duped. We were threading our way through some modern slums, which looked like the Chinese equivalent of the Isle of Dogs. 'Where is the hospital? This is no hospital,' I said.

'Yes, yes,' the taxi-man replied, 'we are going to hospital, number one doctor.'

We stopped by a row of shops and the taxi-man got out. I jumped from the car and seized him by the arm, shouting: 'I said number one hopsital. You lie. You cheap charlie. You number ten thousand Saigon.' We were surrounded by children, in the pouring rain, the taxi-man tugging himself free, and me gripping him by the arm. It was left to the woman, carrying the little bundle of tarpaulin, to find out exactly where the doctor lived. Finally I gave in, and followed her up some steps, then along an open corridor lined with tailors and merchants. At least, I thought, when the baby dies I can't be blamed. And once I had had that thought, it turned into a wish: a little cough would have done it, a pathetic gurgle, then silence, and my point about Western medicine would have been proved to my own satisfaction. I should have behaved very well, and would have paid for the funeral.

In retrospect it was easy to see how the establishment would command confidence: the dark main room with its traditional furnishings, the walls lined with photographs of ancestors in traditional Vietnamese robes, a framed jigsaw of the Italian lakes. And in the back room (it would, of course, have to be a back room) a plump, middle-aged lady was massaging the back of another plump, middle-aged lady. They paid hardly any attention when we came in. There was not the slightest element of drama. Indeed, I began to see that I was now the only person who was panicking. When she had finished the massage, the doctor turned her attention to the baby. First she took some ointment from a dirty bowl at her elbow, and rubbed it all over the little grey body. Then from another bowl she produced some pink substance resembling Euthymol toothpaste, with which she proceeded to line the mouth. In a matter of minutes, the child was slightly sick, began to cry, and recovered. I had never been more furious in my life. To complete my humiliation, the doctor refused any payment. She provided the old woman with a prescription wrapped in newspaper, and we left.

We drove to the miserable shelter in which the old woman lived.

'Sit down,' she said, indicating the wooden bed which was the only feature of her home apart from the roof (there were no walls).

In any other mood I might have been moved by the fact that the only English she knew beyond the terrible pidgin currency of the beggars was a phrase of hospitality. But I so deeply hated her at that moment that I could only give her a couple of pounds, plus some useless advice about keeping the baby warm and off the pavements, and go.

I left the taxi-man at a garage not far from the Royale, where I also gave him some money towards repairing the split tyre.

'You number one, Saigon,' he said, with a slight note of terror in his voice.

The weather had cleared up, and I left him, strolling along past the market stalls. Here, you could buy US army foot-powder in bulk, K-rations, lurp-rations (for Long Range Reconnaissance Patrols), souvenir Zippo lighters (engraved 'Yea though I walk through the valley of the shadow of death I shall fear no evil, for I am the evilest sonofabitch in the valley'), khaki toothbrushes and flannels, and model helicopters constructed out of used hypodermics. You could also buy jackets brightly embroidered with the words 'When I die I shall go to heaven, for I have spent my time in hell—Saigon,' and a collection of GI cartoons and jokes called *Sorry 'bout that, Vietnam.* Five years ago, there had been over 500,000 American GIs. Now there were none.

As I approached the hotel people began asking how the baby was, and smiling when I replied, 'Okay.' I began to think: Supposing they were all in it together? Suppose the old woman, the taxi-driver, the man whose van stalled, the engine-driver—suppose they were all now dividing the proceeds and having a good laugh at my expense, congratulating the child on the way it had played its role? That evening I would be telling the story to some old Saigon hand when a strange pitying smile would come over his face. 'You went to Cholon, did you? Describe the doctor . . . uhuh . . . .Was there a jigsaw puzzle of the Italian Lakes? Well, well, well. So they even used the toothpaste trick. Funny how the oldest gags are still the best . . . .'

Indeed I did have rather that conversation a few days later, with an American girl, a weaver. It began: 'You realize, of course, first of all that the taxi-driver was the husband of the old woman....' But I do not think there was a conspiracy. Worse, I should rather conclude that the principals involved were quite right not to trust the hospital doctors with a beggar's child. It was for this reason that the hotel receptionist had countermanded my orders to the taxi-man, I learned afterwards, and many people agreed with her.

When the old woman came back on the streets, I hardly recognized either her or the child, who for the first time looked conscious and well. 'Babysan okay now, no sick,' she said, gazing at me with an awful adoring expression, though the hand was not

57

stretched out for money. And when I didn't reply she turned to the child and told it something in the same unctuous tones. This performance went on for the rest of my stay: whenever I was around the child would be made to look at the kind foreigner who had saved its life. I had indeed wanted to save the child's life, but not in *that* way, not on the old woman's terms.

I was disgusted, not just at what I saw around me, but at what I saw in myself. I saw how perilously thin was the line between the charitable and the murderous impulse, how strong the force of righteous indignation. I could well imagine that most of those who came to Vietnam to fight were not the evilest sons-of-bitches in the valley. It was just that, beyond the bright circle illuminated by their intelligence, in which everything was under their control and every person a compliant object, they came across a second person—a being or a nation with a will of its own, with its own medicine, whether Fishing Pills or pink toothpaste, and its own ideas for the future. And in the ensuing encounter everything had turned to justifiable ashes. It was impossible in Saigon to be the passive observer. Saigon cast you, inevitably, into the role of the American.

Elsewhere it was possible to breathe more freely, but I was conscious always of following in somebody else's footsteps. On a trip to Quang Tri, the northernmost city in South Vietnam, I asked my driver how far away was the town. 'This is the main street,' he said, indicating the overgrown rubble. We stopped and walked to the edge of the river, looking across to the liberated zone and the still figures of the soldiers on the Other Side. I had heard endless stories of people's exploits in Quang Tri, but it meant nothing to me. There was no point in my being there. I was more at ease in Hué. I walked around the Imperial City in the rain, through the beautiful, shabby grounds that looked like the vegetable gardens of an English country house. But I was nothing more than a tourist. Once, I thought I was actually going to meet someone important when a Vietnamese took me to see a woman. But the woman was his girlfriend, whom he was hoping to marry. She worked in a chemist's shop, and when we arrived the drill was simply that I should go in, buy some aspirin or something, look at her, and tell her boyfriend what I thought. He waited outside for my opinion. I gave the girl a warm recommendation.

I went also to Dalat, a village in the Highlands that, because it was once a resort, had been spared from attack. I walked through the forests where the tall poinsettias were in flower: the Vietnamese called them the Man of Genius Tree. In my hotel room, there were poems scrawled in ballpoint on the walls:

I am a fairy from the moon.
You are my happiness.
When the sun sets
The river will be without water
And the rocks will scrape.
Our promises will be forever.

There was a war going on, but the nearest I got to it was in Gia Nghia, a former American base in the Quang Duc region. It had been a great feat of engineering: the wide roads of red earth cut through the jungle, the vast clearing. There were little signs of America everywhere, the half-caste children, even the dogs of the area were mongrels from the American trackers. There was a dog's footprint on a concrete floor, with the words 'Our Mascot (MACV)' scratched beside it. There were drunken Montagnards wandering round, and in the market-place, which sported two billiard saloons, a soldier was smoking marijuana through a waterpipe made out of an anti-tank shell. There was music and the sound of motorbikes from the Wall of Death, but when we went in the evening and asked them to open it up we found the family asleep on the track.

The USAID compound had a commanding view of the town. A Montagnard soldier, with huge stretched earlobes, stood on guard outside. Inside, leaning over a short-wave radio, was Ed Sprague, the local USAID official and the only American I ever met in the field. He was marking positions on a map. There was a rifle propped against the wall and a neatly polished revolver on the table. The rest of the room was magnificently equipped, with photos, souvenirs, stereo tape-recorder, cocktail bar, Montagnard girl, soft furnishings. Above the bar, engraved on copper and nicely framed, were the sayings of Sprague himself:

The Special Forces have done so much for nothing for so long that now we are expected to do everything for nothing for ever.

And:

> If you kick me once in the back when I'm not looking I'll
> kick you twice in the face when you are looking.
>
> —Sprague '71

He was very polite, but the USAID compound had no room to put us up, so we went to the local hotel in town. The South Vietnamese helicopter pilots were billeted there, and I spent the evening playing Co Tuong ('Kill the General'), the Chinese and Vietnamese version of chess. The round wooden pieces were engraved with Chinese characters, and the board was made of paper. A river flowed down the middle of the board, separating the two rows of GIs, who had to move forward, one square at a time, until they crossed the river, after which they might move in any direction. Just behind the GIs lay the two artillery pieces, which might fire in straight lines at any of the pieces, as long as there was some single obstruction in between. The horses made knights' moves, and could cross the river, as could the tanks, which were the equivalent of rooks. But the elephants, which always moved two squares at a time, diagonally, were unable to cross the river and were reserved for the defence. The general was protected by his officer escort. He lived in a compound of four squares. The red general must never 'see' the black general—that is, there must always be something in between.

'This is the black general,' said my teacher: 'He is Ho Chi Minh. This is the red general. He is Thieu.'

'But Ho Chi Minh is dead.'

'I know. I killed him in the last game.'

I also spent some time in the billiard saloons, collecting Vietnamese jokes from the pilots. The jokes were different in character from Cambodian jokes, which were all about sex. Here is a typical Cambodian joke. A mosquito is caught in a storm and takes shelter in an elephant's cunt. (Roars of laughter.) After the storm, the mosquito meets a friend.

'Did you know what that was you were sheltering in just then?' says the second mosquito.

'What?'

'It was an elephant's cunt.' (Further roars of laughter, particularly from the women.)

'Oh,' says the first mosquito, flexing his muscles, 'a pity I didn't know that. If I'd realized it was an elephant's cunt I might have done something about it!' (Hysterical laughter, old men clutch their sides, tears course down the faces of the women, food and wine are produced and the teller of the joke is asked for more.)

Vietnamese jokes were all about tactics. This is one: during the Tet Offensive in 1968, the Vietcong blew up the central span of the main bridge over the Perfume River, and for some time afterwards planks were put across, and the bridge was very dangerous. A young and beautiful girl was walking home from the school in which she taught (nods of interest, audience leans forward and is very quiet) when she fell into the water (smiles), which was most unfortunate because she could not swim (smiles disappear). So she started calling out, 'Help me, help me,' and a large crowd gathered on the river bank, but none of the young men wanted to help her (expressions completely disappear). So the girl called out: 'If anybody jumps in and saves me, I will marry him.' (Smiles.) At this point all the young men rushed forward, but every time one of them reached the edge of the water (smiles) another man pulled him back, because every one wanted to marry the young girl (smiles disappear, anxiety expressed on faces of young men). And so the girl was very near to drowning, when an old man succeeded in getting into the water and saving the girl.

At the wedding, he was asked by the press: 'How come a weak and ugly old man like you managed to win the girl, when all the young men were trying?'

And the old man replied: 'Every time a young man tried to get in, he was pulled back by another. But when an old and ugly man like me appeared on the scene, they didn't bother to pull me back. In fact they pushed me in.' (End of joke. Heads nod. There is a little laughter.)

Later when I was in the city Hué, I tried this joke out, and the effect at the end of the story was striking. First, there was a silence. Then I was asked to repeat the punchline. Then all hell broke loose, and I thought for a moment that I might be chucked into the Perfume River myself. After several minutes of animated conversation the company turned back to me. They had two comments: *Primo*, the young men were right in the first place not to jump in—after all, they might have been killed. *Secundo*, the story was not true.

While not collecting jokes or playing Chinese chess I was trying to find out about the war. This was difficult. Some of the small outposts that now represented the division between North and South and that were dotted around the mountains—they had names like Bu Prang and Bu Bong—were under attack. The helicopter squadron with which I was staying was here to give support to these outposts. There was a low-level campaign on the part of the Vietcong to wipe out these little impediments, which were used by the South Vietnamese as listening posts along the region of the Ho Chi Minh trail, and which had been set up largely by the Special Forces in which Sprague had served. Now the campaign was under the aegis of Saigon, and these outposts were beginning to fall. At one point my chess-master produced a hand-drawn map and started to show me what was happening, but he didn't get far before somebody came into the room, and he shoved the map quickly into his pocket.

We slept seven or eight to a room, and in the middle of the night I awoke to the sound of rifle fire. There was an extraordinary noise going on, and I suddenly thought—Good God! They're attacking Gia Nghia. They're coming into the camp and blowing whistles. Why are they all blowing whistles? They're blowing whistles in order to tell each other where they are, perhaps to create a panic in the camp . . . . Panic!

I got up and went to the window. One of the soldiers burst out laughing. There was no gunfire any more: a soldier had shot at a shadow, perhaps. The noise of whistles, though it continued, was nothing more than the noise of the jungle. Go back to bed, you idiot.

During this period, moving from one outpost to another, I often suffered from nightmares. It was as if some great spade was digging through my mind, turning over deep clods of loam. If Saigon was a nightmare by day, it was to Phnom Penh that my thoughts returned at night. In Saigon, I was shown some photographs that had come in from Cambodia, which Associated Press had decided were too horrible to use. In one, a smiling soldier was shown eating the liver of a Khmer Rouge, whom he had just killed; from the expression on his face, he could have been eating anything—the liver was obviously delicious. In the next photograph, a human head was being lowered by the hair into a pot of boiling water—but it was not going to be eaten. In the third photograph, decapitated corpses were being dragged along the road behind an armoured patrol carrier.

My nightmares were about war and torture and death. I remember one particularly vividly. We were standing, myself and a friend who was a poet, at the edge of a battle. The landscape was hilly, but belonged neither to Cambodia nor to Vietnam; it seemed to be northern European. The soldiers had taken several prisoners, and there were wounded and dead lying all around. Their features were Cambodian. As the prisoners were brought in, it became obvious that they were about to be beaten up and killed. The soldiers gathered round them. The poet began to shout out: 'No, no, this isn't happening. I'm not here, I'm not here.' When the beatings began, all the bodies of the dead and wounded rose into the air, and began to travel around the sky above the hill.

'Look,' I said, pointing to the hill, 'isn't that interesting? Those figures. They look just like the shepherds in that van der Goes altarpiece in the Uffizi.'

'I say,' said a journalist at my elbow, 'that's a rather good image. But I suppose you'll be using it in your story.'

'Oh no,' I replied, 'have it by all means. I'm not filing on this one.' Here the dream ended.

After a month, I returned to Saigon. I was due to go to Laos, and my visa was coming to an end. I paid up at my hotel, and by the time I was through immigration at the airport I had no currency left. I was badly in need of a coffee, and I was absolutely terrified that the plane would not come. Suppose I had to stay in Saigon any longer? The neurosis came back alarmingly. I got talking to a Chinese businessman, whom I had helped with his luggage. He bought me a coffee and began a lengthy chat about the virtues of South Vietnam as a source of raw materials. Raw materials were very much needed in Hong Kong. He dealt in anything he could find—here was his card—in timber, scrap iron, swatches . . . .

'What are swatches?' I asked.

'Rags,' he said, 'like these,' and indicated my clothes. Then he left for Hong Kong.

I just did not believe that my plane would go. As it taxied along the runway, a cockroach scuttled along the floor in front of me. I thought, This plane is hopeless, it'll never make the journey. We flew for some way along the Mekong, and the neurosis subsided. Then suddenly I looked out and—what! We were flying over the sea! Something's gone wrong, I thought, the pilot's got lost, he's going to turn back and go to Saigon. It's all going to happen over again. But then I looked down and saw that the sea effect was a mirage. We were indeed flying over Laos, and we were beginning to lose height.

South Vietnam as It was: December 1974

'Ask him why he paints his little fingernails.' And it wasn't just the fingernails. It was the little toenails as well— carefully pedicured and varnished a deep shade of red. This seemed most inappropriate in a professional soldier. What would his officers say on parade? In the British army, I reflected patriotically, the offending nails would have been ceremonially torn out.

As the question was asked, I watched his face. A slow and secret smile came over it. He looked down at the table and mumbled inaudibly. The face was like a baby's, quite unmarked by the experience of war. It went, in a way, with the painted nails, but not with the Ranger's uniform. In any event, he didn't want to answer, so I asked him what he thought of the war.

We were sitting in a café in Go Da Hau, a small town near the Cambodian border, on the Saigon-Phnom Penh road. He desperately wanted to talk, but found it difficult. Finally, he said that the war was like a guttering candle. Occasionally it would flare up, but before long it would be entirely extinguished.

And what did he think of that?

There was nothing now that he could do. He would become a monk, he said. He would never marry. There was no job he could do, and little possibility of earning money except by soldiering. If the war ended, that was that.

He was an orphan. His father had died in Dien Bien Phu, and his mother soon afterwards. He had been educated at military school and served in the army ever since. No wonder he was still prepared to fight. No wonder, despite what people said, the Saigon army was still prepared to fight. For many of the soldiers there was simply nothing else they could do.

The Ranger talked sadly until late into the night. For the most part, he did not know how to express himself. His features strained with the burden of something very important that he wanted to say. Finally, a couple of Vietcong were sighted just outside town. Gunfire burst out all around us. The family who ran the café gave us shelter in the back. The Ranger straightened himself up, put on the look of a professional soldier, and disappeared into the blackness of the street.

Conversations in the dark, sad rambling discussions which always led back to the war, shy officers who told you one thing by night but begged you not to remember it the next day. Conducted to the accompaniment of Chinese chess, the tongues loosened by Vietnamese alcohol, which tasted like meths and probably was. Click, click went the chess-pieces, as the dead GIs lined up on either side of the board, the tanks crossed the river, and the officer escort moved around the compound—always diagonally—to protect the general. I developed a theory of journalism, on which I hoped to build a school. It was to be called the Crepuscular School and the rules were simple: believe nothing that you are told before dusk. Instead of diplomatic sources, or high-ranking sources, or 'usually reliable sources', the crepuscular journalists would refer to 'sources interviewed last night', 'sources at midnight', or best of all 'sources contacted a few hours before dawn'. It would be considered unprofessional to interview the general on the morning of the battle. You would wait till the evening, when he was reviewing the cost. Crepuscular stories would cut out the bravado. Their predominant colourings would be melancholy and gloom. In this they would reflect more accurately the mood of the times.

For the war was not guttering out yet by any means. It was a year since I had been in Vietnam, and, if anything, military activities had increased. In a matter of three weeks the equivalent of the population of a small town was killed or wounded, or went missing. District towns fell, remote outposts fell, enormous enemy losses were claimed—little of it was ever seen. If things were going badly, the military did not want you around. If well, no interest was shown. It was, again, difficult to locate the war, difficult to get to it. Indeed most of the journalists in Saigon had given up trying. The same editor who would have insisted on maximum-risk reporting when the Americans were fighting now considered such journalism a matter of minority interest. And so the idea grew up that ARVN, the Saigon army, was simply not fighting; an idea that as far as I know was never tested against the reality of the time, although later it received a sort of retrospective justification.

I really wanted to meet the Provisional Revolutionary Government, the PRG, but I was beginning to think that the chances of 'going across' into the areas it occupied were rather slim. The problem was simply the transition: in 'going across' you were likely to be fired at by the South Vietnamese troops both when you tried to go in and, of course, when you came out. The problem was not to locate the Vietcong areas. It was simply a question of accreditation and opportunity. In the end, I took a long short cut.

I had returned to Saigon where I was introduced to a man by the name of Jean-Claude. Jean-Claude had been to Vietcong areas several times before, spoke a bit of Vietnamese and was a sort of Vietcong groupie. He had been educated, he said, at an English borstal—and much admired the film of *The Loneliness of the Long-Distance Runner*—had been active in 1968 in *les événements*, was now a member of the French Communist Party and lived as a freelance photographer-cum-reporter-cum-entrepreneur. The emphasis was very much on the entrepreneur. I never knew how much of what he said was sheer fantasy and how much was true, but the fact remains that when he finally left Saigon it was in an official limousine provided by the People's Revolutionary Government of South Vietnam. He 'made things happen'.

Our intention was to hire a car and travel from Saigon to Quang Tri, taking in en route every major town and covering a large part of the Central Highlands. At points along the way, we were bound to come across the PRG; indeed we intended to go through areas they controlled, and to drop in on them as the occasion arose.

We left Saigon with great relief: the city was in a festive mood; the loudspeakers were blaring 'Angels from the Realms of Glory'; there were toy Christmas trees, Stars of Bethlehem, tanks and machine-guns on sale, and the street-vendors were being very insistent about the merits of the most hideous Christmas greetings cards.

The first village of interest we encountered was on the main road that had been napalmed a couple of days before. The Vietcong had come into the village to cut off the road, and had been trapped there along with many of the villagers by the Saigon troops. The village had then been destroyed by a force obviously capable of creating enormous heat. I noticed a pile of bananas that had been charred right through, although they preserved their original shape. They looked like something discovered and preserved in Pompeii.

We went on through landscapes as varied as their inhabitants— the coffee plantations near Djiring, for instance, which were worked by a Montagnard race whose language sounded curiously like Italian. We stayed the first night as the guest of an Italian missionary, who had married a Montagnard and was working in agriculture. He told us of the Montagnard resistance movement, *Fulro*—how it was growing, and how it maintained an uneasy, informal liaison with the Vietcong. We met a French planter, whose factor was Vietcong (there was an 'arrangement' as in all rural areas). And we gave a lift to a Frenchman known as Raquin, the Shark, who made his living by selling his own brands of French cheeses and Pernod, which he concocted in a small shack next door to the American Embassy in Saigon. Raquin was on the road distributing his wares to the various Frenchmen dotted around the country, so we dropped in with him to share a rum punch with an old Martiniquan soldier living just south of Dalat.

At Dalat, much less than halfway between Saigon and our destination, we hit the edge of a typhoon. Mist and pouring rain accompanied us as far as the coast and the seaside resort of Nha Trang, where we spent a gloomy Christmas Eve. It would be nice, would it not, to get to the PRG on Christmas Day?

'You know, my friend,' Jean-Claude would say, crossing his legs as he drove, steering with one hand, lighting a cigarette with the other, and giving me what appeared to be the full benefit of his attention, 'you know, my friend, we're going to see some great things, for sure. For sure. Yes, man.' And occasionally, looking out across the paddy-fields of the coastal strip, he would say, Yes, we were getting warm, and then, No, we were getting cold.

At one point we came upon what had been a large military base, one of those that disappeared overnight when the Americans left, torn down by a thousand tiny hands and carted away for building materials. There were large roads and runways beside the dunes, and at the edge of the sea a single standing arch marked '*Das Schloss*'. Beside it stood a village, surrounded by a thorn hedge, where our arrival caused something of a stir. 'This is it, my friend,' said Jean-Claude, 'they're here, for sure, I know it.' But of the group of elders who came out to meet us nobody seemed willing to talk, and they said there was no food to be had in the village. There were no government soldiers, no Vietcong to be seen, and no flags of any kind. The only notice in the village had come from the military base, and now formed the wall of a house: 'Rabies Suspected—No Unauthorized Personnel.' We left disappointed.

And continued up the coast, and through a steep valley which had been almost entirely defoliated. The mountains were strewn with huge boulders, and the white stumps of the dead trees pointed up out of the returning scrub. Several of the rocks had been decorated with the skull and crossbones, and under these sat groups of Saigon soldiers sheltering from the rain, high up the hillside. We drove until evening, when the light began to fade, and we were determined to get to Bong Son that night or fail in the attempt: a failure meaning that we would thus have come across a Vietcong checkpoint. But no such luck. We passed through several astonished and frightened groups of Saigon soldiers, bivouacked by the bridges, and the road was just closing up altogether for the night when we entered Bong Son. An officer in his jeep, *en tenue libre* for the evening, was chatting up the girls in the main street. He asked us what we were doing, explained there was no hotel and invited us to spend the night at his headquarters. He turned out to be the District Chief, a certain Major Bang.

The major, as his name so painfully suggests, was very keen on artillery. He explained to us at supper—shouting over the sound of his own weaponry outside—how scrupulously he was adhering to the Paris Peace Agreement: he was firing only defensively, and only at known targets. I concluded, by the end of an ear-splitting night, that he must have been very much on the defensive, and that his *deuxième bureau* must have been working round the clock to provide him with new co-ordinates for the known targets. Either that or, as in the majority of such camps meant to guard strategic bridges and bases, the tactic was simply to fire enough ordnance to give an impression of strength. We ourselves were not fired at once during the night. Major Bang also told us that the people of the area, after their experience of the Vietcong, loathed and despised the communists. We had an opportunity to check up on this statement the next day.

The soldiers told us that three bridges had been destroyed just up the road, and that the flood waters from the typhoon had rendered repairs impossible for some days. This meant that our plan of driving to Quang Tri—or indeed to Danang or Hué or anywhere else in the northern provinces—was spoiled. It was therefore in a mood of some frustration that we drove up to the first bridge to check the damage for ourselves.

There had been a small battle the night before between the Vietcong and the guards beside the bridge, and one of the Vietcong had been killed. His body lay there. The face had been completely stoved in and the whole corpse lacked blood. It looked as though it had been dragged through the water; round its waist there was still a length of rope. As we stood there, a battalion of soldiers arrived by truck, dismounted and began to climb along the broken bridge. They were about to begin an operation to flush out the Vietcong from the area, and they were in a rather bloodthirsty, hysterical mood. There was tension too among the large crowd of local villagers and travellers who had assembled by the bridge. One of the soldiers took a stick and prised open the mouth of the dead man.

'We go kill too many VC,' the soldier said. There was in the soldiers' manner a mixture of satisfaction and fright.

Jean-Claude was angry enough at the reversal in our plans, but the scene by the bridge roused him to furious action. 'You know, my friend,' he said, 'the VC are all around here, that's for sure.' If we weren't going to get as far north as Quang Tri, we might as well 'go across' at the earliest opportunity. We drove a little way back down the road, and came to a pathway where we could leave the car fairly inconspicuously. Then we simply started walking across the fields. We met a peasant, and Jean-Claude asked him the way to the 'Giai Phong' (liberators). He gave a vague indication with his hand. When we had crossed a couple of small fields, and were still only about a hundred yards from the road, we came to a small stream and a broken bridge. I was just wondering why the bridge had not been repaired when, looking up, I saw a soldier in green peering over the hedge. He beckoned to us to come quickly and pointed to the part where the stream was shallowest. We waded through, and found that we had crossed into the liberated zone.

The soldier carried an American M-79 grenade-launcher, and wore an American jacket with pouches for the grenades. From his lack of insignia or helmet we took him to be Vietcong, but there was no particular way of telling. He had a transistor radio slung from his belt. Behind where he stood there was a large pond, and beyond the pond another hedgerow. Behind the hedgerow, looking to see what on earth was happening, was a row of green pith helmets. The first soldier indicated that we should be careful as we could still be seen from the road. We hurried through the pond, avoiding the bomb craters that he pointed out to us, and emerged, dripping with mud and sweat and trembling with excitement, where the group in the pith helmets were waiting. During the whole process, nobody had pointed a gun at us and, although we had dropped in unannounced, nobody seemed at a loss as to what to do. They took us into a small hut and gave us a couple of coconuts to drink.

'Fuck me,' said Jean-Claude, 'we've made it, didn't I tell you we'd make it, my friend?'

It dawned on us that, although we had got so far, we were now in a considerable quandary. After all, we were only about a mile from where the operation to flush out the Vietcong was supposed to begin, and only about two miles or so from Major Bang.

'You know what, my friend,' said Jean-Claude, 'we're going to have to leave that car. They'll see it on the road in no time. But you know what, I don't care, man, I don't fucking care. If we have to walk to Hanoi I don't mind. We can't go back to Saigon now, my friend, that's for sure.' I was too elated by having actually got across to be much worried by this talk. It was as if we had just stepped through the looking-glass.

The first thing I noticed, with slight dismay, was how well-dressed and clean everyone was. Their clothes were for the most part of Chinese cloth, rather well-cut. Their watches came from Japan and were set to Hanoi time. The Northerners among them wore pith helmets and Ho Chi Minh badges, but otherwise they were in mufti. Most carried the regulation guerrilla rifle, the AK-47, but one had an American M-16. One man unzipped the embroidered pouch in which he kept his transistor, and turned on Radio Hanoi. A solemn voice, which I afterwards learned belonged to Miss Elizabeth Hodgkin, said: 'I'm a teacher. I-apostrophe-M. A. T-E-A-C-H-E-R. *You're* a student; Y-O-U-apostrophe . . . .' But the thing that struck me most was the number of ball-point pens they wore.

I mention the ball-point pens because they seemed a rather important part of everyday life. When they conversed with us, either in English or in Vietnamese (there were no French-speakers among them), they seemed much happier when committing their thoughts to paper. Jean-Claude said that the Vietnamese they wrote was highly elegant and classical. My conversation was rather less satisfactory. It showed, I thought, that their conception of education, or perhaps Miss Hodgkin's conception, might lean a little far on the rigid side. It went like this. First the soldier wrote: 'HOW ARE YOU?'

Then I wrote: 'VERY HAPPY TO BE HERE.'

The soldier looked mistrustfully at this for some time. He almost crossed it out, but then he wrote underneath: 'FINE THANKS, AND YOU?'

Clearly, as an English-speaker, I had failed at the first hurdle.

While we were thus conversing, a meal of chicken and rice was brought by the villagers, who crowded round to watch us eat. There was intense curiosity, but very little noise. Authority seemed to

71

come very easily to the older soldiers, and the children responded to them at once. Several of those who had been at the bridge came back to tell the soldiers what was happening. One boy of about sixteen seemed particularly moved by what he had seen. He sat on the floor and talked about it for some time in a low voice. Everybody spoke quietly, almost as if they might be heard by the Saigon soldiers on the road. Apart from the odd rifle shot, the only noise was that of the military traffic going up to the bridge. One might have been lulled, by the confidence in everybody's manner, into a sense of total security, had not the political officer politely told us after lunch that it would be dangerous to stay any longer.

Thinking of Major Bang's pronouncement the night before, that the people of the area loathed the communists, I wondered whether I could be completely mistaken in thinking that it was quite false. Two things stayed in my mind. First, the Saigon troops that we had seen that morning were clearly frightened, conscious perhaps that they were in hostile territory. The second was the sight of a small child among the villagers who had crowded round us: he wore the uniform of the local school from where we had just come. Every day he must have had to cross the lines and would have been imbued with Saigon propaganda. Crossing the lines was obviously no problem, but did it not argue a certain political confidence on the part of the People's Revolutionary Government that the child was allowed to do so?

A little girl showed us an easy path back to the road and we made towards where we had left the car. There, to our horror, stood a couple of Saigon soldiers. We walked up as calmly as possible.

'You,' said one of the soldiers, 'why you not obey me? You go see VC.'

We had our excuses prepared. We had wandered innocently into the paddy to take photographs, we said, and we had been stopped by the VC. 'Beaucoup VC,' we said, spiritedly, 'with guns, same-same you.'

'I no VC.'

'No,' we said hurriedly, 'you no VC. Hey, we very scared. VC take us, not let us go. We have to talk, many hours.'

One of the soldiers, a warrant officer, was particularly angry because he had apparently been shouting at us, telling us not to go.

72

Finally we said to him, would he and his friend like a beer? Yes, he said angrily, so we took him to the nearest village, where he made a great scene about buying the drink. Then we took him and the beer back to his friend. I put some money in his hand.

'What's this?' he said.

'English custom,' I said, 'It's called Boxing Day, give beaucoup money to friends. Look, if you tell Major Bang we go VC, beaucoup trouble for us, maybe trouble for you. You no say nothing, okay?' And we left him standing by the roadside, suspiciously eyeing the money and the beer.

Driving as fast as we dared back towards Bong Son, we came again upon the body of the dead Vietcong. It had been dragged down the road and dumped near a small market, no doubt as a warning to the local populace. The rope was still around its waist, but the arms, which previously had been stretched out, were now bent into an embrace. I was surprised. I hadn't thought you could do that to a corpse once it was cold. Jean-Claude brought the car to a near-halt. 'For Christ's sake,' I said, 'let's just get out of here as quickly as possible.' Above all, I did not want to meet Major Bang again, after we had so shamefully abused his hospitality.

D oubling back on our tracks, we drove south and inland, up into the Central Highlands to Kontum—still almost 275 miles north of Saigon. The road was permanently blocked a few miles north. We stood on the hillside looking down into the valley, where a couple of burned-out trucks across the road indicated the front line. On our right was a strangely pleasant camp that looked like a fortified *Club Méditerranée*. There were straw huts and wooden tables and chairs set in the shade, and you hardly noticed the ingenious system of trenches and foxholes leading to the officers' bunkers. Painted faces with plucked eyebrows emerged from the trenches, while from the bunkers came the sound of female laughter and one or two other things. It was widely feared at the time that the Vietcong might attack Kontum. This camp would be their first obstacle.

'You must spend the night with us,' said the medical officer, 'in order to share something of the life of the soldier.' We were happy to accept.

Most of the officers had 'wives'. The major's wife prepared a meal, after which another one of the wives sang a mournful song. Then we all sang songs apart from the major, who produced a cassette radio and played us a medley of dreadful Vietnamese tangos. As it grew dark, the soldiers gathered round to watch us, from a respectable distance. You could see their cigarette ends glowing through the trees. Sometimes, as they began to get drunk on rice spirit, the soldiers would abruptly disappear from sight, falling into foxholes or disappearing into trenches. When the officers retired underground with their wives, we were invited to drink with the other ranks.

Their drunkenness had an edge of desperation. They shouted a lot and staggered blindly outside the perimeter fence, saying that they were about to go off on an ambush. Then they leaned forward and were quietly sick. On one occasion a gun went off by mistake, which didn't frighten me nearly so much as the thought that all this noise must be perfectly audible to the Vietcong in the valley below—the shouts, the laughter, the songs, my fearful rendition of *The Water is Wide* (in the Britten arrangment). Having been on the other side only the day before, I was more conscious than ever of the forces patiently biding their time. Suppose they suddenly decided that the time was ripe? Supposing they came down, or rather up, the mountain like a wolf on the fold—what would one, as it were, do?

The soldiers were also conscious of enormous preparations being made on the other side. On most nights, they said, they could hear the tanks and Molotova trucks of the North Vietnamese Army manoeuvring on the road that was being built in the mountains, the road that would link the Ho Chi Minh trail with the coast. But there were other things that made them depressed. Some of them had not seen their families for two years. They didn't get any leave. They didn't find it easy to live on twenty dollars a month. They didn't like having to go out on patrols, from which their comrades often did not return. They didn't like the fact that the local version of malaria can kill a man in two months, and they didn't like the bitterly cold nights. They slept in makeshift bivouacs, with a sack of rice as a pillow, protecting their food from the numerous rats. In contrast to the officers, they were not allowed 'wives', even if they could have afforded them at the going rate of three dollars a night.

The guard on the north gate was a Cambodian from the Delta. He had very much liked serving under the American officers in the Special Forces, but said that with the South Vietnamese Army everything was a fuck-up. I sat up with him most of the night, hoping to hear the movement of the tanks and trucks. From time to time an old man, also Cambodian, came round with a stick to make sure that the guard was awake. This man was in a good mood: in two weeks, after a service of twenty-five years, he was due to retire. As it happened, he came from one of the villages near Wat Champa, which I had visited on my earlier trip. So I was able to tell him that his home was now in a contested area and very likely to be taken over by the Vietcong. He didn't seem at all worried or surprised by this. He was going to retire—and that was that.

But the guard on the north gate was young and had no option to retire. He wanted to leave the army. There were so many things he wanted to do, he said, if only he wasn't a soldier. When I asked him exactly what it was he wanted to do, he was at a loss to say. We sat and shivered and talked. The quiet landscape was brilliantly lit by the moon. To our left we could see the mountains through which the Ho Chi Minh trail used to run, and ahead of us the site of the new road. Although there was no noise of tanks or trucks, there was no particular comfort from the silence.

'Sometimes,' said the guard, 'I think I will go AWOL —I did it before but the military police arrested me.'

I told him that I thought it would be a very good idea to go AWOL. Some days later, when I was leaving Saigon, I received a visit from him in my hotel room. I was packing. The guard had come to Saigon because he was about to be moved on to some new operation. He didn't know where he was going, and he asked if I had any civilian clothes to spare.

'I want you to write,' said the director of the Open Arms programme whom I saw the next morning in Kontum, 'that the people of Kontum are not afraid of attack by the VC.' The idea of an attack was very much in the air. In Saigon it was feared that the coming dry season—January to May—would see a renewal of hostilities in the Central Highlands, and that Kontum, a well-known city, difficult to defend, would be a tempting target. It is surrounded by mountains and forests. 'You see that mountain,' said the director, as we drove aimlessly around the city, 'you see that mountain? It belongs to us.' But precious little else in Kontum belonged to Saigon.

We drove on south from Kontum through Pleiku to Ban Me Thuot, on a road that was alive with possibilities: we were told to expect bandits, Vietcong, the North Vietnamese Army, Montagnard guerrillas or the South Vietnamese. As the road deteriorated, it rose through thick forests to a clearing that commanded a panoramic view of Laos and Cambodia, and the fields where the Montagnards cultivated their rice. The road was quite free of traffic except at one point when a military convoy of empty trucks appeared, guarded by a helicopter. We were at pains to keep our distance, not wishing to be ambushed. First we overtook it, then we had a puncture and it passed us by. By the time the wheel was changed, we were quite alone.

We were alone, but it did not feel as if we were. At regular intervals along the road there were checkpoints, but none of them, on this day, seemed to be manned. Who had built the checkpoints was a matter for conjecture, and it gave one an eerie feeling, to say the least, to wait around at each, in order to make sure it was possible to pass. The checkpoints were beautifully constructed bowers, woven out of the tall grasses that grew on the edge of the road, and the ground showed clearly that they had only recently been made and only recently abandoned. At one point, outside the checkpoint, a gleaming new B-41 rocket stood on its tripod. This suggested the presence of Vietcong—and yet it was uncharacteristic to leave good ammunition behind. Were they simply unwilling to show their faces? At another point, three stuffed mannikins of Saigon troops, with GI helmets, lay overturned on the road. This suggested magic, some terrible Montagnard curse perhaps.

'Fuck me, my friend,' said Jean-Claude, 'they're here somewhere, you know, that's for sure.' Sometimes, when it looked as if a checkpoint was very recent indeed, we would stop the car, get out and call into the forest—in French, in English, in Vietnamese. If the convoy had frightened them off, surely the convoy was now past. If they were listening in the bushes, they must have thought our behaviour was most singular.

Towards Ban Me Thuot—where some of the most recent battles had been fought—the road gradually improved. The sun began to sink and the villagers were returning from the fields in long columns, carrying sacks of rice on their shoulders. We saw one soldier marching in a column, but when he saw us he jumped off the road and scurried behind a hedge. Further on, we came to a Montagnard graveyard and stopped the car. On the other side of a small valley, there was a large fortified settlement. The cattle were being brought in for the night, and we could hear them lowing in the distance. It was a beautiful sight, in the sunset. One of the villagers recognized Jean-Claude from a year before, when he had been in military hospital. He told us that after being wounded, and after the South Vietnamese had disbanded the Montagnard units, he had decided to get out. We asked him whether we could spend the night in his settlement. He said no, it was not possible. He was a little shifty about his reasons, but I thought I understood them well enough.

Everything we had seen, everything we had been told, should have made it clear to us that something was about to happen. That night, in Ban Me Thuot itself we met an officer from the *deuxième bureau* who told us of the latest military disasters in Phuoc Long province. He said that he thought Ban Me Thuot would be attacked next, and that it might last at most three weeks. In Pleiku that morning, we had been told at length how reduced the ability of the South Vietnamese Army was, and how they would be unable to withstand any concerted attack. We were sceptical. We knew that South Vietnam was calling out urgently to America for more funds, and that it was therefore convenient to paint as gloomy a picture as possible. It also seemed highly improbable that with all those soldiers and all that material—the fourth largest air force in the world, the tanks, the trucks, the convoys we had seen, all that expensive equipment—well, it just seemed impossible that the whole show would be over in such a short space of time. In the *end*, yes—but if someone had come up to us and said, 'The Saigon regime has exactly four months left,' we should never have believed him.

As a matter of fact, someone did tell us just that, almost, on New Year's Eve, the last night of our journey together.

'**M**an proposes, God disposes,' he said, by way of opening the conversation. We were slightly taken aback. He was a cyclo-driver in Nha Trang, whom we had invited to join us at dinner to celebrate the New Year. 'Yes,' he had said, accepting our invitation, 'if you have the goodness,' and he took out his long trousers from under the seat, where, as was customary, they were kept ready pressed by the weight of customers. As he put on his trousers and joined us at the table, he seemed to grow in stature before our eyes. The servility left him, and he became garrulous in excellent French. It was as if everything he had ever learned during his French education and his period as a government employee in Tonkin had swelled up inside him and was now bursting out. He had a store of proverbs to meet every situation. When we asked him whether he resented being a *cyclopousse* after having been a *fonctionnaire*, he told us that every man must work in order to repay his debt to society, and that there was no such thing as stupid work, only stupid people.

The evening passed. He recited a poem about the poor in winter, and some verses about a princess weeping under a tree. After every line, he would give us a perfect paraphrase, in case the slightest shade of meaning had escaped us. Then he declaimed a poem by Lamartine, whom I vowed at once never to read. He sang a Boy Scout song (he was a keen Boy Scout, or had been) about the life of the matelot and its attendant dangers. Finally, with terrific flourish and style—you could almost hear the piano accompaniment—he sang a song called '*Tant qu'il y aura des étoiles*': though we are only beggars, the song went, and although our life is utterly wretched, as long as there are the stars, we shall be blissfully content with our lot. He seemed at this point to be the paragon of supine virtues. And he had, of course, a thing or two to say about communism: violence, deception and lying are the methods employed, he said, by those who wish to attain a classless society. When we asked him, however, what he *thought* about the possibility of a classless society, he affected not to understand. Finally, using a phrase of Ho Chi Minh's which had become a password for Vietnamese communism, Jean-Claude asked him: 'Don't you think that nothing is more precious than independence and liberty?'

At this point he underwent his second transformation of the evening. He looked down at the tablecloth and paused dramatically. Then, as he began to speak, his mouth twisted into the most extraordinary snarl. 'I think that Vietnam has been a prey,' he said, 'a prey to foreigners. We could not do anything about it in the past because we were too weak and feeble. But things are changing now. The future, the future will show you'—and here he raised his voice to the climax: '*L'avenir vous montrera. Je ne peux pas dire plus que ça.*'

The Fall of Saigon: April 1975

On my return to Saigon from this trip, I learned that the Khmer Rouge had launched their New Year offensive against Phnom Penh. Cambodia was my chief interest, and I went immediaely to report on the death-throes of the Lon Nol regime. During this time, the situation in Vietnam changed very fast. Ban Me Thuot was overrun by the North Vietnamese, and President Thieu decided to abandon the Central Highlands. His troops were decimated as they retreated, and the general collapse of the southern regime soon became inevitable. President Ford attempted to secure funds for both Vietnam and Cambodia, but in the end even he had to write off the Phnom Penh regime. The American Embassy left Phnom Penh the day after Ford made the announcement in which this was implied. The majority of the press corps went with them. We were helicoptered to the *USS Okinawa* in the Gulf of Siam, and from there I made my way to Bangkok. I was angry with myself for having left Cambodia, and wondered what to do next. The question was—whether or not to go to Saigon? I knew that if I went I would not want to be evacuated by the Americans yet again. I would want to see this story through. So I took all the advice I could, and then decided I would go to Saigon and stay.

James Fenton

On 24 April 1975, the day before my twenty-sixth birthday, I boarded the plane for Saigon. In the seat next to me was a man named Garth W. Hunt, the Field Secretary for Asia of Living Bibles International, who was on his way to get his team out of Vietnam. His team was a 'hard core' of ten to fifteen translators who produced the Vietnamese *Living Bible*, plus a 'broad base' of theological and stylistic reviewers. Then there were the consultants ('men of stature, recognized in their own field') including literary consultants, exegetical consultants, theological consultants, technical consultants and editorial consultants. Each of these had a family and dependants and most of them wanted out.

Living Bibles International is an evangelical organization with strong, unmistakeable political leanings. 'God loves the sinner but he hates the sin,' said Mr Hunt, and in this case the sin was communism, which God certainly despised. So did Living Bibles International: at the present moment, their powerful transmitters were broadcasting the Chinese translation of the *Living Bible* at *dictation speed* into the People's Republic. 'International boundaries', said Garth W. Hunt, 'can't keep out God's message.'

They'd had no luck in North Vietnam, although they had asked to work there. But in the south they had always had tremendous co-operation from the government. A translation of *The Gospel According to Saint Mark*, the only thing this vast organization had so far completed, had already sold 120,000 copies. It had been broadcast over the radio, and was distributed in camps and refugee centres. An earlier book, produced by a sister organization, had been distributed to every psychological warfare officer in the country, and also to every Vietnamese embassy and consulate throughout the world. 'This book,' said Mr Hunt, 'became the most influential book in Vietnam, apart from the word of God himself.' It was called *God Still Performs Miracles*.

My reading-matter for the journey, in addition to my complimentary copy of *The Living Bible*, was *Time* and *Newsweek*. *Newsweek* contained a story describing Khieu Samphan as he entered Phnom Penh: 'When he returned to Phnom Penh last week, Khieu Sampan [*sic*] was dressed in a simple black pajamas suit and *krama*. No one would have guessed from his peasant look that he had spent the last eight years plotting—and carrying out—the overthrow of the Cambodian government.' The story was written by Fay Willey in New York with *Newsweek*'s reporter-in-the-field, 'Paul Brinkley Rogers in Hong Kong', who may have written the footnote explaining that Samphan's *krama* was a 'traditional Cambodian cotton scarf that can be worn as a turban, a towel to protect the neck or as a loin cloth.' The thing that puzzled me was where this story came from. No correspondent or newsagency had reported seeing Khieu Samphan entering the city, and there was no evidence that he was even there. But somebody in New York must have assumed that he had been, looked up his photo, and written up the story nevertheless. This was an unusually vivid example of a tendency in American magazine journalism to embellish . . . ever so slightly. I think it was six weeks before that *Newsweek* described the Khmer Rouge as prowling through the humid jungles around Phnom Penh. There are no jungles around Phnom Penh. It is likely that, if there had been jungles, they would have been humid, and it is possible that the Khmer Rouge, if anybody had been able to watch them, would have been prowling. So, given the jungles, everything else followed, more or less. Without the jungles, things were a little different.

The two magazines were run in a manner similar to that adopted by Living Bibles International: by committee. There was an army of researchers and rewrite men, the key figures, who stayed in the office. And given the fact that each magazine had its own journalists on the spot, it was surprising how often the stories originated in New York. Each week, someone in the office would read all the papers and wire services, and each week he would send out long lists of questions to the reporters and stringers. Steve Heder, the Phnom Penh *Time* stringer, once received a questionnaire for that week's story which included the thoughtful query: 'Do the homeless, poor, maimed etc. of Phnom Penh huddle under flimsy straw lean-tos. Know they have these in Saigon, but are they also in Phnom Penh?' You could see the idea forming in the guy's mind, and, being a scrupulous journalist, he wanted to make quite sure that there were some flimsy lean-tos for his homeless, poor, maimed etc. to huddle under. He was guarding against error, but he'd overlooked one point. The weather was very hot, and no one huddles under a lean-to when it is very hot.

Newsweek now makes it perfectly clear that the man on the spot is only *helping* someone in the office, whose name comes first. Occasionally, if a reporter does something rather spectacular, he is allowed to tell the story as he saw it. But this is a great honour. There was one such story in this same copy of *Newsweek*. It was about the fall of Xuan Loc, and pretty nasty stuff it was too. But the author, Nick Proffitt, told me that evening that even that story was touched up. He had had a pair of crutches lying in the road. Somebody in New York had decided it would read better as a *forlorn* pair of crutches. The chances that the crutches might have been anything other than forlorn—hilarious, for instance—were remote.

We landed in Saigon, and I got my tourist visa without any trouble—they seemed to be giving the things away. But the customs man confiscated my *Time* and *Newsweek*: it was at last impossible to allow too many Saigonese to see the wretched things. One of the covers had a photo of a Saigon soldier with a target drawn over his heart. It was headlined 'Target Saigon'. The customs man asked, 'Do you think . . .?' and made a sign as if to slit his throat. I told him not to worry. Everything was going to be okay, no sweat.

I checked in at the small hotel near the market where I had stayed before, and went off to dinner at the Continental. The garden was crowded—*tout le monde* was there. *Le Monde* was there. The famous Dr Hunter S. Thompson was there, surrounded by admirers, and was rumoured to have bought a gun. All the Indochina hands were back for the last act, which to the Americans meant the evacuation. The *Washington Post* staff had now been ordered, under pain of dismissal, to leave with the Embassy. The *New York Times* had also ordered its journalists not to say behind, and the American networks were planning to evacuate. Everyone was talking about the secret password, which would be broadcast when the time came: an announcement that the temperature was 105 and rising, followed by the song 'I'm Dreaming of a White Christmas'. It was all very jolly: I had a good meal, and sloughed off some of the misery of Bangkok.

I was woken the next morning by a sharp rap on the door. In came a rather beautiful Vietnamese girl, who plunged, without preliminaries, into a passionate speech: She had been a night-club dancer, and now she simply must leave Saigon, and I must help her. It was early in the morning and I was rather gruff. She redoubled her efforts. 'How can I live with the communists?' she wailed. 'I can't spend my money and I can't wear my clothes. I have to wear Vietcong clothes.' Then she kneeled on the floor beside my bed and pretended to cry—or gave what was, at best, a terrible imitation. 'Please help me,' she whined, 'please help me leave Saigon.' She was offering 300,000 *piastres*—a large sum for her, but with the soaring black market rate it amounted only to forty pounds. To earn this money I had only to say that she was my sister, then the Americans would give her papers. She would go to Hawaii, where she would automatically be given a US passport. She had a house in Singapore, which she could sell for $100,000. In addition, she already had $1,500 in greenbacks. The last figure she mouthed with respect and wonder. I decided that the house in Singapore was probably a fiction, and pointed out that the greenbacks would not last very long in the United States. But she had it worked out. She would live in Hawaii and set up a Vietnamese restaurant. There were so many Vietnamese going to Hawaii. She would be able to sell spring rolls and things like that. President Ford had said that two million Vietnamese could go to America. They could go this month, but after that it would be too late. I avoided giving her a definite answer, and she left the room in great distress.

300,000 *piastres*? people said scornfully. Oh *we*'ve been offered far more than that. Wherever you went, Saigon was using its most ingenious methods either to get out or to make money out of those who were leaving. It was said that the Americans were also running the rackets. Hopeful young girls would be relieved of their savings and then left stranded. The bars of Tu Do Street had been combed by the talent-spotters of the Phillipines. An enormous number of people were caught up in a craze for leaving. In a friend's hotel, I met a youth of about twenty rushing around asking for help. He had suddenly remembered something his father had given him—the torn end-paper of a book on which was written an American name and address. In his other hand, he carried the wording of a cable:

'Please send a cable to American Embassy Saigon accepting responsibility for . . . .' It seemed highly unlikely that the addressee would have any recollection of either father or son. Nevertheless we told the boy to send the cable with that wording. He didn't know how to send a cable. He did not know why he wanted to go; he knew only that he had to. He confessed that his head was in a spin. From his manner it seemed as if he had about five minutes to get out, or face the firing-squad.

This mad dash for the planes had begun about a week before when it was noticed that the Embassy had started rounding up the people they believed to be in danger when the communists took over. The calls had been carefully conducted under cover of darkness, in the manner of a Stalinist arrest. The criterion was broad. As one of the embassy personnel put it, 'The kind of people who know us are the kind of people who would be in trouble.' The Embassy was clearing out everyone in its address book, but to do so they also had to take their wives and families, and the families got larger and larger. The rich Vietnamese also wanted to take their maids. Sometimes this would be challenged at the airport: it was not customary in America to have maids. So the rich Vietnamese would then turn round and dismiss their maids with a wave of the hand. Then there was a flood of letters to the Embassy from Americans and Vietnamese living in America . . . . Discreet diplomats would pad up the stairs, knock quietly so as not to arouse the neighbours, and deliver the message: 'Your son-in-law says you must leave. Can you be ready this time tomorrow night?'

'I don't know. I haven't got a suitcase.'

'Couldn't you buy a suitcase?'

'Yes, I think so.'

'All right then?'

'What shall I wear?' And so on.

Sometimes these visits must have been welcome. At other times they shattered a few illusions. A man, living not far from my hotel, was a member of the local defence force. I sat up late one night with him and the other members of the force, drinking Vietnamese spirit and chatting about what was going to happen. They were clear about one thing: they would not lift a finger to defend the area from the Vietcong. They had seen the writing on the wall; when the Vietcong arrived, their duties ended. They all talked with admiration for the other side, and there was not a trace of the usual intransigence or panic of Saigon.

The exodus was continuing at a rate of about 10,000 a day. It was estimated at the time that out of each day's departures, 3,000 had Embassy connections, 1,000 were relatives of Americans and 1,000 were friends or contacts of Americans. What about all the rest? When I went to Tan Son Nhuot airport to watch the processing of the evacuees, I found very few who had a clear notion of why they were leaving. Some were North Vietnamese refugees from the 1950s, others were going because they had once worked in PX stores or as ancillary staff on American bases. One woman just did not know why she was going. Her husband had left the north as a young student. Her sister was married to an American, who had insisted that the family should leave. She did not want to do so at all. She was leaving so much behind. For instance, she had saved up for five years in order to buy her son a piano. It had only just arrived. Another man did know. He claimed to have led the National Revolutionary Movement in the days of Diem. 'Obviously,' he said, 'as a journalist you will know what it means to live under communism. No? Then you should not in that case be a journalist.'

There were snackstands at the entrace to Tan Son Nhuot, set up to cater for the waiting crowd of refugees, many of whom slipped past the guards without any papers. Processing was done in the Defence Attache's Office Compound, one of the last bits of pure America left in Vietnam. The last hurdle was in the gymnasium, under the basketball net. There were old notices reminding you not to bring in your pets, and not to put your hands on the walls. The forms were filled in by sour-looking GIs in olive drab, with daggers hanging from their belts. The prevailing atmosphere was of general menace.

While the American evacuation accelerated, the Vietcong, we later discovered, were filling the place up with their own troops. The operation was haphazard. The soldiers came in wearing Saigon uniforms, in military trucks that had been acquired during the last few months, as the Southern army had retreated in disarray. But the soldiers had no identity cards and must have lived continually on the verge of discovery. They took up positions near important installations, in order to take control swiftly when the time came. The students' groups were also working out what to do in order to help in the takeover, and the Chinese, the shrewdest businessmen in Saigon, were already manufacturing the three-coloured flags of the National Liberation Front, in readiness for a quick sale. There must have been a tremendous run on the haberdashers. When red, blue and yellow cloth ran out, they used coloured plastic.

One night I was awakened by the sound of three large crashes, and I realized that the rocketing had begun. I went up to the top floor of my hotel (once a bar and billiard room for GIs) where I had a good view over the roofs. Already there was a large fire, fuelled no doubt by the petrol kept in the houses of the poor. Soon a whole block was ablaze, and the fire was spreading. I watched it with mixed feelings: the Vietcong had announced their proximity—the fire, though distant, spelled an immediate danger; nevertheless a city fire, far enough away, has a terrible splendour. The fire attracted me. The next day I walked around the burnt-out area, a huddled group of make-shift shacks built on an old Catholic graveyard. The fire brigade had refused to put out the blaze until massive bribes had been produced, and a large number of poor people's homes had consequently been destroyed. All this I might have guessed at the time, and yet I was excited by the fire. It seemed to be the curtain-raiser for the last act.

The next morning, 28 April, began dramatically enough. I went out to the edge of the city at about six-thirty, where I found that the Vietcong had come to the very outskirts of Saigon and had closed the road on the other side of the bridge. There were, it turned out, only a few of them, but they served their purpose, calling down a massive amount of firepower where they were ensconced. Saigon brought out all its weapons, and the helicopter gunships blasted away all day. It was not until evening that the road was cleared of a few brave men. After watching this scene for a time, I went back to my room and was reading a book when, without warning, the city became ablaze with rifle fire. I thought: that's it. The insurrection has begun.

Once again, I went up to the top floor, but this time there was nothing to see. There was simply a noise, a massive, unvaried, unstinting noise. It was too uniform. There was meant to be grenades, machine-guns, more variety. I asked a member of the hotel staff. Perhaps a coup d'état, he said, shrugging. That, again, was possible. But then, as suddenly as it had started, the firing ceased. I walked out into the deserted street. No dead bodies. Nobody much around. On the corner I met a soldier, and gave him a quizzical look. 'Sorry about that,' he said, and turned away.

President Minh, at this time, would have just finished his speech, calling on the Americans to leave, and on the other side to negotiate. The other side would have been answering that this was not enough—there had to be total unconditional surrender. For it was at the same time, for the first and last time in the war, that the Vietcong air force was brought into play. It had been a masterly piece of timing. These planes had been picked up in the previous months, having been left behind as the provinces north of Saigon had fallen in swift succession and in such disarray. Now these same South Vietnamese planes were used to bomb the Saigon air force. There was no other way in which the Vietcong could ever have used an air force except against an air base. To have done so at that moment was to announce imminent victory, and to make sure that the victory cost them as little blood as possible. As for the firing I heard outside my hotel, the troops had been told of enemy planes on the attack, but they were confused. The plane they were firing at was in fact civilian. It got away.

The incident unnerved people. It was a foretaste, we thought. From now on, anything could happen, and happen swiftly. And when something did happen, there would be nothing we could do about it.

The next morning I was woken by the ancient doorman of the hotel, who walked straight into my room carrying one loaf of French bread, two large chunks of palm sugar and a bottle of Coca-Cola. He returned a little later with ice, and insisted I get up and eat. I gathered from a rather complicated conversation that there was still a curfew, and that these were the siege rations. The bread was wrapped in what appeared to be an American Embassy report. As I attempted to eat the sugar and the bread, there was another knock. A young man came in, looking for an American who

87

had promised to get him out of the country. He had been planning to leave from New Port the night before, but the place had been under attack. Now his father, a captain in the army, was waiting outside. We talked for a while. The young man had an infinitely sad face. He was not pushing. He probably knew already that he had missed his last chance. Anyway, he was unclear about why he wanted to leave Vietnam. I told him that he should not leave, since this was his country, and if he left it now he would never get back. He said wistfully, 'I like going to the country. My family always goes to the country for holidays. We go to Rach Gia and Ha Tien.' I said that Ha Tien was now in the hands of the Vietcong. He said: 'Do you think people are happy in Ha Tien?' I said I thought so. We discussed what would happen to his father, and I tried to reassure him. But he left as sadly as he had come in.

The curfew did not seem to be very strict, so I set out to find the other journalists and see what was happening. Saigon looked beautiful that morning, with its deserted streets. Everyone was smiling. There were families standing in the doorways, smiling. A group of soldiers passed, smiling. A beggar girl in a tattered silk blouse, to whom I gave some money, ran laughing along beside me. She was young, with an idiot look and no teeth. Clearly the curfew did not apply to idiots. There was a Sunday morning atmosphere. I felt very happy, as if I were in some English town, setting out to buy the Sunday papers. On the way I met one of my friends from the local defence force, who told me that the airport had been attacked during the night. I appeared to have slept through everything.

At the Continental all the journalists were talking about the previous night's fighting at the airport. They had seen planes shot down with Strela missiles and this, coupled with the previous day's panic when the airport had been bombed, convinced several people that they should leave. Others who had not intended to stay on were having difficulty making up their minds. I felt very excited, but did not consider going. The same principle that had taken me from Phnom Penh would keep me in Saigon. I had made my decision in advance. But I can't deny that I felt a certain superiority to those rushing around, paying their bills, gathering their stuff together, or dithering.

There was a strong move that all the British journalists remaining behind, one of whom was keen to acquire a gun, should stick together. The main worry for those staying on was that the 'friendlies' might get nasty. One of the calculations of those leaving was that the Vietcong would certainly be nasty. As a Beaverbrook reporter said to me, 'I wouldn't like to be interrogated by them. You know, they have methods. . . .'

'I doubt if it would come to that,' I said.

'Have you ever done any work with the Americans?' he asked.

'No, I was never here with the Americans.'

'Well, I can think of things I've done, places I've been and so on, that I'd find very difficult to explain away.'

I never found out exactly what he meant. As the hotel emptied I looked at the garden and was reminded of Coleridge: 'Well, they are gone and here I must remain, This Lime-tree bower my prison.' I said: 'Won't it be nice to have the place to ourselves.' This remark was considered incredibly irritating.

I had to get my possessions and bring them to the Continental. As I walked along the street people asked me why I had not left yet. 'Are you French or Australian?' they asked. One small restaurant was open, in which a group of lieutenants were sitting eating Chinese chicken and drinking Johnnie Walker Black Label. They invited me to join them, which I did with some diffidence since they were obviously out to get drunk, and might therefore become aggressive. They began by explaining that they would sit there until they were killed. I tried to say that I thought they were wrong, but when I explained why, I saw at once that I had gone too far. Ice formed over the conversation. 'How long did you spend with the communists?' they asked. I said I hadn't been with the communists. Hitherto we had been talking in English. Then we switched to French. They were amused, they said, that when I started speaking in French I began to tremble.

I was afraid that I had fallen into the hands of precisely those 'friendlies' who were supposed to turn nasty. I reached out for a piece of chicken and nonchalantly picked up the head. It was not the part I had had in mind, but I bit into the eyeballs with great gusto, and sucked out the brains. The ice was finally broken when one of the officers asked in Cambodian whether I spoke Khmer. A little, I said, and we exchanged a few phrases. These men belonged to a breed that was just on the verge of extinction—the nattily-dressed, well-groomed, gun-toting, sunglass-wearing, American-style, narcissistic junior officer. The weight of their impending extinction bore down upon them.

Inevitably, the conversation returned to the impending take-over. I asked them why they were afraid. They were well aware, they said, that in Phnom Penh the people had greeted the Khmer Rouge with open arms. But they said that that was just for appearances. Afterwards there would be a settling of accounts. They insisted again that they were going to die. I bade them farewell. They repeated that they were going to sit there drinking all day, until they died.

Some people get rich on others' misfortunes, and it appeared that I was one of them. I became, during the course of the day, acting bureau chief of the *Washington Post*. *I* had a bureau! The keys were waiting for me in the office, together with a charming farewell note from the staff. I had a pleasant young Vietnamese assistant, who was good enough to show me how to open the drawer to get at the office petty cash. The office was well equipped; I could have moved in to live. Nice bathroom, plenty of books, fridge, bottle of Polish vodka in the fridge. I settled down to work, assuming that the evacuation had begun, since there was now a fairly large amount of helicopter activity over the city. I had also assumed that the operation would be conducted as quickly as it had been in Phnom Penh. But this was not so. A few moments later I got a phone call from the *Washington Post*'s former Bureau Chief, David Greenway. He was at the US Embassy. They were stuck. Nobody had come yet, and Embassy staff were getting nervous that the place might be shelled. Oh, and did I want the car keys? They had left the Volkswagen by the Embassy gate.

I went round to the Embassy. The crowd outside had grown, but it had not yet reached the alarming proportions of later in the day. There were shady Koreans, a few stranded Americans and several hundred Vietnamese waiting around or attempting to argue with the Marines on the gate. South Vietnamese Army Officers in mufti would come up and, producing an Embassy visiting card, say,

'Excuse me, I'm a good friend of Mr So-and-so. Do you think I could get in?' Greenway appeared on one of the Embassy's turrets and threw down the *Washington Post* car keys. He had the look of a man convinced that he was about to be shelled, but was far too polite to mention the fact. I went to the car, and found that I lacked the knack of turning the key in the ignition. It had always been troublesome, and I had never driven the thing before. In fact, I had never, I remembered suddenly, learned how to drive. As I tried to start it I became nervous at being so close to the Embassy. There was a sound of rifle-fire nearby, and around the Embassy the police would occasionally shoot in the air when some angry man became too importunate. I decided to abandon the car.

Before too long the large helicopters, the Jolly Green Giants, began to appear, and as they did so the mood of the city suffered a terrible change. There was no way of disguising this evacuation by sleight-of-hand, or, it appeared, of getting it over quickly. The noise of the vast helicopters, as they corkscrewed out of the sky, was a fearful incentive to panic. The weather turned bad. It began to rain. And as the evening grew darker, it seemed as if the helicopters themselves were blotting out the light. It seemed as if the light had gone forever. All the conditions conspired against calm. All over Saigon there were people who had been promised an escape. There were others, like the officers of the morning, who thought that they would definitely die. And there were others still who for no definite reason went into a flat spin. Always the beating of the helicopter blades reminded them of what was happening. The accumulated weight of the years of propaganda came crashing down upon a terrified city.

The crowd around the Embassy swelled and its desperation increased. It became dangerous to go out on the streets. The looters were out and the cowboys were on their Hondas: who knew what grudge might be worked out on the white face of a passer-by? The first major looting took place at the Brinks building, which had served as a billet for American officers from the earliest days of US involvement in Indochina. It proved a rich source of booty. To add to the confusion of the city, the electricity cut out at around seven in the evening. It was then that I had to make my second move of the day, from the Continental to the Caravelle Hotel across the square, where it had finally been decided that we should all stay together for however long it took for order to be restored. A mere matter of lugging a few cases across a small square—but I remember finding it an arduous and frightening task, as the Honda boys drove by shouting 'Yankee, go home!' I cursed the Embassy for its bungled withdrawal, and began for the first time to admire John Gunther Dean, the American Ambassador in Phnom Penh who had evacuated at such speed. But here: always the sound of the helicopters, stirring the panic, making things worse.

Indoors it was all right. Finishing my work in my new office that evening, I came across a note from my nice Vietnamese assistant. It informed me that the office was most likely to be looted by the soldiers, and that the assistant had therefore taken home the petty cash. This was the last time I saw the man. Well, easy come, easy go, I thought. I went to the fridge, and broached the Polish vodka. It turned out to be water.

The power cut turned out to be a godsend, since by the time light was restored the majority of the crowd had gone home and the police had regained control of the streets. As the lights went on in the Caravelle Hotel, they found our gallant press corps in the best of spirits. We didn't know how long we would be holed up in the hotel, or in what manner the city would fall. Most people I think were envisaging a rather slow and bloody take-over, but this did not spoil the brave mood of the evening. We had a distant view of the war. Towards the airport it appeared that an ammunition dump was exploding. Great flames rose up and slowly subsided. It went on for hours, like some hellish furnace from Hieronymus Bosch. If you went up on to the roof itself you could hear the war from every direction. But the city centre had calmed down.

I had one more story to send out. In the foyer of the hotel I found a policeman in mufti, and arranged to walk with him to the Reuters office. It was okay at first, but as we approached the dark area around the cathedral we both became more and more apprehensive. Turning left, we walked down the middle of the road, hand in hand, to keep up each other's spirits. We exhibited all the heroism of children in the dark. To any Vietcong agent, watching us from the top branches of the trees, I should say we must have looked too touching to kill.

Early on the morning of 30 April, I went out of my hotel room to be greeted by a group of hysterical Koreans. 'The Americans have called off the evacuation!' said one. The group had been unable to get into the Embassy, had waited the whole night and had now given up. Of all the nationalities to fear being stranded in Saigon, the Koreans had most reason. I went up to breakfast in the top-floor restaurant, and saw that there were still a few Jolly Green Giants landing on the Embassy, but that the group on the Alliance Française building appeared to have been abandoned. They were still standing there on the roof, packed tight on a set of steps. Looking up at the sky, they seemed to be taking part in some kind of religious ritual, waiting for a sign. In the Brinks Building, the looting continued. A lone mattress fell silently from a top floor balcony.

There was one other group at breakfast—an eccentric Frenchman with some Vietnamese children. The Frenchman was explaining to the waiter that there had been some binoculars available the night before, and he wanted to use them again. The waiter explained that the binoculars belonged to one of the hotel guests.

'That doesn't matter,' said the Frenchman, 'bring them to me.'

The waiter explained that the binoculars were probably in the guest's room.

'Well go and get them then!' said the Frenchman. It seemed extraordinary that the Frenchman could be so adamant, and the waiter so patient, under the circumstances. I had orange juice and coffee, and noted that the croissants were not fresh.

Then I went to the American Embassy, where the looting had just begun. The typewriters were already on the streets outside, there was a stink of urine from where the crowd had spent the night, and several cars had been ripped apart. I did not bother to check what had happened to mine, but went straight into the Embassy with the looters.

The place was packed, and in chaos. Papers, files, brochures and reports were strewn around. I picked up one letter of application from a young Vietnamese student, who wished to become an Embassy interpreter. Some people gave me suspicious looks, as if I might be a member of the Embassy staff—I was, after all, the only one there with a white face—so I began to do a little looting myself, to show that I was entering into the spirit of the thing. Somebody had found a package of razor blades, and removed them all from their plastic wrappers. One man called me over to a wall-safe, and seemed to be asking if I knew the number of the combination. Another was hacking away at an air-conditioner, another dismantling a fridge.

On the first floor there was more room to move, and it was here I came across the Embassy library. I collected the following items: one copy of *Peace is not at Hand* by Sir Robert Thompson, one of the many available copies of *The Road from War* by Robert Shaplen, Barrington Moore's *Social Origins of Dictatorship and Democracy* (I had been meaning to read it for some time), a copy of a pacification report from 1972 and some Embassy notepaper. Two things I could not take (by now I was not just pretending to loot—I had become quite involved): a reproduction of an 1873 map of Hanoi, and a framed quotation from Lawrence of Arabia, which read, 'Better to let them do it imperfectly than to do it perfectly yourself, for it is their country, their way, and your time is short.' Nearby I found a smashed portrait of President Ford, and a Stars and Stripes, mangled in the dirt.

I found one room which had not yet been touched. There were white chairs around a white table, and on the table the ashtrays were full. I was just thinking how eerie it looked, how recently vacated, when the lights went out. At once, a set of emergency lights, photo-sensitively operated, turned themselves on above each doorway. The building was still partly working; even while it was being torn to pieces, it had a few reflexes left.

From this room, I turned into a small kitchen, where a group of old crones were helping themselves to jars of Pream powdered milk. When they looked up and saw me, they panicked, dropped the powdered milk and ran. I decided that it would be better to leave the building. It was filling up so much that it might soon become impossible to get out. I did not know that there were still some marines on the roof. As I forced my way out of the building, they threw tear-gas down on the crowd, and I found myself running hard, in floods of tears.

Although the last helicopter was just now leaving, people still thought there were other chances of getting out. One man came up to me and asked confidentially if I knew of the alternative evacuation site. He had several plausible reasons why he was entitled to leave. Another man, I remember, could only shout, 'I'm a professor, I'm a professor, I'm a professor,' as if the fact of his academic status would cause the Jolly Green Giants to swoop down out of the sky and whisk him away.

There was by now a good deal of activity on the streets. Military trucks went to and fro across town, bearing loads of rice, and family groups trudged along, bearing their possessions. As I finished writing my Embassy story, the sirens wailed three times, indicating that the city itself was under attack. I returned to the hotel roof to see what was happening. The group on the Alliance Française building was still there, still waiting for its sign. Across the river, but not far away, you could see the artillery firing, and the battle lines coming closer. Then two flares went up, one red, one white. Somebody said that the white flare was for surrender. In the restaurant, the waiters sat by the radio. I asked them what was happening. 'The war is finished,' said one.

I looked down into the square. Almost at once, a waiter emerged from the Continental and began to hoist a French tricolour on the flagpole. There were groups of soldiers, apparently front-line troops, sitting down. From the battlefield across the river, the white flares began to go up in great numbers. Big Minh's broadcast had been heard—offering unconditional surrender—and in a matter of minutes the war would be well and truly over.

Under such circumstances, what does one do? For the poor of Saigon, the first reaction was to loot as much as possible. For most of the soldiers, it was to give in as quickly as possible, and make oneself scarce. For the victorious troops, for the students and Vietcong sympathizers within the city, it was a question of taking control as quickly as possible. For the reporter, there was a choice: go out and see what was happening, or write about it. It was a cruel choice, but it was clear that the lines would soon either be jammed or go down altogether. For a stringer, the burden of the choice is even greater, since it is during such moments that he earns the fat off which he has to live during the lean years. The first two laws of stringing are: the more you file the more you earn; and, the more you file the less you learn. I mention this because, throughout the remainder of the day and in the days that followed, all my reactions were underscored by a worry about getting the thing written up, and not just written up but sent out. Whereas all my instincts were not to write at all. In the end the instincts won, hands down.

I took a lift with Brian Barron of the BBC along with his small crew, who had remained after their American counterparts had already left. We went out towards the Newport Bridge, in a small car driven by a Vietnamese. The Union Jack was flying from the aerial, and the BBC sign was clearly displayed. As we drove along past the lines of anxious faces, it became clear to me that I had come with the wrong crew. The soldiers whom we tried to film thought that the BBC had been on the side of the Vietcong. It had been denounced by Thieu, and now, in the moment of defeat, was no time to be flying the Union Jack. There was a large amount of military activity on the roads: truckloads of soldiers returning from the front. There was one bulldozer racing back from the bridge, with a whole platoon sitting in the scoop. The tanks were waiting by the tank-traps, many of them with their crew still in position. As we stopped to film them, I noticed one soldier fingering a grenade, weighing it thoughtfully in his hand. In the doors of houses, families waited nervously. By Newport Bridge itself, the looting of the American stores was still going on, a desperate last-minute effort which would hold up, in parts of the city, the advance of the victorious troops. The first thing the North Vietnamese and Vietcong saw as they came into Saigon was crowds of looters dragging sacks of rice and cartons of luxury goods. It must have justified their view of the degeneracy of the city.

But they had not yet arrived. Walking up to the top of the bridge, we wondered whether to go on to meet them, or retrace our steps. Then we were called back to the car by the Governor of Gia Dinh.

He looked exceedingly angry and unpleasant—he and one of his officers laden down with pistols and grenades, ready perhaps to make their last stand against the encroaching communists. They were fat men, with twisted faces, gripped no doubt by the bitterness of betrayal.

Where had we been?

To the top of the bridge.

No, they said, we had come from the Vietcong.

We replied that we had been to the bridge because we wanted to film.

'I don't want to hear any more,' said the Governor, 'how much did they pay you? How much did the Vietcong pay you?'

'Look,' said Brian Barron, 'I'm not Vietcong. I'm afraid of the Vietcong. When the Vietcong start shooting, I lie down.'

'Why do you lie to me?' said the Governor of Gia Dinh.

I thought, 'This is it. He's going to kill us.' And apart from the fear of death itself, there seemed to be something particularly bitter and unfair in being killed as a traitor after the defeat. But instead of killing us, the Governor told me to remove the Union Jack from the car, and ordered one of the film crew to take the BBC label off his camera. The Union Jack was stuck to the aerial with Elastoplast and I remember wondering whether my trembling hands would ever get the thing off. The Governor then ordered us to push our car between two tank traps, where it was later found, completely squashed by a tank.

I wanted to get back to the city centre as quickly as possible—we were now going to have to walk—and I couldn't understand why Barron was taking such a long time. He seemed to be looking for something in the car, and later he told me what it was. A few days before, he had been reading Ho Chi Minh's works, and had shoved them under the back seat, out of sight. Now he was afraid that they would suddenly find the book, and shoot us on the spot. He therefore decided to get the thing out and shove it under his shirt. He went back to the car, put his hand under the seat, and discovered that the book was gone.

By now there was chaos on the streets. The trucks which had passed us in one direction as we were coming out of Saigon appeared to have returned. Clearly nobody knew where to go. There was gunfire at the crossroads just ahead, and I think that we all felt, having lost our car, in great danger. We were saved by a taximan who dumped a load of customers and offered to take us back for four thousand *piastres*. I would have paid whatever I had. We got into the car, put our heads down, and sped back to the city centre.

In the Reuters office I was writing an account of what I had just seen when Barron came in again.

'I don't know what's happening,' he said, 'I've just seen a tank with the flag of the National Liberation Front.' I went to the door and looked out to the left, in the direction of Thieu's palace, and saw the tank. Without thinking, I ran after it and flagged it down just as it turned towards the palace gates. The tank slowed down and a North Vietnamese soldier in green jumped off the back and went at me with his gun, as if to hit me. In my confusion, I couldn't remember the NLF salute, or how to explain to the soldier that I wanted a ride. I tried everything—a salute, another salute, a clenched fist, a hitch-hiker's thumb. Finally (after, that is, a few extremely nervous seconds) I held out my hand to shake his. He took my hand abruptly and indicated the back of the tank. I remember worrying, as I climbed on, that I might touch something very hot. Then, as the soldiers told me to keep my head down, I idiotically produced my passport, which they dismissed scornfully. The tank speeded up, and rammed the left side of the palace gate. Wrought iron flew into the air, but the whole structure refused to give. I nearly fell off. The tank backed again, and I observed a man with a nervous smile opening the centre portion of the gate. We drove into the grounds of the palace, and fired a salute.

I had taken a ride on the first tank to reach the palace, but it was not until several weeks later that I realized this was the case: looking up from my crouching position at the back, I saw another vehicle in the grounds (which turned out to be a South Vietnamese tank). Damn, I thought, I was on the second; still, never mind. I wondered whether I was under arrest. I tried to talk to the soldiers, but I did not notice that some of them were captured troops of the South Vietnamese Army who had been co-opted in order to show the way. On the top of the tank was an open carton of Winston cigarettes, which struck me as odd. No doubt it had been thrown up from the looting crowd. I also remember noticing that another tank was passing behind us on the lawn. Its tracks crushed the verge of a flower bed, and I remember thinking: that was unnecessary. Also, I noticed an extraordinary number of dragonflies in the air.

I was very, very excited. The weight of the moment, the privilege of being a witness, impressed itself at once. Over and above my self-consciousness, and the trivial details which were made all the more interesting by the extraordinary nature of the event, there was the historical grandeur of the scene. Events in history are not supposed to look historical: no eye perceived a battlefield at a glance, no dying leader composed his followers around him in the neo-classical manner; many war photographs, even some of the great ones, are said to have been rearranged. The victors write, rewrite, or retouch their history. Indeed in one western account of these events, I noticed that the tank I have just described was meant to have knocked the palace gate to the ground 'like a wooden twig'. The man who opened the gate, a civilian guard, has in this account been subbed out. The guards themselves have fled. Nothing is allowed to interfere with the symmetry of the scene, or interrupt the conquest with wild, flailing arms.

And yet the North Vietnamese do not merely touch-up history. They also enact it in the heroic manner. This was the first time I had seen their genius for imposing their style upon events, for acting in the manner of their propaganda. The spectacle was tremendous and, as one of their officers realized, not to be missed. He ran up to a British cameraman filming the arrival of the tanks, and begged him: 'You take film for us? You take film for us?' The tanks rolled on to the lawn, and formed automatically into a semicircle in front of the palace, firing a salute into the air as they did so. Soon the air became full of the sound of saluting guns. Beside the gate, sitting in a row on the lawn, was a group of soldiers, former members of the palace guard. They waved their hands above their heads in terror. An NLF soldier took his flag and, waving it above his head, ran into the palace. A few moments later, he emerged on the terrace, waving the flag round and round. Later still, there he was on the roof. The red and yellow stripes of the Saigon regime were lowered at last.

I thought, I shall know if I'm under arrest when I jump off the tank. There came suddenly to mind a story of a plane which went through an electric storm: when it touched down, all the passengers were electrocuted on contact with the earth. I jumped off, and noticed that I was still alive and free. The palace grounds filled up with soldiers, and trucks were arriving all the time. The broad avenue towards the cathedral became the centre for the arriving troops. Their vehicles and helmets were covered in leaves, their uniforms were green. A great wave of greenery swept over the city. It blended into the grass and the trees of the avenue. Only the red armbands and the red tags on the guns stood out. Everything had changed in a trice.

For the Westerners present, it was an occasion for overt celebration. I saw Jean-Claude running through the palace gates, his hands over his head, his cameras swinging hectically around his body. Old colleagues greeted each other with delight. We felt bound to congratulate each other, as if we had a right to partake of the victory. For the National Liberation Front troops, on the other hand, such satisfaction as they felt was completely suppressed. They sat down and lit up North Vietnamese cigarettes, like men who had simply done a good day's work—they were justified and did not need praise. Sometimes they shook hands with the foreigners, occasionally they smiled, or waved from the trucks, but never once did I see them lose their self-control.

I walked past the cathedral, and came upon a North Vietnamese soldier in a condition of extreme embarrassment. He was facing a wall, secretly looking at something. I thought he was embarrassed by having to relieve himself in front of a group of interested onlookers, but in fact he was consulting his compass, unsure of where he was supposed to be. The group realized his difficulty, and gave him directions. At this moment the fire brigade drove past, lights blazing, horn blaring, waving their hats in the air, in expressions of wild delight. Further down, along Tu Do street, I met a friend and we walked together to the Ministry of Defence, which was in the process of surrendering. At these ceremonies, a salute was always fired over the building, and so the city must have been full of falling lead, and yet I never heard of anyone being injured from such fall-out. This was one of the many curious features of the day.

The most dramatic change that had taken place was the complete disappearance of the Saigon army. All round the streets one would come across piles of clothes, boots and weapons. Some of the piles were so complete it looked as if their former occupant had simply melted into his boots. And then, in the doorways, one would see young men in shorts, hanging around with an air of studied indifference, as if to say, 'Don't look at me, I always dress like this—it's the heat, you know.' Where groups of soldiers had been caught and told to surrender, they were made to take off their clothes and sit down. I came across one such group by the town hall.

Slowly the streets were beginning to fill up again. Occasionally the requisitioned jeeps of the former regime came past, full of cheering youths in gear that was intended to look like Vietcong attire. These new revolutionary enthusiasts were immediately distinguished in appearance and behaviour from the real thing. Some of them were disarmed on the spot. Others were to carry on for several days or weeks before being identified, but for the moment they had a great fling, cheering, shouting and riding around. Most people were still indoors, wondering what would happen to them. The first to appear on the streets and talk to the soldiers were the old men, women and young children. They brought out tea to the tired troops, and sat with them, firing questions about what would happen next. The reassurance they received spread visibly throughout the suspicious city, and in a short while the areas where the troops were concentrated (around the palace and the port) took on the air of a massive teach-in.

The sorts of questions being asked were: Would there be revenge? Would those who had left North Vietnam at the time of the division be forced to return? Would the women be forced to cut their hair? Would those with painted nails have them pulled out, *without anaesthetic*? Would the women be forcibly married off to the crippled soldiers of the North? To all such questions, the answer was a gentle no. Another question was, what did the North Vietnamese eat? The fact that such a question could be put shows the ignorance of young Saigon about Hanoi, since the answer of course was rice.

I was getting very hungry and thirsty after the exertions of the day, so I wandered down to my old hotel by the market. The manager was pleased, and rather surprised, to see me. She had obviously assumed that, whatever I said, I would in fact leave with the Americans. I told her what was happening outside. 'We are very pleased to welcome the liberation forces,' she said, through clenched teeth. The night-club dancer, whom I had failed to assist to leave, was also there. She gave me some very sick looks. She had dressed simply, in black pyjamas, and done up her hair in a bun, in what she imagined would be a manner suitable for receiving the forces of liberation. The landlady and the old doorman produced from the siege rations a meal of bread, olives, walnuts, cheese and beer. It was the first and last time that the landlady ever let me have anything for free.

A phrase ran through my mind, from the time of the arrival of the tanks, and on through the day as I wandered round the streets, meeting people I knew, watching the chatting groups, and seeing how the whole place settled down. The phrase was: 'a permanent and marvellous disgrace'. It seemed to me evident, and bitterly ironical, that all the talk of what the North Vietnamese would do when—*if*—they took Saigon, all of it had been wrong. During the whole of the day I saw only three or four corpses. The North Vietnamese Army were clearly the most disciplined troops in the world. They had done nothing out of order, and it could not be that they were just waiting till the foreigners were out of the way before setting about the rape and pillage which many had prophesied. You could not fake the sort of discipline they had shown, nor could the events of the day be depicted (even by the most bigoted critic) as anything other than a triumph—a triumph that exceeded the expectations of their warmest, most bigoted, admirers. Consequently when the story was told (by now the lines were down), it would disgrace those who had predicted otherwise. It would be a permanent and marvellous disgrace; the CIA and Pentagon boffins, a generation of hawks, would be made to stand forever in the corner, wearing the dunce's cap. I did not think that Saigon had been liberated in the way that would shortly be made out. I did not think that there had been an uprising—I had seen no real evidence for such a thing. But the victorious army had justified itself by its behaviour alone. That I will never forget.

Peace had come, more or less. In the afternoon one desperate group of South Vietnamese soldiers had made a last attempt at a fire-fight right in the centre of town, and sometimes in the distance one would hear explosions, for which I never found the reason. Along the outskirts of the town the looting continued wherever any wealthy establishment had been abandoned, or wherever the troops had not yet arrived to take control. I went to the Buddhist University, where the students were already organizing the collection of the enormous number of arms that had been abandoned on the streets. Nguyen Huu Thai, the student leader, greeted us and gave us a form of identification which would serve for the next few days. Were we not impressed? he asked. Was it not like the Paris Commune of 1871?

As we drove back, we passed the Taiwanese and Malaysian Embassies, which were being very thoroughly looted. People were stealing everything, including the chandeliers. The young students who had taken it upon themselves to stop the looting tried to do so by firing into the air. When this did not work, one of them adopted a most terrifyingly effective technique. Holding a rifle in his left hand and a pistol in his right, he pointed the pistol at a looter and fired his rifle into the air.

Back at the Caravelle Hotel, I watched the landscape settle down in peace. The flares still went up, on and on into the night. The intense excitement of the past days subsided into an irritable exhaustion. I had a bitter argument with one of my greatest friends, and went to bed in the worst of spirits. As my head sank into the pillow I burst into tears.

After the Fall

May Day 1975 was probably an occasion for world-wide celebration of the liberation of Saigon. I don't know. In Saigon itself, indeed throughout Vietnam, May Day was not celebrated. It had been cancelled by Hanoi, as part of the war effort, and now, the day after the war was over, it was too late to organize. May Day would have to wait.

I went out at dawn on May Day morning. The flares were still going up, and the flags of the National Liberation Front had already appeared on public buildings. NFL washing hung from windows. The soldiers were breakfasting by the parked tanks. They had dug foxholes in the public squares, and slept in Saigon as if in the jungle. The trouserless soldiers of the defeated army wandered around with nothing to do. There were beggars in the doorways, and an old woman asleep and a young girl beside her looking through a work of lurid pornography. There was litter everywhere, military and domestic, and piles of incriminating documents and letters and, in one case, a large stack of seventy-eight gramophone records.

There was a pair of nuns on a motorbike, sporting the NLF flag. Sightseers. Saigon was coming out to see the NLF, and the NLF was being conducted around the city in trucks, gazing up at the buildings. It had been told of the poverty of Saigon. It had never seen such wealth. As yet the spivs, beggars and prostitutes had not come out. But I saw one cripple from the Saigon Army dressed in what he clearly conceived to be the outfit of a guerrilla.

As yet, very few of the guerrillas, the true Vietcong of the South, had appeared. They strolled in in twos and threes, with strangely shaped bombs tied to their belts, and antique weapons. They sometimes had no holsters for their guns, but carried them in their hands or in trouser pockets. Some were barefooted. They wore the same range of cheap man-made fibres in blues and browns. They wore either pith helmets or floppy hats. When I asked them about the difference between these two forms of headgear, they replied that the pith helmets were hard, whereas the floppy hats were—floppy.

I put out my hand to shake that of a Vietcong. He thought I was trying to take the revolver from his hand. Prudently he put the gun behind his back.

Most of the regular troops seemed to come from the north. They arrived in trucks, and all but the officers abandoned their arms. Then they wandered hand in hand through the streets. We rushed down to the port to marvel at the navy in their nineteenth-century suits. At Tan Son Nhuot, the air-force arrived, wearing wings and speaking Russian. Near the still smouldering remains of the DAO compound, these elusive aristocrats of the air could be found drinking Chablis and American beer.

The Saigon bourgeoisie, to meet the occasion, dressed themselves up to the nines and drove round and round the city for days on end, until they were stopped by the price of petrol. Many cars had been destroyed, and lay at the side of the roads. The bourgeoisie then came round and round on Hondas. They were at last admitted to the bar of the Continental Shelf, where they came to be seen. The café crowds came back to their old haunts, and cowboys resumed work, stealing watches and handbags: they thought it good sport to snatch cameras from the necks of NLF soldiers. People were said to have been shot for stealing, but the reports did not deter the criminals.

After a time the beggars returned to their usual patches, and an unusually large number of prostitutes started hanging around the hotels. As Saigon got used to the new soldiers, and realized that their orders were not to intervene, the hope grew that the city might draw these saints into its aged corruption.

It was easy to pick out the stalls of looted goods. Drink was cheap, and since many Embassy wine cellars had been ransacked the quality was high. It was in liberated Saigon that I learned what happens to aged champagne, how it loses its sparkle and turns to a nutty dessert wine. The French residents of Saigon—there were many—descended on the street-markets early and got the best wine home and out of the sun. The journalists—of whom there were not a few—picked off the bottles of genuine spirits: it had been foolish to try to buy whisky in Saigon before; now the real thing was as cheap as the imitation. Over the next three months, the depletion of stocks told you a lot about drinking habits: it was clear, for instance, that since the Americans had left, no one in Saigon could stand tequila, or knew what to do with it. I tried it, and tried to imagine what it would be like with a salted rim. Ten years later the thought still disgusts me.

The chief customers in the market were the NLF. The soldiers had been paid on arrival in Saigon, and with the North Vietnamese *dong* standing at four to five hundred *piastres* (the panic rate) they were richer than they had ever been in their lives. They bought several watches and might wear them all. They bought cigarette lighters with tiny clocks concealed inside them. And the more they acquired, the less they resembled the nineteenth-century army of the early days of liberation. Once they had bought the dark glasses, they had taken on something of the Saigon look.

There were no wounded soldiers. They were not allowed to visit Saigon. The soldiers we met were appalled by what they saw: the beggars, the painted faces of the women, the dishonesty. They spoke of a future in which they would turn Saigon into a beautiful city. They compared it unfavourably with Hanoi.

The soldiers had a mission to perform, but they did not have a missionary's reforming zeal. They knew it was best to take their time, and they had time on their hands. Saigon society slowly returned to abnormal, out of gas and freewheeling downhill. Everyone knew the situation could not last. Nobody knew what would come next.

In those initial days it was possible to travel outside the city, since no formal orders had been given. Indeed it was possible to do most things you fancied. But once the regulations were published restricting us to Saigon, life became very dull indeed. The novelty of the street scenes had worn off, and most journalists left at the first opportunity. I, however, had been asked by the *Washington Post* to maintain its presence in Vietnam until a replacement could be brought in. I allowed the journalists' plane to leave without me, then cabled Washington stating my terms, which were based on the fact that I was the only stringer left working for an American paper. The *Post*, on receipt of my terms, sacked me. I had thought I had an exclusive story. What I learned was: never get yourself into an exclusive *position*. If the *New York Times* had had a man in Saigon, the *Post* would have taken my terms. Because there were no rivals, and precious few Americans, I had what amounted to an exclusive non-story. By now, I was sick of the East, sick of travel, sick of the journalistic life. But I was stuck. I crawled back to the *Post*.

When there was nothing to write about, I described myself, but as this was against house style in an American paper, I had to be thinly disguised: '"It's like a spa at the end of the season," remarked a dejected Englishman, sitting on the empty terrace of the Continental Palace—this abandoned, echoing, colonial hotel. The rains have begun, leaving the air cooler and clearer. Most of the foreigners are preparing to leave.' And I went on to record how the old Assembly building had been turned back into an Opera House, where a brute of a conductor leaped around in tails, and where the mixed evening always included the same programme: a movement of Beethoven's Fifth, some Strauss, and a rendition in Russian of *La*

Donna è Mobile, sung by a Vietnamese tenor with an idea of how to smile like an Italian. The NLF soldiers would listen relaxedly, sticking their bare feet over the gallery. It appears to be an idea common among conquerors that what a fallen city needs is a good injection of culture. After the capture of Berlin, every sector was immediately featuring Russian dancing and lectures by T. S. Eliot. Hanoi sent down pretty well everything it could transport, including massed choirs and an archaeological exhibition of a strongly nationalistic bent.

In early June I went to a reception at the Presidential Palace, to mark the sixth anniversary of the founding of the Provisional Revolutionary Government. Nowadays, I believe, you will find that Vietnam has written the PRG out of history. The process was just beginning then. A particularly frank and cynical guerrilla told me that the talk about the PRG was nonsense. Hanoi called all the shots and it was stupid to believe otherwise. And yet I believe that the members of the southern movement did generally believe in the authority of their own existence. The excitement was, on this occasion, to spot the PRG leaders, such as Huynh Tan Phat, with his face wreathed in smiles, dressed in the kind of khaki suit favoured by foreign correspondents in the tropics, but with the addition of a matching khaki tie.

The person we all wanted to meet was General Tran Van Tra, Saigon's military chief. He was in a terrific mood, and laughed and laughed when we reminded him of some of his previous activities. We would ask: the Americans say you masterminded the Tet Offensive from headquarters in Thu Duc; is this true? And he would reply that he couldn't remember. I'd been reading Lucien Bodard's extraordinary *The Quicksand War*, in which Tran features as having organized a patriotic liquidation campaign against the French. Was that true? He said he wouldn't elaborate. All he would say was that he had been in the environs of Saigon since before 1945.

There was a sense that the life work of such men was coming to fruition, that the plan of years could now be implemented. And the implementation could proceed at its own proper pace. The centre of Saigon was losing its significance. The shops of Tu Do, dealers in luxury goods, were now also soup-stands. But Tu Do itself was deserted. It reminded me of an old French photograph, with a couple of blurred figures in the middle distance, and a cyclo-driver snoozing in the shade.

In the suburbs, by contrast, the mobilization of the youth groups had got under way. They sat around awkwardly singing revolutionary songs, clapping in unison and not wearing jeans. They had turned the task of sweeping the streets into a ceremony. They were tearing down the old police posts, but not all the barbed wire, not all the barbed wire by any means.

The major effort was to get people back from urban squats to their homes in the country. A truck would come through the streets bound for Quang Nam, its destination written in large chalk letters along the side, together with the words 'We drive by night'. That was an astonishing novelty. For over twenty years the golden rule in Indochina was not to be on the roads at night.

Something had to be done about crime. Saigon had lived on crime, all kinds, from the petty to the most highly organized. With the fall of Saigon, prisons were opened, all prisoners released, and judiciary suspended. I spoke to one judge, an opponent of Thieu and yet part of his criminal court. He said that after the liberation he and about a hundred other former judges had presented themselves and asked for pardon. The pardon had been given, after they had informed on their fellow judges. Since that time they had gone to their place of work every day, and waited for the arrival of the new Minister of Justice. Finally he came and looked round the tribunal, delivering himself of one sentence: 'Comrades, continue your work.' So a hundred judges sat around and waited. In the provinces it was said that they received unwelcome visits from men they had sentenced.

Justice took to the open streets, and in one week the official newspaper (the old papers had been closed down) gave two front-page stories showing robbers executed by the liberation forces. Both accounts emphasized the popular support for the executions. In the first case, a Honda-cowboy was killed trying to escape. Support was *ex post facto*. In the second, the photograph showed a former 'puppet soldier' tied to crossed planks in the manner of Spartacus. Public support preceded the action. The man had been caught attempting to steal a watch at gunpoint, had resisted arrest, and, not having repented when finally caught, had committed further 'savage' actions. So: 'In order to protect the tranquil life of the Saigon population and in accordance with the aspirations of the people, the revolutionary law shot the thief Vo Van Ngoc.'

In another case, three thousand people assembled in order to judge three thieves. They climbed up on buildings to witness the popular tribunal, which sentenced one of the culprits to death. He was shot 'before the joy of the people', whom the newspaper showed in a rather blurred photograph waiting for the event.

That a thief had not repented was a serious point to be held against him. In the judicial and moral climate of the day, repentance was of prime importance, and obstinacy was a political category. Re-education, *Hoc Tap*, was under way, and everyone was talking about it. It appeared that the private soldier or NCO could go along for the three-day political education session: if he performed well he would be praised, whereas if he was uncooperative he would be told to emulate those singled out for praise. It sounded an absurdly lenient programme—perhaps merely a way of filling in the time and keeping idle officers off the street. But later on, the same people who had spoken with modest pride of their good performances in *Hoc Tap* came back to say that *Hoc Tap* was not yet over. It was becoming inexorable; it was impossible to extricate oneself from the guilt of being associated with the Thieu army. In South Vietnam, men of military age had had no choice but to join the army: they were conscripts. And yet they seemed to be asked to share the guilt of Thieu.

It was, in fact, over the question of re-education that the new regime showed its true character, and it brought to an end the long period in which the Saigonese were prepared perhaps to give their conquerors the benefit of the doubt. One morning my Vietnamese assistant burst into my room. 'It's sensational, all the officers have to leave home for a month's course. They're going to be re-educated.'

I got back into bed, crossly, and asked why that was so sensational.

'Don't you think it's harsh? They're to be separated from their families for thirty days.'

I replied that in the case of the generals I thought the whole thing pretty lenient.

The details of the announcement were extraordinary. You were told exactly how much money you would need for the course, for the purchase of food, and you were advised to bring three kilos of rice as emergency rations. In addition, you needed a change of clothes, blanket, towel, mosquito net, mat, raincoat, pullover, toothpaste, toothbrush, bowl, cigarettes (if a smoker), paper, pen, health card and medicines. It seemed to indicate a trip to the Central Highlands, and looking at the list I was foolish enough to express the wish that I was going too.

That there was a ten-day course for junior officers seemed to indicate that the duration of the course was seriously meant. The officers put on their raincoats and went off to their departure points, joking that if they tell you to shower and don't provide the soap you are not to go in. They left, and as long as I was there they didn't come back.

The officers had been duped, and you might almost say that the deception was justifiable: there were decades of corruption in an army that was going to be extremely difficult to incorporate into the new society. But the ruse was exacerbated by the way it was reported. In the days of Thieu there had been a press of sorts, and spokesmen of the Provisional Revolutionary Government used to be eloquent in its defence. Then, with the end of the war, they came in and closed the papers down, replacing them with *Giai Phong*.

The new official press hated mentioning disasters of any kind. A friend of mine sent a report abroad concerning a road accident. This was censored, and the rumours began. There was a rumour that two truckloads of former officers had been ambushed, or had hit a minefield, somewhere near Tay Ninh. The rumour grew until I was assured by one woman that two thousand former officers had been killed. The women of Saigon went into shell shock. There were gatherings, real demonstrations in the streets, and slanging matches between the innocent soldiers of the north and the very down-to-earth wives of Saigon. The women wanted to know from General Tran Van Tra what had happened. The soldiers seemed completely unnerved. Worse, there were more officers waiting to leave on similar 'courses', and so there was always a group of tearful women waiting behind the Post Office to learn when their husbands were due to go. I was told that four officers had returned from re-education in coffins.

It was becoming impossible for me to work as a journalist. Up to now my stories had all had the theme of life returning to normal, but when the censorship began it was very difficult to describe normality truthfully. I wrote a story about how a fishnet factory had been ordered to stay open with full employment, even though there was no nylon thread for the nets (the implication being that the employer would soon become impoverished). No one questioned the truth of the story, it was that they wanted me to say simply: the factory has been ordered to stay open *despite all the difficulties*. If they could not admit that there was no thread, how could they allow us to say that no one seemed to have returned from the re-education camps? And if one could not write such a story, how could one justify giving a general impression of normality in other stories? In one I mentioned that a man had committed suicide in the ruins of an old military monument. But the outside world was not allowed to know that there had been a suicide in Saigon.

I began to wonder if there was a code word to explain to my employers on the *Washington Post* that my copy was being censored. The thought, judging from the subjects they asked me to write about, hadn't occurred to them. I had retained from the *Post*'s bureau (before I handed it over to the authorities) a copy of a handbook for the paper's correspondents. I looked up censorship. There was no entry. I looked up Moscow, where the most I learned was that a correspondent should beware of making unflattering personal references to Lenin and to the way Jews were treated in Russia. I decided to solve the censorship problem by stopping writing and applying to leave. It was not a solution, but I could no longer bear Vietnam.

I had a spacious but gloomy old flat in Tu Do street. If I looked out of my window any time during the day, there would be a bum swinging in the window opposite, which belonged to a body-building club. If I looked down at the street to the corner slightly left, my eye would immediately be caught by a tiny cyclo-driver in a panama hat, who had decided that I was the only generous customer left in the city, and that he might as well specialize. I was under a kind of commercial house arrest, genial enough, but unrelenting. If I told the cyclo-driver I was walking today, I would still have to go past my spastic beggar, the one who was all smiles and whom I was supposed never to let down. But he was generous enough in a way. One day I carefully crossed the street to avoid him on my usual walk. I was studiously pretending not to be anywhere near him when I happened to see he was doubled up in laughter. He knew exactly what pressure he was putting on me every day, and he seemed to think it well within my rights occasionally to refuse.

Early in the morning at, say, 5.30, you would hear the bells ringing in the military billets. Then there was a noise—a great tearing sound—which I thought must belong to some extraordinary contraption for removing the surface from the road. I rose and threw open the mosquito blinds: it was a company of soldiers sprinting along the street in their Ho Chi Minh sandals. The soldiers were relaxed and cheerful at this time of day. They shouted a few slogans, exercised, listened to what sounded like a little pep-talk for about ten minutes and then went off to breakfast.

These soldiers—the *bo doi*, as we all now called them—were members of the best army in the world, disciplined in war and extraordinarily well-behaved in peace. But they had no gift for drill—even their gymnastics were uncoordinated—Saigon rooked them something rotten. The stall-holders persuaded the *bo doi*, when they suspected the dud watches they had been sold, that the only foolproof test was to put a watch in your mouth, block your ears and close your eyes. If you could hear it ticking, it was kosher.

The *bo doi* hated keeping order. They did at one stage execute thieves in the street, but that was at the height of the crime wave in May. Later I saw a robber trying to escape from a pursuing crowd. The *bo doi* were appealed to, but were reluctant to interfere: because the *bo doi* had a great deal of sympathy for the poor of Saigon, and all the people they had put out of work by winning. They believed their own propaganda. They *were* heroes. A story was told in the early days after the fall that a *bo doi* had been driving a truck carelessly and had killed a child. His commanding officer said to him: you have been a good soldier and have sacrificed much for the revolution—the time has come to make the final sacrifice. Whereupon the *bo doi* shot himself. The fact that the Saigonese told these rumours says something for the reputation of the *bo doi*. Even so, they were sometimes stabbed in the back streets, and once or twice one would hear gunfire at night.

If I had been able to talk to the *bo doi*, Saigon would have been the most interesting place in the world. But I mean really talk. They were forbidden to chat to *us*. Once one told me: 'I always liked going into battle because the atmosphere was so good. Everybody knew they were going to die. They had no food, and nothing to drink for days. If a man had something to eat, he would share it with you, and if you had nothing to give in return, you would show him the letter you had just got from your wife. Everybody loved each other, because they all knew they were going to die.' But then he became embarrassed at confessing all this to a foreigner.

Part of our admiration for the *bo doi* derived from what, in contrast, we were now learning of the Khmer Rouge after the fall of Phnom Penh. Large numbers of refugees had been making their way from the evacuated Cambodian capital across the border into Vietnam and, in some cases, to Saigon itself. The stories they told made it clear that the Khmer Rouge had not just instigated a bloodbath, they had no plan for the governing of the country they had won. If you could persuade a Vietnamese officer to talk about the Khmer Rouge, the best he would say, with a shudder, would be that they do not respect the laws of Ho Chi Minh. But it was obvious now that the regime was one of unparalleled savagery, and the Vietnamese were shocked by what they knew of it.

What was happening in Cambodia meant far more to me personally than the events I was witnessing in Vietnam, and I spent some time cultivating contacts with those who had escaped the Khmer Rouge regime. In particular, there were nine officers who had been associates of Son Ngoc Thanh, the former Cambodian prime minister and leader of the Khmer Krom (the ethnic Cambodians from South Vietnam). They had now requested asylum in Vietnam, as they were terrified of repatriation. But nobody knew precisely what the relationship between the authorities in Saigon and the Khmer Rouge would be.

The officers were living with their families in a Cambodian pagoda not far from the city centre. They were free to go around town. One day, one of them came to see me in the hotel. He asked if he could borrow my spare bed. I asked him why. He explained that over the last few days a particular car had been arriving at the pagoda and taking people away. The pretext was that the officers and the head of the monastery, the Venerable Kim Sang, were to meet with Son Ngoc Thanh himself. Four people went and did not return. Nobody knew if they had been arrested by the Provisional Revolutionary Government, or if Khmer Rouge undercover agents were involved.

I told the officer that he could stay the night, but he would not be able to continue in the hotel for a long time, or he would draw suspicion on both of us. We sat up and talked until late into the night. As it happened I had Sihanouk's memoirs with me, which included a long attack on the CIA and Son Ngoc Thanh for undermining his regime. The officer agreed with much of Sihanouk's account, and admitted to me that he had been involved with the CIA. I asked him a number of times where Son Ngoc Thanh was now. It took a long time before he would say. Finally, he admitted that Son Ngoc Thanh was in Saigon. I said that it seemed very strange, if the man had been an associate of the CIA, that he should have stayed on in Saigon. The officer replied that Ho Chi Minh and Son Ngoc Thanh, both being nationalist leaders, had a respect for each other, and that there was a stipulation in Ho's will that Son Ngoc Thanh must not be harmed in any way. He had nothing to fear from the PRG.

Once his story was out, the officer began to talk about his fears that the Khmer Rouge would catch him. He recounted his escape from Cambodia. He talked about the screams he had heard from the undergrowth, when they had taken away suspected officers. He talked about the beatings. He was still pleading for help and he believed that I had influence. I remember his soft voice from the next bed asking if I could imagine what it was like to be put in a cage and left all day in the sun, 'like a wild animal, like a wild animal.'

That night, every time I fell asleep, there was a loud knocking at the door. I would wake fully, then wait, my heart beating, to see whether the knocking was real. I would doze off again. Then the knocking would resume. The next day the officer left to find a new hiding place.

I was out of my depth entirely, and confided my problem to a colleague who was not only very curious to know who had spent the night in my room and why, but also seemed very well-connected. A few days later he came rushing into my room and said that if I could find my lieutenant-colonel, the one who was supposed to have done stuff for the CIA, he couldn't guarantee anything but he just might be able to help him. But it had to be straight away. I said it was impossible. I couldn't find him. He was in hiding.

Later on, the desperate officer came to see me in my flat. His wife, who was still at the pagoda, had been threatened by the same mysterious men in the car; if her husband did not come with them, they said, she would be beaten up. It was I think on this visit that the officer found something I had not told him I possessed—a copy of the last will and testament of Ho Chi Minh. I had not told him about it because I knew that in the published version at least there was no reference to Son Ngoc Thanh. He flicked through the little pamphlet desperately, and had to agree that unless there was a secret codicil, his hero and mentor was entitled to no special protection from the Vietnamese. And that meant perhaps that his position was even worse than he had thought.

I still do not know what to make of this story. I do not know why Son Ngoc Thanh stayed on in Saigon, or who was causing the disappearance of the Cambodian officers. But the reason I tell the story is this: those who actually set out to see the fall of a city (as opposed to those to whom this calamity merely happens), or those who choose to go to a front line, are obviously asking themselves to what extent they are cowards. But the tests they set themselves— there is a dead body, can you bear to look at it?—are nothing in comparison with the tests that are sprung on them. It is not the obvious tests that matter (do you go to pieces in a mortar attack?) but the unexpected ones (here is a man on the run, seeking your help—can you face him honestly?).

115

At that time in Saigon there was a craze for a cheap North Vietnamese soup called *bun bo*. All the shops in Tu Do seemed to be serving it in the hope of attracting military customers. Some friends called on me and suggested we should go for lunch in one of these establishments. As we were crossing the road, I bumped into the Cambodian officer, with his pockmarked face and his pleading smile. Something very important has happened, he said, I must talk to you. I told him I was going with some friends for a bowl of *bun bo*. He was welcome to join us. No, he said, this was very urgent; and he added meaningfully that this might be the last time we met. He had hinted at suicide before, and on this occasion my heart hardened. I told him I was going with my friends for a bowl of *bun bo*. The incident was over in the time that it took to cross the road, and I never saw the officer again. But I can remember where I left him standing in the street.

It takes courage to see clearly, and since courage is at issue I know that I am obliged to address myself to the questions raised at the outset of the journey. I went as a supporter of the Vietcong, wanting to see them win. I saw them win. What feeling did that leave me with, and where does it leave me now? I know that by the end of my stay in Saigon I had grown to loathe the *apparatchiks*, who were arriving every day with their cardboard suitcases from Hanoi. I know that I loathed their institutional lies and their mockery of political justice.

But as the banners went up in honour of Lenin, Marx and Stalin, I know too that I had known this was coming. Had we not supported the NLF 'without illusions'? Must I not accept that the disappearances, the gagging of the press, the political distortion of reality was all part of a classical Stalinism which nevertheless 'had its progressive features'? Why, we supported unconditionally 'all genuine movements of national independence'. I must be satisfied. Vietnam was independent and united.

In my last days in Saigon I began to feel that it had all been wrong. But when, on a plane between Vientiane and Bangkok, I learned from a magazine that Solzhenitsyn had been saying precisely that, and condemning the Americans for not fighting more ruthlessly, I was forced to admit that I still believed in the right of

Vietnam to unity and independence. The French had had no right in Vietnam. The Japanese had had no right in Vietnam. The British had had no right to use Japanese troops to restore French rule in Vietnam. Nor had the Americans had any right to interfere in order to thwart the independence movement which had defeated the French. Many of my bedrock beliefs were and are such as one could share with the most innocent *bo doi*. 'Nothing is more precious than independence and liberty'—the slogan of Ho that had driven me wild with boredom in the last few months, broadcast over the p.a. system through the streets, and emblazoned on all those banners—but it is a fine motto.

But the supporters of the Vietnamese opposition to the United States had gone further than that, and so had I. We had been seduced by Ho. My political associates in England were *not* the kind of people who denied that Stalinism existed. We not only knew about it, we were very interested in it. We also opposed it. Why then did we also support it? Or did we?

I was forced to rethink this recently when I read a remark by Paul Foot: 'No revolutionary socialist apart from James Fenton was ever under the slightest illusion that Vietnam could produce anything at all after the war, let alone socialism.' My first thought was: what about the poor old *bo doi*? Do *they* count as revolutionary socialists? And my second point may be illustrated by an editorial in *New Left Review* ten years ago: 'In achieving the necessary combination of national liberation and social revolution the Vietnamese Communists drew on many of the best traditions of the international workers' movement which produced them.'

The editorial—written by Robin Blackburn, a Trotskyite as influential as Paul Foot in securing the support of my generation for the liberation struggle of the Vietnamese—never mentions that the victory of the Vietnamese was a victory for *Stalinism*, because to do so would have muddied the issue. The great thing was that the évents of ten years ago represented a defeat for American imperialism. The same issue of *New Left Review* quotes Lukács: 'The defeat of the USA in the Vietnamese war is to the 'American Way of Life' as the Lisbon earthquake was to French feudalism . . . . Even if decades were to pass between the Lisbon earthquake and the fall of the Bastille, history can repeat itself.'

Stirring words, and—look—we don't have to support the Lisbon earthquake in order to support the Fall of the Bastille.

Blackburn's editorial ended by saying that the success of a socialist opposition against such odds would have 'a special resonance in those many lands where the hopes aroused by the defeat of fascism in the Second World War were to be subsequently frustrated or repressed: in Madrid and Barcelona, Lisbon and Luanda, Milan and Athens, Manila and Seoul.' An interesting list of places, and a reminder of the variousness of political change. The example of Madrid, for instance, would I think be much more inspiring to anybody in Seoul than the example of Saigon. We seem to have learned that dictatorships can be removed without utter disaster. Is this thanks to the Vietnamese? Maybe in some very complicated and partial way. But Madrid has not yet been 'lost to capitalism' like Indochina.

While I was working in Vietnam and Cambodia I thought that I was probably on the right track if my reports, while giving no comfort to my political enemies, were critical enough to upset my friends. I knew something about the thirties and I absolutely did not believe that one should, as a reporter, invent victories for the comrades. I had the illusion that I was honest, and in many ways I was. What I could not see in myself, but what I realize now is so prevalent on the Left, is the corrupting effect of political opportunism. We saw the tanks arriving and we all wanted to associate ourselves, just a little bit, with victory. And how much more opportunistic can you get than to hitch a ride on the winning tank, just a few yards before the palace gates?

When the boat people later began leaving Vietnam there was an argument on the Left that this tragic exodus was a further example of the pernicious effects of US foreign policy. Yet it is striking that for three decades after the Second World War such a mass departure did not take place. It is only in the decade since unification that people have been trusting themselves to flimsy vessels in the South China Sea. A recent report described a group of North Vietnamese villagers who acquired a boat and were setting out in the dead of night when they were noticed by another village. The second group said, Let us come too. The first group did not have enough space for safety, but they were afraid that if they did not agree the other villagers would raise the alarm. So the boat was impossibly crammed.

The boat people are not merely 'obstinate elements' or Chinese comprador capitalists on their way to new markets. They are simple people with no hope.

For two months after the fall there had been no banking facilities in Saigon. Petrol was expensive and it was not unusual to see students directing the traffic in streets where there was no traffic to be directed. Everything changed when the authorities allowed the withdrawal of small amounts of cash, and when petrol prices were reduced. The rich brought out their cars again. The Hondas reappeared. And the whole bourgeoisie went into the café business.

You borrowed an old parachute from a friend. You got hold of a few small stools, brought your crockery from home and you were in business. Every day I walked the length of Tu Do, looking to see if my name had come up on the departures list at the Information Ministry, and one day I counted seventy of these stalls, excluding the allied trades—cake vendors, cigarette stands, booksellers, manufacturers of Ho Chi Minh sandals, and the best example of Obstinate Enterprise, the man who sat outside the re-education centre making plastic covers for the new certificates.

The parachutes were strung between the trees for shade. With their varying colours and billowing shapes, they made the city utterly beautiful. The tables had flowers. The crockery was of the best and the service—inexperienced. It was all an economic nonsense. There was a group of students who ran a bookstall but spent all their time in the café across the street, watching for custom. During the day they might just make enough money for soft drinks. If more, they moved further up the street to drown their sorrows in a spirit called *Ba Xi De*, 'the old man with the stick'. With this they ate dishes of boiled entrails, and peanuts which came wrapped in fascinating twists of paper—the index of an English verse anthology, or a confidential document from some shady American organization.

In Gia Long Boulevard, by the tribunal where the judges were twiddling their thumbs, proprietors and clients came from the legal profession. The proprietor of 'The Two Tamarind Trees' told me she made about a thousand *piastres* a day. Previously she had made two hundred thousand *piastres* a case (755 *piastres* to a dollar). On the street beneath the Caravelle Hotel, there was the Café Air France, known to us as Chez Solange. Solange came from a rich family. She was beautiful. One day she brought two rattan bars and a set of bar-stools from her house, and set up shop. I was one of her first clients, and she told me over a breakfast of beer and beer what it had been like to become a barmaid.

Her elder brothers had told her she was mad to try it. They dropped her off with her things, but later would have nothing to do with her. Her younger brothers had been more helpful. But: 'This morning when the first customer came for coffee, I was so ashamed that I couldn't serve him. And then when I did serve him, I couldn't decide how much to charge him.' But once the business was established, the elder brothers relented and were to be seen lounging at the bar most of the day, except during the heat.

Solange had come down in the world. There was a thing called *bia om*, meaning beer and a cuddle, a half-way house to prostitution. The client ordered the beer. With it he paid for the company of an attractive girl. The open-air cafés were not great places for a cuddle, but the suggestion was still there. The new slang term was *caphé om*, coffee and a cuddle, reflecting the diminishing spending power of the bourgeoisie.

The morality of the cafés was attacked in the newspapers, particularly on the grounds that the bourgeoisie were procrastinating. What role were they going to play in the future society? I sometimes asked these people, particularly students, why they didn't try going to the countryside as teachers or in some professional capacity. Of course they were horrified. One man told me that he wanted to stay on in the capital in order to read foreign newspapers (there were no foreign newspapers). Another girl said she couldn't teach in the countryside because peasant children didn't go to school (they did go to school).

The *bo doi* occasionally came along with loudhailers, clearing the cafés away. But a few days later the obstinate economy was back in place. And it was still there when I finally got permission to leave.

The majority of the emigrants at this stage belonged to the French community, and it was obvious at the airport that they had spent their last *piastres* very well. We were going out on a plane provided by the United Nations High Commission for Refugees. You should have seen the kind of refugees we were. I had a Leica and two *Washington Post* typewriters. That was my loot. They, the French, had ransacked the market for hi-fi systems of the very highest quality, and they had snapped up the best of the leather jackets and coats in Tu Do, where for some reason you could get very good calf. Their photographic equipment was luxurious, but the thing that held us all up was the censorship of photographs.

Vietnam had become known throughout the world through photos of a kind which emphasized the grain of squalor. The *bo doi* did not like these photographs, and they weren't fools either: if they found a print of an unacceptable image, say a poor woman squatting, they took the print and insisted on a search for the negative. Everyone's attempts to be better than Don McCullin were confiscated, and the process took a long time. There were more mysterious reasons too: I was told that a *bo doi* confiscated a photo of a flower: when asked why, he explained that there was a kind of powder on the flower; if you enlarged the photo enough, you would see a grain of the powder, and if you enlarged that grain enough— you would see a photograph of the whole of Vietnam.

As I waited for the French to clear their loot, a panic seized me which was just like the panic I had had all those months before. I would never escape from Vietnam. The *bo doi* would never get through all those enormous suitcases. And besides the runway was absolutely dancing with rain. We would be sent back to Saigon, and then we would be forced through the whole process again. It had happened to others and it could happen to us. I wished those fucking French would get a move on.

And then at last we were let through. The man in front of me had too much hand-luggage and I offered to help. I took from him the French Embassy's diplomatic bag and we all ran together across the tarmac through the cloudburst. My last memory, as we entered the aircraft, is of the overpowering smell of tropical rain on very expensive new leather.

MARILYNNE ROBINSON

THE WASTE LAND

On the coast of Cumbria, in the Lake District, there is a nuclear reprocessing plant called Sellafield, formerly Windscale, that daily pumps up to a million gallons of radioactive waste down a mile and a half of pipeline, into the Irish Sea. It has done this for thirty-five years. The waste contains caesium and ruthenium and strontium, and uranium, and plutonium. Estimates published in *The Times* and in the *Observer* are that a quarter of a ton of plutonium has passed into the sea through this pipeline—enough, in theory, according to *The Times*, to kill 250 million people; much more than enough, in theory, according to the *Observer*, to destroy the population of the world. The plant was designed on the assumption that radioactive waste would lie harmlessly on the sea floor. That assumption proved false, but the plant has continued to operate in the hope that radioactive contamination may not be so very harmful, after all. If this hope is misguided, too, then Britain, in a time of peace, has silently, needlessly, passionlessly, visited upon us all a calamity equal to the worst we fear.

Everything factual that I will relate in this article I learned from reading the British press or watching British television. But it would not be accurate to say that I know, more or less, what a reasonably informed Briton knows about these things, because there is a passivity and a credulousness in informed British opinion that neutralizes the power of facts to astonish.

To understand what I will tell you, you must imagine a country where, though the carcinogenic properties of radioactivity in general and of plutonium in particular are gravely conceded, it is considered reasonable, in the best sense, to permit the release of both of these into the environment until the precise nature of their effect is understood. This notion of reasonableness is, I think, extremely local, but the consequences of such thinking are felt in many places. The Danes object to plutonium on their beaches, as do the Dutch. And of course the Irish, a volatile people at the best of times, are now very much exercised by elevated rates of childhood cancer and Down's syndrome along their eastern coast. They have leaped to the very conclusion the British find too hasty—that the contamination of the environment by known carcinogens is detrimental to the public health. No one disputes that the

125

contamination of these coasts is surely and exclusively owing to British reasonableness, since the Irish have not developed nuclear energy—nor have the Danes, who consider it unsafe—and since the only other fuel reprocessing plant known to release waste into the sea, at Cap de la Hague in France, releases only one percent of the radioactivity that enters the sea from Sellafield.

When I realized what I was reading, I began to clip out articles every day and save them, and I brought them back to America, knowing that my uncorroborated word could not be credited. Travellers to unknown regions must bring back proof of the marvels they have seen. Perhaps the most incredible part of this story is that it has fallen to me to tell it. American scholars and scientists go to Britain in platoons. Many live there. Probably all of them look at the *Guardian* now and then, or *The Times*. Perhaps most of them are more competent to understand what they read there than I am, better schooled in such matters as the particular virulence of plutonium, or the special fragility of the sea. No one had ever hinted to me that for thirty-five years Britain has knowingly befouled itself and its neighbours with radiation, and nothing I had heard or read had prepared me to discover a historical and political context for which the one vivid instance of Sellafield could well serve as an emblem. Yet Sellafield does not depart from, but in fact epitomizes, British environmental practice. This is only to say, read on. This is a tale of wonders.

In November 1983 a family was walking along the beach near Sellafield—it is a major tourist and recreational area—when a scientist who worked at the plant stopped to tell them that they should not let their children play there. They were shocked, of course, and raised questions, and sent a letter to their MP. The scientist was fired, amid official mutterings about his having committed an impropriety in disclosing this information. No doubt he had violated the Official Secrets Act, though so far as I know the matter was not couched in those terms. British workers in significant nationalized industries—for example, British Aerospace, the postal system, and the nuclear industry—are obliged to sign the act, which imposes on them fines and imprisonment if they reveal without authorization information acquired in the course of their work. Only death can release them from this contract. Employees of private industries are in the same position, to all intents and purposes, since the unauthorized use of privately held information is prosecuted as theft. In the democratic kingdom, the exercise of judgement and conscience is the exclusive prerogative of the great.

But I digress. Though the renegade employee was dismissed, the issue of the safety of the beaches was called to public attention, with a number of consequences. A woman who lived in a village near Sellafield sent a bag of dust from her vacuum cleaner to a professor in Pittsburgh, who found that it contained plutonium. Divers from British Greenpeace tried to close the pipeline but were unable to do so because the shape of its mouth had been altered. They discovered an oily scum on the water that sent the needles of their Geiger counters off the scales. The divers and their boat had to be decontaminated. The radioactive slick was said to be the consequence of an error at the plant that had disgorged a radioactive solvent into the sea—an accident that, unlike the normal functioning of the plant, raised questions of competence and culpability. That is to say, this matter was put into the hands of the Director of Public Prosecutions, and quite appropriately. However, it is a curious feature of British law and practice that silence descends around any issue that is about to become the subject of legal action. A judge may remove this restriction in particular cases; murder trials, for example, are reported in lascivious detail. But a newspaper that publishes anything relating to matters prohibited as *sub judice* is subject to catastrophic fines. The manufacturers of thalidomide, the sedative that caused many British children to be born without limbs, kept the question of their liability before the courts for seventeen years, and therefore unresolved and out of public awareness, until the *Sunday Times* defied the law and broke the story. The newspaper took its case to the European Court of Human Rights, and won, but this has had no effect on British law or practice. British justice, which is cousin to British reasonableness, grows squeamish at the thought that the legal process should be adulterated by publicity.

As a third consequence of the attention drawn to Sellafield, Yorkshire Television sent a team there to look into worker safety.

The team discovered that children in the villages surrounding the plant suffered leukaemia at a rate ten times the national average. This revelation fuelled public anxiety to such an extent that the government was obliged to appoint a commission to investigate. It recently published its conclusions in the so-called Black Report, named after Sir Douglas Black, president of the British Medical Association and the commission's head and spokesman. Dr Black startled some by assuring a television interviewer that people fear radioactivity now just as they feared electricity one hundred years ago.

The report offers 'a qualified reassurance' to those concerned about a possible health hazard in the area. The *Guardian* said: 'Recognising that radiation is the only established environmental cause of leukaemia in children, "within the limits of present knowledge," the Black team calls for new studies to provide additional potential insights.' Again according to the *Guardian*, 'Despite the high rates of cancer close to Sellafield, the report stresses: "An observed association between two factors does not prove a causal relationship."' This is certainly true. And this is the darling verity of the British government. Souls less doughty than these might feel that exposure to radiation around Sellafield, together with an elevated cancer rate, testifies to a causal relationship between these two factors, but we're not dealing with a bunch of patsies here. In environmental issues, a standard of proof is demanded that makes the claims of the Flat Earth Society look easy.

What do we have here? The better college sophomore has learned that this world does not yield what we call 'proof' of anything. That so weighty an edifice as public policy should be reared upon an epistemological abyss is truly among the world's marvels. Are these decision makers, known to wags as the Good and the Great, cynical connivers, imposing upon what can only be a frighteningly naive and credulous public? Or are they themselves also frighteningly naive? I cannot think of a third possibility. Whatever the cause of their behaviour, its effect, like the effect of the Official Secrets Act and the contempt laws, is to shield government and public and private industries from suspicions of error or wrongdoing, and to blur, fudge, and frustrate questions of responsibility and liability.

You will note that the laws and practices and attitudes I describe here have existed over decades, and have persisted while governments rose and fell. For example, in 1974 the government passed the Control of Pollution Act. To have a proper understanding of 'pollution' in this context it is essential to realize that in Britain, no legal control is exerted over agricultural chemicals or sprays. DDT is still in general use, as are Aldrin and Lindane. I know of no reason to imagine that policies towards industrial pollutants are any less indulgent in effect. Inspectors politely inform manufacturers of their intention to visit, so control of effluents can hardly be stringent. And we are not speaking here of soapsuds. In any case, part two of this Control of Pollution Act is now to be implemented, reports the *Guardian*. The article goes on to say, 'The new measures are expected to have a big impact on the problems of Britain's dirty beaches.' This seems to me a remarkably cheerful thought, considering that, to quote again, 'the measures only apply to new sewage or trade effluent discharges, however. Existing discharges will continue, but "consents" already granted will be subject to public scrutiny.' Well, this looks to me like an act designed to confer legality on the very sources of pollution that already dirty Britain's beaches. However, the act must have a fang, if only a small one, because for ten years it was not implemented. Why? The article offers an explanation from William Waldegrave, Under-Secretary of State for the Environment, who said that 'one of the factors that had held back successive governments was the fear of increasing costs to industry.'

How is one to understand the degradation of the sea and earth and air of the British homeland by people who use the word *British* the way others of us use the words *good*, and *just*, and *proud*, and *precious*, and *lovely*, and *clement*, and *humane*? No matter that these associations reflect and reinforce the complacency that allows the spoliation to go unchecked; still, surely they bespeak self-love, which should be some small corrective. I think ignorance must be a great part of the explanation—though ignorance so obdurate could be preserved only through an act of will.

The issue of Sellafield is complicated by the great skill the government has shown in turning accidents to good account. You will remember that the Greenpeace divers surfaced through highly radioactive slime. If they had not had Geiger counters with them, no one would have known that an accident had taken place. *Ergo*, one cannot know that *other* accidents have *not* taken place. From which it follows that these accidents, and not the normal functioning of the plant, might be responsible for the cancers and other difficulties and embarrassments. As the *Guardian* said, in its sober and respectful paraphrase of this startling document, the Black Report, 'The possibility of unplanned and undetected discharges having delivered significant doses of radiations to humans via an unsuspected route could not be entirely excluded.' The implication of all this is that the plant can be repaired, improved, and monitored, and then the hazards will go away. Number eight on the list of ten recommendations by the Black inquiry team suggests that 'attention [be] paid to upper authorized limits of radioactive discharges over short periods of time; to removal of solvent from discharges and adequacy of filter systems'—in other words, if occasional splurges are avoided, the level of radioactivity will remain safe and constant. That might well be true, if the substances put in the sea decayed. But as the *Observer* has noted, plutonium remains toxic for at least 100,000 years.

Another accident that has had great effect on the way this affair has been managed is the fact that Yorkshire Television focused its attention on leukaemia among local children. This is understandable, since the deaths of children are particularly vivid and painful to consider. But the limiting of the discussion to childhood cancer in the Black Report is clearly arbitrary and possibly opportunistic. Seascale, the village nearest the plant, where seven children have died of leukaemia in a period of ten years, has a population of 2,000. Children living there are said to have one chance in sixty of developing leukaemia, but the sample is considered too small to be reliable—coincidence might account for the high incidence of the disease.

But why are we talking only about leukaemia? I noted with interest, and added to my collection, a brief report about an inquest into the death of a Sellafield worker from bone cancer. An environmental group (not named) had pointed out that Dr Geoffrey Schofield, the plant's chief medical officer, 'did not mention the three most recent deaths from bone cancer at Sellafield.' The article continues, 'Dr Schofield, quoting a 1981 report on mortality rates among British Nuclear Fuels workers at Sellafield, referred to four cases of myeloma, a bone cancer. These figures over the period 1948 to 1980 were comparable with national figures. Since that report three more workers have died from myeloma and a fourth appears to have contracted the disease.' How do these cancer deaths relate to the cancer deaths among children in the area? Doesn't the concentration on the young actually focus attention on that portion of the population least likely to have developed cancer?

But officially preferred hypotheses are invoked to preclude lines of inquiry that might produce data that would discredit them. What harm could there be in checking for lung cancer deaths in areas downwind of Windscale?* These would certainly be equally relevant to the question of public safety, the real issue here.

---

*A striking feature in all this is the seeming difficulty of obtaining and interpreting information. One would think that a country with a national health service would enjoy centralized and continuous monitoring of health data. One would expect it to encourage preventive practices at both public and individual level, if only on grounds of economy. But the British government has actually suppressed reports on alcoholism and on the relation of cardiovascular disease to diet—the second of these was leaked to the *Lancet*; the first, though joked about in the press, has been dubbed an Official Secret, and its findings may not be published. The British government saves money in the most direct way: by refusing to spend it. In the European Community only Greece spends a smaller share of its wealth on health care. Yet the British are proud of their health system. Margaret Thatcher is fond of saying they get 'good value for money,' and one often sees statements to the effect that indicators of general health show the British system outperforming the big spenders. If this is true—if, with poverty and unemployment and all the problems that attend them; if, with rampant abuse of alcohol and heroin, a polluted

The conclusion reached by James Cutler, the Yorkshire Television producer who first made public the high incidence of leukaemia in Seascale, and the great fear of the chairman of British Nuclear Fuels, who really is named Con Allday, is that anxiety among the public signals a defeat for proponents of nuclear power. Now, I think nuclear power has proved to be a terrible idea, but I do not think the practices associated with Sellafield should ever be spoken of as if they were characteristic and inevitable aspects of its development. To do so would be to obscure the special questions of competence, of morality—of sanity, one might say—that Sellafield so vividly poses. But as I said earlier, I do not wish to imply that what has been done at Sellafield departs radically from the *British* nuclear establishment's behaviour. Ninety percent of the nuclear material that has been dumped in the sea world-wide has been dumped by the British. They have deposited it off the coasts of Spain and France and, of course, Ireland, and elsewhere—in containers, supposedly, though their methods of disposal at Sellafield do not encourage me to imagine that their methods elsewhere should be assumed to be particularly cautious.

I suppose the British make lots of money cleaning spent fuel rods from all over the world, and from their own facilities. To be a source of a substance so prized as plutonium must bring wealth, and influence too. It is certain that they do not do it for their health. Exactly contrary to the universally held view, Britain is an island of unevolved *laissez-faire* plutocracy characterized by unregulated (my translation of the British 'self-regulated') commerce and industry. So far from being lumbered with the costs of runaway socialist largesse, Britain ranks near the bottom in Europe not only in health spending but also in spending for education. In workers' wages and benefits, it has never approached the levels achieved by

---

environment, and immunization policies so casual that Britain still has rubella epidemics; if, with a slow rate of decline in cigarette smoking and rates of breast and lung cancer at or near top of the charts—if Britain still does better than countries that devote more generous portions of larger resources to populations whose conditions of life are distinctly more consistent with well-being, then the National Health Service beggars any praise.

West Germany, Sweden, or the Netherlands. The British seem rather fond of their poverty, which I think is a social and economic strategy rather than the mysterious, intractable affliction it is presented as being. It effectively excuses the state from responsibility for the conditions of life of the poor, and for the quality of life of ordinary people. While lowering public expectations, this 'poverty' justifies the astonishing recklessness of British industries, public and private, and makes it entirely acceptable for government and industry to be in cahoots to a degree that boggles the American mind.

Avoiding costs to industry is treated as an unquestioned good—Britain being so poor, after all. That very little trickles down from these coddled industries is a fact blamed squarely on the British worker, of all people, who, if he is lucky, toils for bad pay in a decaying factory and hopes that his children's lives will not be worse. Only consider: Britain is the world's fourth-largest arms dealer, a major exporter of petroleum, a major exporter of drugs and chemicals, a major centre of banking and insurance, a major centre of tourism. And it has access to the vast literatures of research and technology produced in the United States, the application of which in other countries is slowed and complicated by the problems of translation. This seems to me to be the basis for a presentable economy. But no, Britain is 'poor'—because its workers are sullen and Luddite, or because its governing classes are too haplessly genteel and fair-minded to cope in the hurly-burly of the market-place, or because the national character has grown idle in the embrace of the Welfare State, or because the great forces of entropy and decline have at last overtaken this noble civilization. Or because neither law nor custom encourages the sharing of wealth. Consider: university students are almost entirely subsidized. But only five to seven percent of secondary-school students are admitted to universities. Since nothing is done to compensate for the advantages children of privileged backgrounds bring to examinations and interviews—such education is expensive, and Britain, after all, is poor—the subsidies go to the children of the prosperous. The cost per student of the university system to the state justifies its being kept very small—and this magnifies the value and the prestige that attach to university degrees. That is British socialism.

My point is simply that all the talk of decline, along with the continuous experience of austerity, creates an atmosphere in which the granting of enormous latitude to corporations, whether private or public, seems urgently necessary, and the encumbering of them with codes and restrictions a luxury embattled Britain can scarcely afford. Economic considerations have an importance and a pervasiveness that startle. The *Sunday Times*, reporting on a critical study of the British diet that had been suppressed, laid the blame on a government fear of a negative impact on the food industry, and also on an awareness on the part of the government that old people are expensive: 'Civil servants representing the social services . . . point out that healthy and long-lived citizens will increase the number of old-age pensions.' Britain, you must always remember, is poor.

What a thoroughly miserable business. What arrogance to save a few quid by allowing Sellafield to spew and haemorrhage, again and again, on and on. According to the *Sunday Times*, a spokesman for British Nuclear Fuels agreed that it was 'in everybody's interests to get discharges down as low as possible' but argued that the cost was 'prohibitive.' He said, 'We would have to pass the cost on to our customers, which would mean higher electricity prices. We are already spending £500 million on reducing our discharges. We have reduced them considerably over the past ten years.' Reduced them from what, *to* what? Note how 'everybody's interests' are put in the scales against cost, and with what result. Why should expenses at a fuel reprocessing plant raise the price of electricity, rather than of plutonium? And why should the cost of recycling spent fuel for Japan—to pick a name out of the air—be subsidized by consumers in Britain? The idea is preposterous. We are hearing the same old song: *Shackle us with restrictions and you will pay dearly for it.*

Con Allday, chairman of BNF and, as one may glimpse him through the dark glass of British newspaper journalism, a man of views as emphatic as they are liable to be consequential, and who was quoted in the *Guardian* as saying that 'There is little point in spending additional money simply to be safer than safe,' is well deserving of some attention, while we are on the subject of thrift. This gentleman, according to the *Guardian*, 'announced a new feasibility study into how the company can reduce radioactive discharges into the Irish Sea to "as near zero as possible."' I am quoting this so that you can share my admiration of the language. 'He said: "Public acceptability of nuclear power is so important and the time-scale needed for a swing-round of public opinion is so long that we must be realistic and accept that our discharges must be reduced to very much lower levels than hitherto planned." This was "even though there is no rational, cost-effective basis for doing so on risk assessment grounds."' Weighing cost against risk again. That really is an interesting exercise—quite theological, I think. Considering that the expense involved in running a nuclear plant safely is truly vast, is it possible to say that the value of a given number of lives is exceeded in cash terms by the expenditure that would be required to prevent their loss? Clearly for these purposes the answer is yes, a fact all the more disturbing since the question is gravely distorted by the association of this slovenly enterprise with 'nuclear power' and by the insistence—based on what?—that anyone, least of all an island of coal in a sea of oil, needs nuclear power in any case. Note Allday's impatience with the idea that discharge levels lower than Sellafield's should be achieved. Does this give us insight into the environmental standards maintained at other facilities?

Even Dr Black, whose report found that the connection between radiation and leukaemia at Sellafield was 'by no means proven,' was quoted by the *Guardian* as having said that 'the risks of living near Sellafield were no greater than many of the risks everyone faced in their daily lives.' He compared the increased risk to that of someone who used a private car rather than public transport. This unctuous little simile translates into an admission that there is some measurable risk involved in living near Sellafield. (Risk of what? Leukaemia, surely, among other things. Then is not the presence of leukaemia this very risk actualized? By no means proven!)

How has this happened? I can only speculate that within a tiny community of specialists, where esteem, advancement, and influence travel through a very narrow channel, and where over the life of a new discipline such as nuclear technology the views of a very few people are reflected in policies of great magnitude and consequence, dissent would have little practical or emotional reward. Choices have been made, by scientists, industrialists, and politicians, that have reflected their willingness to accept human deaths at a certain rate, to put a part of the earth at risk, and the sea, contaminating them irreversibly. They have presumed so far on the basis of notions about the hazards involved that they admit to be conjectural. This is an appalling presumption, truly unpardonable if their notions prove wrong. It ought to be expected, therefore, that their standards of proof would be exceptionally rigorous.

Certainly the development of these policies has been very much affected by the dangers, political and diplomatic, of the issues involved. The British would know the effects of radioactivity if they had monitored the Australians who lived in the path of fallout from the huge, misbegotten hydrogen-bomb test at Monte Bello; or the aborigines who drifted across Maralinga, in South Australia, where radioactive detritus was left behind after British weapons testing; or the populations affected by the fire and the radioactive cloud that drifted south-east and west from Sellafield in 1957. They have given themselves many opportunities to look into this question and availed themselves of none of them, no doubt because to do so would undermine their claims that nothing serious has really happened.

There is, as I have said, the continuing threat of economic erosion to keep the public mind focused on the short-term and the local; and there is the image of the government battling to recoup Britain's losses and restore her scanted dignity; and there is the educational system, which trains very few people and these very narrowly, greatly enhancing the authority of specialists while diminishing the content and forcefulness of public debate and the numbers involved in it. And there is the secretiveness that permeates British life, which allows the Foreign Office to impound the records having to do with Argentina's claims to the Falklands;

which prohibits journalists from reporting what they see in prisons; which conceals the identity of those on the committees that choose Britain's magistrates (the magistrates have no legal training—they simply suit some anonymous notion of worthiness); which leads the governing bodies of cities and counties to conduct their business behind closed doors. The Official Secrets Act is simply the most conspicuous manifestation of all this. Granting that it is used as the basis of prosecutions, and assuming that the *Guardian* is accurate in its accounts of mail-openings, phone-tappings, and break-ins practised by MI5, the British secret police, against groups such as Greenpeace, the Friends of the Earth, and the National Union of Mineworkers—nevertheless, it seems to be that the English, at least, have the government they deserve, that they prefer not to know, and that they have very little capacity for exerting power and influence. I think they feel—deeply feel—that their moral rectitude is preserved intact by this means. The Greenham Common women will never encircle Sellafield, though Britain could desist unilaterally from its war against the sea, which is not a terrifying threat, but a terrifying fact.

Then there is the absence of American reaction to consider—especially puzzling since both Greenpeace and the Friends of the Earth have been involved with Sellafield. British Greenpeace was given a heavy fine—paid by public donations—for tampering with the pipeline, and was induced to intervene to prevent Danish and Dutch Greenpeace ships from sending divers down by the threat that all its resources would be sequestered by the court if they did. Why Greenpeace has chosen not to galvanize public opinion outside the range of such restrictions, I cannot imagine. Perhaps regional patriotism has stood in the way of global matriotism. Or perhaps British environmentalists, like many Europeans of advanced views, believe that American public opinion is too brutish to be enlisted in any good cause. It is a treasured faith among Europeans of the Right and the Left that America is a nation of B-movie villains laying waste to the continent and to one another by any means that come to hand, in a sort of frenzy of capitalist rapacity.

Europeans on the Left enjoy the opinion that they are very advanced thinkers. In fact they are simply intellectual cargo-cultists, to whom accident now and then delivers an elaborated policy, a sophisticated idea, or half of one. That crude, capitalist America should enforce higher standards of public conduct than humane, socialist Europe is not to be imagined. So our example in environmental matters is almost never consulted, and our research and experience are almost never invoked.

We in America are greatly at fault in this. There is a streak of pure yokel that reaches straight to the top of American intellectual life, widening as it goes, and it is deference towards all things 'English'. We cannot believe that the English could be stupid or corrupt. We think of them as our better selves, and the source of our most precious institutions—a slander on the dark and the ethnic and a disparagement of the noisy public dramas of advocates and adversaries that provide us with the legal and ethical capacity for discrimination and judgement. We are capable of outrage and we are capable of shame, like a living soul. If we are fortunate in one thing it is in the knowledge that we *can* do evil, and we *can* do injury. A country incapable of scandal is like a mind incapable of guilt or a body incapable of pain.

On 24 July 1984, the *Guardian* concluded its editorial on the Black report, titled 'Lingering Particles of Unease,' with a call for 'one group of inter-disciplinary experts who do nothing else but shadow it round the clock.' In the editorialist's affable view, 'life with [Sellafield] is a tumultuous and ongoing affair.' On 30 July, the *Guardian* wrote that Charles Haughey, the former Irish prime minister, had called the report a whitewash. He said: 'If there is a high incidence of leukaemia in an area where a nuclear plant is situated, surely to God the obvious interpretation is that the plant was responsible for it. These figures alone would in my view justify closing down the plant immediately for further investigation, and certainly putting a lot of people in gaol who have clearly been telling us lies over the past four or five years about this matter.' The words we have longed to hear. But from the wrong side of the Irish Sea.

GERMAINE GREER

WOMEN AND POWER IN CUBA

I came to Cuba with my heart in my mouth. Ever since my first contact with the 'Third World', in Jamaica in 1971, I had been aware how burningly important it is for the developing nations that Cuba not be a fraud or a failure. As the years passed and I wandered through slums in Bombay, past windowless huts in Morocco, Tunis and Yucatan, through the dust of Uttar Pradesh and the infested dirt of the Brazilian north-east and the menace of Bogota and the Guatemalan highlands, every step showed me that paternalist development aid is worse than useless. In the eighties, as the external debts of the developing countries mushroom over them while their people grow steadily poorer and the number of landless multiplies daily, the need of a genuine alternative is agonizing. If Cuba had shown me nothing but the institutionalized poverty and bureaucratic rhetoric and repression that Western mega-media taught me to expect, a brain-washed militarized population living by hypocrisy and fear, the dark future would show no sign of dawn. If Cuba's was really a revolution of the people, then even if a malignant power should blast Cuba out of the Caribbean, its people will be invincible.

My arrival coincided with the Fourth Congress of the Federation of Cuban Women, the FMC. Billboards and posters announced it all over Havana. *Toda la fuerza de la mujer en el servicio de la revolución* ('The entire women's force in the service of the revolution'). The logo was an art nouveau-ish montage of Kalashnikov rifles and Mariposa lilies. I was not keen on the implications of either. On the Rampa, the flood lit exhibition pavilion was turned over to the exploits of women. Banked television sets showed colour videos of the history of Cuban women, and a succession of booths displayed everything from the techniques of screening for breast cancer to scent and hair curlers. Women whose bottoms threatened to burst out of their elasticized pants tottered round the exhibits on four-inch heels, clutching their *compañeros* for support. Their nails and faces were garishly painted. Their hair had been dragged over rollers, bleached, dyed and coloured. Their clothes, including their brassières, were all two or three sizes too small and flesh bulged everywhere. Most people rushed past the educational exhibits to where a painted, conked, and corseted trio bumped and ground its way through an amorous rhumba. At the sight of an unattached woman, the loose men began a psst! psst! and beckoned to me, as if I had been a dog.

The next day, my minder from the Ministry of Exterior Relations came to take me to the Palacio de Congresos for the first session of the FMC Congress. Security was tight. I was directed to a press box in the back of the vast auditorium, with no facilities for simultaneous translation. A policeman ordered me not to put my tape-recorder up on the parapet. Later I discovered that one such instrument had been accidentally knocked off and narrowly missed braining a delegate seated thirty feet below, but then and there it seemed that Cuba was determined that I would see little and understand less. The whole day was taken up with the reading of the *informe central*, the 157-page official report to the congress. The reader was Vilma Espín, president of the FMC, alternate member of the Politburo, member of the Central Committee of the Communist Party, and wife of Raul Castro, Fidel's brother. She read correctly and quietly, a calm, matronly figure hard to associate with the slender girl who had organized the medical support system during the *lucha clandestina* and joined the guerrilla fighters in the Sierra Maestra. I complained that she was hardly a charismatic speaker. 'She doesn't have to impress us,' answered one of the delegates. 'We know her. She is our Vilma.'

Alongside her, in the front row of the serried ranks of office-bearers on the dais, sat Fidel Castro, quietly reading through the report. I expected him to make some formal rhetorical statement, as befits a totalitarian figurehead, putting in a token appearance for the Association of Townswomen's Guilds before leaving to take care of more pressing matters of state. To my surprise, he sat there quietly the whole day long, reading, caressing his beard, thinking and listening. The next day he was there again. As one of the delegates waxed eloquent on discrimination against women in the workplace, a man's voice interjected. 'This is the heart of the problem, isn't it? Women's access to work!' I looked about, wondering who owned these mild, slightly high-pitched tones. It was Castro, whom I soon learned to call what every Cuban calls him, Compañero Fidel. He was leaning forward earnestly, intent on participating in the debate, not leading but participating. If anything, the discussion became less formal and more spontaneous, as delegates held up their hands for recognition and described precise problems of access to work. The women claimed that they were considered more likely to absent themselves from work, because of their family responsibilities. Fidel pointed out that men still refuse to shoulder their part of the burden of housekeeping and child-rearing as laid down by the Cuban Family Code. The women pointed out that in fact the absenteeism of women workers was often less than that of men, and certainly no greater. Fidel pointed out that women shoulder a double duty, which is unequal, and the women argued that they were not prepared to give it up. Sometimes when the head of state wagged his hand for recognition, the chairperson ignored him. At other times, the delegates noisily disagreed with him, crying, 'No, no!,' some even booing.

I had been prepared for the chants of Fidel! Fidel! but nothing had prepared me for this. I thought ruefully of Margaret Thatcher and Indira Gandhi, each incapable of listening, especially to someone who disagreed with her. And all the time Fidel made jokes, selected funny comparisons, continually pressing the delegates to give concrete, living examples. Their carefully prepared statements went all to pieces. We discovered that women did not want men to have the same leave to absent themselves from work for family reasons, because they would abuse it and use the time to visit other women—or at least the delegates thought they might—and thus one of the most fascinating contradictions in Cuban sexual politics was drawn out in a public forum of 1,400 participants.

All afternoon the debate surged on, with Vilma at the helm steadily working through the order paper. And all the next day. When delegates complained that if the day-care centres closed down for any one of a hundred reasons—lack of water, pollution of the water supply, sickness of staff, deterioration of the building, communicable illness—women were called away from hospitals and factories, schools and voluntary work, to take care of their children. Because the day-care centres did not operate on the free Saturdays, which fall every two weeks, women were effectively prevented from undertaking the extra voluntary work that led to distinction and party membership. Fidel noticed that the Minister of Labour and Employment and the Minister of Education had not bothered to attend the Congress.

'They should be hearing this,' he said.

'Watch,' said one of the Cuban journalists.

After lunch the chairs on the dais had all been moved up, and lo! the ministers in question had appeared to answer the women's demands. When the Minister for Education complained of lack of trained infant teachers, Fidel reminded him that he was using statistics from the Second Party Congress and up-dated them for him, thus destroying the excuses. Everyone but the ministers, who could fall back only on silly compliments and party slogans, enjoyed it enormously.

When the sessions rose, the women leapt to their feet, waving the coloured nylon georgette scarves and matching plastic flowers they had all brought with them, pounding maracas, bongos, conga drums and cowbells, clapping their hands and singing fit to bust, *Para trabajar, para estudiar, para defender nuestra libertad! Firmes con Fidel! Firmes con Fidel!* Hips gyrated, scarves flashed, flowers wagged. The syncopated thunder roared round the huge building, sucking the tiredest professional congress-makers out of their offices to watch as the women put on a turn that would have shamed a Welsh football crowd into silence. They were so delighted—with the occasion, with Fidel, but above all with themselves—that I forgot how clumsy some of the women looked in their harsh-coloured and badly-made synthetic suits and the crippling high heels they thought appropriate to the situation. I abandoned my posture of superiority and let myself be impressed.

Each lunchtime, 1,400 women swarmed into the commissaries of the vast building and forty minutes later they swarmed out again into group and regional meetings in preparation for the afternoon sessions. They gave hundreds of interviews for Cuban television, to be used gradually over the ensuing months, for daily papers, for women's magazines, for regional newsletters, for books. The youngest delegate was sixteen, the oldest ninety-something. They were ready to work all day and all night if necessary. My questions to Vilma Espín had to wait ten days for answers, but late on a Saturday afternoon I was called to her office, to spend two hours discussing what the questions meant. The written answers and tape-recording of our discussion were delivered to me first thing on Monday morning.

The first evening the delegates were taken to a ballet. They arrived stomping and chanting, sat chatting eagerly about the day's doings, and when the dancing had started and silence was finally imposed, a good proportion of them went straight to sleep, waking up only to applaud wildly. While exhausted *delegadas* slumbered around me, I watched Dionea, a man-eating plant composed of Josefina Menendez and the *cuerpo de baile*, to music by Villa-Lobos, as it ate three male dancers dressed as glittering mothy creatures, with horribly erotic gestures. This was followed by the world *première* of *Palomas,* a ballet choreographed by the Chilean exile Hilda Riveros especially for the Fourth Congress of the FMC. The story ran straight down the party line; the dancers mimed birth, the mother mimed ecstatic admiration of her child. She was joined by her mate and mimed ecstatic admiration of him. They simulated spontaneous conjugal relations on the floor. She then went off for her militia training, and mimed something rather like *kung fu* in strict unison with the *cuerpo de baile.* Then she and her fellow soldiers were joined by their mates and mimed heterosexual fulfilment in unison.

The delegates snored through the whole thing but woke up with a start to watch the eighth wonder of the world, Alicia Alonso, sixty years old and virtually blind, dance a *pas de deux* with Jorge Esquivel to music by Chopin. Her line was exquisite, and if once or twice things went slightly wrong, such as when she slid out of a lift and down Jorge Esquivel's nose, so that his eyes streamed with tears, the audience had no intention of feeling, let alone showing, any dissatisfaction. Alicia Alonso came back to Cuba at a time when artists and skilled technicians were leaving in hordes. She promised her people a world-class ballet and she kept her promise. She danced in complete confidence on a stage she could no longer see, borne up less by Esquivel's strong arms than by the love and loyalty that surrounded her.

This was early days, but already I could feel something unfamiliar and very special about Cuba. The absence of theatricality that I noticed in Vilma and Fidel was part of a complex of attitudes. People did not sell themselves as they do in consumer society. Life was not soap opera, but real. There was no competition or character assassination, as people jockeyed for limelight. They spoke not to persuade or bamboozle, but to explain. They had not our prurient interest in domestic and sexual affairs. No one was quite sure how many children Fidel might have had, or, for that matter, Vilma. Public functionaires were assessed on their performance of their public duty, and did not have to drag their bed partners around with them, miming domestic bliss. Life without gossip magazines and advertising seemed wonderfully uncluttered. There was no equivalent of Princess Diana's latest outfit or Elizabeth Taylor's latest wedding or the American president's haemorrhoids. Doubtless there are some Cubans who think life would be more interesting if murder and rape were reported in the newspapers and convicted criminals were paid a working man's earnings over ten years to describe their activities in lurid detail, but most of the people I met know the other culture from glimpses of Miami television and find it crazy and perverse. The slice of American culture they get from Miami includes late-night pornographic videos, which do nothing to improve the US image. Some Cubans, the ones who steal designer jeans off foreigners' clothes-lines in Miramar and offer to change pesos for dollars, giving five times the official exchange rate so that they can buy ghetto-blasters in the dollar shops, obviously envy the hyper-stimulated life-style of capitalism, but all the Cubans I met and talked to were more interested in Ethiopia and Guatemala than in Michael Jackson.

A Chilean exile explained to me, 'I could have stayed in West Germany. They were paying me a fortune, but what could I do with it? Invest in the latest parsley cutter? Life is exciting here, even if I have very little money. There is always something to do, and it's exciting. People are creating their own future. If I got sick in Germany I could lie and rot. Here, if I don't show up at the *tienda* for my rations, people are straight round to help.' Her bath was kept permanently full of water to flush the lavatory, for Havana has a chronic and crippling water shortage, just another minor inconvenience that women have to deal with, but it made no dent in Elisabeth's fierce loyalty to Cuba. As we sat on her tiny balcony, drinking *añejo sobre las rocas*, while people flowed in and out of the tiny apartments above, beside and below us, and the old red buses, affectionately known as *guaguas,* groaned and shrieked down the hill, disgorging streams of workers, she said, 'It's a hard life, but a good life.'

146

The Cubans are involved after all in a much bigger adventure than sex, speed and smack could possibly supply. Their morale is towering, even if their energy should occasionally flag, as they negotiate the daily obstacle course which is life in a poor country, cursed by an irreplaceable investment in a single crop—sugar—and strangled by the American blockade which has cut off the only cheap source of supply for all the goods a single-crop economy does not produce. Every Cuban will tell you that underdevelopment is a feature of minds and hearts as well as economies. As Cubans struggle to develop logistical and communicative skills, they encounter inefficiency and confusion at all levels of social organization. The response is not irritability and hostility, but tolerance and mutual assistance.

Because of rationing, limited supplies of essential commodities and the unreliability of transport (given shortage of vehicles and spare parts), queueing is a way of life, but Cubans do not try to jump queues or stand guard to see that no one else does. Instead they have developed a characteristic solution to an intolerable situation. When you arrive at the *tienda,* to find fifty people already waiting for their ration of rice, beans, oil, crackers, fruit juice or whatever other commodity is on sale that day, you simply ask who is *el último.* When another person arrives, and you are asked the same thing, you are free to go about other business and return when the queue has moved up. People less pressed chat, criticize the authorities, flirt and clown around. When you come back the person who was behind you will call you to your place. This ad hoc system involves co-operation and a degree of awareness of other people, neither often found in rich countries. Even on my last day in Cuba, when I found a hundred people queuing at the hotel cashier's desk, I could hardly prevent myself from panicking, thinking I had no time to pack because I would be queuing for two hours or so (given the mean speed of such transactions in Cuba). However, I tried asking *el último* and went about my other chores. When I came down, the honeymooners behind me waved me to my place, by now only four from the head of the line. As I had screamed and ranted at the hotel management about their inefficiency, while they politely defended a system I condemned as hopeless, I felt truly ashamed.

It may seem that all this has little to do with women and political power in Cuba. In fact, it has everything to do with it. The people meet constant daily frustrations with calm and co-operation because they do not feel that they are the result of corruption, caprice or incompetence on the part of a separate ruling class, but aspects of problems which afflict a twenty-five-year-old nation with a heritage of ignorance, disease and poverty.

The first priority of the Cuban revolution was to combat illiteracy, disease and malnutrition, thus bringing the Cuban population to a condition in which they could exercise the duties of popular government. Despite the enormous drain of human and other resources in maintaining a convincing defence posture, they have achieved those basic aims, largely by voluntary work undertaken alongside the desperate struggle to make the sugar economy profitable despite falling world prices, and to cope with the effects of the US blockade.

My first duty in Cuba was to check the validity of Cuban claims about health and education, so I hired a car and slipped off into the countryside, driving through town after small town, checking the *policlínico* (the community hospital), the water supply, the electricity cables, the health status of the inhabitants, the intensity and productivity of the industry and agriculture. I turned up back streets, wandered into sugar mills and factory forecourts, stopped to watch militia training and the volunteer brigades grubbing up garlic and packing tomatoes in boxes. Nobody stared, nobody tried to beg, but people by the roadsides cheerfully accepted lifts. *La guagua está mal*—'The bus isn't working'—was the usual explanation. Everyone I saw was healthy, busy and quietly self-confident. Occasional unpleasantnesses helped me to realize that I was not dreaming. A boarding-school cook, coming back from collecting his daughter who spent the weekend with her psychologist mother and lived with her father during the week, told me he would not let her marry a *negro*.

'Oh, popi,' said the ten-year-old indulgently, shaking her head at this foolishness.

Everyone was interested in the progress that was being made. They explained to me about the difficulties of industrializing sugar production—'humanizing the work,' they called it. Questions about plant genetics and animal diseases got intelligent answers, if not from parents then from the children.

In all Cuba's struggles, women have been in the front line. During the *lucha clandestina* women organized medical supplies and treatment and taught school in the Sierra Maestra. Fidel has always acknowledged that without the help of women in building up the underground organization which victualled, supplied and protected the guerrillas in the fifties, they would never have been successful. Celia Sánchez, who was waiting with supplies, petrol and transport for the arrival of the yacht, *Granma,* which brought Fidel back to Cuba in 1956, became his aide in the closing years of the war, and took part in several battles. She chose to work as Secretary to the Council of State when the Revolutionary Government was set up. Every little girl in Cuba grows up with an impressive series of role models, going back more than a hundred years before the revolution: Rosa La Bayamesa, a captain in the war of independence; Paulina Pedrosa and Carolina Rodriguez, supporters of José Martí's revolutionary party in the 1890s; Emilia Rodriguez, leader of the *Partido Popular Obrero* (The Workers' Popular Party) in the 1920s, and dozens more. The struggle to oust Batista threw up more still, like Lydia Doce and Clodorinda Acosta Ferrais, who were only twenty years old when Batista's police threw their bullet-riddled bodies into the sea. The all-woman *Peloton Mariana Grajales,* formed in September 1958 and named after the mother of the *maceo* who led the Revolutionary War of 1868-78, held one of the most exposed positions on the highway between Havana and Santiago de Cuba and was involved in some of the bitterest fighting of the war. Women fought at the Bay of Pigs; Cira García Reyes, leader of the FMC in the region, lost her life there.

On 23 August 1960, the female network which had contributed so much to the rebel effort was officially instituted as the Federation of Cuban Women, the FMC. By spreading out over the countryside, they were to consolidate the revolution by convincing the passive and fearful that they could construct a new society. Peasant women like Nadividad Betancourt Marten led groups of women who travelled from village to village in their regions, politicizing women like themselves. The FMC organized the push for literacy in Cuba, working as volunteer teachers in peasant huts up and down the island, teaching more volunteers who taught others. Women conducted the 'Battle for the Sixth Grade', and when that was won, they went on to help all kinds of people achieve the standard of ninth-grade education.

The US blockade is a disaster which popular endurance and initiative have turned into a blessing, for nothing less brutal could have protected Cuba from becoming another impoverished would-be consumer nation. The ridiculous attempt to invade, known by the Cubans as the Victoria de Girón and by the Americans as the Bay of Pigs débâcle, gave all Cubans a sense of external threat and national heroism. The strangely explosive epidemic of haemorrhagic dengue fever, involving a mutant strain similar to one that is normally found in Asia, which swept through the province of Havana in 1981, producing thousands of cases within a week, was met by mobilizing all the mass organizations to isolate cases and run improvised field hospitals in all kinds of public buildings. The hypothesis of germ warfare was obvious, but the Cubans wasted no time in investigating whether it was another gift from the CIA dirty tricks department; they were more interested in their own preparedness and efficiency in overcoming it, as they did. The disease vanished from Cuba as suddenly as it came.

It would be quite wrong to imagine, however, that there was no resistance to the full incorporation of women in the development process. For many people the only notion of the good life was derived from the bourgeois example; moreover, the legacy of the past included male unemployment, especially during the seven months of the year when the cane was not being cut, while women struggled to feed their families by domestic work, by working in the tobacco industry and by prostitution. Slave women had not been protected from brutalizing toil, therefore the right to manual labour was not one that Cuban women were on the whole particularly anxious to win. There had been opposition to the presence of women fighters in the Sierra, but for some reason, perhaps his dependence on Melba Hernández and Celia Sánchez, Fidel insisted on women's full participation in the struggle, in the victory and in the glory. In 1965 he was already defining women's liberation as 'a revolution within the revolution.' It is generally assumed that the authority for the revolutionary Cuban conception of women's role is the writings of Marx and Lenin, against 'the base, mean and infamous denial of rights to women' and inequality of sexes. To be sure, Cuba follows the Russian line on abortion, contraception, neo-Malthusianism, women in the workplace, divorce, child care, education and maternity leave. But there are aspects of sexual politics in Cuba that are distinctly Cuban, and owe nothing to the Russian paradigm.

Sexual politics in Cuba are complex. It is not enough to say that the Cuban man is macho or even extremely macho. Chances are that whatever the Cuban male is, his mother has had far more to do with the development of his personality than his father. A joke in a Cuban girls' magazine sums the conundrum up perfectly. 'Your boyfriend is terribly macho,' says one. 'Yes,' simpers the other. 'Aren't I lucky!' Cuban sociology does not express itself in detailed examinations of the psychopathology of everyday life, so it was difficult for a visitor to gain any clear idea of the reality behind the body language of male-female interaction. Officially, Cuba is a totally heterosexual country. There are no homosexual partnerships, no people living alone, no one-parent families. There are no published figures to illuminate the reality behind this impossibility, just as there are no figures on rape and crimes against women or sex-related offences generally. Certainly, when work is over, the streets of Havana fill with couples, hand in hand, kissing, giggling, wandering through Coppelia (a complex of pavilion and garden covering a whole block and totally given over to the sale and consumption of ice cream) or attending any of the dozens of free amusements that socialism supplies—museums, aquaria, literary *tertulias*, concerts....

The situation is complicated by a severe housing shortage, with a typically Cuban solution. People in need of privacy to make love can go to one of several *posadas*, where at very reasonable rates they can hire a room, a bed and clean sheets by the hour, and order food and beverages to the room. Nobody asks questions about the couples, who may be married to each other, married to others, unmarried, engaged or one-hour stands. The only inconvenience is that, as with everything in Cuba, there is a wait, sometimes a three-or four-hour wait. Couples sit in the waiting-room, smoking, necking, chatting, until the next horizontal space becomes free. Anyone who remembers Lenin's scornful dismissal as bourgeois the demand of feminists like Inessa Armand and Alexandra Kollontai for the right of free love will see that, in this matter at least, the Cubans have gone their own way.

The Cubans have accepted that adultery is their national sport. Men boast of it. A man otherwise intelligent, cultivated and reasonable will tell you that when a pretty girl works for him or near him he will do his best to get near her and 'be with her' as often as he can, but his attentions to his wife will continue at the same intensity. The implication is that he can satisfy both, and there can be no significant objection to the spreading of so much happiness by his so potent art. The men seem to be totally caught up in this fantasy, which explains why they have the temerity to call unattached women across to their sides as if they were loose puppies. A foreign woman alone in Havana might well interpret the staring and gesturing of men as signs of aggression, hostility and low esteem for women, especially if she is accustomed to the North American or north European version expressed in whistling, cat calls and sexist comments.

Cuba's boast of advances in its progress towards complete equality for women seemed to me invalidated by the overt interference by Cuban men in my freedom to sit in a darkened cinema by myself or stand waiting for the lift in a hotel lobby. However, after a few days I began to realize that male aggression in Cuba was different. If I clearly expressed my displeasure or lack of interest in the proceedings, the men appeared startled and embarrassed and tended to disappear or, indeed, flee. Men told me that Cuban women quite enjoy approaches of this kind and often flirtatiously provoke them, and I did see some evidence for the truth of this claim. Women on the other hand told me that if I had protested, when I was harassed in the cinema, the people sitting around me would have taken my part. One of the men involved might have found himself the victim of a citizens' arrest and eventually subject to up to fifteen years' detention in a work centre. This is a rather different reason for not creating a scene than what prevails in England, where the people around me would most likely dismiss the uproar as evidence of my hysteria and exonerate the man for lack of evidence other than my protest.

It stands to reason that male aggression towards women would be modified by the salutory reflection that any woman may be a salaried officer of the Fuerzas Armadas Revolucionarias. Most women are trained in the militia and actively involved in the public surveillance duties of the *Comités para la Defensa de la Revolución*. However, male-female relationships in Cuba are different from those I grew up with, principally because, like Cuba itself, they are Afro-Latin. The Africans who were shipped to Cuba left behind them intricate family structures in which the relationships of siblings and cross-cousins through the female line were at least as important as patrilineal relationships, and the mother-child relationship possibly the most intense and durable of all human bonds.

In the slave society, where men and women were bought and sold like cattle, women were used as brood animals, often fecundated by their owners rather than the men of their choice and prevented from setting up any viable, legitimate family structure. The legacy of this persists in all Afro-American societies, where first births are often very early, where the nuptial bond is fragile and mothers—and mothers' mothers—supply the only stability in the child's experience. Doubtless, feminist chauvinists will sneer at an impression based on two weeks' acquaintance; nevertheless I must say that there seems to me to be less hostility in male-female relations in Cuba than, say, in northern Europe. Cuban women would agree. They staunchly refuse to entertain a notion of sexual politics which postulates any significant degree of male-female hostility. Even when Compañero Fidel suggests that the greatest obstacle to women's complete equality is the attitude of men to the work traditionally done by women, the women prefer to stress other 'objective' factors. Cuban men, for all their flirtatiousness, seem to like and respect women. One way of interpreting the emphasis on men's strength—machismo, as Cubans are themselves ready to call it—is as an attempt to counter-balance the dominance of women in family and kin relations.

It is notable that one of the sources of friction in the day-to-day workings of the friendship between the Cuban cockerel and the Russian bear is the Russians' treatment of women. Almost more important than Marx and Lenin in the genesis of the Cuban revolution is the figure of José Martí, the national hero of Cuba, a man of high culture and clear and coherent political ideology, who adored women. He died fighting with the Mambi Army in 1895, but his personality permeates Cuba still. When accused of being a Marxist after the attack on the Moncada Barracks in 1952, Fidel claimed that the sole designer of the attack had been José Martí. Martí believed that no cause that women supported could be defeated, and no side could be victorious which did not have the support of women. Martí's feminism was based on a chivalrous ideal of the pure, cultivated, disinterested woman, an ideal drawn from bourgeois notions of women as weaker, nobler and less sexual than men, but which had a special relevance in a society in which women had never been protected from degrading physical toil. His notion of male/female complementarity relied upon an extreme polarity, but he also argued that one source of the brutality of capitalist society was that it suppressed feminine feeling in women *and* in men. He found American feminism erring in its over-emphasis on the same coarse self-seeking that characterized the perversion of the American dream of a free and egalitarian society. If they achieve their aims, he asked, *Dónde éstará el aroma de las rosas?* ('Where will the roses' scent be?') Present-day Martí scholars argued with me earnestly that society needs the feminine qualities, which when pressed they defined as self-abnegation, sensitivity, enthusiasm, '*espirito*' and tenderness. *Cuál es la fuerza de la vida y su única raíz sino el amor de la mujer?*('What is the force of life and the only reason for living, if it is not the love of a woman?')

To Martí's enduring influence, then, we may attribute the emphasis that Cuban feminists lay on feminity. Women who have been trained to kill will be wearing pearlized nail polish and lipstick when they do it. The perennial shortage of acetone in Cuba probably means that the nail polish will be chipped, unless the solider has had time to got to the beauty parlour, for acetone is supplied to the nation's manicurists. Even the heroines of work, who cut cane, go down the mines and drive huge cranes, are depilated, deodorized and scented. One of the first problems tackled by the FMC was devising a way of supplying Cuban women with the resources for making pretty clothes out of the scanty fabric supplies. Seamstresses and tailors were trained and given the facilities for carrying on trade as licensed artisans in a state scheme. At the FMC Congress, some of the foreign journalists were intrigued that so many women were wearing suits of various styles in a particular shade of kingfisher blue Courtelle. Was it a uniform of some sort, they asked. In fact it was simply that the blue was one of the few vivid shades available, and literally hundreds of women had chosen it.

For a feminist like me who considers that the combination of dazzle with drudgery is one of the most insidious ways in which women in our society are subject to stress, the multiplication of contradictory demands upon the Cuban woman is a cause for concern. Women who are expected to be prepared to kill are also expected to be flower-like; the Mariposa must accompany the Kalashnikov. The brain surgeon, the politburo member and the chief of police must also be ready to sit by their children's beds in hospital, comforting and caring for them, their attention for the moment undivided. The Cuban women are proud that they can handle all this. They see theirs as the force of the flower that in growing towards the light shatters the rock. To Martí's question, *Hay hombres que se cansan, cuando las mujeres no se cansan?* ('Are there men who tire when women do not?'), they answer yes.

As I travelled around the provinces of Havana, Matanzas and Pinar del Rio, alone in a hired car, I talked to dozens of women, hitch-hiking without fear in their own country, to join their parents, their *novios*, their husbands, separated from them by the demands of the revolution. They were shy, but not frightened to talk.

Pilar was typical. She is twenty-three, and has nearly finished her studies in medicine at the University of Havana. Next will come work in a remote part of the island or *internacionalismo*. She had hitched a ride with me to visit her husband, studying a hundred kilometres away at the University of Matanzas. When I suggested that so much separation now and a prospect of indefinite separation to come was a bit hard on a marriage, she said, 'We can handle it. We were sweethearts for eight years, and it was always like this.' I pushed a little harder, saying how hard it was to give men the attention they demanded after a week's hard work. She grinned and I noticed how pale she was and how white were her gums.

'Sometimes, I've been in the operating theatre all night and I have to grab my bag and get out here on the road. I haven't time to wait for the *guagua* and it's always so crowded—I just can't face the trip standing up.'

I probably should have concentrated on the pot-holes and let her go to sleep, but instead I asked if she might not have been anaemic.

She seemed slightly startled by the thought. 'Possibly. I've got an IUD.' She knitted her brows. Cuban girls can be fitted with IUDs on demand if they are sixteen or over. Pills, some made from steroids derived from locally-grown hennequin (sisal), are also available, and there is a move to switch to them. IUDs in a young population are always problematic, but absolutely no publicity is given to such matters in Cuba. Juvenile pregnancy is such a pressing problem that the emphasis is all on prevention.

We talked about housework.

'A man wants a wife, doesn't he? Not a maid,' she said stoutly. I got to know other women like Pilar, hard-working party members, serious and committed in everything, including their sexual relationships. As I watched her walking towards her husband's dormitory over the burnt grass, I hoped she would find his room clean and his clothes washed when she got there. The older women told me, 'Oh no. If she wanted to be at all comfortable, she would have had to set to and clean him up.' The young women said, 'Of course,' but it sounded more like ideology than fact. As Pilar walked away, I called out, 'Take care of yourself!' She gave me a white smile, and slightly ironic shrug.

It would be perfectly possible to argue that Fidel Castro's revolution exploits women. Socialist revolution exploits everybody. 'From each according to his capacity, to each according to his need.' Every ounce of courage, patience, energy, determination and intelligence is needed if Cuba is to realize her own aims.

The burden ought to fall on men and women impartially. In addition to their salaried and professional work, men and women both undertake voluntary work in the service of the revolution. Men and women are involved in the constant watch kept in Cuban streets by day and night, so that in the event of an attempted insurrection or invasion or an epidemic the Cuban people can be mobilized from the street up; as a by-product, crime has disappeared off their streets.

Men and women volunteer to clean the streets and plant public gardens in their free time; on a Sunday morning in every town in Cuba, you may see gangs of women, gangs of men and mixed gangs sweeping away leaves, burning waste paper, hauling trash. Such voluntary work is particularly onerous for women because in addition to their paid work, they are also working unpaid in the home. As the level of general culture and the standard of living has risen, the amount of housework to be done has increased exponentially. Cubans are fanatically clean. When it became possible to wash garments every time they were worn, because water, soap and garments were all present in sufficient supply, all Cuban garments were so washed. The traditional Cuban diet involves a good deal of preparation and long cooking, as well as the the hours of waiting at the *tienda* for the monotonous supplies. The state helps by providing meals at the place of work, and in schools and day-care centres, where pre-school children stay from seven to seven p.m. and eat two full meals and two snacks. Working women carry a card which enables them to go to the front of the food queue, not because they deserve some free time but to make it possible for them to cram all the duties expected of them into the inelastic twenty-four hour day.

There is very little time left over for even more voluntary work in the grass-roots organization of *Poder Popular,* the ultimate legislative power in Cuba, even if we do not take into account the time and money the Cuban woman must spend on her other duty of keeping pretty and attractive. It is the more remarkable then that two million members of the FMC voted to be allowed to train with the *Milicia de las Tropas Territoriales*, the volunteer home guard, who train one Sunday a month. Women's record as *cumplidoras*, with full attendance at work and invariably fulfilled production quotas, is consistently higher than men's. And yet at the first sign of *fiesta,* the Cuban woman is ready to stick a frangipani behind her ear and rhumba the night away. Even the Cuban sugar allowance, four pounds of sugar per person per month, could not generate this kind of energy in a disaffected population, although it clearly goes some way to causing a serious health problem of massive obesity, especially in women over forty.

Germaine Greer

Those people who ask, 'But in Cuba are men relinquishing political power so that women can take it up?' are projecting a curiously corrupt notion of political power on to the post-revolutionary process in Cuba. Revolutionary socialists are involved in re-making political power in such a way that it is genuinely wielded by the masses. While enemies of the revolution may persist in believing that power is still concentrated in the hands of an oligarchy, the people themselves are working hard to create the administrative structures which will promote the expression of the collective will and translate it into state policy.

Outsiders may assume that Cuba is actually a dictatorship masquerading as a democratic republic and that real power is vested in the politburo or the Central Committee of the Communist Party; such in fact is not the case. In 1976, Cubans voted in a referendum to accept a socialist constitution which enunciated the principle by which the popular assemblies became the ultimate legislative power in the land. Those of us accustomed to seeing democratic processes subverted by lobbying, patronage and secret government would assume that the huge machinery of *Poder Popular* could do little but rubber-stamp legislation originating in the inner recesses of the Communist Party. In fact, the grass-roots-level assemblies do originate the legislative process, follow it through and participate actively in the drafting of legislation. For such a cumbersome system to work, the enthusiastic participation of large numbers of people for frequent and long sessions is indispensable, yet the system has produced the new housing law in Cuba, which has less to do with socialist ideology than the pragmatic expression of the people's will. Rather than nationalize housing, the Cubans have chosen to own their own homes, amid a multitude of special considerations regarding leasing, letting and inheritance, all designed to protect the right to own one's home and prevent speculation or profiteering.

Democratic centralism, if earnestly undertaken, is the system which produces the least return for the most massive expenditure of human resources. Frequent long meetings, with the intervening struggle to study unfamiliar matters, such as housing law, contract, equity, conveyancing and alternative adminstrative systems, as in the case of the 1985 *Ley de las Viviendas* (Housing Law), must arrive at unanimity, much as juries do, by long argument and counter-

158

argument. The amateur legislators—for only the full-time functionaries are paid—must struggle to keep the process under control, agreeing agendas and then following them through. The process demands what Cuban women have least of—time—yet, even so, twenty-seven per cent of delegates in *Poder Popular* are women. This is more significant than the presence of women on the Central Committee of the Communist Party; nevertheless of 119 members and seventy-one alternates, twenty-seven are women, seventeen of them full members. Women formed twenty-two per cent of the delegates elected at the Second Party Congress, an increase of fifty per cent over the First Party Conference. The Third Party Congress this year will probably be attended by a high proportion of women and elect more female members of the Central Committee.

If we look at the profile of women's participation in leadership activities, contradictory trends emerge. From their first participation in the youth movement of the José Martí Young Pioneers, we will see that little girls are fifty per cent of the members and 66.3 per cent of the troupe leaders. In the *Federación de los Estudiantes de las Escuelas Medias* (The Federation of Secondary School Students), women are fifty-seven per cent of the membership and sixty-one per cent of the leadership, while at university level they are fifty-nine per cent of the student enrolment but only forty-eight per cent of the leadership. Thus, as women become numerically dominant in the rank and file, they are outnumbered in the leadership. Women are only forty-one per cent of the Young Communists, the highly selective organization and training ground for future members of the Communist Party of Cuba. The disparities can be understood in two ways: the increasing proportion of female leaders in the younger age groups may reflect a general tendency to increasing female participation in the future; the troupe leaders among the Young Pioneers may continue as leaders until they find themselves on the Central Committee of the CPC. (In December 1984 the FEEM elected a national committee composed of six women and three men with women for president and vice-president.) The negative interpretation of the same data leads to the conclusion that as little girls approach puberty their ascendancy over the boys, who develop social and communicative skills more slowly, disappears, to be replaced by passivity and participation only in an ancillary capacity, in proportion as they become aware of and involved in sexual activity.

The price Cuban women pay for teenage sexual activity is very high: analysis of statistics supplied in the *Anuario Estadístico de Cuba* (1981) shows that not only were nearly 52,000 of the nation's 187,500-odd births in 1976 to mothers aged between fifteen and nineteen, but a further 10,000 of the total were unaccounted for, probably to mothers below the age of fifteen, the only category not specifically mentioned. Abortions have settled at about 100,000 per year, and about a quarter of them are carried out on women under nineteen. More than 400,000 girls of less than nineteen years old are already married, accounting for the largest proportion of divorces, currently running at about 3.2 per thousand per year, while marriages stand at about thirteen per thousand. Of the nation's 3,371,000 women over fifteen, about 1,400,000 are legally married, while half as many are living in informal unions. Of Cuba's 575,000 or so girls under nineteen, 52,000 are already legally married, while 87,000 are living with a man, and a further 25,000 describe themselves as divorced or separated.

The data are incomplete, but they point to a situation in which young women find themselves with domestic and family responsibilities just at the time when they should be gaining professional experience and qualifications. To the problems of evolving sexuality and the contradictoriness of the female role as both active comrade and sex object are added the divided attention of the young mother and the unavoidable drain upon her time and energy. The state gives all the help that legislation can provide, with free birth control, free abortion on demand and free day-care facilities, but it cannot alter the emotional reality of juvenile marriage, parenthood and divorce and the young women's own attitudes towards them. Babies are accepted in day-care from forty-five days old, but mothers are not, and should not be constrained to give them up for twelve hours a day, an impossibility in any case if they wish to breast feed.

It must not be thought that it has taken an outsider to detect the series of interlocking factors militating against women's full incorporation in the development of the Cuban state. The FMC is a high-relief organization, with vociferous representation at all levels of local, provincial and state administration. Its members, *las federadas*, are known throughout the country, and although their demands may cause consternation, as does their present campaign to allow husbands to be granted leave from work to accompany sick children in hospital, it is understood that they will eventually have to be met. Cuba's commitment to the full social, political and economic equality of women is a fundamental aspect of Cuban socialism. Insofar as the system is not one of draconian imposition, but of pragmatic accommodation of the people's will and transformation of social realities at a pace with which the ordinary people (who are the ultimate cause and purpose of the revolutionary process) can keep up, women's full emergence into political life depends upon their own redefinition of their life aims with a consequent alteration of the psychopathology of everyday life. Put in the simplest terms, this means that women will have to demand more of men.

There are some indications that the young Communists are leading the way in this. In sex education discussion groups involving both sexes it is generally agreed that emotional relationships should be built on a more intimate and committed basis. Cuban feminists have begun to reject the idea that men should help with women's work, and have begun to demand sharing all aspects of family building, involving men much more in the activities of parenting than has traditionally been the case. It is understood that progress towards women's equality is a struggle against entrenched attitudes and obsolete but enduring concepts of appropriate sex roles. An older Cuban man may tell you that he accepts the idea of his responsibility towards his children and their mother or mothers, and yet give curiously vague answers to direct inquiries about how often he sees his children and how much time he spends with them. He may tell you that his wife accepts his absenteeism and his sporting attitude to extra-marital conquests, but it is unlikely that his wife will agree with him. The *delegadas* stoutly maintain that as women have economic independence they no longer have to tolerate humiliation and would reject any husband whose infidelity was discovered, but their anxiety about male fickleness could not be concealed. When I argued that male adultery was impossible without serious flaws in female solidarity, they refused to see the point. They would not agree either that if women were really monogamous men would be unable to find partners for adultery, or that men's promiscuity was anything but 'natural'. *Él es hombre* is the sexist explanation they give for male perfidy. They could not see that women's vulnerability to men's infidelity was an aspect of sexual colonialism. The Cuban woman has all her emotional eggs in one basket; she is psychic one-crop economy, direly threatened by male sanctions, in particular the withdrawal of affection and intimacy, but the suggestion that she protect herself by cultivating other kinds of emotional satisfaction and other sources of esteem was not taken. There was very little emphasis placed by the FMC on sisterhood. No one ever discussed the single woman, a rare creature in Cuba in any event.

There is an inherent contradiction in Cuba between the socialist ideals of the revolution and the bourgeois paradigm of the nuclear family, which is what most Cubans take as the basic unit of the modern state. In the nuclear family the child is confronted by only two adults contrasted by sex. The tendency towards polarization is unavoidable. The duplication of effort in the nuclear family is directly connected to the family's role as the principal unit of consumption in consumer society. Each household is destined to acquire a complete set of all the consumer durables considered necessary for the good life, and per capita consumption is therefore maintained at its highest level. In sex as in consumption the nuclear family emphasizes possession and exclusivity at the expense of the kinds of emotional relationships that work for co-operation and solidarity. Even the best-educated Cubans seem unaware of the arguments of Marx and Engels against monogamy. They regret the instability of marriage, and work towards enculturating young people to delay the formation of exclusive sexual partnerships until they should be mature enough to undertake long-term commitment, when perhaps they ought to be spending more time reducing the psychic damage done to young people, young women especially, by the breakdown of these early relationships, so that they are less vulnerable in future.

One of the heroines of the revolution, Haydée Santamaría, killed herself after her husband began a public affair with a younger, more glamorous woman. Although she was the founder of the Casa de las Americas, and widely respected throughout Latin America, she could not recover from this blow to her self-esteem. Yet Cuban feminism shows no signs of any attempt to reduce women's psychic dependence upon their success in heterosexual relationships by strengthening cameraderie among women or teaching them that in order to live with men they must learn to live without them. As the standard of living rises women's work increases, and their dependence upon the sexual relationship with their husbands will increase as households diminish in size.

There are difficult days ahead for the Cuban woman, but as long as the ideology of revolution is lively and sincere, ways will be devised to deal with the new stresses. In the meantime Cuba remains the only country in the world where women may take any job they wish to do at the same rate of pay as a man, earn any qualification they are prepared to study for, carry their own weapons in the army and rise to the rank of colonel, dress as they please and accept or refuse men's attentions as they please, terminate or continue a pregnancy as they think fit, knowing that they will have help to carry out whichever course they should decide to follow.

Perhaps the true extent of women's power in Cuba is best illustrated not by quoting numbers on the central committee, but in a homely example which shows how important women are to Cuba. Every sexually active woman in Cuba at risk of contracting cervical cancer is given her smear test every two years. Every year hundreds of women's lives are saved by prompt treatment, while in England, Equal Opportunities Commission or no, women are dying because they have not had their smears, because they did not have them often enough, and because they were not informed when the cells were seen to be abnormal. The British health service could not cope with the demand if all the women who should ask for smear tests did, and presented themselves for further treatment. Yet little Cuba manages it. Follow-up and recall are carried out at street level by the FMC and the Committee for the Defence of the Revolution, while the state institutions supply the technical facilities. This may not be evidence of power as it is commonly perceived by capitalist societies, but access to the technology in order to save your own life is the kind of power women want. It is real power, unlike the authoritarian fantasies that pass for power in most of the world. And the women of Cuba struggled for it, defined it and exercise it on their own behalf. It remains to be seen now whether Cuban women will raise their own standard in the world forum and show the other emergent nations how to harness the strength and tenderness of women in the remaking of our tired and guilty world. As Cuba's leaders have always realized, survival is too desperate a matter to be left to half the world's population. We need to see Federations of Women of every nationality mobilizing in the streets of every city, town and village in the world, *para trabajar, para estudiar, para construir nuestra libertad!*

Joseph Lelyveld

Forced Busing

W hen they are out to demonstrate their decency and good-will, to themselves as well as others, white South Africa's racial theorists are inclined to lose themselves in a riot of euphemisms, analogies and fatuous forecasts. A lot of words get spilled as the urge to be understood clashes with an aversion to being understood too well. But when being understood is no longer an issue, language can be used sparingly. The letter informing me I had a week to clear out of South Africa was a model of economy, unencumbered by explanations. 'You are hereby instructed,' it said, 'to make arrangements for yourself and your family to leave the Country on or before the 28th April, 1966.'

We had been there for only eleven months, but the message had long been expected, ever since an official had cancelled a lunch in Pretoria, privately explaining that he would be compromised if he were seen again with someone the Cabinet had decided to expel. When the snub was finally made official, my immediate reaction was relief. A weight had been lifted, and as we walked out of the terminal at Jan Smuts Airport to our plane for Rome—two days ahead of the official deadline—I had a feeling of lightness, of freedom as a palpable sensation, such as I had never known before. Possibly it occurred to me at that moment to wonder whether I would ever set foot in South Africa again. But since I had now been officially certified an enemy—'one of South Africa's most notorious enemies in the world,' an Afrikaans-language newspaper would later say, honouring me beyond my deserts—that would have been tantamount to wondering whether the regime would crumble and fall in my lifetime.

Fourteen years later, when the suspicion that I might be reconstituted as a *persona grata* in South Africa hatched itself almost instantly into a compulsion to return, I could remember the sense of relief and lightness I felt on leaving as vividly as I could recall anything about the place. It was a memory I willed upon myself almost daily to check my headlong flight from Manhattan, where I thought I really belonged, and another uprooting of my family. The white regime hadn't crumbled, and even with the transformation of Rhodesia into black-ruled Zimbabwe, then taking place on its northern frontier, it wasn't about to do so. But the whites' old urge to be understood, coupled with their need to believe their own propaganda about how much had changed, gave me a slight opening; at least that was my calculation. My work as an editor in New York occasionally brought me into contact with South African diplomats who seldom failed to say the diplomatic thing: that my expulsion had been an aberration, or that those had been the bad old days, or that I would be astonished by the changes. Getting carried away, they sometimes seemed even eager to make me a witness. What may have been intended as no more than a courtesy—or, at most, a suggestion for a brief visit—I took as a sporting wager, even a dare.

U p close, apartheid had been not only a caste system but a statement about reality amounting to a denial, which then sought to be self-enforcing. That statement insisted, against all the evidence that met the eye, that there was such a place as 'white South Africa.' It existed as a legal concept, reflecting the solipsism of the dominant minority, but not anywhere in the external world that I could find. The first story I filed from Johannesburg concerned a black choral group that had been denied permission to sing Handel's *Messiah* to a white audience because it had been scheduled to perform with a white orchestra. In the mind of some white official, that constituted illicit race mixing. When the sponsors of the concert proposed as a compromise that the chorus be accompanied by an organist instead of an orchestra, official permission was forthcoming, though the only available organist was also white. 'We had to promise that he would play only on the white keys,' one of the sponsors wisecracked. Apartheid in those days was often nearly funny; the reality it created seldom was.

In the fourteen years after my expulsion—the headlines in the Afrikaans press had proclaimed that I had been *uitgeskop* ('out-kicked') as if it were a triumph for patriotism and morality—I had lost much of the feel of the place, remembering mainly my own tautness and alertness when I lived there; forgotten, too, its physical and cultural scenery and most of its political rituals and arguments. What had lodged near the surface of my mind, available for ready excavation along with a wad of yellowing clippings, was a series of stark images and, because reporters remember quotes, small shards of dialogue. Two in particular involved blacks in courtrooms.

One was from a visit to a pass-law court, where black men were

168

prosecuted for the crime of being in a 'white area' without a stamp in their reference books, the domestic passports they all had to carry, to show they were 'authorized to seek work'. Then, as now, the 'white areas'—as opposed to the former tribal reserves known as homelands—accounted for slightly more than eighty-six percent of the land.

These trials, which have been taking place in South Africa one way or another since 1708, when the first passes were issued to Malay slaves, were fundamental to its way of life, the balance-wheel of the political mechanism. The rationalizations could change from decade to decade, but the trials went on. Few blacks could go through a lifetime without an experience of these courts, as either an accused or a relative of an accused; fewer whites cared to know where they were or how they worked, let alone to visit them. The trials themselves could be, still can be, measured in minutes or sometimes seconds. An hour could be long enough to get through thirty or forty cases in open court. The context was something I would have to learn all over again, but one brief exchange was graven in my memory. 'Why were you in Johannesburg?' asked the presiding officer, a white civil servant in black robes known in those days as the Bantu commissioner.

'I was looking for my child,' the accused replied.

'Where is your child?'

'Lost.'

'Fourteen days,' the commissioner ruled.

In the other scene of black men in the dock, there had been fifty-six of them, wearing large numbered placards around their necks so they could be identified. Their trial, on charges of belonging to an underground black movement called Pogo, took place in a courtroom in Port Elizabeth on the Indian Ocean coast. It was earlier coverage of trials in that area involving the outlawed African National Congress that appeared to be at the root of my difficulties with the authorities. But it was the Pogo trial that I remembered because of the cynical line of cross-examination the white prosecutor had pursued. The accused came from the same small dorp, or rural town, where they represented a significant fraction of the adult black males. In the dock, they were a scruffy, undernourished lot ranging from post-adolescent to doddering. The prosecutor's tactic was to

169

demonstrate that they were dissatisfied with their lives and therefore likely 'terrorists'. In response, the defendants attempted to deny that they could ever be unhappy as black men in South Africa.

'You have no objection to being ordered around by white men?' the prosecutor taunted.

'I have become so satisfied that my health keeps improving,' number 23 replied.

'Are you satisfied with your wages?'

'I have never complained, not on a single day.'

'Do you want better wages?'

'No, Your Worship.'

'Are you satisfied with your house?'

'It's a very beautiful house.'

'Are you satisfied with the pass laws?'

'Yes, entirely.'

The white prosecutor's scornful questions showed that he knew it was reasonable for black men to rebel, unreasonable for them to claim they could be happy; that they were held in check only by the power of the state, which he represented. Every other white in the courtroom had to know it, too.

The cross-examination of number 23 was a caricature of the political exchanges blacks could have in that period. Conversation was inexplicit, steeped in irony, with kernels of meaning hidden between sardonic throwaway lines. A few weeks before I received my expulsion notice, white South Africans went to the polls to give their leader, Hendrik Verwoerd, the strongest mandate he had yet received to go on building apartheid. Several hours before the returns were due, I went to one of the illegal drinking establishments known as shebeens in Soweto, Johannesburg's black annex, to see if I could elicit some black reflections on the spectacle of white democracy. What I got was typically roundabout. 'What were you doing at that polling station this morning?' a black man who said he was an undertaker asked another drinker.

'Voting, of course,' came the reply, right on cue.

'Who for?'

'Well,' the other man gibed, 'that's between my conscience and myself, but if you must know, the candidate's name was Hendrik Verwoerd. He's my man.'

What kept conversation in check was the seeming omnipresence of informers, known among blacks as *impimpis*. Invariably, when there was a political trial or wave of arrests, someone discovered the exorbitant price of trust. While visiting Port Elizabeth for the Pogo trial, I met two blacks at the seaside cottage of the playwright Athol Fugard. Because he vouched for me to them, and them to me, we were able to speak with more than normal candour. How was it, I asked, that black security policemen and the state witnesses in political trials were never assaulted in the black townships? 'To do something like that,' one of the men said, 'you would want at least two men, wouldn't you?' Pausing to indicate that my question was hypothetical and not intended as incitement, I gestured towards the only other person in the room, the man's best friend. 'How do I know,' came the mumbled reply, 'that he is not an *impimpi*?' No one who was not in jail or house arrest under what was called a banning order could ever be immune from that suspicion. So pervasive was it then that the authorities could compromise stalwart black nationalists by seeming to ignore them.

Under the circumstances I had little or no direct experience of black politics in that time and relied largely on intuition and observation for my sense of what it was like to be black in the apartheid society. Many whites never tired of explaining to a foreigner that blacks had their own distinct cultural values as Zulus, Xhosas and so forth, that it was impossible to try to see the world through their eyes. But it seemed to me a reasonably safe assumption that these cultures did not absolutely require the decimation of black family life that apartheid entailed; that most blacks were aware that they had nothing to say about the shape of the system; that some occasionally wearied of white bossiness; and that when I saw a newspaper photo of nine black schoolgirls in uniform, each holding aloft a placard with one of the letters that spell out A-P-A-R-T-H-E-I-D as part of a welcome to a touring white Cabinet minister, I was witnessing something other than a flowering of indigenous culture.

Of course, a global perspective is easily used to belittle the sufferings of particular groups, to deny the significance of their history and particular circumstances. If it can be shown that someone in Gdańsk or Kampala or Lahore is worse off than someone in Cape Town, then anyone in Cape Town who vents his unhappiness is convicted of a lack of global perspective. I was never impressed by the line that racial tyranny was easier to bear than Leninist totalitarianism. It struck me as an unseemly calculation for anyone who has never borne either. I didn't have to be reminded that I was not South African and not black. Nevertheless, from the distance at which I was following these events, it was the emergence of the student protests and of Steve Biko rather than their suppression that stirred me. Once again blacks were making themselves heard. This was the generation that Verwoerd had intended to educate for a life of meagre privileges and low horizons in the 'homelands' since, as he put it, there could be 'no place for [them] in the European community above the level of certain forms of labour.' A system of 'Bantu education' had been designed to save the 'Bantu' from the frustration that came with exposure to 'the green pastures of European society in which he was not allowed to graze.' And now it turned out that they had read Franz Fanon and Aimé Césaire, some of them at least, and were standing up to denounce the legacy of the great white seer and demand their birthright. Without Verwoerd at the helm, the Afrikaners seemed a bit wobbly in their response, uncertain of how to justify the system he had elaborated. They had changed, were changing, would change; so they said. The tenses blurred, and so did the promise, but ideologically, at least, they seemed to be in ragged retreat. More inward? It didn't seem so anymore. More fragmented? More dreary? I couldn't begin to imagine what it was.

On the strength of that uncertainty, I asked my editors if I could explore the possibility of returning. The matter was taken up discreetly in Cape Town by John Burns, who had gone to South Africa a full ten years after my expulsion as the first resident correspondent *The New York Times* had been allowed to station there after me. In that sense Burns was to be both my predecessor and my successor. 'Do you think, Mr. Burns,' the foreign minister, Pik Botha, asked once my name had been broached, 'that a condemned man has the right to choose the witnesses at his execution?'

I took the joke to be doubly ironic, a way of promising that I would be disappointed if I thought I would see the crumbling of white power. But I also took it as an accolade. Five months later my visa finally came through.

M y time machine seemed to have landed me in Oz. Or was it Brobdingnag? No, it was Bophuthatswana. This was to be my first weekend in South Africa in nearly a generation, and now, I was given to understand, I was not in South Africa at all. I was in the Tswana 'national state', which I had never heard of in my first incarnation because it had not existed except, possibly, as a gleam in Verwoerd's eye. Then there had been something called the Tswana Tribal Authority, but I don't think I had ever heard of that either; if I had, I certainly had not thought of it as a place. Bophuthatswana—now alleged to be a sovereign and independent nation for the two million black South Africans of Tswana origins who, by virtue of its existence, were no longer deemed to be South Africans—was not exactly a place either. It was at least seven places, scattered across three South African provinces, surrounded on nearly every side of each fragment by the huge holdings of white ranchers and farmers. Three times on the drive from Johannesburg I had crossed its border without running into anything that remotely resembled a border post. There were small 'Bophuthatswana Border' signs, but they were superfluous; a glance out of the window could always tell you which country you were in. If you saw fields that were empty except for cattle and grain, it was obviously South Africa. If they were full of people in tribal villages and desolate shanty towns, it was the 'national state'. But now I was in neither a village nor a shanty town. I was in a glossy casino resort called Sun City that seemed to have taken some of its decorative cues from the Peachtree Plaza Hotel in Atlanta. Here, where whites and blacks mixed as freely as they might there, a black and a white were to fight for one of the world's two heavyweight championships. Hendrik Verwoerd, I wondered, where is thy sting?

From the ringside it seemed likely that Verwoerd was revolving in his grave over this bizarre fulfillment of his vision, which nonetheless was turning into a festival of white South African, mainly Afrikaner, patriotism. Gerrie Coetzee from Boksburg, South Africa, was to fight Mike Weaver from the wrong side of the tracks in Gatesville, Texas, and a crowd of about 17,000, who had consumed about 100,000 cans of Castle or Lion Lager, screamed in good-natured frenzy as the theme from the movie *Star Wars* blared over huge quadraphonic speakers and a chorus girl from an ensemble called the Sun City Extravaganza, dressed mainly in orange ostrich plumes and sequins, danced down the aisle, bearing the South African flag as honour guard to the contender. Another chorus girl brought Weaver and the Stars and Stripes. These were followed by chorus girls with the Bophuthatswana flag and even a flag for Sun City itself, until finally there was a line-up of eleven Extravaganza dancers, mainly but not exclusively white, swinging their bottoms and kicking their heels in the ring. Floyd Patterson, the last black heavyweight champ to be defeated by a white, got a cheer as he climbed through the ropes wearing a T-shirt that advertised Old Buck Gin, a local distillate. Then came the anthems, including that of Bophuthatswana, with the thousands of whites standing at solemn attention. Finally, when the chorus girl holding their flag gave the signal by thrusting its staff into her navel and raising it high, they burst into a full-throated and passionate rendering of their own 'Die Stem' ('The Call') so that Coetzee would be left in no doubt of his duty:

> *At that call we shall not falter,*
> *Firm and steadfast we shall stand,*
> *At thy will to live or perish,*
> *O South Africa, dear land.*

The poor lug perished in the thirteenth, dropping with a thud in a stunned and suddenly silent arena. To those of his countrymen who had been intent on viewing the fight as a racial allegory, he had presented a chilling foreshadowing of their destiny. For eight rounds their hero, their white hope, had seemed cruelly invincible, but the black man proved to be more patient, more determined, and finally just stronger. In far-off Soweto blacks were rejoicing over the Afrikaner's defeat. A mood sodden with anticlimax and regret descended on the casino resort in the independent homeland. Yet there was no apparent bitterness of a racial kind as Afrikaners and Tswanas brushed shoulders at the slot machines and fast-food stands. On the platforms cantilevered over small lagoons in the dimly-lit lobby, a few voluble young whites threw themselves into earnest, boozy colloquies with young blacks, which gathered intensity as the evening wore on but seemed to be largely one-sided. Out on the patio a middle-aged Afrikaner tried to catch the eye of a black barmaid.

'Mrs Weaver, Mrs Weaver,' he called in a bantering tone. She took his order with a wary smile that seemed to show there had been no offence.

The nearest thing to a confrontation occurred at the entrance to the casino when a uniformed black security man informed a leather-jacketed young Afrikaner that he could not proceed farther in running shoes. It was not far-fetched to imagine that it was the young man's first encounter with black authority.

'Why can't I?' he demanded, asserting his whiteness but looking around with noticeable uncertainty for support from his friends.

'That's our rule,' the black man said.

'What's the reason for the rule?'

'Look,' said the guard, who was trying to unclog the entrance and get the line moving, 'I don't want to talk.'

Not knowing how to step back without humiliating himself, the young white persisted. 'What did those shoes cost?' he asked, pointing to the cop's brogans. 'Mine cost nineteen rands.'

'That's cheap,' said the black.

'What do you mean cheap? What did yours cost?' And when that was met by silence: 'Don't you want my money?'

The man in uniform was now insulted. 'I don't need *your* money,' he replied. 'I get paid.'

The kid in the leather jacket was now as beaten as Gerrie Coetzee. His forefathers had fought blacks for half a century and built one of their frontier republics in this area on a constitution prohibiting 'any equality…either in church or state', then had been ground down in a filthy war with the British and lost their republic, but had clung to the principle so hard and nurtured their grievances and sense of destiny so fiercely that decades later they reversed the tide of history. 'The blindest heathen and unbelieving creature,' the patriarchal Paul Kruger said in the nineteenth century, 'must acknowledge that it is God's hand.' But now the long struggle had brought the Afrikaners to the point where a fairly upstanding, at least erect, young member of the tribe could be turned away from a casino entrance by a black cop. Was that also God's hand?

If I had paid more attention to the designer emblems and signatures that many of the whites in the casino were flashing on their sleeves and pockets, I might have realized that there was a sumptuary code operating in reverse throughout the land. DRESS SMART CASUAL, warn signs at the entrances to most drinking and eating establishments that aspire to be more than commonplace. Or, absurdly, ELEGANT CASUAL. Or, packing all the anxieties of a class of arriviste Puritans into three words, STRICTLY SMART CASUAL. Independent Bophuthatswana, the borders of which could not be guessed at in the darkness as I drove back to Johannesburg in the early hours of the morning with Allister Sparks, a fellow journalist and old friend, aspired to be 'smart casual', too. Sparks lost his way in the vicinity of two Transvaal hamlets, Hartbeespoort and Hartbeeshoek. It was three in the morning; there was no traffic, and we had no map. The authors of the highway signs that appeared in our headlights every thirty miles or so had obviously never heard of Johannesburg or Pretoria, only towns named after antelopes, either hartebeests or elands. In my mind they all merged into a mythical Hartbeespoortfontein. The points on our wayward compass made us laugh all the more as we pronounced them. 'I think this is Hartbeespoortfontein now,' I would say. 'No,' Sparks would say, 'I think it's Bophuthatswana.' So one blind heathen laughed most of the way back, as he had never laughed before in South Africa, without being able to say what was really so funny.

In a period in which South Africa is alleged to be changing and phasing out apartheid, the expansion of the Putco bus company into the *bundu,* or bush, of a soon-to-be-independent homeland called KwaNdebele provides as accurate a measure as can be found of the real thrust of change. The bus company had to draw its own maps, for its new routes were on roads that had just been cut; its buses came in right behind the bulldozers. In 1979 Putco started to run two buses a day from Pretoria to the resettlement camps of KwaNdebele. By 1980 there were sixty-six a day, which jumped to 105 in 1981; to 148 a day in 1981; then 220 a day in 1983 and 263 a day in 1984, when the government was expected to pay Putco a subsidy of £18.8 million to keep its buses rolling to the homeland. That worked out to about £18 a head a week, more than £700 for each 'commuter' a year: a negative social investment that went up in diesel fumes when it might just as easily have gone into new housing for the same black workers nearer the industrial centres, if that had not violated the apartheid design. It was the price the white government was willing to pay—and go on paying, year after year—to halt the normal process of urbanization. The KwaNdebele bus subsidy—the government's largest single expense in the development of this homeland—was higher than the KwaNdebele gross domestic product. This is basic apartheid economics. It had to be so high because KwaNdebele, a state supposedly on the way to independence, was utterly devoid of a productive economy or resources. The racial doctrine sets the priorities: first you invent the country; then, if you can, an economy. In the meantime, there are the buses to carry the homeland's citizens to jobs in the nearest industrial centre. In KwaNdebele's case that meant Pretoria, which is fifty-five miles distant at the homeland's nearest point.

The first time I saw KwaNdebele, it was a rash of 'closer settlements' spotted over open veld that had previously provided grazing for some thirty white farmers. At a place called Kwaggafontein, I came upon the Nduli family, who had just been evicted from their kraal on a white farm near Middelburg, about fifty miles away. I found them with their paltry belongings on a plot white officials had staked out on a grassy hillside, which was fast being blighted by squalid shanties. Rose Nduli was literally sitting on the veld while her son, Kleinbooi, wearing a brown shoe on his right foot and on his left a black boot laced with copper wire, chipped away with a shovel at the dry stucco-like earth in order to prepare the ground for a shelter. Kleinbooi said they knew none of their neighbours. He knew that he had landed at a place called Kwaggafontein, but he hadn't been told that KwaNdebele was supposed to have deep significance for him as his homeland. When I asked who brought him there, he replied simply, 'GG'. The initials are the first two letters of the official licence plates on the government trucks used to move blacks out of white areas. Throughout the rural Transvaal and Natal it has become the universal shorthand among blacks for the white government, its pervasive authority and its arbitrary ways, which seem to be beyond ordinary comprehension. GG is as predictable as natural calamity. GG scoops you up when you least expect it and drops you somewhere you have never seen, leaving it to you to patch together the torn and ragged pattern of a life. And like natural calamity, it evokes depression and resignation, rather than resentment. 'The law is the law,' Rose Nduli said, 'and we have nothing to say about it.'

I heard only one angry voice at Kwaggafontein on that visit. It belonged to a man named Jim Masetlana, who started his working life as a tenant on a white farm and then was moved three times by GG in nineteen years. Without meaning to do so, I had uncapped his resentment by offering the cold comfort that he probably would not be harried any more now that he was in a homeland. 'This is no homeland,' he said, waving his hand at the dreary refugee camp growing up around him. 'It's just a township. Where I grew up was really a homeland. I had land. I could plough. Even the white farmers give you land to plough. This type of homeland I have never seen. They have no business taking us from the place of our birth.'

Kwaggafontein made as little sense to me as it did to the people who had been dumped there. But I saw a lot more of resettlement in South Africa and its effects. By the time I went back to Kwaggafontein, I could make a dubious boast that, to offer a wild guess, probably fewer than one hundred South Africans could match: I had been to each of the ten homelands, and I had seen most of the major 'closer settlements'. I did not expect to be surprised again. I thought I understood that this process—known euphemistically as resettlement, bluntly as removal, and cynically as repatriation—represented a final stage in a campaign to alienate blacks from their land that had already gone on in the Transvaal for 140 years. For seventy years it had actually been illegal for blacks to purchase land in more than eighty-six percent of the territory the world still knows as South Africa. For thirty-five years they had been forced, cajoled, and squeezed off 'black spots', land to which they had secured proper title according to the white man's law, prior to the passage of the Native Lands Act in 1913. I knew that resettlement was central to the government's audacious plan to redefine the bulk of the black population, if not all of it, as foreign. At first I had thought this was just an ideological word game, not to be taken seriously. But the misery and endemic malnutrition I had seen in out-of-the-way resettlement camps from Thornhill, in supposedly sovereign Ciskei in the south-east, to Rooigrond in supposedly sovereign Bophuthatswana in the north-west, had long since cured me of the easy notion that this programme of exclusion and partition existed only on paper.

I thought I understood all that, but I was not prepared for the visual shock of what Kwaggafontein had become in two and a half years. It was no longer just a spot in a rash of 'closer settlements'. Now it was a part of a nearly continuous resettlement belt. You drove through the Pretoria suburbs and then through more than forty miles of rich farm country before you hit it; then you could drive another forty miles, and it was seldom out of sight: a serpentine stream of metal shanties and mud houses the metal roofs of which were typically weighted down by small boulders to keep them from blowing off in the Transvaal's violent hailstorms. Such sights can be seen in other countries, usually as a result of famines or wars. I don't know where else they have been achieved as a result of planning. The hillside where the Ndulis had been dropped was now as densely settled as Soweto. It no longer looked like a hillside. What it had become was a slight swell in a sea of shanties. I turned off the highway there and followed a dirt road for five miles to see how far into the *bundu* the settlement now extended. This brought me to a place called Frisegewacht that seemed to be near the homeland's outer edge, for when I looked past the last shanty to the next rise, all I could see was open, unspoiled, empty grassland belonging to a white cattle farmer.

To catch the first Putco bus out of the Wolverkraal depot in KwaNdebele, the photographer David Goldblatt and I calculated, we would have to leave the Bundu Inn (a white hostelry that went 'international' after finding itself in a homeland) no later than one-thirty in the morning. It is then that KwaNdebele's first 'commuters' start to stir. Wolverkraal was even farther from Pretoria than Kwaggafontein or Frisegewacht. The black settlers of the new state who boarded the bus near there had to ride about ninety-five miles before transferring to local buses that would take them to factories where they worked, in areas where they were forbidden to live. That meant a minimum of 190 miles every working day in buses designed with hard seats for short hauls on city streets. They were fortunate in a sense—they did have work—but they were spending up to eight hours a day on buses. The distance they travelled annually, I calculated, came to more than a circumnavigation of the globe.

179

The Putco depot was just a fenced-off clearing in the bush with a tiny shack for the dispatcher and nothing else: no floodlights; no time clocks; no coffee machines; no grease pits. Rain during the night had cleansed the air and drained a layer of clouds that had glowered over the veld at sundown, leaving a light breeze and a full moon to limn the hulks of the ranked buses. I counted fifty-two of them. Two others, I was told, had left the yard at one in the morning to round up the drivers who stayed in nearby 'closer settlements'. One of these staff buses had then got stuck in the mud, so Putco was going to be a little behind schedule this morning in KwaNdebele. The engine of the other staff bus, which had rescued the stranded drivers, was the first night sound I heard.

It was about twenty past two when the lights inside the buses at the depot started to blink on one by one. Number 4174, which we boarded after being told that it would be the first out of the yard, had one bulb glowing dimly inside a red globe, another in a green globe, casting together an eerie light into a gloom made Stygian, despite the clear night outside, by the coating of caked mud on the bus's windows. A sign near the cage in which the driver was encased declared that number 4174 was certified to carry 62 sitting passengers and 29 standing. I did another quick calculation: the fifty-two buses represented roughly one-fifth of the homeland's daily convoys to the white areas; the number of 'commuters' who were thus being subsidized by South Africa to live beyond the pale—the pun was inadvertent but hard to erase—came to roughly 23,000 on the KwaNdebele run.

At two-forty in the morning, number 4174 left the depot and headed north and east, *away* from Pretoria, to pick up its first passengers at a place called Kameelrivier. In the Ndebele homeland, it seemed, all place-names were still in Afrikaans—the names, mostly, of the white farms the state had bought up in order to ghettoize the bush. The headlights showed six men and four women waiting patiently beside the dirt road, in what appeared to be the middle of nowhere, when the bus made its first stop, ten minutes late, at two-fifty. At that place and that hour, the sight of a couple of whites on the bus was as much to be expected as that of a couple of commuting walruses. Momentarily it startled the passengers out of their drowsiness. Once our presence was explained, it became possible to ask a few questions as the bus rattled to its next stop.

180

John Masango, the first man to board, said he worked six days a week at a construction site near Benoni, an industrial town forty miles on the far side of Pretoria, taking three buses each way. Even at the concessional rates arranged by the authorities for KwaNdebele, the total bus fares he paid out in a week gobbled up one-quarter of his wages. He was fifty-three years old, and on days when he was not required to work overtime, he could get back to Kameelrivier by eight-thirty at night. Only on Sundays did he ever see his home or his family in the light of day. Most nights, after washing, eating, and, as he put it, 'taking care of family matters', he was able to get to sleep by ten or ten-fifteen. With four hours' sleep at home and a couple of hours' sleep on the bus, he managed to stay awake at work. It was important not to be caught napping; you could lose your job. While I was still thanking him for his patience, John Masango reached into a bag he was carrying and extracted a little rectangle of foam rubber about the size of a paperback book. He then pulled his blue knitted cap over his eyes and, leaning forward, pressed the foam rubber to the back of the seat in front of him; in the final step in this procedure, he rested his forehead against the foam rubber and dropped his hands to his lap. As far as I could tell, he was out like a light.

Emma Mokwena was on her way to a part-time job as a cleaning woman for an Afrikaner family called the Van der Walts who lived in one of the new suburban developments burgeoning on the veld between Pretoria and Johannesburg. She was expected at work by seven in the morning, in time to prepare breakfast for her employers, who rose to face the new day four and a half or five hours after she had to get up in KwaNdebele. She did not, however, have to serve the Van der Walts tea in bed, as live-in servants are often still expected to do in South Africa. She worked for them two days a week, for other families in the same suburb on other days. Usually she worked for seven hours, leaving at about two in the afternoon, in time to return to Kameelrivier to prepare dinner for her five children aged fourteen down to two and a half. In a month she earned about £85, of which a little more than £21 went in bus fares. It could have been worse, but fortunately her employers underwrote the 85 pence she spent each day getting from Pretoria to their homes and back. When she saw I was finished with my questions, Emma Mokwena pulled her blanket snug over her shoulders and unfolded the collar of her turtle-neck sweater so it covered her face. She then leaned back in her seat, half-slumped against the woman with whom she had boarded, now similarly mummified.

By this time it was only three-twenty, and number 4174 had yet to reach the narrow ribbon of asphalt that connects KwaNdebele to Pretoria. But it had stopped by enough 'closer settlements' to fill all its seats; anyone getting on beyond this point was bound to stand, not just this morning but every morning in the week. There were still nearly two and a half hours to go to Pretoria. Thus some people *stood* on the bus nearly twelve hours a week. These calculations were beginning to make me more tired than the ride, which was grim enough, especially since I had lost my seat and was now standing, too, squeezed in next to a man who was managing to doze on his feet.

Another 'commuter', a construction worker whose job was at a site in a section of Pretoria called Sunnyside, stood long enough to tell me that he had received several reprimands, each formally inscribed on his work record, for falling asleep on the job. This man represented a particularly telling example of the dramatic changes that have occurred in the lives of some South African blacks, for his family had been landowners in a 'black spot' called Doornkop, from which they were expelled along with 12,000 others in 1969. The compensation his family got from a government that never ceases to profess its devotion to principles of private enterprise came to less than £220. The man smiled bitterly as he mentioned the figure. Then, excusing himself, he removed a folded piece of newspaper he had been carrying under his jacket and spread it neatly on the floor between his feet. Next, with the suppleness of a yogi, he collapsed himself into a seated position on the paper with his knees drawn up to his chin and dropped his head.

I looked around. Aside from the driver and one man who was smoking about four rows from the rear of the bus, David and I and a black Putco official who had graciously come along with us appeared to be the only persons out of more than ninety who had not now dozed off. The centre aisle was packed with bodies wound around themselves like anchovies in a can. The motion of the bus threw some chance couples, men and women who got on at different stops, into intimate contact. A young woman's head slumped on the shoulder of the man seated next to her, who was too far gone to recognize his good fortune. Nearer the front a young man clutched restlessly in his sleep at the sleeping woman next to him. Some of the heads lolled backward, but most of the forms were bent forward like that of the man who carried the foam rubber. By three forty-five the bus had reached the highway, and the ride was now smoother. Their heads covered, blankets over their shoulders, the passengers swayed like Orthodox Jews in prayer. Or, in the eerie light of the two overhead bulbs, they could be seen as a congregation of spectres, souls in purgatory.

Twice they were jostled into consciousness: once when number 4174 pulled off the highway onto the hard shoulder for a routine Putco check; another time when the driver slammed on his brakes, barely missing a truck that had stopped by the side of the road as if to let him pass, then eased its way forward directly into our path. Shaken, our black driver got down to yell at the black driver of the truck. A small crowd gathered in the dark patch between the two sets of headlights. The truck driver expressed remorse. He had been giving a lift to three women, who were crowded into the cab of his truck with him, wrapped in blankets like the women on the bus, and asked the one who was nearest the window to tell him whether the coast was clear. Apparently without looking, she had mumbled something that he took to mean 'go.'

The first streaks of dawn showed on the outskirts of Pretoria. We saw plenty of blacks heading for work but no sign of white life as number 4174 proceeded through the first of several white neighbourhoods until we came upon a jogger, a hyperventilating grey-haired man in his fifties wearing a T-shirt that had, stencilled on his chest in red as a greeting to all comers, including the passengers on a Putco bus, a blank 'happy face' with a turned-up smile. Posters strung up on lamp-posts and trees by extremist white parties resisting the new constitutional proposals also seemed to mock the 'commuters', who were excluded, in any case, from the supposed 'new dispensation'.

PROTECT OUR FUTURE, the posters exhorted. REMEMBER RHODESIA.

It was October, and Pretoria's splendid jacarandas were in full blossom, but seen from the vantage point of a black commuter bus, the sight left me indifferent. It was like looking at Bali or the Himalayas in tourist posters for holidays you would never take. It was only a few moments now until we turned into Marabastad, once a teeming black residential neighbourhood at the very edge of Pretoria's downtown, at present a stretch of razed, overgrown real estate lying as a no-man's-land between the capital's commercial centre and a tiny enclave of Indian-owned shops adjacent to the terminus where the buses from KwaNdebele disgorge their black passengers. Number 4174 ended its ride there at five-forty, exactly three hours after it had begun in the *bundu* at the Wolverkraal depot.

This left us leeward of a lavish new temple of apartheid: a combined rail and bus terminus called the Belle Ombre station, which will function one day, according to the dreams of the social engineers who do South Africa's long-range planning, as the hub for a series of bullet trains to the homelands. The first of these, a high-speed rail line into the nearest section of Bophuthatswana, had just begun operation, bringing back to Marabastad on a daily basis many of its old residents, or their descendants, in the status of aliens. At a quarter to six in the morning, there was piped music at the Belle Ombre station to cheer the homeland blacks on their way. A high-pitched pavilion with airy esplanades and structural piping painted in bright primary colours, the station seemed to exert a gravitational pull that sucked the groggy KwaNdebele 'commuters' down its ramps to waiting Putco buses that would carry them on the next stage of their journeys to work.

The South African official's wife put together a couple of bits of information and came up with a strange result that left her incredulous. 'Is it true,' she asked with friendly curiosity, 'that you are actually writing a book on KwaNdebele?'

My wisecracking reply, delivered at a diplomatic party in Pretoria, struck me—but only me—as very funny. Its references were cross-cultural, yielding blinks, squints and blank stares. 'Yes,' I said, 'I'm calling it *The Boys on the Bus.*'

IAN JACK
GIBRALTAR

L ying half-asleep in my room at the Holiday Inn one night I listened to a song I hadn't heard in twenty years. The tune was 'Marching Through Georgia', but the words did not belong to the American Civil War. I last heard them rising from the crowd at the Glasgow Rangers football ground, where every alternate Saturday the chant is probably bellowed still:

> Hello, hello, we are the Billy Boys!
> Hello, hello, we *are* the Billy Boys!
> We're up to our knees in Fenian blood,
> Surrender or you'll die,
> For we are the Brigton Billy Boys.

I went to the window. Members of the British popular press were walking unsteadily towards the hotel. Great drinkers and pranksters, these chaps from the tabloids. Already in Gibraltar we'd enjoyed a fortnight of jokes. The first fashion was for water-pistols, which to be strictly accurate was started by the men of Independent Television News (or at least it started at their party, shortly before their guests were thrown into the swimming pool). You might be sitting innocently in a bar or walking down the street when the challenge came from behind, 'Stop, police, hands up!' and you'd turn sharply—very much, I imagine, as Danny McCann and Mairead Farrell turned—and receive a small jet of water straight in the chest. This was the English journalists' reconstruction of the role of the Special Air Service Regiment as executioners of the members of the Irish Republican Army. The role of the Irish Republican Army itself had to wait for the second fashionable joke. A couple of Japanese transmitter-receivers were purchased—the kind of thing strolling British policemen use, the kind of thing we'd been shown in court as an IRA bomb-detonating device—and then demonstrated whenever an evening looked as though it might close unpromisingly in an exchange of civilities. Once, at the Marina, I came across a drunken couple shouting into these machines outside a quayside restaurant. 'Shitbag calling fuckface, shitbag calling fuckface, are you receiving me, over?' 'Fuckface to shitbag, fuckface to shitbag, I am receiving you, over . . .' And now, two weeks into the inquest into the killings of three Irish republicans, this Orange song rolled around the lanes of Gibraltar at one in the morning. 'Hello, hello, we are the Billy Boys . . . up to our knees in Fenian blood.' The only surprise was that Englishmen seemed to know some of the words of a song born of sectarian gang-fighting in Glasgow of the 1930s. But then the English these days are a surprising race.

I write as a Scot, and one with too much of the Protestant in him ever to empathize much with the more recent traditions of Irish republicanism, as well as an ordinary level of human feeling which precludes understanding of the average IRA bomber. But the longer I spent in Gibraltar, the more difficult it became to prop up a shaky old structure—that lingering belief in what must, for lack of a more exact phrase, be called the virtues of Britishness. Both the inquest and its setting played a part in this undermining; perhaps this is what the British government meant when it said that it feared 'the propaganda consequences' of such an inquiry and set up an informal cabinet sub-committee (which included Mrs Thatcher) to combat the eventuality. As it turned out—and who knows what part the informal committee played—the government need not have worried. They got the verdict they wanted, the great mass of British public opinion applauded it and the proceedings were minimally covered in the only foreign media which matter to Britain, which lie in New York and Washington. The government then pressed ahead with 'the war to defeat the terrorist' by banning IRA spokesmen and their political sympathizers from radio and television, where in any case they had scarcely ever appeared, and renewed attacks on the television programme that had ventured to suggest that the Gibraltar killings raised questions which needed proper investigation.

And that, so far as the British government was concerned, closed the Gibraltar affair. One or two journalists remained sceptical, but a week after the verdict the topic had vanished even from the letters columns.

What is Gibraltar? John D. Stewart, in the only decent book about the place, wrote that

it may symbolize steadfastness to some and arrogance to others, the British bandit or the British policeman, according to the point of view. But the strongest of all the Rock's suggestions . . . is that concept which used to be called Military Glory, and which we have come to reassess as the slaughter of young men for causes

vaguely understood and rapidly discredited and cast
aside.

Stewart wrote that more than twenty years ago. Since then
Northern Ireland and the Falklands War have intervened to recast
the military's position in British life, and the disparaging
reassessment of 'military glory' which seemed so enduring to
Stewart in 1967 has now itself been reassessed. Who, in 1967, had
heard of the Special Air Service Regiment? Who could imagine that
in less than two decades its initials, SAS, would comprise a 'sexy
headline' for the British tabloids (as an SAS officer told the
Gibraltar inquest)? And who could foresee that the *Sun*, then a
faltering broadsheet of mildly Labourite views, would become the
tabloid-in-chief and cheer-leader of a born-again chauvinism for
twelve million readers? Its front-page headlines are inimitable. Of
the IRA in general: 'STRING 'EM UP!' Of the three who were shot in
Gibraltar: 'WHY THE DOGS HAD TO DIE.' Then again, who in 1967
worried about the fate of Northern Ireland other than the Northern
Irish, or about the gerrymandering and discrimination against its
minority which kept the province intact? Or who could imagine an
ensuing twenty years of terror and counter-terror which, at its last
great manifestation on the British mainland, nearly killed a British
prime minister and many of her cabinet?

I don't want to go back further. Let's avoid Oliver Cromwell and
the potato blight. But is there anything which the head—rather
than the gut—can latch on to in this pernicious cycle of cause
and effect, some handhold on fairness and reason? One such
handhold should be the rule of law, which has always found great
favour with the British establishment who speak of it like a
sacrament, inviolable, invulnerable to prejudice or political
influence: the rule that sets the state morally above those who
oppose it by violence. It would follow that the rule of law would be
served by truth and that truth—the truthful reconstruction of
events—would be the objective of any disinterested and open
process of inquiry.

It was the duty of the Gibraltar inquest to use such a process to
discover the truth of what happened and thus to see whether that
discovery conflicted with the principles of the rule of law—in other
words, to establish whether what was true was also legal, whether it

was the symbolic British policeman or the symbolic British bandit who shot three unarmed people to death on the streets of Gibraltar on 6 March 1988. It was not a trial, it was an inquest, and was in many people's view a sadly inadequate forum to determine what happened, but the British government insisted that it would be the only one. Six months after the killings, on Tuesday, 6 September, the coroner called his first witness into court. For the next four weeks he heard evidence and argument in a courtroom which, oddly enough, also heard the inquiry into the fate of the crew of the *Marie Celeste* after that abandoned barque was towed to port in Gibraltar in 1872. Sometimes during those four weeks it seemed we were in the presence of a mystery of equal proportions. There was rarely a day when a saying of one of Mrs Thatcher's own party men did not come to mind: in the words of Jonathan Aitken MP, when you try to reconcile effective counter-terrorism with the ancient rule of English law, the result is 'a huge smoke-screen of humbug'.

2

Gibraltar has only one overland entrance and exit. A large lump of Jurassic limestone, it points south into the Mediterranean from Spain. Sea surrounds it on three sides. Only to the north does water give way to land—a flat, low strip of plain about one mile long and half as wide joins Gibraltar to the sweep of the Costa del Sol. The airport runway crosses this strip from east to west, while further to the north are the fences and guard posts which mark the half-mile width of Gibraltar's land frontier. The road into the colony bisects the fences and then the runway. Before visitors can reach the town by road, they must first pass through Spanish and British immigration control and then, if they are unlucky, wait at the traffic lights which control movement across the runway.

S ean Savage, Danny McCann and Mairead Farrell arrived by this route on Sunday, 6 March 1988. Savage came first. He drove a white Renault 5 across the border around 12.30 p.m. and parked it ten minutes later near Ince's Hall at the south end of the town. At 2.30 p.m. McCann and Farrell crossed on foot. By 3.45 p.m. all of them were dead.

It seems likely (no, certain) that we shall never know their exact purpose on that day. None the less, certain aspects of it are beyond dispute. Within hours of their deaths, the Irish Republican Army in Belfast claimed all three as 'volunteers on active service', attached to a unit of the IRA's General Headquarters staff. The next day the IRA admitted that the three had 'access and control over' 140 pounds of explosives. What the IRA would not divulge was the intended target, though on this particular point the British government's scenario has never been seriously challenged. News bulletins on British radio and television on the evening of 6 March quoted briefings in London and Gibraltar which identified not only the target but also the place and time. According to several reports the three dead had intended to blow up the band of the Royal Anglian Regiment, which had recently served in Northern Ireland, as it assembled for the weekly changing of the guard ceremony outside the Gibraltar Governor's residence two days later, on Tuesday, 8 March, at eleven in the morning.

As a description of intention, that may be entirely accurate. It was, however, a minor accuracy embedded in a larger untruth. Throughout Sunday evening and Monday morning the same reports also asserted that a bomb had been found in Gibraltar. The earliest reports were the most circumspect. At 6.25 p.m. on the television news, the BBC's Madrid correspondent said that troops were searching Gibraltar's main street, 'following a report that a bomb had been planted near a public hall . . . but it's not known if that report is genuine.' Three hours later all circumspection was cast aside. At nine o'clock the BBC reported that 500 pounds of explosives had been packed inside a Renault 5 and, according to 'official sources', timed to kill British troops when they assembled for Tuesday's parade. At 9.45 p.m. Independent Television News had further details. Three Irish terrorists had been killed in 'a fierce gun battle'. Their bomb had been defused by 'a controlled explosion'. It was becoming more evident, said ITN's correspondent, 'that the authorities came desperately close to disaster with a bomb being left in a crowded street and a shoot-out when innocent civilians were in the area.'

Monday's newspapers all carried similarly certain accounts, though the size of the bomb varied from 400 to 1,000 pounds. On the BBC's morning radio programme, *Today*, the Minister of State for the Armed Forces, Mr Ian Stewart, again spoke confidently of 'the bomb' and its timing for Tuesday's parade. And yet this bomb was a fiction. There was not and never had been a bomb in Gibraltar, neither had the crowded streets of Gibraltar witnessed a gun battle.

At 3.30 p.m. on Monday afternoon, the Foreign Secretary, Sir Geoffrey Howe, rose to make a statement in the House of Commons. No bomb had been found; neither were the suspected terrorists armed. However, Howe added, 'When challenged they [the dead] made movements which led the military personnel operating in support of the Gibraltar police to conclude that their own lives and the lives of others were under threat. In the light of this response, they were shot.' What Howe then went on to say is worth examination, because its confusing mixture of hypothesis and reality echoed through the Gibraltar affair for the next six months and in fact formed the basis of the British government's case at the inquest:

> The suspect white Renault car was parked in the area in which the band of soldiers would have formed for the Tuesday parade. A school and an old people's home were both close by. Had a bomb exploded in the area, not only the fifty soldiers involved in the parade, but a large number of civilians might well have been killed or injured. It is estimated that casualties could well have run into three figures. There is no doubt whatever that, as a result of yesterday's events, a dreadful terrorist act has been prevented. The three people killed were actively involved in the planning and attempted execution of that act. I am sure the whole House will share with me the sense of relief and satisfaction that it has been averted.

The whole House did, for who would not want to prevent a carnage of innocents? When George Robertson, the Labour opposition spokesman, got to his feet, he seemed oblivious to the fact that the carnage would have been wrought by a bomb which in the course of Howe's speech had quietly ceased to exist. Robertson congratulated the military on their 'well-planned operation':

The very fact that this enormous potential car bomb was placed opposite both an old folk's home and a school underlines the cynical hypocrisy of the IRA . . . This House speaks with one voice in condemning unreservedly those in Ireland who seek to massacre and bomb their way to power. These people are evil. They kill and maim and give no heed to the innocents who get in their way. They must be dealt with, if any democratic answer is to be found.

Consider the statements of both men. Howe admits that there was no bomb; at the same time the shooting of three people prevented 'a dreadful terrorist act' because such an act had been planned in the minds of the dead who at some point in the future would have tried to implement it—had they been alive. This could be read as a confession to a lethal pre-emptive strike. Robertson, in reply, is understandably confused by the semantics of what has gone before. The car bomb seems to him still real and a cause for moral outrage; it is only 'potential' because it has not gone off.

Today it may be easy to separate the various elements in this extraordinary fudge, but at the time the government got away with it, aided by further semantic horseplay from the Ministry of Defence, a credulous media and an impolitic volubility from the IRA. We now know from the bomb disposal officer who gave evidence at the inquest that, if members of the British army in Gibraltar had ever imagined Savage's car to contain a bomb, they knew by 7.30 p.m. on Sunday that it certainly did not. And yet throughout that night and the following morning the Ministry of Defence in London cultivated (or, at the very least, did not correct) the impression that a bomb had been found. At 4.45 p.m. on Sunday the Ministry of Defence confirmed that 'a suspected bomb had been found in Gibraltar.' At 9.00 p.m. a statement was issued to the effect that 'military personnel dealt with a suspect bomb.' The following morning the Ministry was still repeating that 'a suspected bomb had been dealt with.'

There is a strong temptation here, a temptation to use the word 'lie'. Writer (and reader), resist it. According to the Ministry of Defence, the phrase 'suspect bomb' or 'suspect car bomb' is 'a term of art'. As the army's bomb disposal officer explained to the inquest it means no more than a car which, for whatever reason, is thought to contain a bomb. Hence you 'find' a suspect bomb by finding a car and suspecting it. Hence you 'deal with' a suspect bomb either by confirming its presence and defusing or exploding it, or by discovering that no bomb exists. Bomb disposal officers are brave men; nobody need mock the terms of their art. But unfortunately neither the British media nor Mr Ian Stewart, a defence minister, quite grasped the subtleties of their definitions. 'Dealt with' so easily became 'defused', while the size of the notional bomb grew in the minds of reporters in Gibraltar whose only source of information was the gossip of excited Gibraltar policemen. (That night, Ronald Sinden, assistant to the deputy governor, was appointed official press spokesman. He said memorably: 'I am the only source of information, and I have no information.')

These 'facts' had a formidable effect on the IRA, and the two statements it issued tried to correct what were rightly perceived to be untruths. The first did it no harm: 'There could have been no gun-battle because the three volunteers were unarmed.' The second immeasurably helped the British government because, four hours before Howe's statement, the IRA admitted that the three had 'had access and control over' 140 pounds of explosives. This was meant to correct reports of bombs six times that size with the consequent potential carnage, in the belief that the British government or media were simply exaggerating the size of a bomb that had actually been found. But of course, as Howe was to admit, no bomb had been found; the IRA, by misunderstanding the radical nature of the lie it was trying to correct, confessed to a bomb thirty hours before the Spanish police found it forty miles away on the Costa del Sol. From the IRA's point of view, an opportunity to embarrass the British government for thirty hours had been wasted.

Little of this information was ever presented to the inquest as evidence—perhaps rightly; much of it is after and outside the facts. But here, only twenty-four hours after the killings, some lessons can be drawn and kept in mind. One, the British government and its servants are no fools. Two, there are already reasons to distrust the British version of events. And three, London, rather than its colonial outpost, Gibraltar, pulls the strings.

3

One day in Gibraltar I tried to buy a map. This was in early May, a couple of months after the killings. Maps are not hard to come by in Gibraltar, in fact the tourist office gives them away, and these are perfectly good if you want to find your way to the feeding grounds of Gibraltar's famous apes, or the Holiday Inn, or any of the bits and pieces of old military science—steam-driven artillery, stout fortifications, labyrinthine tunnels—which are Gibraltar's chief contribution to history. These maps specialize in the past. About the present they are more reticent. Naturally, I didn't expect them to fill in the details of the naval base or the munitions dumps or the copse of radar and radio masts stuck high on the rock above the town; these are contemporary military secrets. But even with ordinary civilian geography they were vague, as though when it came to housing estates and dual carriageways the cartographer had unhooked his jacket from the back of the chair and taken the rest of the day off.

Farrell, Savage and McCann died in the middle of the civilian quarter. Without a good map it was difficult to follow the arguments about who saw them die, from where. I asked a woman in Gibraltar's bookshop about ordnance survey maps: 'They are not available to the public.' Not knowing Gibraltar, I found this hard to believe. Whatever the vices of the British Empire, one of its virtues is the legacy of careful cartography (imperialism needed to be sure of what it owned) still found in the old British capitals of Asia and Africa and even, I am sure, among those forgotten islands—Pitcairn, St Helena and others—which together with Gibraltar, Hong Kong and the Falklands form the rump of the colonial empire.

Eventually somebody suggested the Public Works Department. There I met the chief draughtsman who asked me to choose from a fine selection of maps of different scales. I picked one, and he went off to have it photocopied. Another man approached.

Would this have anything to do with the shootings?

Only indirectly, I said. It was simply a journalistic exercise to show the exact location, and in the interests of accuracy it would be good to work from the best available map.

The man nodded and went away. I heard him making several telephone calls, successively marked by a rising tone of deference. He returned. 'I am sorry but the Attorney-General has refused me permission to sell you a map.'

The Attorney-General himself! This struck me then as the kind of absurd infringement of liberty that might happen in Evelyn Waugh's Africa. But the better I got to know Gibraltar the more typical it seemed. Gibraltarians do not suffer from an over-developed sense of freedom, and this is not just because they are colonials. Their whole identity is antithetical: to be Gibraltarian is *not* to be Spanish; to be free is *not* to be Spanish. Therefore to be free and Gibraltarian is to be British, because Britain is all that stands between them and a successful Spanish reclamation of their rock. Spain is only a mile from the centre of the town, and yet bread is imported from Bristol (it comes frozen, in lorries) and newspapers from London. No Spanish newspapers can be found; nobody in Gibraltar reads *El País*; the local radio and television stations broadcast only in English. And yet Spanish is the first language of the Gibraltarian, who speaks it at home and in the street (and badly only to Spaniards). To judge by their names, many if not most Gibraltarians are as Spanish as any man or woman from Cádiz or Seville. And yet they mock Spain. Echoing the tabloid xenophobia of the mother country ('dago' and 'wop'), they call Spaniards 'slops' and 'sloppies'. Every weekend they drive out to the resorts of the Costa del Sol and then come home to complain. 'Too many slops on the beach today, Conchita.' 'Let's stay on the Rock next weekend, Luís.' Nor do they believe that Spain has changed. To them it will always be Franco's Spain, rich only in cruel policemen and opaque bureaucrats. But surely, I asked a shopkeeper one day, Spain was now prospering, freer, much more democratic? 'Maybe so, but Spaniards don't understand the word freedom like we do. To them it means the freedom to take drugs and screw around, to behave badly, which they couldn't do under Franco. It's not British freedom or democracy like you and I know it.'

Freedom! Democracy! Executive authority in Gibraltar is vested in the Governor, by tradition a retired British military man, who is appointed by the British Foreign and Commonwealth Office 1,200 miles away in London. The Governor represents the Queen and retains direct responsibility for the colony's defence and internal security. A Council of Ministers, drawn from an elected House of Assembly, looks after lesser domestic matters, but even here the Governor is free to poke a finger in: the list of ministers must first be submitted to him for approval, and he can intervene later if he thinks that any of their policies are a threat to the colony's stability.

Few Gibraltarians object to this semi-autocracy. Could a government in distant Madrid deliver more liberty? And in any case to object is to be pro-Spanish, and the colony owes everything, its origins and continued existence, to Britain. Its limited local democracy is a recent invention: not until after World War Two did the civilian population have any say in its colony's affairs. For 200 years its citizens had been there only to serve the British army and navy, who together with the Dutch had seized the fort from Spain in 1704. Nine years later the Treaty of Utrecht ceded it in perpetuity to the conqueror. The local Spanish were expelled and new camp-followers drawn from Malta and Genoa and the Jewry of Morocco. By the nineteenth century, recurrent sieges and the Rock's bold outline, prickling with guns, had found Gibraltar a firm place in the imperial imagination: 'as safe as the Rock of Gibraltar.'

This historic symbolism is still powerful; 'Free since 1713' says the graffiti on Gibraltar's walls, in the same pugnacious red, white and blue as the slogans ('Remember 1690') of Protestant Belfast. But even more potent are the contemporary facts. Today Gibraltar has a civilian population of about 29,000—20,000 Gibraltarians, the rest British or immigrant Moroccan labour—all of whom squeeze into 2.25 square miles of territory, much of it uninhabitably steep (the Rock rises to 1,400 feet), half of it owned by the Ministry of Defence. The Royal Air Force controls the airport and the Royal Navy the harbour while the army spreads out in barracks to the south. Regiments come here after tours of duty in Northern Ireland, in part for rest and relaxation but also to keep in shape for further tours: according to reports, one of the Rock's large caverns contains a mock Ulster village made of wood—a main street, four side-streets, two shops, a Roman Catholic church called St Malachy's, a school and a women's lavatory. What goes on here under artificial light? Raids, sieges and patrols, one assumes, stun bombs thrown into the ladies' loo, the school stormed, sanctuary denied at St Malachy's.

At night the troops come out to play. The usual sights and sounds of a garrison town: rounds of English lager in the Gibraltar Arms, the Olde Rock and the Angry Friar, chips at Mac's fish bar, maybe a disco down at the RAF base. By eleven the military police are cruising down Main Street. By two in the morning only the brain-dead are left, bumping into shop windows, moaning, crying. "Oo you fackin' callin' a cunt, Kevin? You fackin' cunt you.' Gibraltarians do not complain; these lads are their bread and butter, less an ancestral burden than an heirloom. When the novelist Thackeray visited Gibraltar in 1844 what struck him mainly was the sight of befuddled seamen. But the British Mediterranean fleet was long ago disbanded, and these days respectable young Gibraltarian women no longer weight their handbags with stones. Life in a sense has improved.

This then is the town in which Farrell, Savage and McCann spent the last hour or two of their lives. Had they lived and returned and managed to detonate their bomb, then the result would be what British Intelligence knows as 'a spectacular', worth ten times the publicity of ten bombs in Belfast or County Armagh. As it was, they died among memorials to the enemy's history—Farrell and McCann on the pavement of Winston Churchill Avenue, Savage just below King's Lines—having first been watched from the tombstones of Trafalgar Cemetery, the forecourt of the Anglican Cathedral and a small shop called the Imperial Newsagency where Gibraltar queues up for its air-freighted copies of the *Sun*.

4

Of course they had been watched for months.

According to statements made by the Spanish government

soon after the killings, McCann and Savage were first spotted at
Madrid airport arriving on a flight from Malaga on the Costa del Sol
in November 1987. They were travelling under the aliases Reilly
and Coyne. Around this time the Spanish police also detected a
third IRA member in Malaga, a woman—not Mairead Farrell—
who used the alias Mary Parkin. She, along with Savage and
McCann, returned to the Costa del Sol again in February.

In the meantime the Gibraltar authorities had abruptly
cancelled the changing of the guard ceremony scheduled for
Tuesday, 8 December—the guardhouse, they decided, needed
repainting—and did not resume it until 23 February. It was also on
that day, according to British intelligence, that 'Mary Parkin' once
again visited Gibraltar, to attend the ceremony; she returned the
following Tuesday, 1 March. She then disappeared.

Four days later, on Friday, 4 March, McCann and Savage
reappeared for the third time on the Costa del Sol and were joined
there by a second woman, soon identified as Mairead Farrell. All
three came from Belfast, and exhibits produced during the inquest
(a boarding pass, an air ticket and an airline timetable) suggest that
Farrell took three flights to reach Malaga: from Dublin to Brussels
by Aer Lingus, from Brussels to Madrid by Sabena, and then on to
Malaga by an internal Spanish flight. McCann and Savage may well
have come the same way; the man who drove McCann to Dublin
airport was stopped on his way home to Belfast by British troops at
the border on Thursday evening, 3 March. It seems unlikely that
they would risk travelling on the same series of flights on the same
day—very imprudent terrorist behaviour—but with the question of
the exact sequence of their arrival in Malaga the story reaches
another large contradiction.

Of course they had been watched. Or had they?

In the weeks after the killings, there seemed to be no doubt. On
9 March the Spanish Interior Ministry issued a communiqué which
said that the Spanish police had 'maintained surveillance on the
suspects' until they left Spain and entered Gibraltar. On 21 March
Señor Augustín Valladolid, then the senior spokesman for the
Spanish security services, went further. In a briefing to Harry
Debelius, an American correspondent based in Madrid, Valladolid
said that Spain had accepted a commitment in November to follow
the IRA unit and to keep the British informed of its movements. On

6 March, therefore, Savage, driving a white Renault, was followed all the way down the coast road to Gibraltar. To quote the affidavit later sworn by Debelius, Valladolid said that:

> The method of surveillance used was as follows: (a) four or five police cars 'leap-frogged' each other on the road while trailing the terrorists so as not to arouse suspicion; (b) a helicopter spotted the car during part of the route; (c) the police agents were in constant contact with their headquarters by radio; (d) there was observation by agents at fixed observation points along the road.

Debelius's affidavit also states that Valladolid told him that the Spanish police sent 'minute-by-minute details' of the Renault's movements directly to the British in Gibraltar. Later, in a telephone conversation, Valladolid told him that two members of the British security services had also worked with the Spanish surveillance teams in Malaga.

These statements from members of the Spanish government—and many others—are public knowledge.

But: of course they had *not* been watched.

By the time of the inquest, the matter was no longer certain. There were, of course, no Spanish witnesses—not in a Gibraltar court. And every other witness—members of the Gibraltar police, the British military and British intelligence—flatly denied that the three had been watched. Impossible. Their information, they insisted, was limited to a reported sighting of the three in Malaga.

Of course: otherwise how could the bomb—or the car believed to have contained the bomb—have reached the centre of Gibraltar unchecked?

The likely facts are these: the Spanish police followed McCann and Savage, who were both known to them, but either missed or lost Farrell, whom they had never seen before. All three had aliases and false documentation. Farrell flew out of Dublin as Mary Johnson, but entered Gibraltar as Mrs Katherine Alison Smith, née Harper. For two days the Spanish police could not trace her, though by midday on 5 March they at least knew who to look for. Savage and McCann, on the other hand, presented no difficulty. As Señor Valladolid told Tim McGirk of the *Independent* in May: 'We had complete proof that the two Irishmen were going to plant a bomb. We heard them say so.' Under the names Coyne and Reilly, McCann and Savage checked into the Hotel Escandinavia in Torremolinos, a few miles down the coast from Malaga, towards midnight on 4 March and stayed two nights. Farrell did not register, although some women's clothes were found later in the room: she may have stayed with them, or she may have left her luggage there while she drove through Friday and/or Saturday night to collect and deliver the explosives.

Three cars were hired. A man thought to be Savage using the name John Oakes hired a red Ford Fiesta about midday on Friday, 4 March, from a firm in Torremolinos. Spanish police found the car on Sunday evening, a few hours after the shootings, parked in a car-park several hundred yards from the Gibraltar border. Its contents included false documents, a money belt containing £2,000, a holdall covered in dust and soil which looked as though it might have been buried, several pairs of gloves, a dirty raincoat and anorak, tape, wire, screwdrivers and a small alarm clock. The office manager of the car-hire firm retrieved the car and said it had been driven 1,594 kilometres and was covered in mud. A policeman told him that it had been to Valencia and back.

Using the alias of Brendan Coyne, Savage then hired another car, a white Renault 5, from Avis in Torremolinos about eleven on Saturday morning, 5 March. The next day he drove it into Gibraltar and parked it at Ince's Hall, where the band of the Royal Anglian Regiment would leave their bus, form up and fall out again on Tuesday (during the inquest this became known as 'the de-bussing area'). This car became the suspect car bomb. Some time after the three were shot, an army bomb disposal team blew open its bonnet, boot and doors. It contained car-hire literature.

Farrell also hired a car, the third car, using a British driving licence in the name Katherine Alison Smith, from a firm called Marbessol in Marbella, the next large resort down the coast from Torremolinos. Marbessol's manager recalled that she came into the office about 6.30 p.m. on Saturday evening, 5 March, to make a provisional booking and returned about 10.30 a.m. the next morning to collect a white Ford Fiesta. The manager later told a reporter from Thames Televison, Julian Manyon, that she looked exhausted, 'as though she hadn't been to bed.' Spanish police found the car two days after the killings, on Tuesday evening, 8 March, in an underground car-park just off Marbella's main street and about a hundred yards from the Marbessol office. It had been driven less than ten kilometres. It contained 141 pounds of Semtex, a plastic explosive made in Czechoslovakia, wrapped in twenty-five equal blocks; ten kilos of Kalashnikov ammunition; four electrical detonators made by the Canadian CXA company; several Ever-Ready batteries; and two electronic timing units with circuit boards which, according to the evidence of a Ministry of Defence witness at the inquest, bore the same patterns or 'artwork' as previous IRA bombs. The timers had been set for an elapsed time of ten hours forty-five minutes and eleven hours fifteen minutes: a fail-safe device. If set running at, say, midnight on Monday the first would have detonated the bomb at 10.45 a.m. on Tuesday morning. If it failed, the second timer would give the bomb a second chance half an hour later; which represents the difference in time between the Royal Anglian band leaving the bus and preparing to board again.

Events during those few days in Spain, therefore, may well have unfolded like this: Savage hires the red Fiesta and at some point hands it over to Farrell, whom the Spanish police have the least chance of detecting. Savage then meets McCann and the two idle in Torremolinos while Farrell drives 700 kilometres north to Valencia, collects the explosives, and returns. She may have made this journey on Friday night and Saturday, or just possibly (driving hard) on Saturday night and Sunday morning between her two appearances at the car-hire office in Marbella. Then, either on Saturday around 6 p.m. or Sunday around 10 a.m., she parks the red Fiesta and its bomb in the underground car park. At 10.30 a.m. on Sunday she picks up the white Fiesta, takes it for a run round Marbella's one-way traffic system, then parks it underground next to the red Fiesta. She and one of the men transfer the explosives while the third keeps watch. Savage, whom British intelligence insists was 'the expert bomb-maker', checks that the bomb has been safely transferred and then, at about 11.30 a.m., sets out for Gibraltar in his white Renault 5. Farrell and McCann follow a couple of hours later in the red Fiesta, park it, and cross the border on foot. By this hypothesis, Savage is using the white Renault as—in another of the bomb disposal squad's terms of art—'a blocking-car', a car which would hold the parking space in Gibraltar until the white

Fiesta with the bomb was driven into the same position on Monday night.

Given the traffic in Gibraltar, such a precaution makes sense. To make a small diversion into social history: one consequence of the colony's acute land shortage is that most people live in small apartments; one consequence of its military history is that most apartments are owned by the government. Only six per cent of Gibraltar's homes are owner-occupied. Money can't chase property so it chases cars instead. At the most recent count 8,000 households owned 15,000 cars, or 555 cars for every mile of narrow Gibraltarian road. Parking is a problem which 'Mary Parkin' could not fail to have noticed on her reconnaissance trips.

Very little of this information was mentioned at the inquest.

5

The second time I flew to Gibraltar I noticed a man in Club Class reading Doris Lessing's novel, *The Good Terrorist*. He took it up soon after we lifted from Gatwick and didn't put it down again until we were over the Mediterranean for the Gibraltar approach. This was unusual behaviour. Club seats on Gibraltar flights are taken up mainly by off-shore investors and English expatriates who have 'companies' registered in the colony or real estate on the Costa del Sol. Fugitives from British weather and British tax laws, they tend not to be great readers—books not being duty-free.

The man turned out to be a diplomat with the British Foreign Office. A few months later he returned for the inquest. For four weeks he sat in court with a colleague from the Ministry of Defence and at the end of each day both made themselves available to brief the press; sometimes as the equivalent of 'spin-doctors', there to put the best British gloss on the day's proceedings, and sometimes (helpfully) as translators of military or legal jargon. I can't imagine that Lessing's fictional insights into terrorist behaviour played much of a part here. Her characters are muddled, alienated members of the English middle-class whose violent rage against the state springs from domestic roots, smug parents and unhappy childhoods. They are inept at what they do. Nobody in court suggested that Savage, Farrell and McCann were inept. British military and intelligence witnesses spoke of them as 'ruthless', 'fanatical', 'dedicated', 'experienced' and 'professional'. And yet outside the court, in Gibraltar and London, the government's off-the-record conversations stressed their surprising amateurishness. The British had expected professionalism and planned accordingly (so this private argument ran), only to find themselves up against three people who behaved like novices. Had they behaved like professionals—that is, as the British said they expected them to— then their deaths would not have been controversial. Their amateurism had let the British down.

Who were Savage, McCann and Farrell, and how good were they as professional terrorists?

Sean Savage, the unit's technician, was twenty-three and the youngest and least known. He grew up in Catholic West Belfast. When he was four, the houses on the streets around his birthplace were burned down by Protestant mobs. At the age of seventeen, he joined the IRA; according to his obituary in Ireland's *Republican News*, he was 'a quiet and single-minded individual who neither drank nor smoked and rarely socialized,' and who had 'an extremely high sense of personal security.' Savage seems never to have worked, at least outside his business for the IRA, but unusually for West Belfast both his parents have jobs. His family insist that they knew nothing of his involvement with the IRA, though he was arrested (and then released without charge) in 1982. The parents are by all accounts respectable, religious people. His sister Mary engraves crystal in a Belfast factory. According to her, Savage was an enthusiastic cyclist, amateur cook, Gaelic speaker and night-school student of French. He did well at school. His brother has Down's Syndrome and Savage often took care of him. His obituary records: 'His dedication to the struggle was total and unswerving. To his fellow volunteers he was a strong, steadfast comrade, whose sharp and incisive judgement was relied on in tricky situations.'

Daniel McCann, the unit's leader, was thirty and well known to all sides in the Irish conflict. The *Republican News* spoke of him as 'the epitome of Irish republicanism'. He was first arrested as a sixteen-year-old schoolboy and sentenced to six months imprisonment for rioting. He joined the IRA soon after. Between 1979 and 1982 he spent three terms in prison on charges which included possession of a detonator and weapon. Later in 1982 he was arrested and held with Savage and two others after information was passed to the Royal Ulster Constabulary from a man already in their custody. But the charge was dropped and the four released. His family have run a butcher's shop in the Falls Road, West Belfast's main street, since 1905. At the inquest an SAS officer called him 'the ruthless Mr McCann'. His obituary records: 'He knew no compromise and was to die as he had lived, in implacable opposition to Britain's criminal presence in our land.'

Mairead Farrell had become an important public figure in the armed republican movement by the time of her death, aged thirty-one—and perhaps its most important woman. She joined the IRA aged eighteen and went to jail a year later, in 1976, for planting a bomb at the Conway Hotel, Belfast. Of her two male companions on that bombing, one was shot dead by the RUC on the spot and the other died on a prison hunger-strike in 1981. Farrell served ten years in Armagh jail and Maghaberry women's prison and herself became prominent as a hunger-striker, the 'Officer Commanding' other IRA women prisoners and leader of the 'Dirty Protest', smearing excrement on the walls of her cell. After her release in 1986 she spoke at political meetings throughout Ireland and enrolled as a politics undergraduate at Queen's University, Belfast. She defined herself as a socialist; many also saw her as a feminist. Her family are shopkeepers, prosperous by the standards of West Belfast (they own their own house). Neither her parents nor her five brothers have any affiliations with the IRA. Her four brothers are businessmen; a fifth, Niall, is a freelance journalist and activist for the Irish Communist Party, which sets itself apart from the IRA's 'armed struggle'. In a sense Farrell wrote her own obituary in one of her last interviews: 'You have to be realistic. You realize that ultimately you're either going to be dead or end up in jail. It's either one or the other. You're not going to run forever.'

Mary Savage, Niall Farrell and Seamus Finucan, Mairead Farrell's boyfriend, attended the inquest, and sometimes I'd cross the border to their cheap hotel in Spain and meet them for a meal or a drink. They struck me as intelligent and, I think, honest people; it was often easy to share their indignation at what Niall Farrell described as a 'set-up' or a 'fix'. But our conversation had its limits; discussion of the state's morality could not easily be widened to include the moral behaviour of the deceased. Good terrorists? A case might be made for Farrell. Her only known bombing was preceded by a warning; there were no casualties. As for Savage and McCann, we don't know what part their 'dedication' and 'implacable opposition' played in the ending or maiming of life.

But good terrorists in the professional sense? As Farrell had spent most of her adult life in prison and had been free for only eighteen months, it is difficult to see how she could have perfected her trade. Certainly she was careless or superstitious enough to wear a prison medallion—'Good luck from your comrades in Maghaberry'—around her neck when she entered Gibraltar. McCann? His friends describe him as 'charismatic' and 'a natural leader'. But professional? When he was shot, he was clutching a copy of Flann O'Brien's novel, *The Hard Life*. Farrell's bag contained sixteen photocopied pages of a work entitled *Big Business and the Rise of Hitler* by Henry Ashley Turner Junior.

Both had some of the highest profiles within the IRA. To send either of them on a foreign mission which required safe passage through five different border checks and airport controls sounds like ineptitude. To send both smacks of desperation. Soon after their deaths recriminations began to be heard inside the IRA to this effect. But that was in private.

6

The three bodies stayed in Gibraltar for more than a week. First came the autopsy, then the identification by another Farrell brother, Terence, and a representative from Sinn Fein. The embalming posed a problem. Lionel Codali, the undertaker, said that with few staff members at his disposal the process of restoration and preservation would take at least two days. (In Savage's case, though Codali did not say this, there was a great deal to restore.) Eventually they were ready to be air-freighted. But by whom?

Scheduled flights from Gibraltar go only to London; rumours suggested that baggage handlers at both ends, Gibraltar and Gatwick, might refuse to touch the coffins. Irish charter companies excused themselves on grounds of lack of aircraft. At length an English company took the contract. The bodies were loaded by British servicemen from the Royal Air Force and reached Dublin on Tuesday, 15 March.

They were driven north the same evening. Sympathetic republican crowds turned out to see the cortège as it passed through the counties of Dublin, Meath and Louth, but later, over the border, it was stoned by knots of Protestants from the edge of the motorway. That night at a requiem mass for Farrell in Belfast, Father Raymond Murray said that she had died 'a violent death like Jesus . . . she was barbarously assassinated by a gunman as she walked in public on a sunny Sunday afternoon.' On Wednesday, 16 March, several thousand spectators and mourners turned out for the funeral at Milltown Cemetery, Belfast, where the three were to be buried in the corner of the ground reserved for republican martyrs. About 1.15 p.m., as the first coffin was about to be lowered into its grave, a man began to lob grenades and fire a pistol into the crowd. Mourners chased him from the cemetery and on to the motorway nearby. Often he turned to fire at his pursuers, crying: 'Come on, you Fenian fuckers,' and 'Have some of this, you IRA bastards.' A mourner told *The Times*: 'He seemed to be enjoying it. He was taking careful aim and firing at us, just as if he was shooting clay pigeons.' After the crowd caught up with him, he was beaten unconscious and would have been beaten to death had not the police intervened to carry him away. Three men died during the grenade attack; another two people were critically wounded; sixty-six were hurt.

On Saturday, 19 March, another large crowd assembled at Milltown Cemetery to witness the funeral of Kevin Brady, an IRA activist and one of the three killed in the cemetery three days earlier. As the cortège made its way up the Falls Road a Volkswagen Passat drove towards it, stopped, reversed and then got hemmed in by taxis accompanying the funeral. The car contained two British soldiers in civilian clothes, Corporals Derek Wood and David Howes of the Royal Corps of Signals, who were dragged from the car, beaten, stripped and shot dead, amid shouts of 'We have got two Brits.' Spokesmen for the British army said they could think of no reason why Wood and Howes had driven to the funeral, other than misplaced curiosity. Mrs Thatcher described their deaths as, 'an act of appalling savagery . . . there seems to be no depths to which these people will not sink.'

A lethal chain of events which began in Gibraltar on 6 March had ended thirteen days later in Belfast with a total of eight dead and sixty-eight hurt. The last two deaths, however, imprinted themselves on the British imagination in a way the first six never could. They were young British soldiers killed in view of press and television cameras; the most enduring image from that time shows one of their naked carcasses full-length on the ground like something from an abattoir, with a kneeling priest administering the last rites.

It was not a time that encouraged the asking of difficult questions about the killings in Gibraltar. None the less, by the end of the month, Amnesty International announced that it intended to investigate the shootings to establish whether they were 'extrajudicial executions'. The government was contemptuous. Mrs Thatcher told the House of Commons: 'I hope Amnesty has some concern for the more than 2,000 people murdered by the IRA since 1969.' One of her former ministers, Ian Gow, described the investigation as 'a stunt . . . undertaken apparently on the behalf of three terrorists mercifully now dead.' But real government fury had yet to show itself.

The British press had stayed obediently, perhaps slothfully, silent on Gibraltar—this was not one of its more glorious moments. Then in late April Thames Television announced that its current affairs team had made a thirty-minute documentary on the shootings which included eyewitness accounts of how the three had died. The government moved quickly to have it stopped. Sir Geoffrey Howe telephoned the chairman of the Independent Broadcasting Authority to ask him to postpone the programme's transmission until after the inquest. It was the job of the law rather than 'investigative journalism' to throw light on the Gibraltar affair: journalism would simply muddle or prejudice the legal process. We should await a legal verdict, even though Sir Geoffrey Howe himself had not obeyed that stricture when on 7 March he issued his version of events, which had, by its amplification in the press, become the conventional British wisdom.

When the Independent Broadcasting Association resisted Sir

Geoffrey, Tom King, the Northern Ireland Secretary, told Parliament that the programme amounted to 'trial by television'. Mrs Thatcher took up the phrase. 'Trial by television or guilt by accusation is the day that freedom dies,' she told a group of Japanese journalists on the day before the broadcast. When asked if she was furious, as she often is, she replied that her reaction went 'deeper than that'.

The programme, 'Death on the Rock', went out on the evening of 28 April. The response was immediate: an immense uproar, which increased when the BBC, also refusing to bow to government pressure, broadcast a similar investigation a week later in Northern Ireland. Both programmes implied that the government's version of events, as stated by Sir Geoffrey Howe to Parliament on 7 March, was not necessarily complete. Thames Television had found witnesses who said that they had heard no warning before the shots were fired, that McCann and Farrell had their hands up in surrender when they were killed, and that two and possibly all three of them seemed to have been shot again after they fell to the ground. The programme had discovered these witnesses by knocking on the doors of the apartments surrounding the Shell petrol station on Winston Churchill Avenue, the scene of the killings. It is a traditional journalistic method of investigation. It is also a traditional police method, but not one, at that stage, that had been adopted by the Gibraltar constabulary. Several dozen apartments had a good view of the spot where Farrell and McCann died. The programme's researcher, Alison Cahn, found that most of their occupants were reluctant to discuss what, if anything, they had seen on 6 March. Two did, however.

Mrs Josie Celecia said that she was looking from the window of her flat, which faces the petrol station from the other side of Winston Churchill Avenue, when she heard two shots. She turned to look in their direction and then heard four or five more shots as a casually dressed man stood over two bodies.

Mrs Carmen Proetta, whose flat lies 100 yards to the south of the Shell station on the same side of the road, gave a more complete, and even more controversial, picture. She had been at her kitchen window when a siren sounded and several men with guns jumped over the barrier in the middle of Winston Churchill Avenue, and rushed towards a couple who were walking on the pavement near the petrol station. 'They put their hands up when they saw these men with the guns in their hands. There was no interchange of words, there were just shots. And once they [the couple] dropped down, one of the men, this man who still had the gun in his hand, carried on shooting. He bent down and carried on shooting at their heads.'

A third witness, Stephen Bullock, described what he had seen about 150 yards to the south. Bullock, a lawyer, had been walking with his wife and small child when he heard a siren and shots almost simultaneously. He looked in the direction of the sounds, towards the petrol station, and saw a man falling backwards with his hands at shoulder height. 'He was still being shot as he went down.' The gunman was about four feet away. 'I think with one step he could have actually touched the person he was shooting.'

Other evidence from two anonymous witnesses said that Savage had also been shot on the ground, while a retired bomb and ballistics expert with a distinguished army record in Northern Ireland appeared on the programme casting doubt on the possibility that anyone could have believed that Savage's white Renault 5 contained a bomb. According to this expert, George Stiles, it would be obvious to any experienced observer that the Renault was not low enough on its springs—the wheels were not against the wheel-casings—and that therefore the car 'clearly carried no significant weight of explosives.'

The response of the press was curious. Little of its coverage addressed the programme's new evidence. Instead a campaign was begun to discredit the witnesses and the journalists at Thames Television. Two of the government's strongest media supporters—Rupert Murdoch's *Sun* and *Sunday Times*—led the campaign, and the viciousness of their attacks surprised even some of the newspapers' employees. Mrs Carmen Proetta in particular took a mauling. She emerged on the front page of the *Sun* as an anti-British whore ('THE TART OF GIB'), an allegation which had its perilous foundation in the fact that her name had briefly appeared on company documents as a director of a Spanish tourist and escort agency.

The programme emerged as such a powerful challenge to the government and its version of events that the government has not, apparently, forgiven Thames Television. But at the time, the government's complaints wore a nobler face: journalism had no place in the legal process, and that process, as it had said many times before, was entirely a matter for the Gibraltar coroner and magistrate, Mr Felix Pizzarello.

But what had happened to that process? There was still no date fixed for the inquest. Two months went by before the coroner's office finally announced that the inquest would begin on 27 June. For a fortnight or so, this date held good. Then at 11 a.m. on Monday, 27 May, a press spokesman for the prime minister's office announced that the inquest would be indefinitely postponed. The government, said the spokesman, had received this news from Mr Pizzarello over the weekend, adding that the postponement was of course entirely Mr Pizzarello's decision. The government could not interfere with Mr Pizzarello's timetable.

The spokesman, however, was unaware that Pizzarello himself did not know of the decision he had taken. The same morning that the government announced the decision made by Pizzarello over the weekend, Pizzarello was telling Dominic Searle, a reporter on the *Gibraltar Chronicle* and correspondent for the Press Association, that he was considering a postponement—but only considering it. When Searle heard the news from London he went back to the coroner's office, to be told that Pizzarello was still only considering a postponement. Eventually, at 4 p.m., the coroner vindicated Downing Street's prescience and announced an indefinite postponement.

There is a temptation here, a temptation to use the word 'horseshit'. Reader, resist it. Pizzarello had good reason to delay proceedings, and the pressure came from below rather than above. Ten days before, a young Gibraltar woman, Miss Suyenne Perez, had written to the coroner in her capacity as chairwoman of the Gibraltar International Festival of Music and the Performing Arts to remind him that this year's festival was scheduled to begin on 24 June. Four days of it would coincide with the inquest. Perhaps, Miss Perez wrote to the coroner, he would like to consider changing his dates to avoid an undue strain on police resources?

In the event, the festival consisted of one beautiful baby contest, and, in the evening, a number of recitals held in the school halls. Neither the British government nor Pizzarello nor the Gibraltar police ever advanced any other reason for the inquest's postponement. And so the inquest was once again delayed, this time for a further two months, by which time Parliament had gone on holiday—there would be no troublesome questions—and Mrs Thatcher could prepare for a visit to Spain.

7

During late summer a peculiarly local climate overcomes Gibraltar. For several weeks life conducts itself under a thick cloud, while only a mile away Spain sparkles in the sun. Gibraltarians make jokes about this cloud—even our weather is English! They know it as 'the Levanter' and its causes are interesting enough. The prevailing wind in Gibraltar is easterly. From June to September it blows across a thousand miles of warm Mediterranean, gathering moisture on the way, until it strikes the rock's sheer eastern face and soars up 1,400 feet. The air cools rapidly, its moisture becomes vapour, and a dense white cloud tumbles over the rock's escarpment to blot out the sun from the town, which lies in a windless pocket to the west. The effect is spectacular—look up from Main Street towards the ridge and you can imagine a blazing, smoking forest on the other side—but also oppressive. As the colony's historian, John D. Stewart, writes:

> It obscures the sun, raises the humidity to an uncomfortable degree, dims and dampens the town and the ardour and enterprise of everyone in it. It is, inevitably, hot weather—too hot—when this added plague arrives, and now it is hot and humid and without even the benefit of brightness.

It was September, the Levanter season, and we had gathered at last for the inquest. Everybody sweated. The courtroom had a high ceiling from which fans had once been suspended; an effective system of Victorian ventilation helped by the windows high in the walls. But as part of some colonial modernization the fans had been removed, the windows double-glazed and air-conditioning installed. The air-conditioning had broken down.

Sometimes the coroner ordered the doors to be opened; papers would then blow around; the doors would be closed again. Upstairs in the press gallery shirts grew dark from sweat stains.

The court was wood-panelled in the English fashion, brown varnish being sober and traditional, and from the gallery its layout looked like this. Straight ahead and raised above the courtroom floor sat the coroner. A large plaster representation of the royal coat of arms was stuck to the wall above him; the lion and the unicorn, splendidly done up in red, white and blue, picked out in gold, and complete with its legends in courtly French which say that the English monarchs have God and right on their side and that evil will come to those who think it.

To the right sat the eleven members of the jury—all from Gibraltar, all men (women must volunteer for jury service but few do). Counsel shared a bench in the well of the court. On the left, Mr Patrick McGrory, the Belfast lawyer who was representing the families of the dead without a fee. In the middle, Mr John Laws, who represented the British government and its servants in Gibraltar. On the right, Mr Michael Hucker, who represented the soldiers of the Special Air Service Regiment.

The purpose of the inquest was to determine, not guilt or innocence, but whether or not the killing was lawful. The government badly needed the jury to return a verdict of lawful killing. The relatives of the deceased sought to demonstrate that the three had been murdered, and, although dealt with fairly by the coroner, they and their counsel always felt that they were at a disadvantage: inquests, unlike trials, do not require the advance disclosure of witnesses' statements, and so McGrory had no idea what most witnesses would say before they said it. As it was the Crown's inquest, the Crown's counsel read the statement of every witness beforehand. Laws, therefore, could think ahead, while McGrory, always struggling to keep up, had no way of testing evidence he was hearing for the first time against what later witnesses might say.

McGrory was at a disadvantage in other respects. John Laws had been provided with 'public interest immunity certificates' which he invoked whenever the line of inquiry looked as though it might risk 'national security'. So, in the public interest, the inquest learned little about the events in Gibraltar, Spain, Britain or

213

Northern Ireland before 5 March. Nor did it ever discover the true extent of the military and police operation on 6 March, though it clearly involved many more people than appeared in court.

There was some question about who in fact would appear in the first place. Would the SAS testify? Although members of the SAS were servants of the Crown and although the Crown was holding the inquest, the government was, it said, unable to force the soldiers to come to court. Finally—with a curtain round the witness box to protect them from recognition and possible retribution from the IRA—the soldiers, voluntarily, appeared. A total of eighty witnesses passed through the court, but eighteen of them were visible only to the coroner, jury and counsel. These eighteen anonymous witnesses—referred to always by a letter—were drawn from, in addition to the SAS, MI5, Special Branch and the Gibraltar Police.

Soldier A was clearly working-class and from the south of England—perhaps London. This much could be deduced from his accent. He was also the one who fired the first shot—at Danny McCann on Winston Churchill Avenue. Soldier B was standing next to Soldier A, and subordinate to him. Soldier B was the first to shoot Mairead Farrell.

Down the street were Soldiers C and D. They were also working-class but from the north: Soldier C was probably from Lancashire. He was the first one to shoot Sean Savage. Soldier D, his subordinate, then began firing.

Two teams, then: Soldier A and Soldier B, Soldier C and Soldier D. Other teams were on the ground—the inquest heard of soldiers at the airport—but there was no way of knowing their exact number. The two 'known' teams reported to a tactical commander, Officer E, who was in constant touch with them via radio. Officer E reported in turn to Officer F, who was the overall commander of the military operation. Both officers spoke as though they had attended public schools.

Officer F was also assisted by a bomb-disposal expert, an Officer G. This, then, made up the SAS team:

Soldier A: the first to shoot Danny McCann.
Soldier B: the first to shoot Mairead Farrell.
Soldier C: the first to shoot Sean Savage.
Soldier D: Soldier C's subordinate.

Officer E: the tactical commander of the two teams of soldiers.

Officer F: the overall military commander.

Officer G: the bomb-disposal expert.

There was also Mr O, a senior figure in British intelligence whose information instigated the entire operation. But in addition to the SAS there was a large number of 'watchers', in all likelihood drawn from MI5. At the trial their initials were H, I, J, K, L, M, and N. It is probable that there were many more watchers. And finally, although most of the Gibraltar police testified without the curtain, there were three who sheltered behind it: Policeman P, Policeman Q and Policeman R.

The visible witnesses comprised the following: twenty-four members of the the Gibraltar police; twelve experts on pathology and ballistics—seven from the London Metropolitan Police and two from the army; a map-maker from the Gibraltar Public Works Department; and twenty-five people who were, by accident, close to the scene of the killings. But these twenty-five people included five who worked for the Gibraltar Services Police guarding military installations, one who was an off-duty member of the ordinary Gibraltar police, one who was a former Gibraltar policeman, one who worked for the Ministry of Defence, one whose father was in the Gibraltar police, and three who worked for various branches of the Gibraltar government. No more than sixteen witnesses out of seventy-eight, therefore, could be said to be completely independent of either the British government or the administration of its dependent territory.

McGrory also had a problem with money. He had given his services free and had little to spare. The legal authorities in Gibraltar, meanwhile, had decided to charge ten times the usual rate for the court's daily transcripts. Four days before the inquest began they raised the price from 50p to £5 per page—which amounted to between £400 and £500 per day. McGrory couldn't afford it and instead relied on longhand notes made by a barrister colleague from Belfast. McGrory was the only person in court who wanted to ask awkward questions of the official account. But for all these reasons his ability to ask awkward questions was sometimes severely limited.

8

Over the next few weeks I sometimes wondered what Farrell, Savage and McCann made of Gibraltar during their last few hours there. Did they notice, for example, the number of fit young men in sneakers and jeans wandering aimlessly about? Did they realize that few of them were ever far away?

I wonder if they spotted the two young men lounging in the Trafalgar Cemetery. They were Soldier C and Soldier D. They were the two men who would kill Sean Savage. When Farrell looked into the Imperial Newsagency, did she see a man suddenly turn his back? He was Soldier B. Did she glimpse his face, even briefly? He was the man who would kill her. Later, walking down Line Wall Road, looking over her shoulder from time to time (which, we heard, she did frequently), did she think that the two men hurrying behind her were vaguely familiar? They were, once again, Soldiers C and D.

What about Savage? There was the chap who passed him in Lovers' Lane. He was Policeman P of the Gibraltar police. They stared at each other, or, as Policeman P would express it to the court, he and Savage made 'eye-to-eye contact'. Savage had been in town at least ninety minutes longer than the others, doubling back on his tracks, suddenly stopping and watching at the end of alley-ways. Around two o'clock, did he see the fellow hanging about outside the Anglican Cathedral? That was Watcher H of MI5, who likewise spent the afternoon doubling back on his tracks, suddenly stopping at the end of alley-ways. According to Watcher H, Savage employed 'very subtle anti-surveillance techniques.' All three, he said, were 'highly alert and sensitive . . . to all the movements and events that were happening around them.'

The authorities in Gibraltar had been waiting for Savage and McCann, if not Farrell, for weeks and possibly months. The source of their information was Mr O, a senior British intelligence officer and specialist in counter-terrorism and the IRA. Mr O told the court that his representative in Gibraltar (who never appeared as a witness) had briefed the governor, the commissioner of police and military officers with details of the IRA's intention: the time and the target, the method (car-bomb), the kind of explosives that would be used (Semtex) and the names of Savage and McCann. When these details were passed on to Gibraltar's commissioner of police, Mr Joseph Luís Canepa, Canepa then requested military assistance; the assistance would turn out to be an unspecified number of troops from the Special Air Service Regiment which specializes in covert anti-terrorist operations—most famously ambushes—in Northern Ireland.

An advisory group was then established, comprising Canepa, two of his most senior policemen, and the principal parties from Britain: Officer G, the bomb-disposal expert; Officer E, the SAS tactical commander; Officer F, the overall military commander; as well as intelligence officers from MI5. Together they devised a strategy that can be summarized as 'arrest, disarm, defuse.' Secrecy was paramount. According to Police Commissioner Canepa, very few members of the Gibraltar police force knew of the operation. A secret operational headquarters was set up (probably in the Governor's Residence on Main Street, though the location was never revealed to the inquest). There, at midnight, between 5 and 6 March, a meeting of police, military and intelligence officers was told that the three suspects were in Spain and that they could be expected to arrive during the next forty-eight hours.

A secret operational order was issued.

Soldiers and police were briefed about how they would put the order into effect. First, the offenders would be arrested, 'using minimum force'; second, they would be disarmed and their bomb defused; then evidence would be gathered for a court trial. SAS soldiers would make the arrests and hand over the suspects to armed Gibraltar policemen.

By this stage, the operation had a code-name, 'Operation Flavius'. The order for Operation Flavius had many appendices, the most vital being the rules of engagement. The written instructions that Officer F, the overall military commander, was meant to obey included the following:

USE OF FORCE
You and your men will not use force unless requested to do so by the senior police officer(s) designated by the Gibraltar police commissioner; or unless it is necessary to do so in order to protect life. You and your men are

217

not then to use more force than is necessary in order to protect life . . .

OPENING FIRE

You and your men may only open fire against a person if you or they have reasonable grounds for believing that he/she is currently committing, or is about to commit, an action which is likely to endanger your or their lives, or the life of any person, and if there is no other way to prevent this.

FIRING WITHOUT WARNING

You and your men may fire without a warning if the giving of a warning or any delay in firing could lead to death or injury to you or them or any other person, or if the giving of a warning is clearly impracticable.

WARNING BEFORE FIRING

If the circumstances in [above] paragraph do not apply, a warning is necessary before firing. The warning is to be as clear as possible and is to include a direction to surrender and a clear warning that fire will be opened if the direction is not obeyed.

Those were the rules. Here, once again, are the facts. Farrell, Savage and McCann were unarmed; the car Savage had driven into Gibraltar did not contain a bomb; all three were shot dead. Can the facts be made to square with the rules? Can the facts be reconstructed or revealed in a new light, as it were, which would make their pattern on 6 March conform with the law? The recent history of Northern Ireland supplies an answer.

9

Soldiers of the SAS were first dispatched to Northern Ireland in 1976 by the then Secretary of State for Northern Ireland, Merlyn Rees. This year Rees admitted that their deployment had as much to do with public relations as counter-terrorism: the Labour government needed to be seen to be 'getting on top of terrorism', and the piratical, daredevil reputation of the regiment, familiar only to students of late colonial counter-insurgency (Malaya, Borneo, Aden), might therefore be fostered to appease public concern. 'Who Dares Wins,' says the regimental motto. The SAS could be expected to strike first.

Two years later, on 11 July 1978, an SAS unit shot and killed a sixteen-year-old boy, John Boyle, at a cemetery near his home in County Antrim. The previous day Boyle had discovered an arms cache in the cemetery and told his father, who then informed the Royal Ulster Constabulary. The RUC passed on the information to the army, who then 'staked out' the cemetery with soldiers from the SAS. The next day young Boyle was cutting hay in a field near the cemetery and at about ten in the morning went back to see if the arms were still there. The SAS opened fire. Boyle's father, meanwhile, had been warned by the RUC about the stake-out. He ran to the graveyard to look for his son and was joined by Boyle's elder brother, who had also been haymaking in another field. The SAS arrested both men. The army's press office quickly issued a statement: 'At approximately 10.22 a.m. this morning near Dunloy a uniformed military patrol challenged three men. One man was shot; two men are assisting police enquiries. Weapons and explosives have been recovered.'

The SAS version of events did not please the RUC. The Boyles were a Catholic family and therefore an unusual and prized source of important information. The SAS had now shot one of the family dead. In its press statement, the police denied the army's implication that the Boyles were connected with terrorism, prompting a second army statement confessing to inaccuracies in the first: 'Two soldiers saw a man running into the graveyard. They saw the man reach under a gravestone and straighten up, pointing an Armalite rifle in their direction. They fired five rounds at him. The rifle was later found with its magazine fitted and ready to fire.'

There had been no challenge—a warning would have been 'impracticable'.

Eight months later, in the wake of a public outcry caused by the publication of the pathologist's report, two SAS soldiers were charged with murder. Evidence at their trial showed that the rifle had not been loaded, contrary to the army's second statement, and the judge was unable to decide if Boyle had ever picked it up. He concluded that the army had 'gravely mishandled' the operation and that the only SAS soldier to give evidence—one of the two charged—was an 'untrustworthy witness' who gave a 'vague and unsatisfactory' account. The two were found not guilty none the less. Their 'mistaken belief' that they were in danger, said the judge, was enough to acquit them.

O ver the past fifteen years many other killings in Northern Ireland have hinged in court on this question of 'mistaken belief' and the subsequent use of 'reasonable force'. Perhaps the most famous is the case of Patrick McLoughlin, who was shot dead with two other unarmed men as they tried to rob a bank in Newry in 1971. McLoughlin's widow, Olive Farrell, sued the Ministry of Defence for damages in the Northern Ireland High Court, but the jury decided that McLoughlin was to blame for his own death. It had been persuaded by the argument that British troops, in a stake-out or ambush similar to the one that killed Boyle, had shot three men because their commanding officer had suspected, 'with reasonable cause' (though wrongly), that the three were trying to plant a bomb which would endanger life. Shooting was the only practicable, and therefore reasonable, means of arrest. As Lord Justice Gibson, the Northern Ireland judge later to be killed by a republican bomb, commented:

> In law you may effect an arrest in the vast extreme by shooting him [the suspect] dead. That's still an arrest. If you watch Wild West films, the posse go ready to shoot their men if need be. If they don't bring them back peaceably they shoot them and in the ultimate result if there isn't any other way open to a man, it's reasonable to do it in the circumstances. Shooting may be justified as a method of arrest.

The case of Farrell *versus* the United Kingdom was appealed unsuccessfully in the House of Lords and went eventually to the European Commission on Human Rights, where the British government settled out of court in 1984 by paying Farrell £37,500. The payment ensured that the commission's ruling remains confidential, though the British government's submission to the commission has been published. Britain argued that the jury in the Farrell case had been directed correctly because it had been told that it would be unreasonable to cause death 'unless it was necessary to do so in order to prevent a crime or effect the arrest;' and that the concepts of 'absolutely necessary' and 'reasonable' were the same thing when it came to killing a person believed to be a terrorist bomber.

'Belief', 'believed', 'reasonable'. The same words appear in Operation Flavius's rules of engagement. The inquest heard them with dripping regularity. Out of the graveyards of Ulster, one may suspect, reasonably, came the bones of the government's legal case in Gibraltar; a case, like Boyle's and McLoughlin's, of mistaken belief.

10

Could there really have been a bomb activated by a button?

In the months preceding the inquest, the *Sunday Times* became essential reading if only because its reports seemed to reflect so reliably the official leaks that served to strengthen the government's original story: that Farrell, McCann and Savage had all made 'suspicious movements'—suspicious enough to justify shooting the three of them: either they were going for guns or they were about to detonate a bomb with a radio-controlled device. That they had neither guns nor radio-controlled devices obviously diminished the credibility of the government's story, which was diminished further following the statements made for the Thames Television programme by bomb expert George Stiles: that he had never known the IRA to explode a radio-controlled bomb without a view of the target, and that it was unlikely in the extreme that the kind of transmitter used by the IRA could have been sophisticated enough to send a signal a mile from the bomb with buildings in between.

Nevertheless, on 8 May, ten days after the programme, the *Sunday Times* supplied an answer of sorts (REVEALED: WHY THE SAS SHOT THE IRA). According to military sources, the SAS had 'secret intelligence which convinced them that the gang was able to detonate a bomb by using a sophisticated remote-control device.' In the event, the inquest heard of no sophisticated remote-control device. But 'sophisticated' was not the keyword in the *Sunday Times* report. The keyword was 'convinced'. In the face of the apparent facts (no bomb, no devices, no gun) and the Thames

Television programme, the government's case rested on the SAS's conviction that McCann, Farrell and Savage *could* have been carrying radio-controlled devices.

At the inquest Mr O, the senior intelligence officer from London, admitted that while so much of his information had been flawless—names, date, times—he had blundered in three respects: first, the three suspects were not, as he had predicted, armed; second, as he had not predicted, they had used a blocking-car; and third 'when the car bomb was eventually discovered in Marbella it did not contain a radio-controlled device, it contained a timer.'

Why had he been so sure about a radio-controlled bomb?

Because Mr O had overrated the morality of the IRA. The bombing at Enniskillen on 8 November 1987 was central to Mr O's thinking: eleven civilians had been killed and fifty wounded at an Armistice Day parade, eliciting so much protest from so many different parts of the Irish community, north and south, that it had shaken the IRA, and the organization had apologized for 'a mistake'. The bomb, it implied, had gone off at the wrong time. Mr O assumed that IRA would not run the same risk of civilian casualties in Gibraltar, and radio-control was the only way to ensure that the bomb was exploded when the bombers were sure it would destroy the intended target—the British troops. It was unlikely, Mr O said in court, that the IRA would use a timing device, 'because, once a timer is started, it is virtually impossible to stop it [unless the bombers] go back to the bomb and actually disarm it, which is a highly dangerous procedure.'

The only fact that Mr O, or anyone else, could summon to support the assumption that there would be a radio-controlled device was in the discovery by Belgian police on 21 January of a car containing a large amount of Semtex, four detonators and 'equipment for a radio detonation system' of a kind familiar in Northern Ireland. For reasons never disclosed, Mr O assumed the Gibraltar bomb would be of a similar type.

McGrory was puzzled by the statement made by Mr O that a radio-controlled bomb would be 'safer' for the terrorists because they could get away. Wouldn't some form of timer be just as safe for them?

'Yes,' said Mr O, 'but if the parade had been cancelled at the last moment because it rained, which we understood was a possibility, there would have been absolutely no way of reversing the bomb. It would have been set and would have exploded willy-nilly, and the people who would have been injured and killed would not have been military personnel.'

Mr O's answer contained a dramatic implication which went unnoticed at the time, because McGrory, imagining that Mr O thought the bombers intended to detonate their radio-controlled device from Spain, went on to ask Mr O if he had ever heard of a case in which the IRA had exploded such a bomb from such a distance, without 'line of sight' of the target. Mr O said he had not; in fact the army never believed that the IRA would detonate its bomb from Spain in the first place. The Army believed it would be detonated in Gibraltar, with a clear view of the target. What would then be the point of radio-control? To avoid civilian casualties the bombers would need to watch the target. They would need to be, as it turned out, high on the Rock to the east of the car-park at Ince's Hall, hemmed in by buildings and walls on its other three sides.

The bomb-disposal expert, Officer G, and his counsel, Michael Hucker, explained:

Michael Hucker: What would the position on the Renault be? The bomb is planted on the Sunday; the terrorists walk north and stay in Spain. One of them comes back on the Tuesday morning at about ten o'clock and goes to the Rock with a pair of binoculars and one of those [indicating a radio transmitter-receiver]. What would he be able to do?

Officer G: He would be able to maximize the effectiveness and the use of his bomb because he could wait until the band was assembled *in toto*, in that nice clear area of the Ince's Hall car-park. He could wait until they had formed up and from the housing estate [up on the Rock] he could then press the transmit button and destroy them all.

This is the terrorists conforming to what might be called the Dr Jekyll hypothesis. This is the terrorists showing a high regard for the sanctity of civilian life by putting their own lives at considerable risk, entering one of the world's most heavily defended and patrolled military outposts—not once, but twice. They leave a car-bomb in an obvious place for two days, risking the chance that it will be detected, defused and the area staked out. And then, assuming that it has not been detected or defused or the area staked out, they rush to reach Gibraltar's only exit, one and a half miles away, before the authorities close the border in the wake of a massive explosion.

B ut, apart from its improbability, the Dr Jekyll hypothesis contains a serious flaw. If the bombers are prepared to take such care to protect innocent people that they will blow up only a precise military target at only a precise time on a Tuesday afternoon, how are they such a threat to life on the preceding Sunday that they need to be killed? The answer is in the Mr Hyde hypothesis, revealed to the court by Officer F, the SAS military commander of the operation. According to Officer F, it was expected that Farrell, Savage and McCann would carry radio-detonating devices so that, if their operation was 'compromised'—that is, if they thought they were about to be arrested—they would explode the bomb at any time, whatever the consequences to civilian life. In court, McGrory tried to unravel the thinking.

McGrory: Isn't that [the Hyde hypothesis] quite contrary to the other supposition, or deduction, that in fact their anxiety after Enniskillen and all that would be to avoid civilian casualties?

Officer F: Yes, but that's two different deductions. There's one deduction . . . which is that in their terms the perfect operation is where they can use the radio-controlled device in theory to minimize the number of casualties. But the other supposition is that when they are cornered a different set of factors pertain, in my opinion, and when cornered they will have no qualms about either resorting to weapons or pressing a button, knowing that the bomb was there . . . they'd achieve some degree of propaganda success, apart from casualties, of exploding a bomb in the centre of Gibraltar.

McGrory: I'm sorry, I can't follow that, because, if the submission was that Enniskillen caused a propaganda disaster of great magnitude for them, why should they cause another propaganda loss like that, not a propaganda gain that you are talking about?

Officer F: In my opinion, they are adept at turning disaster into triumph in their own propaganda terms, and therefore, if they could claim that they had got a bomb into Gibraltar, that they had . . . successfully exploded it in Gibraltar, I believe that they would claim that to be a propaganda success and would try and derive credit and publicity from it.

McGrory: Propaganda success that had emulated Enniskillen, which was the greatest propaganda disaster? Surely that can't be right?

Officer F: I believe it is.

The jury was being asked to accept that, an hour or so before McCann, Farrell and Savage were killed, the authorities had come to believe the following: that the three would use a car-bomb to be detonated by radio on Tuesday morning; that the car itself was expected to arrive on Monday evening; that a car arrived instead on Sunday which the authorities nevertheless believed to be a car-bomb rather than a blocking-car; that the three bombers would leave and that one (or more) of them would return on Tuesday; that each time the bombers crossed the border and its immigration and customs controls they would be armed and in possession of detonating devices; and that, finally, Savage, using an Irish passport in his known pseudonym of Brendan Coyne, had not been spotted driving the Renault over the border despite the fact that British surveillance teams and the Spanish border police were awaiting his arrival.

This last apparent mistake—the failure to spot Savage as he crossed the border—was crucial to the government's case. Otherwise it would have to explain why it had allowed Savage to drive a car suspected of containing a bomb into the middle of Gibraltar. The lack of surveillance in Spain and hints of some Mediterranean sloppiness at the border itself were the favourite explanations (Charles Huart was the detective constable posted to the border that day to check the passport of everyone who entered, but somehow Savage managed to drive through).

But was it a mistake, an accident? One witness thought not. According to Detective Chief Inspector Joseph Ullger, the head of Gibraltar's Special Branch, the authorities 'were concerned to gather evidence . . . Members of the [British] security service had said that they don't normally give evidence in court . . . so the [police] commissioner spelled it out that evidence was absolutely vital for the subsequent trial of the terrorists.'

McGrory: You said the only way for the operation to succeed was to allow the terrorists to come in?

Ullger: We had the police officers who were going to identify these people, SAS people . . . to assist us in the arrest, so I did not see problems at all. It would have been a problem if we'd told the police officers on duty at the frontier because unfortunately word would have got around . . . and I think there was an absolute need for extreme confidentiality.

McGrory: But you told the Spanish officers?

Ullger: Yes . . . the Spaniards were told because we required the technical advantages, facilities, which they had with computers, simply because of that.

McGrory: But you didn't tell the officers on the Gibraltar side, even to look for a passport in the name of Coyne?

Ullger: No sir, we did not.

Only two conclusions are possible from Ullger's testimony: either the Gibraltar authorities did not seriously believe Savage's car contained a bomb, or that they did, and for several hours risked the lives of Gibraltar's population so that they might gather evidence and make three arrests (remembering Lord Justice Gibson's definition of the word), which legal precedent had established as lawful, and which domestic or international opinion would hardly have found controversial given the presence of a large bomb parked near a school and a Jewish old people's home. Could there really have been a bomb activated by button? The question, finally, was immaterial.

11

But what if Savage's car contained a bomb?

Apparently undetected at the border, Savage then parked his car some time between noon and 1 p.m. Some understanding of the operation awaiting him is suggested by the number of people who spotted him *once* he had entered the town centre.

Watcher N was one of a number of people from MI5 who were meant to study the target area, the car-park outside Ince's Hall, where the bomb was expected. Watcher N said that he had a 'good view of the area, a very good view.' At 12.45 a white Renault 5 pulled into the car-park; the driver was a young man, who remained in the car for two or three minutes. A man was later seen to be wandering near the car-park, and Watcher N was asked to check his identity. He discovered that the man was the driver of the Renault 5 and that it was Sean Savage. Watcher N sent his information by radio to the operations room at 2.10 p.m., and then followed Savage 'for a considerable period.' Savage walked up and down the lanes off Main Street, stopping every now and then, 'trying to draw out stares,' to see if he was being followed. At about 3 p.m., he saw McCann and Farrell who were met by Savage. They were about 150 yards from the car.

Albert Viagas, a Gibraltar constable, was also watching the target area from the offices of Hambros Bank at one end of the car-park. Several other watchers had gathered in the same building. Viagas had two cameras and a radio—his job was to record all movements within the target zone. He did not see Savage drive in, but remembered hearing that at 12.30 p.m. a radio message had said that he had parked. A member of the security forces had commented that 'the driver had taken time and fiddled with something between the seats.' Viagas noted that the man reappeared between 2.00 and 2.30 p.m., walked away and then reappeared at 2.50 with the other two suspects. The three looked at the car and then disappeared again. Headquarters wanted the identities of the suspects confirmed, which the surveillance officers working beside Viagas were able to do: the three were McCann, Farrell and Savage. There were asked to provide further confirmation by a closer inspection, which was duly done, with the suspects positively identified by 3.25 p.m., the time the three returned to their car.

Watcher H of MI5 told the court that he first saw Savage about 2 p.m., when a radio message told him that Savage was approaching his position outside the Anglican Cathedral. He saw Savage stop at the tourist office and look at the notice-board and its diary of local events. He identified him 'with no problem at all,' and then, like Watcher N, began his tour of the alley-ways dogging Savage's heels.

About the same time, Policeman P of the Gibraltar police spotted Savage and they exchanged glances in Lovers' Lane.

By 2 p.m. Savage was being watched by officers of the military, the police and British Intelligence. There were minute-by-minute reports of his progress round Gibraltar. For more than an hour several of these agents had sat studying the car that was meant to contain a bomb of terrible potential. Could they really have believed that a bomb was there in the boot? If so, would they have sat around so casually studying it? If so, would they have done so little to protect the civilian population? After the suspects were shot, it was at least thirty minutes before anyone was warned of a potential bomb, and the first instructions to clear the area were haphazard and slow. If it was reasonable to believe that the Renault contained a bomb, then surely the people who believed it behaved unreasonably. And if it was reasonable, wouldn't somebody have told the man in charge? Until nearly 3 p.m. Police Commissioner Canepa knew nothing about Savage and his car.

12

Canepa made a good impression in the witness box; silver-haired, silver-moustached, quietly spoken, he appeared a round and paternal figure. Fighting terrorism was not his game. None the less the rules of Operation Flavius put him in control, no matter that almost every aspect of the operation—its intelligence, its watchers, its troops, its technology, even the rules themselves—had arrived by aircraft from London. Officer F and Officer E swore he was in control ('I think,' Officer F said in his plummy accent, 'that the chances of me hoodwinking the commissioner are about as good as selling ice-cream to Eskimos'), and Canepa himself grew tetchy when McGrory suggested otherwise. Indeed he seemed to believe he was still in control during the twenty-five minutes when, by his own admission, he had clearly signed control over to Officer F. But that happened later in the afternoon. For most of the day Joseph Luís Canepa was nominally in control of at least a dozen SAS men, an unspecified number of British intelligence operatives, 230 Gibraltarian police and a secret operations or 'ops' room that had been set up to co-ordinate the entire venture.

In control, but rather badly informed. Part of the trouble lay in the sophisticated radio system the military had imported for the operation. The system had two networks—tactical for the SAS soldiers, surveillance for the MI5 watchers—both of which were controlled from the ops room. It was clever, versatile equipment. The watchers and soldiers on the streets could switch into each other's networks; they had tiny microphones stuck to their collars and even smaller ear-pieces stuck in their ears; to transmit they simply pushed a button on their wrist-watches and mumbled into their shirts.

It was unfortunate that Commissioner Canepa could not hear a word. Officer E and Officer F swore that he could if he had wanted to—the information was audible in the ops room. But Canepa, who gave his evidence first, said that all the tactical and surveillance business was conducted by operators with ear-phones, who sat at different desks.

In any case, at 12.30 p.m. Canepa left the ops room and went home for lunch, leaving the acting deputy police commissioner, George Colombo, temporarily in command. It was of course at about that same time that Sean Savage was parking his car in the Ince's Hall car-park, but Canepa must have just missed being informed. So, too, however, did his deputy Colombo. In fact the military and surveillance officers neglected to tell Colombo about Savage for more than two hours.

At 2.30 p.m. Colombo did learn that two suspects believed to be McCann and Farrell had crossed the border. He telephoned Canepa, who stayed at lunch. Then at 2.50 p.m. Colombo was at last informed Savage was in town as well and that he had met McCann and Farrell; all three had been seen looking at the car: 'It was highly suspected that it was a car bomb.' He telephoned Canepa again, and this time the commissioner dismissed prospects of a prolonged siesta and made his way back to the operations room.

What happened in the operations room during the next forty minutes is far from clear, but it would seem that there were some differences of opinion between the police, Canepa and Colombo, and the military, SAS Officer E and Officer F. Under the rules of Operation Flavius the SAS soldiers on the ground had to receive control from the police before they could make their arrests. This required Canepa or his appointed deputy to sign a document which read:

> I have considered the terrorist situation in Gibraltar and have been fully briefed on the military plan with firearms. I request that you proceed with the military option which may include the use of lethal force for the preservation of life.

Canepa or his deputy would be expected to give this to Officer F, who would give the go-ahead to Officer E, the tactical commander of the troops on the ground. After the arrests had been made, Officer F would return control to the police by signing a second form:

> A military assault force completed the military option in respect of the terrorist ASU [active service unit] in Gibraltar and returns control to the civil power.

In the event, it took some time before Canepa finally signed the first document and gave the SAS the control it wanted: it was not in fact until 3.40 p.m., about forty minutes after all three suspects had been seen together and positively identified by numerous watchers.

During the inquest Canepa always insisted that there was no pre-arranged or pre-determined point of arrest, but questions were bound to arise—and perhaps were anticipated—about the forty-minute delay. According to Canepa an arrest had 'nearly been made' before he got to the ops room at 3.00 p.m., when Colombo was still in charge. Soldier A and Soldier B, however, said in court that control had been passed to them twice before 3.40 p.m., and was twice withdrawn.

Why was it withdrawn? Canepa and Colombo said that on the first occasion (they denied a second or third) that, from the direction the suspects were walking, the people in the operations room thought they were not leaving the car after all, that they were going back. At the time, Officer E, along with Soldier A and Soldier B, said the same thing: permission for an arrest had been granted and then rescinded. Real doubt at this moment seems to have existed about a bomb in the Renault.

Soldier C and Soldier D told a different story. Between 2.50 and 3.00, they were in Trafalgar Cemetery, about a minute's walk from the car-park, when the three suspects strolled past. Officer E told Soldiers C and D to get out of the area and make for the airport. It is not clear why; ten or fifteen minutes later, they heard on the radio that Soldiers A and B had been given control for the first time and had been asked to 'apprehend the terrorists,' who were, by then, returning to their car. Soldiers C and D were told to turn back. And, as they did so, control was then withdrawn.

Why this reluctance to allow the military to make its arrests? The evidence suggests that it had nothing to do with the direction in which the three suspects may or may not have been walking. It was because Canepa had returned to the ops room. According to Colombo, one of his chief's priorities was to order that the suspects be 'formally identified.' No watcher or soldier was in any doubt about their identities by then—even Colombo thought they were 'eighty per cent certain'—but none the less two watchers left the hide-out in the Hambros Bank and confirmed the identities of the three around 3.25 p.m.

Soon after, the three began to walk north down Main Street, suggesting to Officers E and F that they were leaving the car behind and making for the border (an oddly certain conclusion: they could simply have been making for the centre of town for a drink). According to Officer E and his soldiers in the field, control again passed to them and was again rescinded, this time more swiftly than before, because, in the words of Officer E, 'The police commissioner wanted to be one hundred per cent sure of the identities of the three terrorists before any arrest was made.' Canepa seems to have been a troubled man; by the account of other witnesses he had been requesting and receiving confirmations of identity for about twenty minutes by now. And yet Colombo's 'eighty per cent' would have been more than good enough for most policemen in most circumstances, and his military and intelligence advisors, who knew much more about Irish terrorists than he did, seemed absolutely sure. What could have been troubling the commissioner? Wrongful arrest? Surely not; three badly scared tourists would have been the only result. Unless, of course, they were to be arrested in Lord Justice Gibson's sense of the word.

231

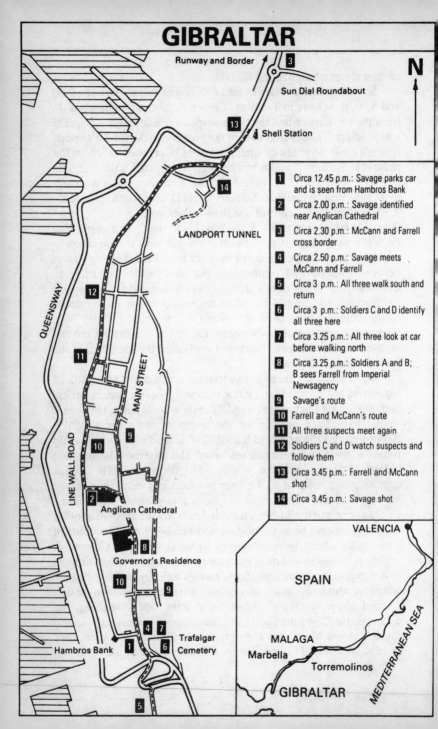

GIBRALTAR

Runway and Border

N

Sun Dial Roundabout

Shell Station

LANDPORT TUNNEL

QUEENSWAY

MAIN STREET

LINE WALL ROAD

Anglican Cathedral

Governor's Residence

Hambros Bank

Trafalgar Cemetery

1 Circa 12.45 p.m.: Savage parks car and is seen from Hambros Bank

2 Circa 2.00 p.m.: Savage identified near Anglican Cathedral

3 Circa 2.30 p.m.: McCann and Farrell cross border

4 Circa 2.50 p.m.: Savage meets McCann and Farrell

5 Circa 3 p.m.: All three walk south and return

6 Circa 3 p.m.: Soldiers C and D identify all three here

7 Circa 3.25 p.m.: All three look at car before walking north

8 Circa 3.25 p.m.: Soldiers A and B; B sees Farrell from Imperial Newsagency

9 Savage's route

10 Farrell and McCann's route

11 All three suspects meet again

12 Soldiers C and D watch suspects and follow them

13 Circa 3.45 p.m.: Farrell and McCann shot

14 Circa 3.45 p.m.: Savage shot

VALENCIA

SPAIN

MEDITERRANEAN SEA

MALAGA

Marbella

Torremolinos

GIBRALTAR

13

Events began to move quickly.

Soldier C and Soldier D, having almost got to the airport, now returned towards the centre and were sheltering behind the Mobil petrol station in Line Wall Road. The three suspects passed walking towards the border. Farrell kept looking over her shoulder. Soldier C and Soldier D began to follow. For the next few minutes soldiers and suspects were in sight of each other. Soldier C and Soldier D were wearing loose shirts, casually covering the nine-millimetre Browning pistols stuck in their trouser waistbands.

At 3.40 p.m. Canepa signed his paper and gave it to Officer F who handed it to Officer E, who then devolved control to his men in the field. According to their evidence, the time and place of arrest were now entirely in their hands. Soldier A and Soldier B took a short-cut through the Landport Tunnel; Soldier C and Soldier D continued walking along the road; both ways were about to meet at the complicated junction where the town of Gibraltar draws together its few roads and sends them forward towards Spain in a short stretch of grandiose dual carriageway: Winston Churchill Avenue. Soldiers and watchers told the court that the three suspects stopped at this junction on Winston Churchill Avenue; some evidence said that Savage and McCann exchanged newspapers here. Two pairs of SAS troops now approached them from behind, all four utterly convinced, so they told the court, that any hesitation on their part could mean carnage a mile to the south.

Approaching Danny McCann, Soldier A was convinced that if he could kill him, he would prevent the slaughter of innocents. His vision was intense:

> At that stage there I thought the man McCann was definitely going to go for a button. Uppermost in my mind . . . was the bomb and the de-bussing area. On that particular Sunday itself I noticed a couple of ships in the harbour, quite a few people around about the area of Main Street. Uppermost in my mind was this bomb. If he had gone for the button to press the button which would

> have detonated the bomb which was in the car or that
> was believed to be in the car . . . So . . . as I said, I was
> drawing my weapon. I fired at McCann one round into
> his back.

Soldier A's conviction about the existence of the bomb was deeply inculcated. But it was not nearly as strong as the conviction felt by Soldier C—which emerged when McGrory began asking him about Farrell. How long had he had her under observation?

Soldier C: On and off for an hour.

McGrory: And during which time Miss Farrell was showing this . . . alertness or nervousness about surveillance?

Soldier C: Very much so.

McGrory: However, you and your surveillance teams were so good at your jobs that she doesn't appear to have twigged, so to speak, that she was being watched closely?

Soldier C: No sir. Well they had just laid a bomb . . .

McGrory: Had just what?

Soldier C: Had just laid a bomb in the Ince's Hall area.

McGrory: No, they had not.

Soldier C [angrily]: I was told by [Officer] E!

McGrory: You are just after saying they had just laid a bomb. You know perfectly well they had not laid a bomb.

Soldier C: I was briefed on that day and categorically told there was a definite bomb in Ince's Hall. I can only operate from that information at that moment in time.

McGrory: It turned out to be rubbish, of course?

Soldier C: At that moment in time I can only react to that information.

McGrory: And at all times you were acting with the information that had been fed into you by [Officer] E?

Soldier C: Fed into me by [Officer] E, yes.

McGrory: Can we get it clear that you are not saying now that there was a bomb?

Soldier C: I don't understand what you are saying.

McGrory: It can't be the fault of my [Ulster] accent this time. I am saying to you, you are not telling his Honour and the jury now that you still believe there was a bomb?

Soldier C: I am not talking about that. I am talking about information I had; on the day there was a bomb in Ince's Hall.

McGrory: I am talking [about] now . . . and would you tell me whether you now believe that now as you stand there, that there was a bomb?

Soldier C: I still believe that there is a bomb in Gibraltar.

The Coroner [trying to clarify]: He still *believed*.

Some conversation between McGrory and Laws, the government's counsel, occurred at this point. Then the coroner intervened again: 'Put it directly to him. "Do you know that there was no bomb?"'

Soldier C: [at last] At this point in time I'd be a fool not to know.

Where did this strange certainty come from?

14

The night before the killings, at the secret midnight advisory meeting, there was a discussion about the two kinds of detonation—timer and radio-controlled. The police witnesses who attended that meeting—Commissioner Canepa, Detective Chief Inspector Ullger, Policeman Q and Policeman R—recalled that a timer *had not* been ruled out. But members of the SAS—both the officers and Soldiers A, B, C and D—attending the same meeting, all believed, and not just believed but *knew*, 'one hundred per cent', that the bomb would be radio-controlled, a 'button job'. Further, they believed that all three suspects would be carrying transmitters or 'buttons'.

One of the small revelations of the inquest was that on certain kinds of operations, including this one, SAS units take an army lawyer with them. The lawyer attending their legal needs in Gibraltar had, it transpired, drawn up the document which Canepa signed to give control to the military. He also accompanied the four soldiers when they went to hand over their guns and their spare ammunition at the Gibraltar police station after the shooting. And he also secured permission, from the colony's deputy attorney-general, that the unit could leave that night for the United Kingdom without first making any statements to the local police. In fact it was not until 15 March, after several sessions with the army lawyer, that the soldiers made statements to British policemen who were acting on behalf of their colleagues in Gibraltar. And it was months before it was even decided that the soldiers would 'volunteer' to attend their trial. No doubt the SAS lawyers had the opportunity to clarify any confusion in the soldiers' minds during this period; which is their right.

Was it reasonable that the soldiers hold these beliefs about the 'button' so firmly? Yes; they had been instilled by their commanding officers. Were the mistaken beliefs reasonable in themselves? Only Mr O knows, but he offered scant evidence to support them. Did they grow more reasonable as the afternoon of 6 March wore on? Hardly, though the crown tried hard to show so.

The important evidence: First, Savage had been seen 'fiddling with something in the car' after he parked it. The watcher alleged to have seen this fiddling (perhaps a seat-belt?) never turned up at the inquest. Second, the three suspects 'stared hard' or 'looked intently' at the car. Hardly proof of evil intention, far less a radio-controlled bomb. Third, the Renault had 'an old aerial' and yet was 'a relatively new car.' Several official witnesses latched on to this conjunction, which came originally from Officer G, the bomb-disposal expert. At about 3.25 G was sent from the ops room to inspect the car, about which he found nothing untoward apart from the aerial. But when the aerial was produced in court it turned out to be a remarkably unsuspicious piece of wire.

15

6 March 1988. Soldier A and Soldier B emerged from the Landport Tunnel with a female witness, known as Watcher J. Soon they saw McCann, Farrell and Savage standing together just north of the zebra crossing on Corral Road. They were talking and smiling. According to Soldier A, Savage broke away from the group and started to walk up towards the soldiers, actually bumping into Soldier A's shoulder as he moved past. Watcher J turned and followed Savage.

Soldier A and Soldier B pressed on towards Farrell and McCann, who were now walking towards the border. According to their evidence, Soldier A followed McCann on the inside of the pavement, while Soldier B took the outer position behind Farrell. The soldiers started to walk fast—'a controlled brisk pace'. By the time Farrell and McCann had walked a hundred yards and were in front of the Shell petrol station, Soldiers A and B were only a few feet behind them. Then McCann looked back—the glance that, by this evidence, killed him, killed all of them, and started a small procession of Belfast coffins.

Soldier A: He had a smile on his face and he looked over at me. We literally had what I would call eye-to-eye contact. We looked directly at each other, and the smile went off McCann's face, and, it's hard to describe, it's almost like McCann had a realization of actually who I was, or I was a threat to him. The look on his face was of alertness and he was very aware. So this came over his face and at that stage then I was just going to shout a warning to stop . . . and at the same time I was drawing my pistol. I went to shout 'Stop!' whether it [the word] actually came out I honestly don't know. I went to shout 'Stop!' and the events overtook the warning. The look on McCann's face, the alertness . . . then all of a sudden his right arm, right elbow, actually moved aggressively across the front of his body . . .

The button.

Soldier A then shot McCann once in the back. 'I then, out of the corner of my eye . . . [saw that] Farrell had a bag under her left armpit at this stage. She had actually moved to the right and was grabbing her bag.'

Another button.

Soldier A then shot Farrell once in the back before switching his fire back to McCann, who was now falling to the ground. He aimed once at his body and twice at his head.

Soldier A did not hear Soldier B fire, though Soldier B heard Soldier A's shots. Soldier B said that as Soldier A was the senior partner he expected him to initiate the arrest. He heard 'a startled yell' to his right and in a split second 'firing, bargh, bargh, firing'. Soldier B was drawing his own weapon at the time. 'At the same instant again Farrell, who I was still watching intently, made a sharp move to her right, and she was carrying a shoulder bag which she drew across her body.'

The button.

Soldier B: I, with the information I'd been given at the time—we were told of their professionalism, their dedication, and of all the car-bombing and other information—I was intently watching Farrell . . . in my mind she made all the actions to carry out a detonation of a radio-controlled device. Uppermost in my mind at that time, sir [to the coroner], was the lives of the general public in that area.'

Soldier B thought he fired one or two rounds at Farrell before he switched his fire to McCann—'Because I didn't know whether Soldier A had been shot, and I perceived McCann as being an equal threat to myself, Gibraltarians and my comrades.' When he returned his aim to Farrell she was going down, but he continued to fire because, he said, he still couldn't see her hands. He did not know how many rounds he had fired at each person, but he fired seven in all and did not miss, he said, with any of them. 'I carried on firing until both the terrorists were laying on the floor, their arms were away from any device or bag, and I decided that they were no longer a threat.'

The twelve shots fired at the Shell station had, according to Soldier C and Soldier D, an instant effect on Savage. He was about 150 yards away and walking back towards town, going up the same path to the tunnel which Soldier A and Soldier B had recently come down. Soldier C and Soldier D had caught up with him and were, according to Soldier C, about five or six feet behind him. Soldier D was to the left and slightly ahead.

Soldier C: There were a lot of people coming towards us . . . My intention at this stage was to effect the arrest but as I was moving forward there were shots to my left rear [at Shell] . . . and when this happened Savage spun round very fast. As he spun round I shouted, 'Stop!' At the time I was shouting, he went down with his right arm to the area of his jacket pocket.

Another button.

Soldier C: At this stage I fired, because at this moment in time it had been confirmed from [Officer] E that there was a device, a bomb, at the Ince's Hall area which could be detonated by one of these three terrorists, more likely to be Savage, because earlier he had been seen in that vehicle, playing around in the front, leaving the vehicle.

Soldier C fired six rounds at 'the mass' of Savage's body and thought that four hit him in the chest and two in the head, as Savage went 'spiralling down . . . like a corkscrew' through his arc of fire. He stopped firing 'as soon as Savage had hit the ground, his arms had flung back to the side and I was sure, at that moment in time, that he was no longer a threat to initiate that device.'

Soldier D said he pushed a woman away with his left hand and drew his Browning with his right, to get 'a clear line of arrest' as his counsel Hucker called it. He had not drawn his gun when Savage spun round and Soldier C shouted stop.

Soldier D: At this stage I had to make a decision as to what my actions would be, and uppermost in my mind at the time was what had been confirmed to me by [Officer] E. He told me there was a bomb . . . I believed that Savage had a detonator and he was going to detonate the device. With all the innocent people up in the area I had to make a decision. There was gun-fire to my left and to the rear. Again, I didn't know what that was. I didn't know if Soldiers A and B had been shot by McCann and Farrell, and I also had a threat to the people who were around me at the time . . . At this stage I had to make a decision, and it was in milliseconds I drew my pistol and I fired at Savage.

And went on firing at him; nine shots as he twisted and fell, all aimed at the centre of his body, apart from the last two which were aimed at his head—'just before he became still, just as he reached the ground.' Soldier C estimated that their total of fifteen shots had been fired from within three to five seconds—fast work with non-automatic pistols—but could not be sure if Soldier D went on firing after he had stopped.

None of this, of course, was supposed to happen. The court heard how the SAS had practised their arrest procedure. Pistols would be drawn, a challenge shouted and the suspects made to lie on the ground with their hands away from their bodies until Gibraltar policemen arrived with handcuffs. Four or five times the challenge itself burst from behind the curtain over the witness box. STOP . . . POLICE . . . HANDS UP. Few in the court (including the coroner, as he later confessed) had understood this challenge when Officer E first demonstrated it. Consonants disappeared, vowels were mangled—it was no more than the kind of frightening noise which professional soldiers perfect on the barrack-square. In any case the challenge was something of a luxury. As Soldier D said, 'In our rules of engagement, if we thought the threat was so great . . . we had no need to give a warning. We knew the fact the bomb was there. We knew he [Savage] could well be carrying the device to detonate the bomb. With him making such violent movements . . . in fact we didn't even need to give him a warning.'

McGrory: Why did you give him it then?

Soldier D: Because we gave him the benefit of the doubt. We told him to stop. He didn't stop. He carried on with the movement.

Loud noises frighten people. They tend to move. No soldier could explain to the inquest, however, why the dead had moved as they were alleged to have done. No buttons, no guns, but three distinct movements, all of them lethal. Was there anything Savage, Farrell and McCann could have done to prevent themselves from being killed that day, apart from rewriting the history of their last few months alive? One thing had always been clear. There was never an intention to shoot to immobilize: soldiers are trained to fire and go on firing until they kill, and in this case they needed to expunge life, to stop the possibility of 'contrived movement', in Hucker's phrase, as quickly as possible. But McGrory wondered what would have happened if Savage, in the middle of the firing, had shouted, 'Stop!

I surrender!' Would Soldier D have carried on killing him?

Soldier D: I would have carried on firing until I believed he was no longer a threat.

McGrory: Even if words of surrender like that had been uttered like that?

Soldier D: He may well have said that and pressed the button at the same time.

McGrory: The startled man was wheeling, and the shout and the shot had come on top of each other. What chance had he to surrender?

Soldier D: He had been given the chance. He had been told to stop and he didn't.

McGrory: You didn't even finish the warning.

Soldier D: Because we didn't have the time to finish the warning.

McGrory: I am suggesting to you, soldier, that you appointed yourself Lord High Executioner of Mr Savage on this day.

Soldier D: That is definitely not true.

16

By Officer E's reckoning Savage, Farrell and McCann had died at 3.47 p.m. He was in the ops room with Canepa, Officer F and others when his men radioed in—somewhere between 3.47 and 3.48 p.m.—that the 'apprehension of the terrorists had taken place.' Officer E said he wasn't sure what this implied—though clarification would surely have been easy enough—and so he left and went to the scene with Detective Chief Inspector Ullger of the Special Branch. By 4 p.m. he had confirmed that the three were dead and that the SAS soldiers were 'safely out of the area'. Canepa himself did not hear about the killings until 4.05 p.m., his first definite information since he handed over control twenty-five minutes before. One minute later Officer F signed the document which restored control to the civil power.

17

There is in police methodology a universal principle known as the preservation of the scene of the crime. It was applied sparingly on 6 March. Within minutes, the Gibraltar police had corrupted, if not quite destroyed, any chance that the killings could be properly reconstructed by the higher standards of legal proof. The spent cartridges were collected without first marking where they had been found. The bodies were removed without first photographing them *in situ*. No one bothered to chalk around the outlines of Farrell and McCann; without the pictures of Douglas Celecia, an amateur photographer whose home overlooks the scene, the inquest may never have known precisely how or where they had fallen (Celecia's photographs, which appear in these pages, were later seized by the police and restored to him, only after a legal action, with every face whited out).

The bodies were then removed to the morgue of the Royal Naval Hospital. A senior pathologist, Professor Alan Watson of Glasgow University, arrived around lunch-time the next day to perform the autopsy. It wasn't an easy job. The hospital had a mobile X-ray machine, but he was never given access to it; X-rays could have traced the track of bullets through the bodies. The clothing had already been removed; torn fabric can help determine entry and exit wounds, while the spread of blood stains could indicate whether the three were upright or prone when they were shot. He found the photographs taken in the morgue inadequate—the police photographer had not been under his direction—and there was no surgical help. Subsequently he was not given any copies of the ballistic and forensic reports, nor the reports on the blood samples he had submitted in London on his return.

McGrory expressed puzzlement.

'Yes,' said Professor Watson, 'it is a puzzle to me too. I am just giving you the facts.'

But wasn't there normally close co-operation between the pathologist and the forensic scientist?

'Yes,' said Watson, 'but here, I repeat, I have had none.'

Why not?

'I cannot answer that question.'

'Are you saying,' McGrory asked, 'that at no stage in the last six months did you become aware that, for instance, it was a matter of importance in this case that it is alleged that some, if not all, of these people were shot as they lay on the ground?'

'Yes, [but] I had expected that you would put those questions to the . . . forensic scientist.'

The forensic scientist was David Pryor of the London Metropolitan Police. He appeared in court on 27 September. Professor Watson had appeared on 8 September. The gap between their appearances made it impossible to combine their complementary evidence, blurring thereby a vital—maybe the most vital—question in the case: Did the wounds, the clothing and the bullets bear out the stories of the soldiers?

Like Watson, however, Pryor had been handicapped. The blood-soaked clothes had been dispatched to him in bags. 'The clothing was in such a condition when I received it,' said Pryor, 'that accurate determination of which was an entry site and which an exit site was very difficult.' What Pryor could say, from powder marks found on Farrell's jacket and Savage's shirt, was that a gun had been fired about three feet from Farrell's back and about four feet to six feet from Savage's chest. And of two bullets found in Savage's head, one came from the gun of Soldier C and the other from that of Soldier D. Watson's evidence, however, proved in the end to be more important than Pryor's, and taken together with 'strike marks'—impressions left by bullets—in the ground it casts a good deal of doubt on the soldiers' stories.

The first body Watson examined was Mairead Farrell's. Farrell had three entry wounds in the back and three exit wounds in the chest. The back wounds were all within about two-and-a-half inches of each other—a cluster—and neater and smaller than the chest wounds, which were higher in the body. The five wounds to her face and neck were produced by two bullet tracks: one from the left cheek to the hair-line below the left ear, producing an intermediate hole just below the left ear; one on the right neck beneath the chin to the left neck just above the collar line. The head wounds were superficial. Farrell had been killed by gunshot wounds to the heart and liver. Watson thought that Farrell must either have had 'the entire body, or at least the upper part of the body, turned towards the shooter' when she was shot in the face and had then been shot in the back as she was going down. Farrell's height was only five feet one inch, said McGrory, so the upward trajectory of the bullets in her back would mean that the gunman would have to be kneeling, or Farrell would need to be close to the ground. Watson agreed.

'Or on her face?'

'Yes.'

McCann had two entry wounds to the back, again close together, and two exits in the chest. Again the trajectory was upward. He had a hole without an exit in the lower left jaw and extensive damage to the back left side of the brain caused by a bullet which appeared to have entered at the top left back of his head and exited in his left neck above the hair-line. The hole in the jaw could have been a ricochet or a bullet which had first passed through Farrell. The bullets in the back and the back of the head would all have been lethal. Watson suggested that the wound in the jaw stunned him and the rest were fired at his back and head 'when he was down or very far down.'

Savage was a mess. His twenty-nine wounds, said Watson, suggested 'a frenzied attack'. He had seven wounds to the head, five to the back, one to each shoulder, five to the chest, three to the abdomen ('and lying there in the depth of the navel itself was a piece of grey distorted metal presumed to be a bullet'), two to the left thigh, two to the right arm, one superficial to the left arm and two to the left hand. Watson recorded the cause of death as fractures of the skull and cerebral lacerations, with a contribution from gunshot wounds to the lungs. He thought sixteen or eighteen bullets had struck Savage, which is at least one more than Soldiers C and Soldier D said they fired. He said that of the seven head wounds, five were probably entries. 'But bullets, with respect, are extremely difficult . . . a bullet does not simply do what you imagine.' The exits and entries to the chest and back were difficult to establish with certainty.

At first sight, Watson's evidence seems to support two civilian witnesses—Mrs Carmen Proetta and Mrs Josie Celecia—in their earlier statements to the press and television that Farrell and McCann were shot from close range as they lay on the ground. That could account for the clusters in the back, the powder marks on Farrell's jacket and the upward trajectory of bullets fired by a gunman standing nearer to their feet. What this supposition overlooks, however, is that all the evidence, including Celecia's pictures, suggest that Farrell and McCann fell backwards, face up.

The wounds to Farrell's face and neck, on the other hand, do support evidence in court from several civilian witnesses that one or more of the gunmen fired from the road rather than the pavement, where Soldiers A and B claimed they stood. She seems to have turned back and to the left—a bullet tearing through the left side of her face from cheek to neck—from her position at the edge of the pavement. In which case the bag on her left shoulder, which contained the notional detonating device, could hardly have been hidden from the gunman's view.

In Savage's case the contradictions are quite impossible to reconcile. Soldier C thought he hit him twice in the head, accidentally, as he fell through the soldier's arc of fire. Soldier D said he fired twice at his head as Savage was close to the ground. Sure enough, a bullet from each gun was found in his skull, and the other two bullets could have gone clean through. But the Gibraltar police, in an unusual moment of efficiency, had circled four strike marks within the chalk outline of Savage's head. Watson saw a photograph of these strike marks for the first time when McGrory showed it to him in court. Did it look as though those bullets were fired into his head as he lay there?

'Yes, that would be reasonable.'

18

This is not the only problem with the death of Savage. Savage died in a busy area—6 March was Gibraltar's first fine Sunday of the spring, with families strolling in and out of town through the Landport Tunnel. Soldiers C and D themselves estimated there were about thirty people in the vicinity. Yet the coroner's office could find only three civilian witnesses to Savage's death, two of whom had been found originally by Thames Television. The picture of the shooting that emerges from them, and from the four MI5 watchers who were also close by, has some extraordinary gaps (see Diagram One).

DIAGRAM ONE: SAVAGE

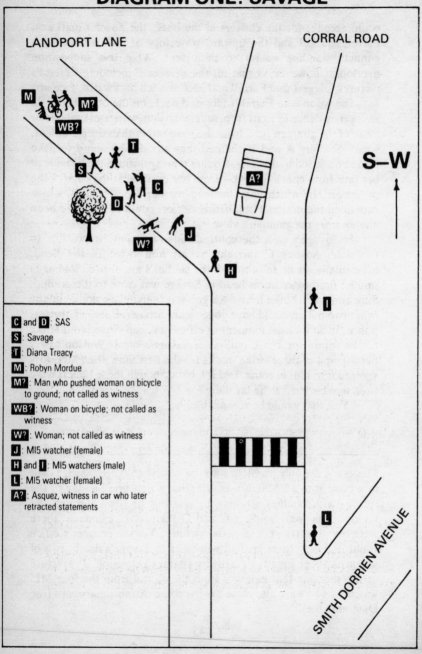

LANDPORT LANE

CORRAL ROAD

S–W

C and **D**: SAS

S: Savage

T: Diana Treacy

M: Robyn Mordue

M?: Man who pushed woman on bicycle to ground; not called as witness

WB?: Woman on bicycle; not called as witness

W?: Woman; not called as witness

J: MI5 watcher (female)

H and **I**: MI5 watchers (male)

L: MI5 watcher (female)

A?: Asquez, witness in car who later retracted statements

SMITH DORRIEN AVENUE

Kenneth Asquez, a twenty-year-old bank clerk, alleged last April that he saw a man with his foot on Savage's chest, firing into him at point-blank range two or three times. Asquez made the claim in two statements, one hand-written and another made before a lawyer, which he refused to sign because, he said, he wanted to protect his identity. Thames Television used seventy-two words from his statements. But at the inquest Asquez—a surprise witness, given his previous anonymity—said he had invented his account under 'pressure' and 'offers of money', the first unspecified and the second unquantified (he received none, in any case). Sir Joshua Hassan, the colony's most distinguished lawyer and former chief minister, represented him in court. Asquez said he was 'confused' about which parts of his statements were true and which parts he'd made up. The coroner said that, retracted or not, his first account should still be considered by the jury.

Then there is Robyn Arthur Mordue. He was a British holiday-maker, walking towards Savage in Landport Lane when the shooting started and he was pushed to the ground by a woman on a bicycle (herself pushed by a third party). He saw Savage fall at the same time. The shots stopped for a time, and then resumed as Mordue struggled to his feet; as he ran for cover behind a car, he looked back to see a man standing over Savage and pointing down with a gun. Mordue was a confused (and perhaps frightened) witness; coroner and counsel examined him ten times before he was released from his oath. He may also have been a confused and frightened witness before he arrived in Gibraltar: in the weeks before the inquest, he received a number of threatening phone calls ('Bastard . . . stay away'). His telephone number is ex-directory.

Diana Treacy, another Gibraltar bank employee, told the court she saw two men running towards her, the second with a gun. After she was passed by the first man, who turned out to be Savage, the gunman opened fire, about six feet in front of her. While Savage was on the ground, she saw the gunman fire another three, four or five shots into him. Professional observers close by managed to see even less.

Watcher J, the woman surveillance officer from MI5, followed Savage round the corner and turned away when he spun round, to avoid eye-contact. She neither saw the shooting, nor heard any of the fifteen to eighteen shots fired. Yet she was only fifteen feet away.

'Is that not,' McGrory asked her during the inquest, 'a very remarkable thing?'

'It may be, sir, but I did not hear them.'

Watcher H, the surveillance officer who accompanied Soldiers C and D, saw Savage spin round with 'an expression of amazement, a quite intense expression'. Then Watcher H too turned away and ran back down the road to warn people to take cover. He saw none of the shooting. When he looked back he saw that Savage was on the ground and that Soldier C and Soldier D had 'stood back' to the right of the lane.

Watcher I said he heard gun-fire in the lane and walked a few paces to have a look. He saw 'one or two shots being fired, by which time the terrorist Savage was on the ground.' He left the scene immediately.

Watcher L, another woman from MI5, heard gun-fire from the lane and 'got to the ground, a natural reaction.'

The woman on the bicycle and the man (possibly a watcher) who pushed her were never identified. Neither was the woman whom Soldier D pushed with his left hand. The only complete account of Savage's death comes from the people who say they killed him.

19

Commissioner Canepa contended that there was no predetermined point of arrest: that everyone happened to arrive on the scene just before the shooting started. Diagram Two illustrates just how many people happened to turn up—at least of those we know. Policeman P, Policeman Q and Policeman R are all members of the Gibraltar police force, armed with .38 Smith and Wesson revolvers. They just happened to form a circle around the scene of the shooting. Policeman P hitched a lift from a foreign-registered Mercedes, and Policemen Q and R rode by their motorbikes. There were others. Watcher K of MI5 had been hiding behind the hedge for some time. There was also Detective Constable Charles Huart, who, after his

DIAGRAM TWO: McCANN AND FARRELL

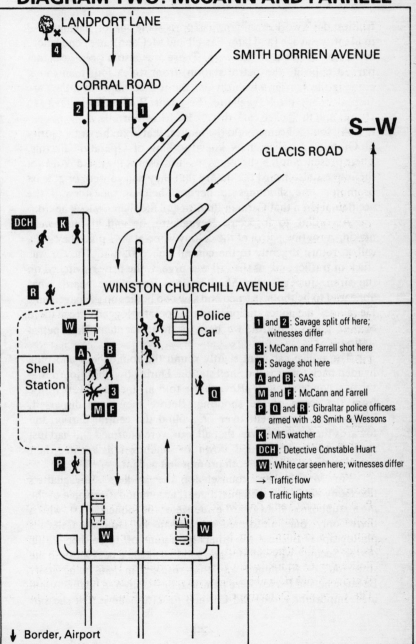

LANDPORT LANE

SMITH DORRIEN AVENUE

CORRAL ROAD

S–W

GLACIS ROAD

WINSTON CHURCHILL AVENUE

Police Car

Shell Station

Border, Airport

1 and **2**: Savage split off here; witnesses differ

3: McCann and Farrell shot here

4: Savage shot here

A and **B**: SAS

M and **F**: McCann and Farrell

P, **Q** and **R**: Gibraltar police officers armed with .38 Smith & Wessons

K: MI5 watcher

DCH: Detective Constable Huart

W: White car seen here; witnesses differ

→ Traffic flow

● Traffic lights

fruitless day's work examining passports at the border, having failed to identify Savage (and later Farrell and McCann), happened more or less by accident to show up. There was also a police car that parked opposite the petrol station, from which four men came, crossing the barrier which divides the two carriageways; they are Inspector Joseph Revagliatte, Sergeant Emilio Acris, PC Ian Howes and the police car's driver, PC Clive Borrell.

All four policemen told the inquest that, like the vast majority of Gibraltar's police, they knew nothing of Operation Flavius. Their presence at the shootings was fortuitous, they said. And yet the inquest also heard the theory that they had caused, or at least prompted, the shootings to begin. Theirs is the story of the accidental siren that Carmen Proetta and Stephen Bullock heard.

According to Inspector Revagliatte, he and his men were making a routine patrol of the colony when at 3.41 p.m. they got a call to return urgently to the central police station. The car was stuck in traffic, and, as the call was urgent, the driver switched on the siren. Just past the Shell station, Revagliatte heard 'what appeared to be shots,' turned and saw two bodies on the pavement. He radioed the police station, and the operator logged the call there at 3.42 p.m.: 'Control, we have firing incident at Shell petrol station.'

The police car went swiftly round the roundabout and then headed back towards the Shell station. During this short journey— thirty seconds at most—Revagliatte told his men to divert traffic from the scene of the shooting. Before they were dispersed, however, all four went over or around the central barrier and towards the bodies. Given that all four were unarmed and had just seen two people gunned down by unknown assailants, their behaviour was certainly both prompt and gallant.

For Mr Hucker, counsel for the soldiers, Revagliatte's testimony was a splendid instrument, accommodating some of the most stubborn and awkward evidence of the inquest. First, why is there only one uniformed policeman in Douglas Celecia's photographs? Because the others have gone off to do their traffic duties. Second, why did McCann suddenly glance backwards in the suspicious or frightened way that resulted in him being shot? Because he and Farrell were panicked by the siren. And finally and most importantly, why did Carmen Proetta believe that she saw armed men attack McCann and Farrell from over the barrier? Because what she saw, and got muddled by, was a group of uniformed, unarmed policemen jump over the barrier some seconds after Soldiers A and B shot Farrell and McCann from the footpath.

Again and again, the counsel for the SAS allowed Revagliatte to demonstrate how his involvement in the killings was accidental:

Hucker: Inspector, I am going to ask you some questions on behalf of Soldiers A to G. The first matter is what your knowledge was of the operation to arrest the terrorists on 6 March. When you came on shift at three o'clock or thereabouts, did you know anything about that operation at all?

Revagliatte: Nothing at all.

Hucker: You thought that life in Gibraltar was totally normal, that what was happening between you and the border was the same as happened any other day of the week?

Revagliatte: Exactly.

In November, eight weeks after Inspector Revagliatte gave this evidence, a startling fact emerged. His name appears on the secret operational order prepared by police Commissioner Canepa for Operation Flavius that was read by certain unnamed police officers at the midnight briefing between 5 and 6 March. The order assigns him a vital role—officer in charge of the two police firearms teams. Each team consisted of three armed policemen, and one consisted of the witnesses known as Policemen P, Q and R, the same policemen who happened to form a circle round the scene of the shooting. Had this fact been disclosed to the court, the jury would would have been asked to conclude:

1. That while Policemen P, Q and R had attended the midnight briefing, their commanding officer for the operation, Revagliatte, had not.

2. That while Policemen P, Q and R knew their role on 6 March, their commanding officer, Revagliatte, did not.

3. That though Revagliatte and Policemen P, Q and R appeared at the scene of the killings almost simultaneously, this was pure coincidence.

The British government may, of course, supply a simple explanation. But as I write, two weeks after the question was first raised in the Irish parliament, it has so far neglected to comment.

So what are we now to believe? If Revagliatte was knowingly involved, the official version of what happened in Winston Churchill Avenue needs to be completely re-examined. We fall back on what his testimony tended to destroy—the stubborn and awkward evidence of the civilian witnesses who first appeared on Thames Television. Carmen Proetta said at the inquest more or less what she said on television: that from her kitchen window she saw a car pull up and one uniformed policeman and three men in plain clothes get out and jump over the barrier; that at least two of the men in plain clothes appeared to have guns; that two people (McCann and Farrell), on the pavement near the Shell station, looked round and raised their hands to about head level; that one shot dropped the girl to the ground; that the man moved as if to shield or help her; that then he too went down in 'a fusillade of shots'. Behind McCann and Farrell, she also saw a fifth man with what looked like a gun; then a man with fairish hair crouched over the bodies with his hands clasped together at waist level, seemingly pointing a gun. She heard more shots. (Josie Celecia, whose husband took the photographs, made a similar observation in court: that she too saw a man standing over the bodies with his hands clasped together, his arms outstretched, pointing downwards, and that she heard bangs—bangs which the soldiers' counsel suggested came from the shooting of Savage.) Proetta then saw a second car draw up, this time on the same side of the road as the petrol station, and men in plain clothes got out and started arguing and 'gesticulating' at the fairish man, who was pulled into the second car by someone in a dark jacket and driven away.

It is worth recalling Stephen Bullock, the English lawyer strolling with his wife and child. He saw a police car stuck in traffic next to him on Smith Dorrien Avenue. He thought its siren sounded at the same time as shooting started. When he looked in the direction of the Shell station he saw a gunman firing rapidly from the edge of the road at another man, three or four feet away on the pavement, who was falling backwards with his hands raised above shoulder height. Something which looked like a heap of clothes was already on the ground.

The siren, however, may not have been a mistake. Perhaps it formed some part of the arrest plan. Shortly before the shooting started a man with a pistol stuck down his jeans pushed past Bullock, saying, 'Excuse me,' and then went on to meet a man similarly dressed and also armed, who was standing near the corner. The men looked at the shooting at the Shell station, and then ran off towards Landport Lane. They were probably Soldiers C and D. Bullock remembers that the man who pushed past looked back at the police car. 'He seemed to have some sort of interest in what the police car was doing.'

And what was that car doing?

Soldiers A and B said that they approached McCann and Farrell from behind by walking briskly along the pavement after them. They have always insisted that they were still on the pavement, side by side, when they opened fire and stayed there throughout the shooting. But if we add the accounts of these eye-witnesses to the forensic evidence—the little, that is, that survives—then at least the opening rounds came from gunmen firing from the road, not the pavement. This small difference poses large questions. Could gunmen have arrived by car? Where did Policemen P, Q and R come from? Were they not, perhaps, in the positions that they told the court? Somebody began shooting from the road not the pavement, and if, as the forensic evidence suggests, Farrell had turned to face them, then there would have been no mystery about the movements of her hand: she would have been clearly in view of the gunmen.

20

On the morning of 30 September the coroner summed up the evidence to the members of the jury and urged them to avoid the ambiguity of an open verdict. They should decide whether Savage, Farrell and McCann had been killed lawfully, 'that is justifiable, reasonable homicide,' or unlawfully, 'that is unlawful homicide.' If they were to conclude that any of the three—though only Savage was mentioned by name—had been shot on the ground simply to 'finish them off,' then that would be murder.

The jury left the court at 11.30 a.m. to consider its verdict and re-appeared again at 5.20 p.m. to say it had been unable to agree a decision. The coroner then told the members of the jury that they were 'reaching the edge' of a reasonable time to produce one, and said he would expect to see them again at 7 p.m. To some observers in the court, this sounded like a deadline. At 7.15 p.m. the jury returned again, and the foreman rose to say it had reached a verdict of lawful killing by a majority of nine to two, the smallest majority allowed.

This was hardly a vote of confidence in the behaviour of the British army on 6 March. None the less jubilation erupted in London among members and supporters of the British government. The reaction of Mr Jerry Hayes, Conservative Member of Parliament for Harlow and secretary of his party's back bench committee on Northern Ireland, was typical. 'This is wonderful news for those brave young men in the SAS who daily put their lives at risk to protect our democracy,' he told the *Daily Telegraph*. After all: 'What greater inquiry could one have than an independent inquest in an independent colony?'

21

That was two months ago now. Today in England another inquiry still continues—the inquiry into how Thames Television came to make its documentary, 'Death on the Rock'. The television company itself instigated this inquiry to appease the government; there was talk that the government might deprive the company of its broadcasting franchise. Already it has lasted twice as long as the inquest itself and its two investigators—Lord Windlesham and Mr Richard Rampton—are still taking evidence. Rampton is a barrister, a Queen's Counsel. Windlesham is a Conservative peer, a former government minister in Northern Ireland and the author of a book entitled *Broadcasting in a Free Society*: they have been charged to discover if the programme was 'responsible' and if it 'performed a public service by contributing information and insight on a controversial matter of public concern.'

What really happened in Gibraltar on 6 March? Many of us who gathered under the Levanter cloud still wonder. Everyone had theories which to a greater or lesser extent conflicted with the story in court. Here is mine.

Nothing in the IRA's history suggests an overwhelming fear of killing innocent civilians, neither are its members suicidal martyrs in the Japanese or Islamic Fundamentalist tradition. The British expected a timed bomb to be driven in and set on Monday evening, and possibly even a blocking-car or some last-minute reconnaissance the day before. A reconnaissance would need at the most two people. To find all three in town on Sunday was a complete surprise, but, as in the old Chinese maxim, no military plan survives contact with the enemy. Over weeks or months the British had devised a plan for a move at the last moment, to catch bombers and their bomb together. The surveillance by this stage would need to be extremely thorough, but then, with the bomb already in Gibraltar and an arrest minutes away, the consequences of watchers being spotted by the bombers would hardly matter. They might make a run for the border and be cut off as they crossed the runway. But could anyone have expected to watch all three on the Sunday, watch them return to Spain, await their re-arrival on Monday? Operation Flavius does not seem to have prepared for that contingency; three bombers and no bomb is amateur behaviour. But how could the man who ran the operation trust that it would still work on the intended day? The bombers looked very 'surveillance-aware'. Perhaps they'd discovered they were being watched; perhaps they would abort the mission. An enormous effort, which had received the highest government sanction, would be thrown away. Whether the British believed the Renault contained a bomb or not, the three would have to be arrested in whatever meaning of the word. But if there was no bomb in Gibraltar, evidence for a trial would be thin.

So what really did happen in Gibraltar on 6 March? A case of mistaken belief? An operation that went wrong? A carefully created opportunity that was too good to miss? Today in Scotland, a new chant rises from the terraces of Glasgow Rangers football club: 'SAS, bang-bang-bang, SAS, bang-bang-bang.'

JOHN SIMPSON

TIANANMEN SQUARE

It was humid and airless, and the streets around our hotel were empty. We had set out for Tiananmen Square: a big, conspicuous European television team—reporter, producer, cameraman, sound-recordist, translator, lighting man, complete with gear. A cyclist rode past, shouting and pointing. What it meant we couldn't tell. Then we came upon a line of soldiers. Some of them had bleeding faces; one cradled a broken arm. They were walking slowly, limping. There had been a battle somewhere, but we couldn't tell where.

When we reached Changan Avenue, the main east-west thoroughfare, it was as full of people as in the days of the great demonstrations—a human river. We followed the flow of it to the Gate of Heavenly Peace, under the bland, moonlike portrait of Chairman Mao. There were hundreds of small groups, each concentrated around someone who was haranguing or lecturing the others, using the familiar, heavy public gestures of the Chinese. Other groups had formed around radios tuned to foreign stations. People were moving from group to group, pushing in, crushing round a speaker, arguing, moving on, passing along any new information.

For the most part these were not students. They were from the factories, and the red cloths tied around their heads made them look aggressive, even piratical. Trucks started arriving from the outskirts of the city, full of more young workers, waving the banners of their factories, singing, chanting, looking forward to trouble.

People were shouting: there was a battle going on between tanks and the crowd, somewhere to the east of the city centre. Details differed, and I had trouble finding out what was being said: I watched the animated faces, everyone pushing closer to each new source of information, pulling at each other's sleeves or shoulders. Tanks and armoured personnel carriers, they were saying, were heading towards the Square. They were coming from two directions, east and west. The crowds that gathered couldn't stop them.

'It's a different army. It's not the Thirty-eighth!' The man who said this was screaming it, clutching at our translator, holding on to him, trying to make him understand the significance of it. 'It is *not* the Thirty-eighth!' It had been the Thirty-eighth Army that had tried to recapture the city twice before. The soldiers had been unarmed: the commander, the father of a student in the Square, had ordered that operations be carried out peacefully.

We pushed our way towards the Square where, despite the rumours and the panic, we saw something very different: several thousand people standing in silence, motionless, listening to a large loudspeaker, bolted to a street lamp:

> Go home and save your life. You will fail. You are not behaving in the correct Chinese manner. This is not the West, it is China. You should behave like a good Chinese. Go home and save your life. Go home and save your life.

The voice was expressionless, epicene, metallic, like that of a hypnotist. I looked at these silent, serious faces, illuminated by the orange light of the street lamps, studying the loudspeaker. Even the small children, brought there with the rest of the family, stared intently. The order was repeated again and again. It was a voice the people of China had been listening to for forty years, and continued listening to even now. But now no one did what the hypnotist said. No one moved.

And then, suddenly, everything changed: the loudspeaker's spell was broken by shouts that the army was coming. There was the sound of a violent scraping, and across the Avenue I saw people pulling at the railings that ran along the roadway and dragging them across the pavement to build a barricade. Everyone moved quickly, a crowd suddenly animated, its actions fast and decisive, sometimes brutal. They blocked off Changan Avenue and the Square itself, and we began filming—flooding the sweating enthusiasts with our camera-light. People danced around us, flaunting their weaponry: coshes, knives, crude spears, bricks. A boy rushed up to our camera and opened his shabby green windcheater like a black marketeer to reveal a row of Coca-Cola bottles strapped to his waist, filled with petrol and plugged with rags. He laughed, and mimed the action of pulling out each bottle and throwing it. I asked him his age. He was sixteen. Why was he against the government? He couldn't answer. He gripped another of his Molotov cocktails, laughing all the time.

That the army was coming was no longer rumour but fact and our translator heard that it would move in at one o'clock. It was half-past midnight. In the distance, above the noise of the crowd, I thought I could hear the sound of guns. I wanted to find a vantage point from which we could film, without being spotted by the army. But the tension that was bonding members of the crowd together did not have the same effect on the members of our small team. It was hot and noisy. We argued. We started shouting, and I headed off on my own.

I pushed through the crowds, immediately feeling better for being on my own. There were very few foreign journalists left in the Square by now, and I felt especially conspicuous. But I also felt good. People grabbed my hand, thanking me for being with them. I gave them a V for Victory sign and was applauded by everyone around me. It was hard to define the mood. There was still a spirit of celebration, that they were out on the streets, defying the government, but the spirit was also giving way to a terrible foreboding. There was also something else. Something I hadn't seen before: a reckless ferocity of purpose.

I crossed back into the main part of Tiananmen Square, the village of student tents. There were sticks and cardboard and broken glass underfoot. The smells were familiar and strong—wood-smoke, urine and heavy disinfectant. A couple clung to each other, her head on his shoulder. I passed in front of them, but they didn't raise their eyes. A student asked me to sign his T-shirt, a craze from earlier days. He had thick glasses and a bad complexion, and he spoke English. 'It will be dangerous tonight,' he said. 'We are all very afraid here.'

I finished signing his shirt, at the back below the collar. He grabbed my hand and shook it excitedly. His grip was bony and clammy. I asked him what he thought would happen.

'We will all die.'

He straightened up and shook my hand again, and slipped away between the tents.

The camp was dark. There were a few students left; most of them had gathered in the centre of the Square, around the Monument to the People's Heroes. I could hear their speeches and the occasional burst of singing—the Internationale, as always. Here, though, it was quiet. This was where the students had chosen to build their statue of the Goddess of Democracy, with her sightless eyes, her torch held in both hands. The symbol of all our aspirations, one of the student leaders called her: the fruit of our struggle. To me, she looked very fragile.

The speeches and the songs continued in the distance. Then suddenly they stopped. There was a violent grinding and a squealing sound—the familiar sound of an armoured personnel carrier. I heard screaming, and behind me, in the Avenue, everyone started running. When I finally spotted the vehicle, I could see that it was making its way with speed down the side of the Square. It seemed uncertain of its direction—one moment driving straight for the Square, and then stopping, turning, stopping again, as if looking for a way to escape. There was a sudden angry roar, and I know it was because the vehicle had crushed someone under its tracks. It then turned in my direction—it was pointed at me—and I felt a different kind of panic. The action was starting and I was separated from my colleagues: it is an article of faith to stay with your camera crew in times of danger.

The vehicle carried on, careering back and forth. It must have knocked down six or seven people. By now it was on fire, having been hit repeatedly by Molotov cocktails. Somehow, though, it escaped and headed off to the west.

Then a second armoured personnel carrier came along Changan Avenue, alone and unsupported like the first. This time everyone turned and ran hard towards the vehicle, knowing that they, with their numbers and their petrol bombs, had the power to knock it out. They screamed with anger and hate as the vehicle swung randomly in different directions, threatening to knock people down as it made its way through the Square. The Molotov cocktails arched above our heads, spinning over and over, exploding on the thin shell of armour that protected the men inside. Still the vehicle carried on, zigzagging, crossing the Avenue, trying to find a way through the barricade. A pause, and it charged, head-on, straight into a block of concrete—and then stuck, its engine whirring wildly. A terrible shout of triumph came from the crowd: primitive and dark, its prey finally caught. The smell of petrol and burning metal and sweat was in the air, intoxicating and violent. Everyone around me was pushing and fighting to get to the vehicle. At first I resisted; then, close beside it, I saw the light of a camera, just where the crowd was starting to swarm. There were only three cameramen still filming in the entire Square, and I knew that my colleague was the only one crazy enough to be that close. Now I was the one fighting, struggling to get through the crowd, pulling people back, pushing them out of my path, swearing, a big brutal Englishman stronger than any of them. I tore one man's shirt and punched another in the back. All around me the men seemed to be yelling at the sky, their faces lit up; the vehicle had caught fire. A man—his torso bare—climbed up the side of the vehicle and stood on top of it, his arms raised in victory, the noise of the mob welling up around him. They knew they had the vehicle's crew trapped inside. Someone started beating at the armoured glass with an iron bar.

I reached the cameraman and pulled hard at his arm to get his attention. He scarcely noticed me, amid the buffeting and the noise and the violence, and carried on filming. He and his sound recordist and the Chinese lighting man were a few feet from the vehicle: close enough to be killed if it exploded or if the soldiers came out shooting. But I couldn't make them step back, and so we stayed there, the four of us, the heat beating against our faces as people continued to pour petrol on the bonnet and roof and smashed at the doors and the armoured glass. What was it like inside? I imagined the soldiers half-crazed with the noise and the heat and the fear of being burned alive.

The screaming around me rose even louder: the handle of the door at the rear of the vehicle had turned a little, and the door began to open. A soldier pushed the barrel of a gun out, but it was snatched from his hands, and then everyone started grabbing his arms, pulling and wrenching until finally he came free, and then he was gone: I saw the arms of the mob, flailing, raised above their heads as they fought to get their blows in. He was dead within seconds, and his body was dragged away in triumph. A second soldier showed his head through the door and was then immediately pulled out by his hair and ears and the skin on his face. This soldier I could see: his eyes were rolling, and his mouth was open, and he was covered with blood where the skin had been ripped off. Only his eyes remained—white and clear—but then someone was trying to get them as well, and someone else began beating his skull until the skull came apart, and there was blood all over the ground, and his brains, and still they kept on beating and beating what was left.

Then the horrible sight passed away, and the ground was wet where he had been.

There was a third soldier inside. I could see his face in the light of the flames, and some of the crowd could too. They pulled him out, screaming, wild at having missed killing the other soldiers. It was his blood they wanted, I was certain, it was to feel the blood running over their hands. Their mouths were open and panting, like dogs, and their eyes were expressionless. They were shouting, the Chinese lighting man told me afterwards, that the soldier they were about to kill wasn't human, that he was just a thing, an object, which had to be destroyed. And all the time the noise and the heat and the stench of oil burning on hot metal beat at us, overwhelming our senses, deadening them.

Just as the third soldier was lifted out of the vehicle, almost fainting, an articulated bus rushed towards us stopping, with great skill, so that its rear door opened just beside the group with the soldier. The students had heard what was happening, and a group had raced the bus over to save whomever they could. The mob did not want to give up its prize. The students tried to drag the soldier on board, and the crowd held on to him, pulling him back. By some mischance the bus door started closing and it seemed that he must be killed.

I had seen people die in front of me before. But I had never seen three people die, one after the other, in this way. Once again the members of the crowd closed around the soldier, their arms raised over their heads to beat him to death. The bus and the safety it promised were so close. It seemed to me then that I couldn't look on any longer, a passive observer, watching another man's skin torn away or his head broken open, and do nothing. I saw the soldier's face, expressing only horror and pain as he sank under the blows of the people around him, and I started to move forward. The ferocity of the crowd had entered me, but I felt it was the crowd that was the animal, that it wasn't properly human. The soldier had sunk down to the ground, and a man was trying to break his skull with a half-brick, bringing it down with full force. I screamed obscenities at the man—stupid obscenities, as no one except my colleagues could have understood them—and threw myself at him, catching him with his arm up, poised for another blow. He looked at me blankly, and his thin arm went limp in my grasp. I stopped shouting. He relaxed his grip on the brick, and I threw it under the bus. It felt wet. A little room had been created around the soldier, and the student who had tried to rescue him before could now get to him. The rest of the mob hadn't given up, but the students were able to pull the soldier away and get him on to the bus by the other door. He was safe.

The vehicle burned for a long time, its driver and the man beside him burning with it. The flames lit up the Square and and reflected on the face of the Monument where the students had taken their stand. The crowd in Changan Avenue had been sated. The loudspeakers had stopped telling people to save their lives. There was silence.

The students sang the Internationale. It would be for the last time, and it sounded weak and faint in the vastness of the Square. Many were crying. No doubt some students joined in the attacks on the army, but those in the Square kept to their principle of non-violence. Although the army suffered the first casualties, it was the students who would be the martyrs that night.

My colleagues and I wanted to save our pictures in case we were arrested, and I told the others that we should go back to the Beijing Hotel and come out again later. I now feel guilty about the decision; it was wrong: we ought to have stayed in the Square, even though the other camera crews had already left and it might have cost us our lives. Someone should have been there when the massacre took place, filming what happened, showing the courage of the students as they were surrounded by tanks and the army advancing, firing as it went.

Instead, we took up our position on the fourteenth floor of the Beijing Hotel. From there, everything seemed grey and distant. We saw most of what happened, but we were separated from the fear and the noise and the stench of it. We saw the troops pouring out of the Gate of Heavenly Peace, bayonets fixed, shooting first into the air and then straight ahead of them. They looked like automata, with their rounded dark helmets. We filmed them charging across and clearing the northern end of the Square, where I had signed the student's T-shirt. We filmed the tanks as they

265

drove over the tents where some of the students had taken refuge, among them, perhaps, the young couple I had seen sitting silently, their arms around each other. Dozens of people seem to have died in that way, and those who saw it said they could hear the screams of the people inside the tents over the noise of the tanks. We filmed as the lights in the Square were switched off at four a.m. They were switched on again forty minutes later, when the troops and the tanks moved towards the Monument itself, shooting first in the air and then, again, directly at the students themselves, so that the steps of the Monument and the heroic reliefs which decorated it were smashed by bullets.

Once or twice, we were ourselves shot at, and during the night the security police sent men to our room to arrest us: but I shouted at them in English, and they went away, uncertain of the extent of their powers. Below us, people still gathered in the Avenue, shouting their defiance at the troops who were massed at the farther end. Every now and then the crack of a rifle would bring down another demonstrator, and the body would be rescued by a trishaw driver or the crew of an ambulance. Below us, the best and noblest political protest since Czechoslovakia in 1968 was being crushed as we watched. I knelt on the balcony, beside the cameraman and a Chinese woman, one of the student leaders.

She had taken refuge in our room because we were foreigners. I shouted at her to go back inside, but she refused, turning her head from me so that I wouldn't see she was crying, her hands clenched tight enough to hurt, intent on watching the rape of her country and the movement she and her friends had built up in the course of twenty-two days. I had seen the river of protest running along Changan Avenue in that time; I had seen a million people in the streets, demanding a way of life that was better than rule by corruption and secret police. I recalled the lines of the T'ang dynasty poet Li Po, that if you cut water with a sword you merely made it run faster. But the river of change had been dammed, and below me, in the Avenue where it had run, people were dying. Beside me, the cameraman spotted something and started filming. Down in the Square, in the early light, the soldiers were busy unrolling something and lifting it up. Soon a great curtain of black cloth covered the entrance to Tiananmen Square. What was happening there was hidden from us.

MARTHA GELLHORN
THE INVASION OF PANAMA

We drove too fast on a dark road; there was no other traffic. Everything had been going too fast from the moment of arrival at Panama's airport. A bent bony little man seized my luggage and ran with it, shouting, 'Hurry, *Señora*, I have no salary, I live on tips!' Immigration and customs were only a pause. The porter dumped my stuff on the pavement. A taxi driver shouted, 'Come, *Señora*, with three it costs only eight dollars to the centre!' I was hustled into his car where two passengers waited. I thought all this rush and noise were hysterical. What was the matter with these people?

The young Costa Rican sitting next to me said he was going by bus tomorrow to buy merchandise in the Free Zone at Colón, at the Caribbean end of the Canal, and if God wills would be back in Costa Rica the next day.

The middle-aged Panamanian in the front seat said, 'Noriega used to run the Free Zone. Now it's a nephew of Endara.' They all laughed. Endara is the new President of Panama, installed by the US Invasion.

Then the panic talk started. I heard a variation of it every day from everyone I met.

'This is a very dangerous place,' said the Costa Rican. 'I do not like to come here. There are robbers everywhere. They have weapons. If you do not give them what they want, they kill you. You should not be travelling alone.'

The Panamanian passenger said, 'Never be out after nine o'clock.' It was now nearly half-past nine. 'Do not walk on the streets alone. If you take money, take only what you need and hold your purse close to your side.'

The taxi driver asked: 'Which is your hotel?'

I said any hotel in the centre would do.

They discussed this and the driver said, 'I will take you to the Ejecutivo; it is clean and comfortable and safe.' *Seguro* was the operative word.

We turned off the wide street by a lighted petrol station. High board fences lined both sides of a narrow street. 'Those stores were looted,' said the front-seat passenger. 'Everyone stole—not only the poor, the rich too.' We stopped in the dark and waited until the Panamanian had opened his front door and gone inside. They

269

dropped me at the Ejecutivo with renewed serious warnings to take much care.

At ten o'clock, I stood on the first-floor balcony of my very clean, very comfortable, safe room and looked at a dead city. No movement, no sound, no lights. The curfew was at midnight. Panama had been famous for its nightlife, a wide-open town. This was almost three months after the Invasion.

I had to change traveller's cheques, and my delightful hotel nestled among banks and closed night clubs. The banks have a Pharaoh complex; there are 140 of them. They are towers or palaces, monuments to money. A mirrored skyscraper, with SWISS BANK in red neon on top, gleamed nearby. Why not be brave and walk? The streets in this part of town were wide and clean, every building opulent, white, with decorative planting. No one was walking.

When I reached the air-conditioned bank foyer I was drenched in sweat, a sensible reason for not walking. To my surprise the Swiss Bank used only a few floors in the middle of the tower. To my greater surprise I found myself in a small, linoleum-floored hall, with a wood shelf and a man behind a dirty glass teller's window. No, they didn't do retail business; this was an international bank, engaged in shipping money around the world. He said that the Invasion had closed the commercial banks for a few days. But 24,000 armed men, attack helicopters, tanks and riotous disorder in the city had not interfered for an hour with international banking.

The commercial bank, very grand, had an armed private guard in front of its locked, iron grille door. The teller gave me a wad of used dollar bills. Money in Panama is American. Due to two years of the US embargo, supplies of new dollar bills ceased. Paper which has changed hands for all this time is so worn and foul that it feels like oncoming skin disease. Now, stiff with cash, I hailed a taxi though the bank was only a few long, hot blocks from my hotel. The taxis are little beat-up cars, like fast water beetles, with room for three passengers; they collect trade as they go. The fare is a dollar for any distance. You flag one down and if it is headed in your direction, you hop in with the others. This taxi driver said, 'Be very careful. Many taxi drivers have been robbed and killed. It is worse than war here.'

I put my fortune in the hotel safe and set out to improve my looks. There was a beauty salon on the side street by the hotel. While her assistant washed my hair, the jolly, blowsy hairdresser said, 'People stole anything, from viciousness not need. Twenty-five beauty salons were robbed of everything, even the wash-basins. Noriega stole and he taught the people to steal. There was such corruption here; it was a sickness. They left this street alone except for the jewellery shop. Where I live was not harmed. Only the houses of the poor were destroyed.'

I was slow to understand the catastrophe of looting that ravaged the whole of Panama City for three days, beginning the day after the US night invasion on 20 December. The structure of the state was wiped out in the six hours of the main attack. US Southern Command, the permanent military establishment in Panama, had created a vacuum in civil order, but did not recognize that it was obligated to patrol and protect the city. The troops had no orders to do so. The people turned into mad locusts, swarming through the streets. At the time it must have seemed like the biggest wildest happiest drunken binge ever known, courtesy of the US Army. The hangover is painful; Panama has not yet recovered. 'I saw American soldiers sitting in a tank, watching,' said the hairdresser.

I asked about the US embargo, which starved Nicaragua and has been a crippling burden on Cuba for thirty years. In Panama, it was meant to cause hardship and popular discontent that would drive out Noriega. She shrugged. 'There was always plenty to eat in Panama. We lacked for nothing.' In fact, the embargo reduced Panama's gross national product by twenty per cent, but hurt mainly the rich, the white business community, since the United States is Panama's major trading partner.

As I needed to buy a plane ticket and there was a travel agency a few doors away, I took my problem to a stylishly dressed, thirty-something business woman, who reserved a ticket quickly on her computer. She said, 'The United States created that monster; they knew Noriega well. They even *decorated* him. He has been in power here for twenty-one years.'

I asked what it was like to live here in those years.

'Nothing happened to people like me under Noriega. If you were neutral it was all right. Mostly the poor favoured Noriega.'

Her facts were not entirely correct. Panama had indeed been a military dictatorship for twenty-one years, which did not disturb the US government until two years ago. Noriega was the intelligence chief of General Torrijos, the previous military overlord. Noriega had been top man for six years, behind a president and legislature and elections, the way the United States likes things to look. But it is correct that American governments knew Noriega well during three decades. Noriega did not suddenly become a drug-dealing fiend in the last two years, after a blameless life. President Carter took him off the CIA payroll; President Reagan put him back.

I asked about the banks: why build those immense, unneeded towers?

'They rented out their extra space for offices,' she said. 'There will be many empty offices now. You know this city was called "the washing machine". Anybody could open an office and be a banker and launder money, no questions asked.' The cowboy bankers may be gone but the useful secrecy laws remain.

The heat was heavy, a weight on your body, and the sun was blinding. I said I must buy sun-glasses and shirts; I would be changing them four times a day. 'Shop around here, on Via España. Do not go downtown. Above all don't go near Central. They will see you're a foreigner: you will be robbed immediately.' Central is the main popular shopping street in Chorrillo, the district that took the worst blast of the Invasion.

There were three giant round-ups while I was in Panama. Before dawn, 500 to 700 American soldiers and the new Panamanian paramilitary police blocked off poor sections of the city with tanks and made house-to-house searches. The first, most publicized round-up netted 726 'anti-socials', largely illegal Colombian immigrants, forty-six revolvers and a minor supply of drugs, average for private use. The triumphant catch was a tall, skinny twenty-year-old black, nicknamed Half Moon, a gang leader 'accused of four assassinations'. The papers carried no further mention of anti-socials in later round-ups and no reports of mugging, armed robbery, not even pickpockets. It was finally admitted that there was no great hidden arms cache in the city, nor any sizeable quantity of drugs. Without reason, the people are certain that Panama is overrun by cut-throat criminals, and the panic talk never stops. I think this pervasive fear was shell-shock from the terror of the Invasion, something like an unconscious mass nervous breakdown.

The traffic of the capital city, which is called simply Panama, hurtles at race-track speed along the streets. There are no traffic-lights. They were knocked out two years ago in a general strike, to disrupt the city. They were not replaced but Noriega had tough traffic cops, armed with .45s, and drivers dreaded fines or prison sentences. In my first days there were no traffic cops. Then a few began to appear with day-glo gloves and vests. These uncertain men, all blacks, belong to the new Panamanian paramilitary police. US Southern Command vetted Noriega's former soldiers on a scale ranging from black (downright bad) to grey (neutral) to white (harmless). It selected a chosen number and gave them a new name. They are no longer the Defence Force; they are the Public Force and their barracks now bear the words Policia Nacional. They have also been given a new humiliating uniform, a loose, belted khaki shirt, baggy khaki trousers and floppy khaki hat, like a sun-hat.

The people, who find this laughable, are told that this force with new commanders and new orders to be polite and helpful, are new men. But wherever authority must be imposing, there are six-foot-tall, white American soldiers, with M-16 rifles, and those somehow ominous boots and camouflage uniforms, and nobody doubts for a minute who is in charge here: US Southern Command.

My watch-strap broke; I went in search of a watch shop. Advised and directed by people on the street, I found a hole-in-the-wall store, looted clean of its stock, including watch-straps. This small businessman was bankrupt. Insurance, if he had any, does not cover acts of war. The city-wide vandalism was the sequel to an act of war. A slim, neatly dressed young man, chatting with the unemployed proprietor, offered to take me to Central on a bus to buy a strap.

The buses, like the taxis, belong to their drivers and are a treat. They have girls' names and fanciful decorations painted on their sides: a puffing steam locomotive, a sylvan scene, a luscious blonde on the rear end. When you want to get off you shout '*parada*', stop, pay fifteen cents and jump down. Juan, my new friend, and I got off at the lower end of Via España, a street more or less comparable to Regent Street. Opposite was the Archaeological Museum and a big Chase Manhattan Bank, both looted. Juan felt awful about the museum. 'It is our history,' he said. 'Now it is gone.'

Central begins here and it looked a mess, litter, garbage, but it is a genuine Panamanian street that still has the charm of liveliness. Every building had been looted and, though some had re-opened and some like McDonald's were operating behind boards instead of window-glass, many remained empty and ruined. The effect was of a recently bombed city. Juan pointed to an untouched shop, offering Oriental wares. 'The owners are Pakistanis; they protected their place with guns.' We found a watch-strap.

Juan insisted on taking me to his flat in Chorrillo. We walked down narrow slum streets, stepping around garbage. The houses here were big, old, unpainted wood boxes, four storeys high, filthy, packed with people, the balconies draped in drying laundry. I heard that these structures were built in the early years of the century as boarding houses for the men who dug the Canal. Chorrillo is the poorest and most densely populated district of a long strung-out city where 600,000 people live. At this end, the poverty is stunning; at the other end, wealth is flaunted.

Juan, an accountant, lives on the twelfth floor of a tower-block, one of several rising above the ancient grey wood warrens. The entry was dark and miserable, but once out on the open walkway that led to the flats, you saw how proudly these people took care of their homes. Juan's spotless, cramped flat was blissfully cool, wind blowing through from the back door to the front balcony. It has beautiful views: behind to green Ancon Hill, HQ for Southern Command; in front to the Pacific and the beginning of the Canal. Juan shares the meagre space with his wife and three infant sons, the fourth well on the way. Here his family, and everyone else in the building, was wakened shortly after midnight on 20 December by the inconceivable noise of bombardment.

'We all ran to the basement,' Juan said. 'We lay on the floor for six hours. We were terrified. The children have traumas.' (Trauma, misused, has now entered the Spanish language in Panama.) When the noise died down they went back to their flats. A machine-gun bullet slashed across one wall of Juan's balcony; the windows were broken. For three days this area was without electricity, for five days without water.

Almost opposite Juan's building, three streets away, Noriega had established his main Cuartel, a compound of headquarters and barracks, set in the midst of the slums. Perhaps Noriega felt most comfortable here because this is what he came from, an illegitimate abandoned slum kid. That Cuartel was the focus for the US Invasion. Noriega was not there and never had been. But the poor were sleeping in their overcrowded tenements all around, and there they died, unless they managed to escape. Juan took photos from his balcony right after the attack. It looked the way any city looks, subjected to modern warfare; like a wilderness of jagged teeth. Juan was most impressed by his photos of crumpled burned private cars.

'What did that?' he asked.

'I'd guess machine-gun fire from helicopters.'

'Do you see the bodies inside?'

American army engineers bulldozed the area, as much as they could, and now it is a grey stony wasteland, about six city blocks in size. Apparently to shift the blame for the death and destruction in Chorrillo, the story was put about that it was the work of Noriega's Dignity Brigade, his special thug bodyguard. While pinned down in the Cuartel by helicopter gunships, rockets, tanks and US infantry, men of the Dignity Brigade are supposed to have crept out and set fire to the surrounding slums.

The magazine *Army*, in its account of Operation Just Cause, prints a photo of a sky-high black cloud which it describes as a fire in a Cuartel building, 'the result of heavy damage inflicted by air support and Sheridan light tanks.' The Cuartel buildings were cement and would not have burned like that, but the dry old wood tenements burned to the ground. Again as reported by *Army*, some of Noriega's troops escaped from the Cuartel and sniped at American soldiers from the upper floors of the tenements. Since when are snipers silenced by erasing whole city blocks crammed with civilians?

After the Invasion, we read in our newspapers first that there were 300, then later 600 dead in Panama. The consensus on the streets of Panama is 7,000 dead. Chorrillo was a death-trap. There was also heavy fighting in San Miguelito, north-east of the airport where another Noriega Cuartel is encircled by slums. 'You cannot see that,' I was told. 'They have their Cuartel there now.' 'They' are always Americans. 'It is closed off by barbed wire. But you could smell the dead, a horrible smell, two days later.' Juan also spoke of smelling the dead in Chorrillo, three days after the invasion. It is a smell you know at once though you never knew it before; and you never forget it.

Y ou are not allowed to see San Miguelito, but any taxi driver will take you to the Garden of Peace, a large, private cemetery near there. The cemetery is an expanse of perfectly tended lawn with identical small, flat marble gravestones. A trench of chocolate-coloured earth runs across the rear width of the cemetery. A mass grave. This mass grave is common knowledge. Rumour says there is another mass grave at Fort Amador, now occupied by US Southern Command. Rumour says that there are several more.

In early January, a group of well-known Americans—lawyers, clergy, civil rights activists, students, trade union leaders—formed the Independent Commission of Inquiry on the US Invasion of Panama. Ramsey Clark, former US attorney general, the Commission's principal spokesman, made several trips to Panama. On 25 January, the Commission sent out a press release: 'Having spoken to hospital personnel, cemetery and morgue workers and others with first-hand accounts, we believe that as many as 4,000 to 7,000 people may have been killed during the Invasion.' No one knows the number of the wounded—hundreds? thousands?—and they are unseen. The Panamanian authorities admit that 15,000 families were made homeless, in one night.

I went out to dinner once, hoping for a good meal, but it was too spooky, only five other people in the restaurant and nerves about finding a taxi to get back to the hotel by nine o'clock. The empty streets suggested that everyone had nine o'clock nerves. At night I read the Panama papers. The news was mostly bland waffle. Every day, the 'fast' of President Endara made the front pages. In these chaotic times, the President had withdrawn to the Cathedral, where he 'fasted', 'out of compassion for the humble people who are suffering hunger' and to gain 'a more spiritual outlook'.

The humble people jeered. They said that the President was a fat man of fifty-three dieting to lose weight for his June wedding to Ana Mae, aged twenty-four. In a brilliantly lit side chapel, whose altar was adorned with a truly hideous plaster statue of the dead

Christ in Mary's arms and big vases of artificial flowers, President Endara received diplomats and delegations and starved on mustard-coloured varnished wood pews. He slept there on a cot. The Presidential piety was much appreciated by the Church. The President fasted for thirteen days, lost seventeen pounds and returned to his offices in the Presidential palace, a handsome white building that faces the sea. Here a small group of protesters, bearing hand-printed placards, camps silently on the cobbles across from the guarded entrance. One placard stated: 'No one talks of fasting who knows hunger.' Another announced: 'Noriega robbed us, Endara locks us up.'

Everyone asks where you come from. I said *Inglaterra* which is true. Now I intended to present myself as a '*periodista inglesa*', an English journalist, at the *Casa de Periodistas*, the modest compound of meeting rooms, courtyard, tatty bar and union offices of Panamanian journalists. I wanted people to talk to me, and I refused to take any responsibility for the Invasion.

The *Casa de Periodistas* buzzed with arguing, sloppily dressed men; journalism cannot be a road to riches here. The first protest demo, called by the National Council of Workers' Organizations, was due that afternoon outside Parliament. I had been gripped by the human misery and the wreckage of the Invasion; I had no idea of its political effect until I met the press.

Upstairs in the union office, a man said: 'American troops went to people's homes; they arrested all union officials within three days. They took them to Clayton [Fort Clayton, the main US Southern Command base] for interrogation. They took our pictures. I was held for three days. Some colleagues for weeks, some we still don't know about. US soldiers moved in here and occupied the place. They only gave it back on 18 January [nearly a month after the Invasion]. About 150 journalists in the private and public sector have been sacked. *Not* Noriegistans, by God, but anti-gringo. I expect to be picked up any day.'

'There are American advisors in every department of the government, telling Endara's people what to do,' another journalist said. 'It is against the Panamanian Constitution to have foreigners in our government.'

An angry man said: 'They sacked 2,000 civil servants, including

277

all the union officials, without any kind of legality. There are 30,000 more unemployed since the Invasion. The worst is that the real hacks, people who took part in the corruption of the Noriega regime, are now part of this new government and saying who should be fired, protecting their own people. If you are against the Invasion, they say you are Noriegista. Soon they will say we are communists. We are *nationalists*.'

This journalist spoke with bitterness. '*Radio Nacional* stayed on the air after the Invasion, telling people what was happening. A day later, a helicopter circled their building three times until it got into position, then it fired a rocket into the seventh floor. That took care of *Radio Nacional*. Then they arrested its director Ruben Dario. The newspaper *La Republica* came out with reports of the dead, after the Invasion. The next day American soldiers went in and smashed up the offices and closed the paper. They kept Calvo, the editor, in Fort Clayton for about six weeks; now he's in the Model Prison. We haven't heard of any charge against him. Southern Command closed two other newspapers and they've taken over TV channels 2 and 4 [Panama channels]. To move freely in our own country we need a press card from Southern Command. We haven't the right to know how many people died because General Cisneros [of Southern Command] took the list. Information is the property of Southern Command, not the Panamanian press. This isn't a democracy; it's a US military dictatorship, instead of a Noriega dictatorship.'

'Noriega is nothing, an excuse,' an older journalist said. 'They can't even bring him to trial. First they said March; now they say January 1991. They'll hide him away and in five years he'll be free to enjoy his millions. This Invasion is about the Canal Treaty. The United States has put in a docile government, the oligarchy, the same class we had in 1968. It has the same interests as the United States. There must be an election in 1994, according to the constitution—though we should have an election now to get a legitimate government—and then again an election in 1997 when the Canal is due to revert to Panama. But the United States will make sure there is still a docile government here. That government can abrogate the treaty, say it's too difficult for us little people to manage, please stay. The Canal isn't the important thing; it's the Canal Zone, the bases, the airfields. The United States dominates all Central America now and geographically Panama is the ideal control point.'

The Canal Zone is a strip of land north of Panama City ten miles wide by fifty miles long, between the Pacific and the Caribbean. It contains the Canal, the extensive civilian administration of the Canal, and a major US military installation, plus all their dependents and recreational facilities. By the terms of the 1977 Panama Canal treaty, this will be ceded back to Panama in 1999 and the treaty forbids the presence of foreign troops on Panamanian soil.

The Invasion was obviously long-planned, waiting for a 'Just Cause', and Noriega, crazy with hubris, obliged. President Carter had forced through the Panama Canal Treaty; it had never suited the military or the Republicans and no doubt they would like to cancel it if they can. Still, nothing explains the preposterous size of the Invasion, the most copious display of force since Vietnam. Unless Operation Just Cause was intended as a very special PR job: to remind every country from the Caribbean basin to the Strait of Magellan that the United States is the last superpower.

My Panamanian journalist colleagues also gave me a sheaf of documents, press releases from various unions and the American Independent Commission of Inquiry on the US Invasion of Panama. The unions accuse the Endara government of denying their rights, won during twenty-one years of dictatorship. The Independent Commission accuses the US government of 'police state tactics', citing cases. The arrest by American soldiers of Dr Romulo Escobar Betancourt, chief negotiator of the Panama Canal Treaty, formerly Chancellor of Panama University and delegate to the UN, who was held incommunicado for five days at Fort Clayton, then turned over to the Panamanian police. The ongoing searches, harassments and interrogation of Panamanian civilians by US military. The arrest order for seventy-four prominent Panamanians, known as lifelong supporters of Panamanian independence, to be charged with 'impeding the renewal of the Powers of the State.' The penalty is five to twenty years in prison and prohibition from holding public office. The Independent Commission concludes that there is 'a clear and continuing effort by the United States government to intimidate and crush any democratic opposition.'

The Spanish word for totally destitute is *damnificado*. The people who ran from their burning collapsing houses in Chorrillo, with the clothes on their backs, saving their lives and nothing else, were *los damnificados de Chorrillo*. I wanted to hear their stories, exactly what happened on the night of the Invasion and what was happening to them now. The Panamanian journalists said they were not allowed to see them; maybe I could get in.

Three thousand *damnificados* are housed at an unused US airfield. The US army built windowless plywood cubicles for most of them in an unused hangar. The cubicles are three metres by three metres. The high, shadowed building is at least cool; the overflow suffocates in army tents. Another 500 *damnificados* camp in two city schools.

I got to the hangar entrance and was stopped. As I had no press credentials of any kind, I made a bullying scene, saying that if I could not speak to these refugees the authorities must have something to hide. The camp director, from the Panamanian Red Cross, conceded that he would let me in if the '*Señora*' the government representative, gave me a letter. I returned to Panama. After infuriating telephone calls, trying to find this lady, she appeared at my hotel, a nice oligarchy aristocrat. She wrote a note and telephoned the Red Cross director to expect me.

I went back. This time I got no farther than the guard post. The camp director came to meet me, all welcoming smiles, and took the note. But the American lieutenant on duty, eight feet tall, white, swathed in bandoliers, hefting his M-16 (a seriously threatening weapon) said: No. I did not have a 'seal' (a press card from Southern Command?); my name was not on his roster.

I observed that the Panamanian authority and the camp director gave me permission to talk to Panamanian citizens and I did not see what the US army had to do with it.

'Anybody can write a letter,' said the lieutenant, holding the note. 'I have my orders.' The camp director, who of course knew the handwriting and knew his superior had agreed to my visit, stood beside the lieutenant, looking at the ground. It was a public humiliation, delivered with indifference. US Southern Command rules, OK.

I said to the camp director, in Spanish, 'You live under an army of occupation.'

He closed his eyes for a second and said softly, 'What can we do?'

I said, 'You have my full sympathy.'

He said, 'Thank you, *Señora*,' and we shook hands.

I walked back to the warehouses where traffic was stopped and found a taxi that had just deposited a passenger, which spared me the long, hot trudge to the main road and a bus. A very young woman, very pregnant, asked for a lift to town. We sat in the back with her five-year-old son between us. The boy was much too thin, pale, dressed in a clean, pressed white shirt and cotton trousers. By chance, I learned from this tired, helpless girl what I had wanted to know. Her story was brief.

'I grabbed the child and we ran through the bullets. We ran and ran until we came to the sea. Now something is bad with baby,' she touched her stomach. 'I must go to the hospital every day. My father gives me two dollars for the taxis. He is a taxi driver. I have no money or anything. Many people were burned up, many, many, old ones and children who could not get out. At the camp they give us coffee and dry bread for breakfast and at five in the afternoon one plate of food.' She sighed and looked at the boy. He sat on the edge of the seat, rigid and silent. 'He is very nervous. If there is the smallest noise, he trembles and cries.'

She had been there in one of those big wood boxes when suddenly her home, her neighbourhood, blazed with fire, and the people tried to escape 'through the bullets'. Her testimony was the reason why Southern Command prevented journalists from meeting the *damnificados*. She cannot have been a special case. All the uprooted survivors of Chorrillo lived through the same fearful night.

We dropped her at the hospital. I wished her luck, wondering what that might be. Not to die in childbirth? Not to produce a deformed or deranged baby?

I went to my room, showered, and drank duty-free whiskey, raging against the Divine Right of US Presidents to do anything they like to poor people in Central America. This arrogance derives from the Monroe Doctrine of 1823, which is no more than a Presidential fiat warning the European powers not to meddle in the

Americas. The United States would then refrain from meddling in Europe. Ever since, US Presidents have meddled ceaselessly in the affairs of sovereign states, south of the US border.

South American states, though tightly entangled in debt to North America, are by now very prickly. After the CIA orchestration of the demise of President Allende of Chile, US Presidents are not apt to interfere flagrantly in South America. But Central America could be described as a free fire zone. Anything goes.

Why have the leaders, the media, the citizens of the Great Western Democracies cared long and ardently for the people of Central Europe, but cared nothing for the people of Central America? Between twenty-seven and twenty-eight million people live in the seven states of Central America. Most of them are bone poor, and most of them do not have white skin. Their lives and their deaths have not touched the conscience of the world. I can testify that it was far better and safer to be a peasant in communist Poland than it is to be a peasant in capitalist El Salvador.

US Presidents, who formulate US foreign policy, never worried about social justice in Central America. The White House tolerates any Central American government if it is loyal to the ideology of capitalism and knows its place, subservience to the national interests of the United States as defined in Washington. Washington likes dictators because they are easier to deal with. US Presidents regularly clamp down on popular rebellions. The demand of cruelly deprived people for a decent life is seen as dangerous to US interests; quite simply, the poor are dangerous. They are capable of saying: Yank Go Home.

No US President ever deposed a dictatorship in Central America or South America either. On the contrary. Noriega is unique. Noriega would still be there if he had not fancied he could be an independent dictator; the fool got above himself. The drug business will continue; North Americans want drugs; drug money will be laundered discreetly. But everything is in order now; the US has taken over Panama in its usual style, with a friendly native government. 'Democracy', which has the sound of silver bells in Central Europe, is a mean joke in Central America.

On the western arm of the Bay of Panama, a forest of condominium skyscrapers rises from untended land. No trees, bushes, flowers, just these massive vulgar buildings. Nearby, luxurious houses are screened by large delightful gardens. This neighbourhood is the golden ghetto of Paitilla, the habitat of the class that the people call *la oligarquía*, the winners of the Invasion.

That night there was a lecture, with three speakers, at the Marriott Caesar Park Hotel, the biggest, gaudiest, most expensive hotel in Panama. It was an oligarchy event. The audience sat in a grandiose salon and listened with rapt attention to two lectures, read by important Panamanians. The subject was: 'Democracy, Sovereignty and Invasion.' The audience, perhaps a hundred people, was mostly men, mostly overweight, wearing good dark suits. Noriega, like Torrijos before him, never touched their money or their lifestyle. But for twenty-one years, they were shelved: they had no active role in government. And they were shamed; it was shaming to be citizens of a state ruled by a squalid crook from the gutter. Upper class Panamanians were the dissidents here. Overnight, literally, Operation Just Cause solved their problems.

The tone of the lectures was creamy satisfaction. To stay awake, I made notes among which I find the well-turned phrase 'pseudo-intellectual bullshit'. Neither speaker mentioned the dead, the homeless, the bankrupted small businesses. I wondered if any of them had looked at the wasteland of Chorrillo. The general sense was clear enough: the Endara government was just fine; the United States was just fine; all was again right with their world.

After two long lectures, the audience needed a rest. They moved to the hall and the meeting became a cocktail party, with drinks from a bar set up for the occasion. The women, now on view, were very chic, in traditional smart little black dresses and appropriate jewellery. Everyone knew everyone else and everyone was white, the flower of Panamanian society.

After the intermission the last speaker was introduced, to applause, as 'the next President of Cuba'. He told his reverent audience that democracy was fragile; Noriegismo was not dead; they must be vigilant to protect their regained freedom. Then he said that Latin America would not have objected to the Invasion if it hadn't been done by the United States. Very odd. Who else would have done it? He ended with an impassioned plea for the liberty of Cuba. Was he urging a US Invasion there? A bloodbath for his countrymen? They gave the next President of Cuba a standing ovation. Some of those here tonight had been in exile in the United States for eight months, from last May—when Noriega violently broke up the election that was going against him—until the December Invasion. But this Cuban had lived in exile in Spain for thirty years; he was their hero.

The University of Panama made a pleasing contrast to the Marriott Park Caesar. It is a sprawl of grimily white cement buildings, inside and out a basic factory for learning. But the buildings, planted in a lovely jungle of trees and flowering shrubs, are linked by colonnaded shady walkways and the kids look bright and shabby and it is a good place. Ten thousand young men and women study here in three daily shifts which start at seven a.m. and end at midnight. Tuition ranges from thirty to forty-five dollars a semester; law and medicine cost the most.

Each faculty has a students' association, with elected officers. I was looking for Literature and found Psychology. The three officers of their students' association sat with me in an enlarged cubby-hole off the small study room; they closed the door. They took turns talking, in low voices as if we were conspirators.

The tall, pale blond said, 'We can say things here we would not say in public. People are afraid to talk. Some professors are in favour of this government. It is bourgeois; all of them born rich; there is no new young blood. When the United States hit us with the embargo we managed anyway; it didn't crush us. The idea of needing identity papers signed by a *norteamericano* general is repugnant.'

The small plump dark one said, 'We are all anti-Noriega but Noriega brought up working class men and gave them positions of power. That was good. This government will keep its own class in the top jobs. We don't think this is democracy. We are nationalists, we want to govern our country in our own way.'

The other dark boy said, 'In this university it doesn't matter if you are the son of a taxi driver or a cabinet minister's son. I think the Invasion was wrong and we ought to have a free election, not this government. The curfew is spoiling our lives. We always went to each other's houses and listened to music and talked or we went to cafés or danced. Now we can't be out after nine o'clock for fear of running into anti-socials or gringo military patrols.'

I asked about drugs; after all, the Invasion was supposed to be about drugs. According to President Bush, drugs are America's number one enemy, threatening its youth, its future, and drugs are not unknown in American universities. They agreed that there were no drugs on the campus and never had been. 'People are motivated to study, the blond said, 'or they wouldn't be here.'

I went to the Law faculty next day, thinking that these future lawyers were most apt to be future politicians. A small, thin young man, elected representative of the law students' association, spoke in a guarded voice. Strangely cautious, like the psychology students: 'All of us here are against the Invasion. The vote last May was against Noriega but not for Endara. We should have had an election now; this is not a legal government. We are not hopeful of the future. We do not think the law will be independent and honest with this government. Already they are appointing judges, magistrates, in the same manner as Noriega, their friends, their relatives. Not on merit. I doubt if there will be an honourable system of justice in Panama for a long time.'

Pedro was the most interesting of the many interesting taxi drivers. I always sat in front, for leg room and conversation. On my last day in Panama, Pedro agreed to drive me around Chorrillo for an hour; many would not, due to the robbery syndrome. Pedro was a little, under-nourished, monkeyish mulatto aged twenty-five or thirty-five. He wore a fixed dazzling smile, as if his face had frozen into this hilarity. Driving down Via España, he said, 'At ten-thirty that night I was stopped by soldiers back there.'

'What soldiers?' The Invasion started after midnight.

'Panamanians. They were stopping cars to carry munitions from their Cuartel to the Cuartel in Chorrillo. but my taxi was too small. One of them fired a shot in the air and said, "Get out!" I tell you the truth, my heart was in my hands! I drove home as fast as possible. I was so full of fear that I stayed there for three days.'

'They knew about the Invasion then?'

'Clearly. But the people did not believe it until they heard the bombs.' We were now in the area of devastation. 'That was the gymnasium for Noriega's officers.' A big building, parts of the walls still standing; inside you could see what had been a basketball court. An old woman sat in the doorway. We drove slowly through the grey wasteland. It had been possible to raze only the stumps of the wood tenements. They must have dynamited the remains of Noriega's Cuartel headquarters.

Pedro stopped before another large building. 'It was three storeys high.'

From what I have seen in war, this building took a direct heavy bomb hit. Nothing else would scoop it out, leaving only jagged sections of wall. *Army*, which gives the most detailed record of Operation Just Cause, states that Stealth fighter planes, used here for the first time, dropped 'concussion bombs'. So we know that planes were in action, and 'concussion bombs' sounds like a cover-up.

'It was a reform school,' Pedro said. 'Boys and girls from five to seventeen. The Cuartel was over there, behind it.'

'They were sleeping here?'

'They were sleeping here.'

I do not see how any of the children could have survived.

'Sad,' Pedro said, his smile brilliant, his voice grieving.

'Let's go,' I said. 'It makes me sick.'

We passed empty yellow tower-blocks, like Juan's, and studied a huge hole near ground-level in a blank side of one building. The burn marks on upper floors were understandable: rockets. I could not guess the purpose of the hole, about five feet in diameter, nor what made it; perhaps some new super-bazooka. 'This is the Model Prison,' Pedro said. 'Look at the wall.' A high solid steel wall surrounds the prison; it too was pierced by a huge hole. 'All the prisoners escaped,' Pedro said, 'now there are other prisoners.'

On a street below the prison, Pedro said, 'This is the School of the Saviour. More than 300 people who lost their homes in Chorrillo live here.' The school had been painted dark red with yellow trim long ago. On the cement front yard, half-naked unwashed kids played and shrieked. Women leaned from the windows shouting at their children and each other. It was very hot. Pedro wiped his face again with a wet grey rag. You could imagine the smell of the place. Being an old slum school, it would have a few old toilets and wash-basins. Across the street the little looted shops were boarded up, except for a re-opened corner grocery store.

'Sad, sad,' Pedro said.

'Yes, but at least they aren't guarded by American soldiers. They can make all the noise they want,' for suddenly I remembered the unnatural stillness in the hangar. 'They can walk to the centre of town; they're in their own neighbourhood.'

'It takes much time for poor people to gain possessions. Then everything they possessed is gone, like that, in a minute. And, who knows, relatives too. Where their houses were they see there is nothing.' He turned his frantic smile and his sorrowful eyes to me, making sure I understood. 'Nothing like this ever happened in Panama. Never.'

William McPherson
In Romania

L ate last December I flew to Berlin with a friend. It was an impulse—I wanted to see the Wall while it was still standing—and for the first time in some years, maybe in my life, I was free to act on an impulse of that sort. My wish was to spend the week between Christmas and the New Year in Berlin, and in return I promised my friend that we would spend the next week in Italy, all of which we did: New Year's Eve at the Brandenburg Gate, a week overlooking the Grand Canal in Venice, then a few days in Florence and Rome. She returned to New York, and I went back briefly to the luxury of Venice, intending to go on to Budapest and Prague, return to Berlin once more and so to home. Pan Am offered a special rate.

But plans have a way of changing. The images of the Romanian revolution—I had seen it on television in Berlin—were still vivid in my mind. I had a few extra days, after all. The country was not far away. I got a copy of a map of Timişoara and secured a visa to Romania. I rented a car and loaded it with bananas, oranges and chocolate. A friend supplied me with some telephone numbers in case of an emergency, a couple of cartons of Kents—for purposes of bribery only; at the time I was not smoking—and two bottles of Johnny Walker Red should the Kents prove insufficient. And then, on 22 January, one month to the day after Ceauşescu had fled by helicopter from the roof of the Central Committee Building in Bucharest, I set off in my newly rented Volkswagen Golf, equipped even with an extra can of diesel fuel: just enough, I was told, to get me through Romania without having to pay the prices the government was charging foreigners for poor quality *motorină*.

I arrived at the Romanian border at four-thirty in the afternoon, darkness already fast approaching. It was very cold. Customs was taking a long time inspecting the Italian aid convoy ahead of me. Finally after half an hour it was my turn.

'Any weapons? Drugs? Ammunition?' the customs official asked.

'No, nothing.'

He inspected the car and asked me to open the hood. I fumbled around under the dashboard in all the likely places but couldn't figure out how to do it. I had neglected to look at the car very closely when I rented it, and now it was dark. I tried to find my flashlight but couldn't, and I felt like a fool.

'Is best you stop your travels tonight in Timişoara,' he said, more in the tone of an order than a suggestion. 'No more far.'

Yes, I assured him, pressing an orange into his hand, the Hotel Continental. 'I have a reservation.'

'Is the best.' He flashed me a V-sign; I returned it, and so I was off, but not for long. A couple of hundred metres up the road a soldier waved me to a stop.

'*Parlez-vous français?*' he asked. His French was about as fluent as mine.

'*Un peu.*'

'*Venez-vous aider la Roumanie?*'

He was rubbing his hands for warmth and looking at the oranges on the seat beside me. I showed my passport again, flashed the V-sign and gave him an orange. And after negotiating another impromptu border check-point, and another, dispensing more oranges and exchanging more V-signs, I was on my way to Timişoara, sixty-five kilometres distant. The road was better than I had expected and free of traffic, but very dark; even in the villages there was no light. All Romania was dark, I was soon to discover, and Timişoara, when I arrived there an hour later, seemed the darkest city I had ever seen.

I turned a corner, lost, and drove directly into the middle of a demonstration. The crowd filling the boulevard looked angry—perhaps a thousand people, maybe more, shouting, shoving, shaking their fists. I did not know if they were for the government or against the government. What was worse, I did not know if they were for or against me. I had no idea what they were shouting. I knew not a word of Romanian at that time, nor did I know that I had come to a stop in front of the former committee building of the district's Communist Party—the Council Building, as it was called. I knew only that I had been driving for half an hour or so in a city without lights and that I was lost. I hoped the people were friendly. They let me pass, in any event, and with relief I continued cruising the streets of Timişoara, searching for the Hotel Continental.

I recognized the triple-towered cathedral from newspaper photographs. On the steps of that cathedral, it had been reported, the terrorists fired on children holding a candle-light vigil, and the cathedral doors were locked against them. The report, I learned later, was a fabrication, but I did not know that then and I was startled by the sudden sight of it, and moved, surprising myself. I decided to give up my search for the hotel for the moment, park the car and go for a walk.

In the long square between the cathedral and the opera, clusters of candles were burning, and here and there dark figures in groups of two and three and four huddled together in the cold, whispering. No one looked at me directly. I passed the burning candles—hundreds of them—and the piles of evergreen boughs and the wreaths for the dead in the square. There were smashed windows and burnt shops and tanks with the soldiers peering out. I was caught somewhere between shock and awe and horror and tears, and I was a little nervous, too. Moreover, I was very cold. I decided to find the hotel.

Children and gypsies and money-changers thronged the parking lot. All of them wanted something: *gume*, *ciocolată*, dollars, especially dollars. One of the money-changers said something that made me laugh. I was grateful for that, but I wasn't going to deal with the first black-marketeer I saw and I continued to the entrance. There were soldiers everywhere: on the steps, at the doorway, in the lobby, around the reception desk. They looked so young, all with rifles casually slung over their shoulders. I showed my documents, registered and was given the key to room 108 where I was to spend the night. When I opened the door I was met by a blast of frigid air. Although it was very cold outside—a damp, penetrating cold—the windows were flung open wide. As it turned out, I spent many weeks in that hotel on four different occasions and with a single exception, when I checked in for only one night, I was assigned to 108, two doors down from the soldiers in 106 who were guarding the radio equipment that was housed, oddly enough, in a room twelve floors above. And the windows were always open when I arrived. Eventually, I grew rather fond of that room, of Mariana who cleaned it, even of the soldiers down the hall, but the first sight was not reassuring. It was too cold to stay there, so I left for another walk. And that is how I met Costel.

Costel was the black-marketeer—the 'businessman'—who had made me laugh. A slight man, in his twenties but almost completely bald, he was waiting on the steps in his sharp Italian jacket when I emerged, and still wanting to change money. The official rate at that time was ten *lei* to the dollar, which made Romania a very expensive place. I did not know what the unofficial rate was, but I was still not interested. I was going for a walk and invited Costel to come along.

Costel had learned his English from films and popular music, and it was primitive at best, but he managed to communicate in a smattering of French, Italian, English and a German word or two punctuated by his all-purpose expletive 'Jesus!', which was invariably accompanied by a sharp blow to the head with the heel of his hand. The expletives were very frequent. We walked to the Opera Square. This time I saw the bullet holes. The Opera itself was opening in two days for the first time since the Revolution with *Cavalleria Rusticana*. We moved on to Liberty Square where the army has its headquarters—more candles and crosses and wreaths marking the spot where the first victim fell in December—and on to the Square of the Union. All was deserted and dark. It was also cold, and I was hungry, so I invited Costel to my room for something to eat.

Costel tried to explain what had happened in Timişoara, 'the first free city in Romania,' from the Day of Sixteen to the Day of Twenty-two—as the days of the Revolution are everywhere called here—but the events were confusing and the language was a problem. We talked about money, an easier subject. The price of bread was five *lei* for a kilogram, and fuel cost nine *lei* a litre. The ration for the month of December was twenty-one litres;

sometimes it was eleven. Life was miserable and money was dear. Naturally he had to 'make business.' I suspect he was quite good at it. Three pages of my notebook are full of his calculations and figures.

I woke up early the next morning. The fog was very thick, and softened and reduced all colour. The outlines of the cathedral loomed at the far end of the square, the green light of its clock like the eye of Cyclops looking down. There were silent people moving past, candles glowing in the mist, and long, slow queues. Having nothing better to do, I joined the longest, which led down a stairway, underground. I could not see what lay at the head of the line—perhaps it was only a public toilet—but when I got down the steps there was a man selling newspapers. I was astonished to see such a long line for newspapers. I bought one of each, perhaps four or five in all. Encouraged by this success, I decided to join every line I saw. One just forming grew quickly to be longer than the first. When I realized that the people were lining up for one-kilogram tins of meat, the gift of an Italian aid mission—four to a person, a great luxury—I left and joined a line for apples. I wanted only one. I held out my hundred-*lei* note. How much? The man wanted to give it to me. I insisted. He refused. I took the apple and ate it as I walked back to the hotel for breakfast.

The coffee was terrible. I wrote in my notebook: next time tea. I look at that note now and suddenly I realize its implications. Had I already decided to spend another night in Timişoara? I had only the morning here. I mustn't waste it. I went into a shop. There were many clerks but only two customers and almost nothing to buy. Outside a man sat down on the pavement and pulled two flapping geese out of a valise. In a food shop, an *alimentară*, the shelves held tomato paste, raspberry syrup and mineral water, nothing else. I moved on, back to the Opera Square, past a poster for *A Comedy of Errors*, past the tanks now laden with flowers, towards the candles, the hastily erected crosses, the wreaths, into the cathedral. I bought a few more candles and lit them. For the Revolution. For the people

who had died in the square. For these sad faces I saw around me.
A boy followed me. He could not have been more than eight or
ten. He was a clever little boy with an engaging but somehow
twisted face. I supposed he had had some kind of injury. He
wanted money. I had only hundred-*lei* notes, and I gave him one.
He brought over his two pals. I parted with 200 more. Then they
asked for *gume-gume* and *ciocolată*. I had neither and I left the
cathedral, but not before surreptitiously dropping another
hundred *lei* on each of the cripples beside the door. By now I was
feeling both guilty for having so much money and foolish for
dropping it for every plaintive face. I had started out the morning
with 700 *lei* in my pocket. I had eighteen and a half left. I decided
to stay another night. I wanted to know what lay behind these
faces—as if another night would tell me.

Another young boy was standing beside me. He was well
dressed, wearing a fur hat. I took him to be about twelve. He was
eating a cookie, and he offered me one from the sack in his hand.
I took it. I was hungry again. I tried to speak with him, but he
spoke no English, no French. He did not utter a word in fact, but
he offered me another cookie, and together we moved on,
walking through the square. I was beginning to feel guilty for
eating so many of his cookies, and by signs I indicated lunch and
pointed towards the hotel. I took him into the dining-room and
we sat down to lunch, in silence. We had not exchanged a word,
but I wanted him to write his name in my notebook. I pointed to
myself and wrote 'Bill'. I pointed to him and handed him the pen.
He wrote in the Romanian fashion, last name first: 'Rotaru
Viorel. *Clasa* VII-A.'

Suddenly Costel, my money-changer from the night before,
rushed to the table. There was someone he wanted me to meet.
George. George spoke English. George had something to tell me.
Something important. He had people I must meet. He was
waiting in the lobby. Come! Come! Costel was pulling at my arm,
and I went to meet George. Costel vanished. The three of
us—George, Viorel and I—set off down the street. I couldn't
figure out exactly who George wanted me to meet, or why, but in
a few moments I was hustled into an old building where two or

three newspapers shared offices and everyone was speaking at once. George was gone. Viorel had disappeared at the door. I never saw him again, and I am sorry about that. Now that I know enough words in Romanian, I would like to thank him for the cookies, I would like to know how he is doing.

The newspaper offices were filled with cigarette smoke. The people there were mostly young, many of them students—writers and editors from a number of papers, including the newspaper *Timişoara* whose first issue I had bought, quite inadvertently, for half a *lei* in the square that morning.

Tell us about democracy! they said.

We know nothing about democracy!

We need books, newspapers about democracy!

This is the first free town in Romania!

They say one in five people here is a *Securist*! Who can we trust?

I was ushered from one room to another. The men and women in those rooms—mostly men—seemed at once diffident and very proud and more than a little anxious. Everything was rushed—there was so little time, they told me, and so much to learn, so much to do. They had started very late. They wanted to talk about literature and art and life in the West and—a question very often asked in Romania—how much had I paid for my camera. They wanted to know which of my country's writers I admired, and why. One young student with a shy but engaging smile told me *Catcher in the Rye* was his favourite book. Some of them had read Steinbeck—the old regime found him more politically correct than most—and they were familiar with Hemingway and Walt Whitman. I thought they knew a lot. And I? What did I know of their country? Was I familiar with the work of Brancuşi? Had I heard of Mircea Eliade? Mihai Eminescu? They asked a lot of questions. They smoked a lot of cigarettes. They laughed a lot, too. There was some joy in Romania after all; or at least a sense of humour.

2

Petru, a reporter for the local student newspaper, *Forum Studenţesc*, was impatient; he had something to show me. He rushed me down the stairs and out the door. We jumped on to a tram. 'No,' he said, when I pulled out some money for the fare, 'I am a revolutionary, I am a student. We do not pay.' So I did not pay either. Over the next few months I rode many trams in Timişoara; I rarely saw anyone pay.

Petru was a very nervous student of engineering, tall and thin with bloodshot eyes. He told me he had not slept for two days and I believed him. He pulled me aside. The document in his hand had been taken, he told me, from the desk of an important officer in the *Securitate*. It was three or four pages long and it contained a numbered list of names, informers—130 or 140 in all—the date each had been recruited and from where, and the amount of money each was paid.

'This is very dangerous. Tell no one. I am dead if they know I have this.'

Dead? Was he serious? I found it hard to believe, but I have since seen many things in Romania, even a suicide, that are hard to believe. 'Why are you showing this to me?'

'You are a journalist. I trust no one here. You must help.'

'But how?' I didn't know if I were slipping into reality or out of it. In Romania, I was beginning to learn, reality has a sliding floor. I looked at the document now in my hand. 'How do you know it's authentic?' I turned the pages. I turned the pages again. The names meant nothing to me. 'Petru, this is a copy. It is very easy to fake a copy.'

'Fake?'

'Falsify. Counterfeit.'

'No! It is veritable. I have a tape cassette, too. More dangerous. In a safe place. Oh! I am a dead man!'

'No, Petru. You're very much alive. I am your friend.' Not, I realized, that that would make much difference; I just wanted it to. 'You will be all right.' I looked again at the document. The list was in chronological order beginning four or five years before. It appeared to be written in the same spidery hand—until the end. There a line had been drawn part way across the page and three more names had been added beneath it, with a darker pen, by another hand. Someone had torn the original in half; the pages had been pieced back together to be copied.

Yes, Petru said, the officer of the *Securitate* was disposing of the document at the time of the Revolution. He had torn it.

'You took it out of his waste basket?'

No, he was in a great hurry. He tore it up and left it on his desk.

'For someone to find?' I asked. 'Look, Petru, this may be authentic, but it looks to me like a plant.'

'A plant?' He took the pages from my hand.

'Someone wanted you to find this.' But what kind of person, I asked myself, would plant such a thing, and what would he hope to achieve? The answer was not comforting.

'No. It is correct.' Petru folded the document and returned it carefully to his briefcase. I regret that I never saw it again. He produced a copy of his newspaper, laying it open before me. His name appeared at the top of the page above three poems. 'I am a poet. Please, I want you to have them.' He looked very proud.

That night there was a big demonstration. George, I noticed, had appeared at my side.

'What's happening, George?'

'The worms are leaving the apple.' George took my pen and notebook. 'I show you.'

He drew two worms abandoning an apple eaten to the core, and labelled it 'PCR'—Romanian Communist Party. The worms were headed for another apple, round and fat, labelled 'FSN'—*Frontul Salvării Naţionale*, the Front for National Salvation. George shrugged. 'The first apple is finished. They're going for the second.' It was as succinct an explanation of what was happening in Timişoara that week—and what had been happening in all of Romania since a few hours after Ceausescu fled—as any I heard.

At that moment in Timisoara there were two factions vying

for power and a third—the army—that seemed to be more or less holding it. The first president of the County Council after the Revolution had resigned—been forced out, really—on 12 January. That day was a day of mourning throughout Romania for the martyrs of the Revolution and one of massive demonstrations against the participation of former Communists in the government. That day the army under General Gheorghe Popescu had taken control of the city. General Popescu, an avuncular looking man with a paunch, had come out of retirement until local elections could be held.

Such a description makes the situation sound so clear. Maybe it was, but that evening and for many evenings to come it was far from clear to me. It wasn't clear to a lot of other people either, which was reassuring in a sense. Soldiers were stationed at the airport, the government buildings, the hospitals, the hotels, the opera—all the important points—but the army in control? The troops looked too young to control anything; the greatest danger appeared to be from one of their rifles going off by accident. The *Securitate* was still at large—there had been shooting, I was told—yet no one knew who or where they were. Who was who was difficult to sort out in Romania.

Two things were clear in Timişoara, however: everyone was a revolutionary, and no one wanted communism. No one wanted to lose what meagre privileges he had, either. And in Bucharest the Council of the National Salvation Front was consolidating its power. Originally, the Council was not a party—it had been only an interim arrangement of the Revolution—but that day it endorsed the decision, contrary to an earlier pledge, to field its own candidates in the national elections, now scheduled for 20 May. They didn't want to lose their privileges either.

Later in the evening, George invited me to his apartment. There had been a large and boisterous demonstration for the 'new' local Front, which was opposed to the previous night's *manifestation* for the 'old' Front, and George tried to explain the difference, again with the help of sketches. The old Front was composed of people who happened to congregate inside the Opera—the centre of the Revolution—from the Day of Seventeen onwards. All sorts of people, George said. Opportunists. Gypsies. Vagabonds. Rubbish people. Some good people, too. They formed the first post-revolutionary government of the county and of the city of Timişoara. But there were problems, and new councils would be elected soon. The elections were supported by Renaşterea, the 'independent' newspaper. It all sounded very democratic, except for the troubling worms in the apple.

The man behind the local elections in Timişoara was George's friend Savu. His given name was Ion, but I never heard anyone refer to him other than by his family name, Savu. Savu was the president of the Front in his enterprise, the detergent plant, one of the largest in Timişoara. Savu was a hero of the Revolution. He tried to make democracy in his factory. He had to run, hide. Even now. Five different houses in four days. 'Come! You must talk to him.' So George and Alec Russell, who had simply hopped a flight to Romania ten days before and was now filing for the *Daily Telegraph*, piled into my car and raced through the streets, black as pitch and dense with fog and riddled with pot-holes, to Savu's block, George shouting directions at the same time as he was shouting politics. I drove over a median strip. I couldn't see it in the fog. At times I wasn't even sure I was on a street. But we made it to Savu's, just as Savu was leaving for the railroad station.

Savu was catching the 11:54 to Bucharest. We sped to the train, jumping aboard with him, his wife and his retinue. There must have been six or eight of us jammed in the small space between the cars.

'Interview him,' George commanded.

I looked at my watch. The train wouldn't leave for more than an hour. 'Why are you going to Bucharest?' I asked.

'Timişoara is the first free town in Romania,' Savu said. I already knew that. 'From the beginning I fought for a real democracy. To fight with all my being for the rights of the people.' The fog was swirling. The locomotives were steaming. George was translating.

'Why are you going to Bucharest?'

'I do not want power. I have no interest in power.'

'But why are you going to Bucharest?'

'One. For an exact determination of political intentions for the short and long term. Two. For help for a real democracy. Timişoara is the . . . ' My notes are scarcely decipherable, but really it made no difference. I had heard many politicians, and although Savu's life might well have been in danger, he sounded like a politician to me. 'One. Really free elections without any pressure from different groups, without interference of private interests. Only honest people. I do not want power.'

'How do you determine who is honest?'

'I was elected by the workers. I am president of the Front in my enterprise. Timişoara will be the first town with democracy in Romania.'

I am not quite sure why I asked the next question. Perhaps I had surmised the situation. Savu had, after all, been living like a fugitive. 'Do you trust anyone?'

'No.'

'No one at all?'

'Only Marton Florin.' (I met Florin a couple of days later. He was a football player, an engineer, and of course a revolutionary. I liked him. A few days after that, he said it was urgent to speak to me. When he came to my room he was so terrified he could not talk, not in my room—it might be bugged—and not outside, either. Maybe I could meet him in Belgrade. I didn't see Florin again for four months, not until after the national elections in May, when he seemed relaxed and quite content. He had been invited to Bucharest where he met Mr Iliescu; he had been made president of the Sports Club of his factory—that was his job. He had voted for Mr Iliescu and life was good and the National Salvation Front was 'the best.')

Savu amended his statement: 'Maybe Marton Florin.' I was learning my first lesson about Romania: no one trusts anyone.

3

As it happened, I did leave Romania—for the afternoon. I drove to Belgrade with Alec, the young journalist from Britain, and Corina, a translator who had never been out of her country. She had never seen shops full of oranges and bananas and chocolate and coffee. She had never seen a city illuminated at night. We went, in short, so that Corina could buy fruit, which she did, masses of it; so that she could use her fresh new passport, her first; so that she could see a city with lights. Belgrade is not Paris by day or by night, and its shops are not luxurious by the standards of London or New York, but it sufficed. After my short time in Timişoara—amazing how quickly the eye grows accustomed to its surroundings—Belgrade looked splendid enough to Alec and me as well. So we all bought fruit, and had coffee and cakes in a café, and then later had dinner in a fairly ordinary cafeteria where, I thought, I lost my red scarf. It was a favourite scarf. I had bought it in London a few years before. We looked around the restaurant, we searched the car. The next day I searched the car again. Someone in Belgrade, I thought, has a very nice scarf. I never expected to see it again, but I did, a few weeks later, when Corina came to visit me in my hotel room where I was recuperating from a particularly virulent case of food poisoning. The scarf was around her neck. I let it pass.

The local elections in Timişoara were held the last Saturday and Monday of January. The new Front replaced the old on the councils of the municipality and the county. No one was surprised, although many were unhappy, and on the Sunday between the two elections there was a very big demonstration. '*Jos Iliescu*! *Jos comunismul*!' the people chanted; 'Down with Iliescu! Down with communism! We are not rats. We do not want a new perestroika. *Libertate*! *Libertate*!'

George, I noticed, had appeared at my side.

'What's happening, George?'

'Nobody knows exactly.'

It seemed to me, though, that a lot of people in Timişoara

303

were objecting to the early retirement of the December revolutionaries—many of them young people—in favour of the considerably older order of Party bureaucrats and chiefs and masters who had run the farms, factories, enterprises and lives of people before, and were about to run them again.

Both days the balloting took place in the Olimpia Sports Hall, under the supervision of the Committee for Free Elections, which the old Front did not recognize. The entrance was guarded by soldiers. Savu was there, plump and proud, making politics in a red tie and pin-stripe jacket. His wife and various other members of the Committee were seated behind a large table on the floor. The elections were not like elections I was accustomed to in the West. The citizens of Timişoara did not turn out to vote. A fellow I had met three days before asked me where I was going that Saturday morning. To the elections, I said.

'What elections?' he asked.

The electoral procedures had been set up in four days the week before; the dates had been established on Wednesday, the day Savu was in Bucharest. The old Communist cells in every factory had disappeared, of course, on 22 December. They were replaced, more or less, by the new and revolutionary-sounding fronts, who chose the delegates—about 1,000 in all—who then chose the candidates and elected the members of the Municipal Council and the larger and more powerful County Council.

But exactly how this system worked was difficult to figure out. 'So every four hundred workers in an enterprise get one delegate for the county elections and two for the city?'

George nodded, but his assent seemed weak.

'And every ten to twenty delegates name one candidate?'

George nodded again. 'Maybe. Is not for sure.'

Few things were 'for sure'. But the voting was very orderly, the ballot boxes were sealed, unsealed, the ballots counted and the results announced. Savu told us we had just witnessed the first free elections in Timişoara, indeed, in all Romania, since 1928, and the first ever done with the help of computers. In making this announcement Savu looked pleased as Punch.

George smiled. He is a good-looking man, and he has an

engaging smile. 'What you see is not true,' he said, 'and what is true you cannot see, only feel. That is what Romania was before, and it still is.' He laughed; George enjoys being cryptic. 'Reality is a secret here.'

'Now we have the celebration,' declared the President of the Committee for Free Elections, his voice jubilant, and late that rainy Monday afternoon we all marched over to the cathedral. Amid the chanting of the choir and the swirl of incense and the flaming candles and the priests in white and gold, my new friend Emil whispered in my ear, 'The bishop who blessed Ceauşescu now blesses the new Council.'

From the cathedral we went to the Council Building where, amid some commotion and many soldiers bearing rifles, the newly elected County Council replaced the old. During this transfer of power—remarkably orderly, under the circumstances—a young man burst into the chamber. 'Something very important is happening on television! They're massing in Bucharest for the Front!'

We rushed out to the television. The Prime Minister, Petre Roman, was speaking from the floodlit balcony. The workers were chanting:

Noi sîntem uniţi
Nu sîntem platiţi!

We are united,
We are not paid!

But everyone else had rushed to the television too, and it was hard to see, and I did not at that moment understand the reference.

Later that night and during the next, I began to understand what I had glimpsed on television. It was not just another manifestation. There had been massive anti-Front demonstrations in Bucharest the previous day, and for the first time the government had responded by calling out the workers for a show of support. Among those workers, though not then in great numbers, were miners from the Valley of the Jiu.

There had been rumours—rumours that the Front carefully planted, it was said—of an orchestrated *putsch*, and that the two principal opposition parties, the Peasant and Liberal parties, had paid the protesters 200 *lei* each. That is why the workers were chanting, 'We are united, we are not paid!' But there were also stories that they were paid a week's wages and given the day off.

Three nights later, three miners appeared on Free Romanian Television, urging everyone to go back to work and let the Front run the government. The Front is the leader, they said, not one or another of the opposition parties. Iliescu himself said he saw no need for more than one party. None the less, the government eventually agreed to form a sort of coalition with other parties in a Provisional Council of National Unity that would rule until the national elections in May. There was little question as to which party—the Front had now declared itself a party—would control the Council.

The miners and various other workers got a raise. The protests briefly subsided, though they did not disappear, and I left Timişoara for a time.

4

I went to Bucharest for a week and then to the historic Transylvanian town of Alba Iulia to visit the parents of Emil, the man who had spoken to me in the cathedral on the night of the local elections. Emil—like many others in Romania—proudly described himself as the son of peasants. His parents had come from a nearby village but had given up their land during the forced collectivization and moved to the city. Emil's father was a shoe-maker and his mother a dressmaker. Emil was their only child. For many years his father had walked to work instead of taking the bus to save two *lei* a day so they could provide some advantages—books, clothes—for their son. They were not poor—they never had been poor peasants, which had caused them some problems—and they owned their three-room apartment. They certainly were not rich, either, though they were fortunate by the standards of most Romanian peasant families. They were intelligent and very generous, and they were concerned about the violence and the confusion in Bucharest. There was a great fear of anarchy and disorder in Romania, a fear the government skilfully played on.

The day I arrived there—Monday, 19 February—the miners had come to Bucharest again. This time there were thousands of them. I was sitting in Emil's parents' living-room watching television. His parents were concerned—not so much about the miners, whose violence was not shown on television, but about the students: 200 putative students had invaded government headquarters on the Sunday before and briefly seized the Deputy Prime Minister. Some armed with clubs devastated offices in the building. Those short, chaotic scenes were shown many times. It was impossible to tell from the television how many students were involved or even if they were students. The word '*putsch*' occurred again. Iliescu said the students were counter-revolutionary, against the national interests. 'We don't know who they were but we will search for them and punish them severely,' he said. In the meantime, 'We appeal to all interested forces, to all clear minds, to protect us, because we are leading the country.'

Emil's father shook his head. What to think?

'A manipulation!' Emil cried. 'Another manipulation!' Apparently the invading students met only perfunctory resistance from the army and the police. Curious. Was this Iliescu's wish, in order to convince the populace that the Revolution was in danger and thus justify the measures he needed to take to stay in power? Were the army and the police plotting something?

'The wolves have changed their fur but not their habits,' Emil said. 'The frames are the same.' Emil's father shook his head again. His mother urged more food on me. We drank a little *ţuica*.

5

One Saturday afternoon in the middle of March I drove to Petrosani, a mining town in the Valley of the Jiu, with Emil and Ionel, another friend. I wanted to see what these miners were like. I wanted to go into a mine. We were having car trouble and while Emil and Ionel peered under the hood—all Romanians are by necessity auto mechanics—I walked up the street. The mining towns were meant to be grim places. Petroşani didn't look that bad to me, but I had been in Romania long enough by then to have grown accustomed to bleakness. There were few people on the streets, but the sun was shining, which always helps.

While I was walking up the street, a taxi-driver had come over to peer under the hood, and Emil had told him I wanted to visit a coal-mine. By the time I returned to the car a man came running up, excited, breathless. He looked about thirty, not tall but husky. A businessman, I thought. He wants to change money. But no. He wanted to practise his English, which he had learned from the movies.

'Los Angeles,' he said. 'California.'

His English was fairly rudimentary. He was a miner and his name was Ion, and he would take me into a mine. He had a mask for me, and a lamp, and clothes. He would show me a real mine; I would see what it was like.

'No problem,' Ion said. 'Just not speak.'

'Not speak?'

'You are miner, not tourist. Most not journalist.'

'Oh.' I pondered that. 'What do you mean? I can't talk?'

'Simple. Be miner. I show you.'

'And if someone speaks to me?'

'Simple. Just not speak.'

'Oh.' I looked at Emil. Emil shrugged. Not his problem. I was the one who wanted to go into a mine.

I'd be going alone, too, or at least without Emil. Ion had only one spare outfit. It became clear that I would have to stay there the whole shift, which began at ten that night. I would go to the head of the mine with Ion, leave my clothes, and put on the suit he had for me. 'Remember, you are Romanian miner.'

'But my clothes, Ion. These aren't Romanian clothes.'

'How much you pay for the jacket?' Ion asked.

'That's what I mean,' I said. Ion looked puzzled.

'How much?'

I was certain now that this adventure was ill-advised. But no. Ion would arrange it. 'No problem,' if only I remembered not to speak. Just pick up my tools and act like a miner. He invited us to his apartment to discuss it, and to tell me his story.

Ion was the son of a simple miner from Moldavia. Like his father, Ion was not a specialist. He showed me his salary slip. He was paid 4,900 *lei* a month, including extra money for night work. Specialist miners are paid double that, and more. This is far above the wage of most Romanians, who make around 3,000 *lei* a month. Miners paid less for electricity too. None the less, I never met anyone who wanted to change places with a miner. Ion's rent for the one-room apartment he shared with his wife and daughter was 200 *lei* a month. The apartment contained, in addition to a glassed cabinet along one wall, a sofa that made into a bed, a table with three wooden chairs around it and a large television set. Ion was proud of the television set. He wanted to be photographed in front of it, with his wife, with the set turned on. He didn't own a car, but he wished for a motor cycle.

One day last August he'd been on a motor cycle. An American from California was passing through. Admiring the motorcycle and eager to practise his English, Ion spoke to him. The American took Ion's photograph on the bike—he showed me the picture—and later that day a member of the *Securitate* came to his door: the photograph had been taken in front of the *Securist*'s house.

The man asked Ion how he knew English and what he had told the foreigner. Then he proposed that Ion work for them as an informer for 800 *lei* a month, in addition to his wages from the mine. Ion refused. The man took his identity card. The next day was pay-day at the mine; to collect his wages, Ion needed his identity card. The *Securitate* man showed up with it. Again he asked him to co-operate, and again Ion refused. Two weeks later two men from the *Securitate* came to his house and accused him of stealing bikes. They then left. They returned and told him they knew he was dealing in the black-market. He had better co-operate.

'Come to my house and see,' Ion had said. 'They see empty bottles of whisky.' He gestured toward the cabinet. 'I picked them out of the rubbish.' The bottles were displayed behind glass, along with spray cans of deodorant and perfume, boxes of Marlboros and Gitanes. All of them were empty. The *Securişti* didn't come again.

I asked Ion if he'd gone to Bucharest with the miners in February.

Yes, he had. A boss had asked him to go and he had taken one of the trains from Petroşani that night. At every station, he said, they were greeted by townspeople bringing them hot bread, yoghurt, coffee and Romanian cigarettes.

'The same food at every stop?'

'Yes.' The same cigarettes too. No, the government didn't organize the people; the people wanted to help.

'They say we were paid by the Front to go to Bucharest.' I hadn't asked. 'No, never. We were never paid. The heart went to Bucharest.'

'Why?'

'I see the television. I see what happened in the government building. It makes me nervous. Upset. How can I go to work, feeling like that? If I make a mistake, 5,000 or 10,000 people are dead. Let's say so.'

It occurred to me to wonder what would happen if I went down the mine that night and made a mistake, but I didn't pursue it. 'What happened in Bucharest?'

'In Bucharest everyone was crying out, "Up with Iliescu! Up with the Front!" My heart went to Bucharest.'

'Do you like Iliescu, Ion?'

'A hard question.' Ion shrugged, thought for a moment. 'Yes, I like Iliescu. He gives us a thirty-day holiday minimum. He tells us we can retire at forty-five. Before, it was fifty-five. He gives us equipment for working. We do not have to pay for it.'

But they had been on strike. 'Why?'

'They had promised us things, and they had not come through. They had promised our wages would go up thirty-five per cent. We got fifteen. After the strike Iliescu had promised us everything, only go to work again. But nothing changed. No changes, only promises. So the miners strike.'

'Only promises,' Emil said. 'They change their name but not their habits.'

'The old Communist mafia is still in power,' Ion said agreeing. 'The mayor, he's one. The directors of the mines, they just switched them to other mines.'

'They changed their mines but not their habits,' Emil said.

'The man who was director of my mine, now he's mayor of the county. It's a better job.'

Ion got up to get me his spare miner's lamp and a mask. I worked the lamp and tried on the mask. It smelled of coal. I tried to imagine myself in the role of a mute Romanian miner. I couldn't quite. 'I do not have an extra safety hat,' Ion said. 'My colleague will give me one.'

'I think I won't go into the mine tonight, Ion. It will be too late, and I must be in Bucharest tomorrow. Perhaps another time.'

'You will come back?'

'I'll try.'

'When you come back, I like Gitanes, postcards, newspapers. But don't ask at the police where I am located. The old mafia still works. Ask at the taxi.'

I took the photograph of Ion and his wife in front of the television, and another in front of the whisky bottles in the cabinet. We exchanged addresses, shook hands and parted. I didn't think to ask Ion if he would return to Bucharest should the need arise. But I suppose the answer was clear. Anyway, I intend to go back to Petroşani. I'll ask him then.

6

The last demonstration in Bucharest was eight weeks long and began on a pleasant Sunday night in April, the same night that a nearly complete version of the trial of Nicolae and Elena Ceauşescu was shown on Free Romanian Television for the first time, keeping most citizens occupied until after ten. That night the demonstration looked no different from any other I had seen in Romania. It was more peaceful than most. At eleven o'clock, when I arrived in University Square, the speeches had ended and the riot police had already left. The demonstrators barricaded the square and had remained there throughout the night. In the early hours, the police returned with dogs and truncheons, and arrested sixty or seventy people. At that hour there were few witnesses.

The next evening 5,000 people were milling in the square. Shortly after midnight a man with a bull-horn said that a colonel of the *Poliţia* had appeared on television and accused the demonstrators of rape, theft, breaking into apartments on the square and damaging buses. The people there—I saw a number I knew—did not look like rapists and thieves to me. They looked like professional people, like students, like the residents of Bucharest one saw on the streets every day. They didn't even walk on the grass or the flowers. They just wanted the old Communists out of the government. That would have meant, of course, the end of the government, because as far as I could tell, everyone from Iliescu on down had been a Communist, most in important positions, although some like Iliescu had fallen into disfavour in recent years.

By the next evening there were 10,000 people. They were being led in a chant: 'Don't be frightened.'

'We won't.'

'Don't leave.'

'We won't.'

'Today the capital!'

'Tomorrow the whole country!'

Ten thousand shouting people make a very loud roar.

That night I was told, when I went into the University

building and up to the balcony of the Faculty of Geography and Geology where the leaders of the protest gathered, that the demonstration had started with a meeting to remember the dead. It had begun at the Cemetery of the Heroes and continued to the University Square, the Roman Square, the television station, where they asked that the decree subordinating the television to the government be rescinded. It was not. It never has been. The marchers returned to the square, where some of them at least remained, night and day, from that Sunday until the morning of 13 June, nearly two months later. Some set up tents near the National Theatre, and a number began a hunger strike. 'In this Square,' one of the leaders said, 'more than three hundred died on the Day of Twenty-one, and maybe two thousand were wounded. We will never leave until the Revolution is finished.'

They didn't, but a couple of days later I did. I wanted to be in Timişoara for the national elections on 20 May. I knew that Bucharest would be packed with journalists and foreign observers. It was already difficult to book a hotel room.

To the surprise of no one, the elections produced a landslide victory for Iliescu and the Front.

I returned to the capital early in the evening of 12 June, with Emil again, and checked into the Hotel Ambassador, some 500 metres up the street from University Square. In my room there, neither the telephone nor the television worked; its only advantage, aside from its justifiably lower price, was the balcony overlooking the Boulevard General Magheru, which becomes the Boulevard Nicolae Bălcescu in the next block. When I arrived, marchers were passing beneath the balcony, chanting: 'Sound asleep you voted in a dictator!' They were headed toward Victory Square and the headquarters of the government. I let them go by. I was tired. I had seen many marches. I was sure that in time they would come marching back, and four hours later they did. Besides, the crowd seemed to have changed. After the May elections the student leaders, in a gesture of conciliation (and because the students had exams to take), had called for official demonstrations only on Thursdays. The hunger-strikers remained, a few students and others, and traffic continued to be diverted around University Square, as it had been since the demonstration began. But the crowds were thin, and at night they seemed to consist less of *opozanţii* than of opportunists. The students—Iliescu's *golani*—had more or less withdrawn from the Square, leaving it to what the Prime Minister, Petre Roman, later described, and accurately enough, as the underworld of Bucharest—the *traficanţi*, the chiefs of prostitution and assorted other lowlife, the *dégradés* and *déclassés* as he called them, with which the city abounds. When I made a midnight visit to the square during a brief stay in Bucharest the week before, I had been offered—for dollars—whisky, cigarettes, two women and *lei*. The crowd was not the same.

The evening of 13 June began with an explosion. Someone had thrown a Molotov Cocktail—then another and another—and Emil and I rushed out to see. But it was raining and I ran back to the hotel room for my umbrella, absurdly enough, which is how I lost Emil.

I left the hotel moments later, running towards University Square, but Emil had disappeared. Buses were in flames, some still exploding. The stench of burning rubber filled the air. I ran faster, to the university building and up the stairs to the balcony.

'Don't go out!' someone shouted.

'But I must see,' and I went out. Burning buses were blocking the square, seven of them. The square itself was almost empty.

Someone from the Student League pulled me inside. 'No one must be seen on the balcony! It is dangerous. The Student League did not organize the violence! We must not be blamed!'

'But I just saw someone on the balcony. What happened?'

This is what happened. In the early hours of the morning, about 1,000 policemen in riot gear and armed with truncheons charged the barricades blocking University Square, forming a cordon and stopping the exits. Military police in combat fatigues then rushed in and, together with an undetermined number of plain-clothes men whom many found reminiscent of the old

Securitate, arrested eight or ten hunger-strikers and various others camped there, between 200 and 300 in all. Some time after five o'clock in the morning, the customary hour for the police to strike, the President of the Student League of the University of Bucharest, Marian Munteanu, was arrested in his home, as well as various others in their homes and at the Institute of Architecture. University Square was cleared of demonstrators, and soon workers were painting fresh traffic lines on the boulevard. By ten-thirty, women in babushkas were turning over the hard-packed earth in front of the National Theatre, in the place where the demonstrators had pitched their tents.

A woman appeared in the square a short time later and was dragged kicking into an unmarked car. An hour later workers from the IMGB, a large heavy-equipment enterprise in Bucharest, appeared and attacked the Institute of Architecture. There were a hundred or so students—some say gypsies, not students; they were probably both—hiding inside. The workers began pounding on the doors, crying that the IMGB was making order. A window was broken. An enormous crowd was forming around the back of the workers, shouting that Iliescu had sent his scandal makers. There was fighting. The police stood by. The workers surged once again towards the Institute, throwing rocks now, windows breaking. The police remained calm.

By late afternoon, demonstrators had become more violent and invaded the square again—thousands of them this time—more stones were thrown, and not long after that the Molotov cocktails. The remaining police ran away, and a few minutes after five o'clock I arrived, just as the student leader Marian Munteanu, who had been released shortly before, was concluding a plea from the balcony. March on the police headquarters to free the prisoners, Munteanu said, but '*Fară violenţe!*' Without violence! And so thousands of people set out for the Municipal Police Headquarters.

When I reached the headquarters, I saw that others had got there before me: the gatehouse was in flames, six vehicles were burning in the stone courtyard and the building itself was on fire. Many windows were broken. The building was dark and apparently deserted. Hundreds, maybe thousands, thronged the street that led to the headquarters' entrance, but the street directly in front of it was relatively clear: a man had been shot in the head there an hour before. Had I known that then, I might have been more cautious. But I didn't know it, and I went into the courtyard for a quick look. Six or eight young men were lounging on the steps, passing bottles of beer among them. They did not look like students.

The Internal Security Ministry was next to the police headquarters; across the street was the *Securitate*, a small, old and rather pretty brick building: they were burning too. Black smoke was pouring from the entrance of the nearby underground garage: more vehicles were on fire down there. A boy ran out, his eyes streaming tears. His four friends were still in the garage. It was impossible to get them out because of the smoke. 'I am the only one who escaped!' he shouted. There was another explosion—from the garage. Where were the police? Where was the army? They had run away, I was told. Strange.

8

It should have been a pleasant evening for a stroll. The air was fresh after the afternoon's rains. Passers-by, many with their children, were chatting, laughing. I walked along the Boulevard of Aviators towards Victory Square. The events of the afternoon, the events that I had myself witnessed, began to seem unreal. Had I really seen buses burning and buildings in flames and a boy whose eyes were streaming tears? 'It's all a movie,' Emil often said, referring to the events of the last six months. It gave a kind of false comfort to think so.

The scene at the massive Foreign Ministry, since the Revolution the seat of the government, was impressive: the darkened building squatting there, the broad floodlit square, the crowds milling. The people had come there, I soon learned, in response to Iliescu's plea that 'all conscious forces gather around the buildings of the government and the television to curb the attempts of the extremist groups to use force, and to defend the democracy that was so difficult to attain.' He had spoken ominously of an organized *coup d'état* in the offing. And so, at ten o'clock, as the long Bucharest twilight was finally giving way to night, there they were, the 'conscious forces', several thousand strong, helping each other don white arm bands.

I found a woman who spoke English. The white band, I said, pointing to her arm. What is it for?

'You don't know?' She seemed surprised. 'We support the Front. We are *Fenişti*. This is our sign.' Then she told me about Mr Iliescu's call to the people, and that a mob had briefly seized the television station, cutting off transmission for more than an hour. 'Now we wait for Mr Iliescu.' I had passed within two blocks of the television station a few minutes before.

'You know what they did at the University Square?'

Yes, I knew.

'It will be a white night,' she predicted, a night without rest.

At two in the morning I was with two young British journalists—the few journalists now in Bucharest seemed all to be British, and most of them were young—and a translator. I had met them at the Hotel Intercontinental. We had all heard gunshots forty-five minutes before and went near the television station to investigate. We met four paratroopers.

No, there was no shooting here,' they said. 'Only rocks were thrown. The police had rubber truncheons only. Go home. We don't need you to write about Romania now.'

We tried another approach to the television station, failed, passed by the Foreign Ministry—'There was no shooting here; only at the television'—and then returned to the entrance to the Intercontinental. Church bells began to ring, then suddenly stopped. Almost immediately there was a round of gunfire. It seemed to be coming from the direction of the Interior Ministry. I ran to the corner of the Square, with Sorin whom I had just met and who was to become my friend. There was an ambulance from *Médecins sans Frontières*. A man had been shot in the chest—he looked near death—and another had been shot in the cheek. Everything was happening so quickly nothing had time to register. We ran across the square to the Boulevard Gheorghiu-Dej, where there was a burnt shell of a bus. Farther down the boulevard we could see tanks and a line of riot police with white shields and helmets and truncheons. We watched. Were the tanks moving? It was hard to tell. The street was dark, and we were looking at the tanks head on. Shots rang out. I saw the flames from the rifles.

'Run! Get down!' Sorin was screaming, pulling at my arm. We ran behind the ruined bus. 'They're using real bullets!' Sorin could hear the ricochet. I could not tell. I had never been in the military. I had never seen a war. The shooting stopped. Another French ambulance drove up, waiting. We moved cautiously out. More gunfire, and we ran again. Were the tanks moving?

'We go,' Sorin said, pulling at my arm again. And we ran around the corner, out of sight of the rifles, the tanks, the sheltering bus, and back to the front of the hotel.

We exchanged stories with the four or five journalists clustered there, watched the troops file across the street by the Geography Faculty. Suddenly the police made a running baton charge—they came within inches of us, out of nowhere. No one had seen them coming. No one saw what they were going after. It was three in the morning. We went to Alec Russell's room, which had a balcony with a good view of the square. Alec asked if I'd like to sleep on his couch.

Yes, I would. I was afraid to walk up the street to the Hotel Ambassador.

As I was drifting off, I thought I heard a strange soft noise, a kind of murmuring. I listened for a few moments, straining to hear—was that a sound, or was I imagining it?—then reluctantly pulled myself from the couch and went to the balcony once more. I looked down. I didn't see anything at first, only shadows. Then I didn't know what I was seeing. I didn't really want to see anything more. But why else was I here?—and I knew that what I saw down there was important.

'Alec, wake up! Come quick! Wake up! Alec!'

At five in the morning, in the hushed first light before the dawn, the first group of miners—only a few hundred then—were swarming down the broad Boulevard Nicolae Bălcescu from Victory Square towards the university. Shrouded in that early half-light, their dun-coloured shapes were muffled, indistinct, grey shadow on grey shadow and discernible at first only by the soft flickering of the lamps in their hands, on their metal helmets, and by the nervous rustling sound and a low buzzing hum that carried from the street to our balcony sixteen floors above.

A quarter of an hour later there were some thousands. Approaching the square the miners marched in phalanxes—several hundred in each—and when they arrived the phalanxes broke up, the flashing beams from thousands of tiny lamps darting restlessly in the shadow.

As the light increased, it became apparent that the miners were dressed for work, carrying the picks and chisels, augers and rubber hoses of their trade, as well as identical long sticks—and clubs, limbs torn from trees, pipes, iron bars, axes, chains—whatever came to hand that might be used to protect their government and restore order to the capital. And the humming voices we were hearing were calling for the objects of their hunt: *Golani! Golani!*

As they reached the Square a black Dacia with yellow licence plates came to a stop near the Hotel Intercontinental. Yellow plates indicate a government vehicle. Two men in suits were walking at the edge of the street, in the same direction as the miners. Secret police everywhere look the same.

A group of the miners broke off and rushed down to the entrance of the university building. Soon several miners appeared on the balcony of the Faculty of Geography and Geology, which occupies the eastern end of the university building, overlooking the square. The student protests, which began almost eight weeks before, were led from that balcony. It is a familiar landmark in Bucharest. A few soldiers—twenty or thirty—were standing casually on the sidewalk beneath it. There were no other army, or police, or riot squads. The miners reached the roof. Six or eight of them had climbed through one of the skylights and were waving triumphantly. The building appeared to be empty.

A few moments later a man wearing a red sweater appeared on the street, began to run and disappeared around a corner and out of sight, pursued by miners wielding sticks. A truck drove slowly into the square. Through a megaphone a voice boomed: 'Don't be afraid, the miners are good people.'

Several people were with us now, Romanian friends and journalists, including Hermann Tertsch from the Madrid newspaper *El Pais*. He had driven through the night from Bulgaria and seen the miners gathering at four-thirty in Victory Square before they began their march down the boulevard to the university. He also brought word from the reception desk: the miners said if they saw anyone taking photographs from the balconies they would come in and devastate the hotel. As we were hearing this, they captured a man near the fountain between the Geography Faculty and Institute of Architecture and beat him to the ground. A few minutes later, a fire was blazing up the street in front of the Liberal Party's headquarters. The flames reached the second storey, and we heard glass shattering, an occasional scream. On the street there was another announcement: 'Those of you who see cameras, catch the people and take them to the cars.' Apparently the 'cars' were the unmarked black and white Dacias we saw here and there around the hotel and the square. But there was no one on the street with a camera. No one would be foolish enough to appear on the street with a camera. No one not already in the street would be foolish enough to enter it.

We heard a rumour that there were 30,000 miners in Bucharest. It was hard to tell how many were in the square, at least 5,000. They were everywhere and more were arriving. By six o'clock the miners had invaded the Institute of Architecture—we could see them through the windows—and five of them now claimed the roof. A voice came over the hotel's public-address system: 'No more cameras.' At the same time, two men in blue suits, white shirts and ties, carrying briefcases, were talking affably to a group of miners, clapping them on their shoulders.

I took the elevator to the lobby. About 150 miners were standing at the door with clubs, logs and rubber hoses. They wanted mineral water and the hotel provided it. I did not go out but instead returned to the balcony in time to see the first marked police car arrive in the square.

By this time the miners had seized a number of people: they either beat them with sticks or dragged them into an unmarked vehicle or both; usually they did both. Someone suggested that their victims were being taken to the government building. I don't know how these rumours were reaching us. None of us had yet ventured outside the hotel. I suppose they were coming by telephone, through our Romanian friends. Cristian Unteanu, the government's press spokesman, was standing beside a car in the centre of the square.

Another announcement from the megaphone: 'All civilians out of the square! This is not a show here. You are not capable of making order in Bucharest. We'll do it our way now.'

At the edge of the square the miners were beating a man in the face with sticks, then they kicked him. They kicked him twice in the face, and then in the stomach, and then they clubbed him in the stomach. He was doubled over, bleeding, trying to protect himself. He was led to one of the waiting cars in the middle of the square. It took a long time because they were beating him. I wondered if this was what it had been like in Nazi Germany when the Brown Shirts were loose. A woman appeared to be on her way to work, but she was knocked to the ground, beaten, forced into a waiting car. Another man was being kicked in the face. The violence intensified, spread like an infection. Miners were shaking their fists at people on the balconies of the hotel, shouting 'Photos are forbidden!' Many were looking at us.

I returned to the lobby. It was seven-twenty. The miners had chased a man into the hotel's revolving door and were beating him with clubs, chains, hoses. He was slumped there, his face bleeding, which he was trying to protect with his hands. He was picked up and dragged to a waiting car. I stood in the doorway for a minute, venturing out a step or two. I wanted to make a list of the weapons I saw. Here is my list: thick chains, miner's drills (one came up to my chest; it was very thick and must have been five feet long), pipes, wooden clubs, tree limbs, rubber hoses with nozzles attached, chains in rubber hoses . . . I left before finishing the list, but in a few moments I went out again and stood under the canopy. I saw a miner carrying one of the distinctive yellow plastic 'Raţiu for President' bags. Ion Raţiu was the National Peasant Party's candidate. I assumed—correctly, as it happens—that they had invaded the party's headquarters nearby.

A little later several of us very cautiously ventured out, farther this time. We were in a group; we were safe, we thought. Stop. A little farther. Stop. More. We reached the steps leading to the sidewalk and the street. A woman in a red pullover and a dark skirt was running towards us, screaming, several miners surrounding her, chasing her, hitting her with clubs, tearing at her clothes. She lost one shoe, the other. Her pullover was ripped, then ripped off. She was naked to the waist, and they were beating her with whatever implements they had. I screamed at them—'Stop!'—but Sorin, the fellow I'd met the night before, clapped his hand over my mouth. All this happened very fast. The woman was running by me, or trying to. She was stumbling and they were beating her. She was no more than a body's length away, between our small cluster and the hotel. As she passed I saw a very large red bruise on her breast, and then I saw her back, which had been beaten raw, to a pulp. I had never seen anyone beaten to a pulp before. It had always seemed a cliché. Her skirt was torn, her legs were bleeding; her face was a blotch. She was pummelled, dragged and then pushed into a waiting vehicle. I was standing with Victoria Clark, a young woman who writes for the *Observer*. Victoria speaks some Romanian, and she had more nerve than I. We walked over to three or four miners and asked why they had beaten this woman.

She was on drugs, they told us. 'There is a lot of heroin here. We found this big bag on her.' With his hands he indicated something the size of a ten-pound sack of flour. None of us had ever seen a drug in Romania. None of us knew any Romanians who had.

'You tore off her clothes.'

'No, we found her like that.' They were carrying long steel augers. 'We are guardians of order, of peace, and we'll stay until we have peace.' And then the old revolutionary cry—Savu said something like it on the Day of Twenty—'We die, we fight to defend you.'

Who were they defending us from?

'Prostitutes, drug addicts, fascists.'

How did they identify them?

'Pistols, drugs, bullets and inflammatory pamphlets—we found on all these people we have arrested.' But the miners didn't show us any.

B eside the entrance to the hotel fifty or sixty pieces of luggage were lined up. Inside, a large group of Japanese tourists, their faces quite impassive, were waiting to leave. The airport, I heard later, was closed. The miners wanted to check the hotel, room by room, for Marian Munteanu, the president of the Student League. He had been arrested the morning before but released to be arrested again. A reporter told us the miners had already found Munteanu. He saw them beating him in the square earlier.

Three or four of us decide to make a foray down the square. We began talking to a miner who showed us what he had confiscated from one of those arrested. (That was the word being used: arrested. It seemed a rather benign way to describe what was happening to people who had been clubbed and bloodied and thrown into unmarked cars and driven off.) He handed me a pamphlet containing the Declaration of Independence and the Constitution of the United States of America. The American government prints them by the millions. Inside was a cheque for twenty-five dollars made out to the Romanian Student League on a bank in Kentucky. The miner had never seen a cheque. He did not know what it was. He could not read English either. I tried to explain that the pamphlet now in my hand was a historical document and not usually considered inflammatory political material—though it was, of course, but that was too complicated to explain. He wanted to tell us about the drugs he found—four sacks of white powder in the university; a doctor from the ambulance said it was heroin. He knew: 'He is a doctor.'

William McPherson

At ten o'clock that morning I spotted two Americans, obviously tourists, approaching Victory Square, cameras hanging from their necks. That two tourists should be sightseeing this day in Bucharest was so bizarre it was ludicrous. What did they imagine they were seeing? Cameras were of course forbidden. Soldiers saw the cameras the same time Alec Russell and I did, and the terrified couple were dragged and pushed and carried behind the cordons of troops around the Foreign Ministry. Alec and I showed our credentials and were allowed through the first line of troops and then the second. An officer was shaking his fist at the couple, then let them go, but not before someone stomped on the man's foot. They walked quickly away. Alec and I ran after them, and just as I asked their names I was grabbed from behind and shoved behind a truck. They then grabbed Alec. We were trying to show our press passes to a major—and the beating started.

During it the major stood about three feet from us, screaming, shaking his fist. He had grabbed our credentials and Alec's notebook; fortunately I had stowed mine in a back pocket concealed by my jacket. Four soldiers and a couple of *Fesenişti* ripped open my shirt. I was very angry. I had never been beaten up before. I remember every blow. There were six of them: a club in the left kidney, another on the shoulder, a vicious uppercut to the jaw that I could still feel a week later, a kick in the back, a club in the chest, a kick in the leg. I felt none of them then or felt them only through a kind of adrenalin rush. They tried to drag us behind another truck, farther out of sight from the street. I was more frightened now. I did not want to disappear behind a truck in Bucharest. I did not want to end up in a hospital in Bucharest. I wanted my credentials back, and these goons had ruined my shirt! One cooler head, I didn't know whose, prevailed and the men were persuaded to release us. The major shoved us off but kept our credentials. We walked away as quickly as possible. They were following us—I could hear their footsteps—but I knew that to turn and face them would be a serious mistake. To run would be worse. We kept walking, cursing. There were no taxis.

A tape has surfaced of a low-frequency police band radio, recorded on 13 June. The government has denounced it as a provocation, but it sounds convincing. The background noise, the sense of urgency, the confusion are all there, and it appears to confirm what many of us suspected: that the terrible violence and bloodshed that began that day, leading to the rampage of the miners on Thursday and Friday were deliberately provoked. On the tape, officer fifty-three says to officer fifty-two, 'Do you see any possibility of informing the president? We are starting to burn all of the buses. This was the agreement.' The recording implicates a Mr Magureanu. Virgil Magureanu is the head of the new Romanian Intelligence Service, whose purpose is 'to gather data and information on the activity of espionage and terrorist organizations against Romania, of extremists or of individuals who plan subversive actions to undermine the national economy, to destabilize the rule of law.' No one in Romania has seen the rule of law for some time; the rule of force and rumour and manipulation prevails. On the tape officer fifty-two says to officer fifty-three: 'I don't know how we can resolve this. Magureanu retreated and we don't know where he is. This was his business. . . The prime minister's orders were to keep order until the workers arrived.' Two people who have listened to the tape insist that one of the voices is that of the interior minister, General Chiţac, who has since been replaced. I did not recognize General Chiţac's voice, so I cannot say.

A few days later, Ion Iliescu was inaugurated President of Romania. The Athenaeum, where the ceremony took place, was ringed by troops and protected by tanks. I skipped it.

Two days later wreaths were laid in the University Square to the heroes of the Revolution. It has been six months since Ceauşescu fled. The Army band was playing the Romanian national anthem. The solemn tune floated up, on to my balcony and into my room at the Intercontinental where I was staying now, for safety reasons. I went to the balcony to watch. The church bells began to toll. All the church bells throughout

Romania were tolling at this hour. I cried. I could not help it.

Six days later I was packing to leave Romania for a time. My friend Sorin came by my room to say goodbye. I have a terrible memory for tunes and I asked him if he would sing for me the anthem '*Deşteoptăte romăne*'—'Romania, Awake!'

No, he said, he could not do it. He would write the words in my notebook. If he sang it he would cry. He wrote the words, but he cried anyway.

A couple of hours later I passed the Foreign Ministry on my way to the airport. Soldiers were still guarding it, but not as many as before. To the east of the building there was a long row of tanks.

17 December 1989: anti-government demonstrators massacred in Timişoara, during a protest against the *Securitate*'s attempt to deport Lászlo Tökes, an ethnic Hungarian pastor.

21 December: street fighting in Bucharest after a Ceauşescu rally turns into an anti-government demonstration.

22 December: Nicolae and Elena Ceauşescu flee from Bucharest.

23 December: the Ceauşescus are captured.

25 December: the Ceauşescus are executed.

26 December: the National Salvation Front name the new government, headed by President Ion Iliescu. The first non-communist political party in Romania since 1947 is re-established: the National Peasant Party.

27 January 1990: first local election is held in Timişoara.

28 January: opponents and supporters of the National Salvation Front clash in Bucharest.

22 April: full version of the trial of the Ceauşescus is shown on Romanian television for the first time. Students and others occupy University Square to remember those who died in the Revolution and protest against the presence of former Communists in the government.

20 May: the National Salvation Front wins a landslide victory in the election. Eighty-five per cent of votes go to the Front, giving them 325 of the 506 seats. There are 600 foreign observers, and allegations of electoral malpractice are made against the Front.

12 June: government deploys armed soldiers and police to quell a demonstration outside government headquarters. The demonstrators accuse the government of continuing the policies of Ceauşescu. The student anti-Front demonstration in University Square enters its seventh week.

13 June: police attempt to end the student occupation of University Square, arresting 263 protesters. At least five people killed in disturbances in Bucharest, which Iliescu describes as an attempted *coup* against the Front.

14 June: thousands of miners from the Valley of Jiu are brought to Bucharest in special trains at dawn.

15 June: Petre Roman, the prime minister, denies that the miners were acting on government orders. He does not condemn their behaviour despite international protest. Hospitals in Bucharest release statistics showing that 296 people have been treated for head injuries and broken bones. The opposition calls for the outside world to isolate the government.

16 June: troops and police patrol Bucharest. Iliescu claims to have averted a fascist *coup*. The European Community expresses 'shock and disappointment' at the miners' brutality.

20 June: Iliescu is formally inaugurated as president at a ceremony boycotted by the US ambassador, who announces that the US will now withhold all non-humanitarian aid from Romania.

14 July: defence minister General Stanculescu announces that former *Securitate* agents are to join the national guard service established after the June demonstrations.

Svetlana Alexiyevich

Boys in Zinc

In 1986 I had decided not to write about war again. For a long time after I finished my book *War's Unwomanly Face* I couldn't bear to see a child with a bleeding nose. I suppose each of us has a measure of protection against pain; mine had been exhausted.

Two events changed my mind.

I was driving out to a village and I gave a lift to a schoolgirl. She had been shopping in Minsk, and carried a bag with chickens' heads sticking out. In the village we were met by her mother, who was standing crying at the garden gate. The girl ran to her.

The mother had received a letter from her son Andrey. The letter was sent from Afghanistan. 'They'll bring him back like they brought Fyodorina's Ivan,' she said, 'and dig a grave to put him in. Look what he writes. "Mum, isn't it great! I'm a paratrooper . . . " '

And then there was another incident. An army officer with a suitcase was sitting in the half-empty waiting-room of the bus station in town. Next to him a thin boy with a crew-cut was digging in the pot of a rubber plant with a table fork. Two country women sat down beside the men and asked who they were. The officer said he was escorting home a private soldier who had gone mad. 'He's been digging all the way from Kabul with whatever he can get his hands on, a spade, a fork, a stick, a fountain pen.' The boy looked up. His pupils were so dilated they seemed to take up the whole of his eyes.

And at that time people continued to talk and write about our internationalist duty, the interests of state, our southern borders. The censors saw to it that reports of the war did not mention our fatalities. There were only rumours of notifications of death arriving at rural huts and of regulation zinc coffins delivered to prefabricated flats. I had not meant to write about war again, but I found myself in the middle of one.

For the next three years I spoke to many people at home and in Afghanistan. Every confession was like a portrait. They are not documents; they are images. I was trying to present a history of feelings, not the history of the war itself. What were people thinking? What made them happy? What were their fears? What

331

stayed in their memory?

The war in Afghanistan lasted twice as long as the Second World War, but we know only so much as it is safe for us to know. It is no longer a secret that every year for ten years, 100,000 Soviet troops went to fight in Afghanistan. Officially, 50,000 men were killed or wounded. You can believe that figure if you will. Everybody knows what we are like at sums. We haven't yet finished counting and burying all those who died in the Second World War.

In what follows, I haven't given people's real names. Some asked for the confidentiality of the confessional, others I don't feel I can expose to a witch-hunt. We are still so close to the war that there is nowhere for anyone to hide.

One night I was asleep when my telephone rang.

'Listen,' he began, without identifying himself, 'I've read your garbage. If you so much as print another word . . . '

'Who are you?'

'One of the guys you're writing about. God, I hate pacifists! Have you ever been up a mountain in full marching kit? Been in an armoured personnel carrier when the temperature's seventy centigrade? Like hell you have. Fuck off! It's ours! It's got sod all to do with you.'

I asked him again who he was.

'Leave it out, will you! My best friend—like a brother he was—and I brought him back from a raid in a cellophane bag. He'd been flayed, his head had been severed, his arms, his legs, his dick all cut off . . . . He could have written about it, but you can't. The truth was in that cellophane sack. Fuck the lot of you!' He hung up; the sound in the receiver was like an explosion.

He might have been my most important witness.

A Wife

'Don't worry if you don't get any letters,' he wrote. 'Carry on writing to the old address.' Then nothing for two months. I never dreamed he was in Afghanistan. I was getting suitcases ready to go to see him at his new posting.

He didn't write about being in a war. Said he was getting a sun-tan and going fishing. He sent a photo of himself sitting on a donkey with his knees on the sand. It wasn't until he came home on leave that I knew he was in a war. He never used to spoil our daughter, never showed any fatherly feelings, perhaps because she was small. Now he came back and sat for hours looking at her, and his eyes were so sad it was frightening. In the mornings he'd get up and take her to the kindergarten; he liked carrying her on his shoulders. He'd collect her in the evening. Occasionally we went to the theatre or the cinema, but all he really wanted to do was to stay at home.

He couldn't get enough loving. I'd be getting ready to go to work or getting his dinner in the kitchen, and he even grudged that time. 'Sit over here with me. Forget cutlets today. Ask for a holiday while I'm home.' When it was time for him to get the plane he missed it deliberately so we would have an extra two days. The last night he was so good I was in tears. I was crying, and he was saying nothing, just looking and looking at me. Then he said, 'Tamara, if you ever have another man, don't forget this.'

I said, 'Don't talk soft! They'll never kill you. I love you too much for them to be able to.'

He laughed. 'Forget it. I'm a big lad.'

We talked of having more children, but he said he didn't want any more now. 'When I come back you can have another. How would you manage with them on your own?'

When he was away I got used to the waiting, but if I saw a funeral car in town I'd feel ill, I'd want to scream and cry. I'd run home, the icon would be hanging there, and I'd get down on my knees and pray, 'Save him for me, God! Don't let him die.'

333

I went to the cinema the day it happened. I sat there looking at the screen and seeing nothing. I was really jumpy. It was as if I was keeping someone waiting or there was somewhere I had to go. I barely stuck it out to the end of the programme. Looking back, I think that it must have been during the battle.

It was a week before I heard anything. All of that week I'd start reading a book and put it down. I even got two letters from him. Usually I'd have been really pleased—I'd have kissed them—but this time they just made me wonder how much longer I was going to have to wait for him.

The ninth day after he was killed a telegram arrived at five in the morning. They just shoved it under the door. It was from his parents: 'Come over. Petya dead.' I screamed so much that it woke the baby. I had no idea what I should do or where I should go. I hadn't got any money. I wrapped our daughter in a red blanket and went out to the road. It was too early for the buses, but a taxi stopped.

'I need to go to the airport,' I told the taxi-driver.

He told me he was going off duty and shut the car door.

'My husband has been killed in Afghanistan.'

He got out without saying anything, and helped me in. We drove to the house of a friend of mine and she lent me some money. At the airport they said there were no tickets for Moscow, and I was scared to take the telegram out of my bag to show them. Perhaps it was all a mistake. I kept telling myself if I could just carry on thinking he was alive, he would be. I was crying and everybody was looking at me. They put me on a freight plane taking a cargo of sweetcorn to Moscow, from there I got a connection to Minsk. I was still 150 kilometres from Starye Dorogi where Petya's parents lived. None of the taxi drivers wanted to drive there even though I begged and begged. I finally got to Starye Dorogi at two o'clock in the morning.

'Perhaps it isn't true?'

'It's true, Tamara, it's true.'

In the morning we went to the Military Commissariat. They were very formal. 'You will be notified when it arrives.' We waited for two more days before we rang the Provincial Military Commissariat at Minsk. They told us that it would be best if we came to collect my husband's body ourselves. When we got to Minsk, the official told us that the coffin had been sent on to Baranovichi by mistake. Baranovichi was another 100 kilometres and when we got to the airport there it was after working hours and there was nobody about, except for a night watchman in his hut.

'We've come to collect . . .'

'Over there,' he pointed over to a far corner. 'See if that box is yours. If it is, you can take it.'

There was a filthy box standing outside with 'Senior Lieutenant Dovnar' scrawled on it in chalk. I tore a board away from where the window should be in a coffin. His face was in one piece, but he was lying in there unshaven, and nobody had washed him. The coffin was too small and there was a bad smell. I couldn't lean down to kiss him. That's how they gave my husband back to me. I got down on my knees before what had once been the dearest thing in the world to me.

His was the first coffin to come back to my home town, Yazyl. I still remember the horror in people's eyes. When we buried him, before they could draw up the bands with which they had been lowering him, there was a terrible crash of thunder. I remember the hail crunching under foot like white gravel.

I didn't talk much to his father and mother. I thought his mother hated me because I was alive, and he was dead. She thought I would remarry. Now, she says, 'Tamara, you ought to get married again,' but then I was afraid to meet her eye. Petya's father almost went out of his mind. 'The bastards! To put a boy like that in his grave! They murdered him!' My mother-in-law and I tried to tell him they'd given Petya a medal, that we needed Afghanistan to defend our southern borders, but he didn't want to hear. 'The bastards! They murdered him!'

The worst part was later, when I had to get used to the thought that there was nothing, no one for me to wait for any more. I would wake up terrified, drenched with sweat, thinking Petya would come back, and not know where his wife and child live now. All I had left were memories of good times.

The day we met, we danced together. The second day we went for a stroll in the park, and the next day he proposed. I was already engaged and I told him the application was lying in the registry office. He went away and wrote to me in huge letters which took up the whole page: 'Aaaaargh!'

We got married in the winter, in my village. It was funny and rushed. At Epiphany, when people guess their fortunes, I'd had a dream which I told my mother about in the morning. 'Mum, I saw this really good-looking boy. He was standing on a bridge, calling me. He was wearing a soldier's uniform, but when I came towards him he began to go away until he disappeared completely.'

'Don't marry a soldier. You'll be left on your own,' my mother told me.

Petya had two days' leave. 'Let's go to the Registry Office,' he said, even before he'd come in the door.

They took one look at us in the Village Soviet and said, 'Why wait two months. Go and get the brandy. We'll do the paperwork.' An hour later we were husband and wife. There was a snowstorm raging outside.

'Where's the taxi for your new wife, bridegroom?'

'Hang on!' He went out and stopped a Belarus tractor for me.

For years I dreamed of us getting on that tractor, driving along in the snow.

The last time Petya came home on leave the flat was locked. He hadn't sent a telegram to warn me that he was coming, and I had gone to my friend's flat to celebrate her birthday. When he arrived at the door and heard the music and saw everyone happy and laughing, he sat down on a stool and cried. Every day of his leave he came to work to meet me. He told me, 'When I'm coming to see you at work my knees shake as if we had a date.' I remember we went swimming together one day. We sat on the bank and built a fire. He looked at me and said, 'You can't imagine how much I don't want to die for someone else's country.'

I was twenty-four when he died. In those first months I would have married any man who wanted me. I didn't know what to do. Life was going on all around me the same as before. One person was building a *dacha*, one was buying a car; someone had got a new flat and needed a carpet or a hotplate for the kitchen. In the last war everybody was grief stricken, the whole country. Everybody had lost someone, and they knew what they had lost them for. All the women cried together. There are a hundred people in the catering college where I work and I am the only one who lost her husband in a war the rest of them have only read about in the newspapers. When I first heard them saying on television that the war in Afghanistan had been a national disgrace, I wanted to break the screen. I lost my husband for a second time that day.

A Private Soldier

The only training we got before we took the oath was that twice they took us down the firing-range. The first time we went there they issued us with nine rounds; the second time we all got to throw a grenade.

They lined us up on the square and read out the order: 'You're going to the Democratic Republic of Afghanistan to do your internationalist duty. Anyone who doesn't want to go, take two paces forward.' Three lads did. The unit commander shoved them back in line with a knee up the backside. 'Just checking morale.' They gave us two days' rations and a leather belt, and we were off. Nobody said a word. The flight seemed to take an age. I saw mountains through the plane window. Beautiful! They were the first mountains any of us had ever seen. we were all from round Pskov, where there are only woodlands and clearings. We got out in Shin Dand. I remembered the date: 19 December 1980.

They took a look at me. 'One metre eighty: reconnaissance company. They can use lads your size.'

We went to Herat to build a firing-range. We were digging,

337

hauling stones for a foundation. I tiled a roof and did some joinery. Some of us hadn't fired a single shot before the first battle. We were hungry the whole time. There were two fifty-litre vats in the kitchen: one for soup, the other for mash or barley porridge. We had one can of mackerel between four, and the label said, 'Date of manufacture, 1956; shelf-life eighteen months.' In a year and a half, the only time I wasn't hungry was when I was wounded. Otherwise you were always thinking of ways to get something to eat. We were so desperate for fruit that we'd slip over into the Afghans' orchards knowing that they'd shoot at us. We asked our parents to send citric acid in their letters so that we could dissolve it in water and drink it. It was so sour that it burned your stomach.

Before our first battle they played the Soviet national anthem. The deputy political commander gave us a talk. I remember he said we'd only beaten the Americans here by one hour, and everybody was waiting to welcome us back home as heroes.

I had no idea how to kill. Before the army I was a racing cyclist. I'd never so much as seen a real knife fight, and here I was, driving along on the back of an armoured personnel carrier. I hadn't felt like this before: powerful, strong and secure. The hills suddenly looked low, the irrigation ditches small, the trees few and far between. After half an hour I was so relaxed I felt like a tourist, taking a look at a foreign country.

We drove over a ditch on a little clay bridge: I remember being amazed it could take the weight of several tons of metal. Suddenly there was an explosion and the APC in front had got a direct hit from a grenade launcher. Men I knew were already being carried away, like stuffed animals with their arms dangling. I couldn't make sense of this new, frightening world. We sent all our mortars into where the firing had come from, several mortars to every homestead. After the battle we scraped our own guys off the armour plate with spoons. There weren't any identification discs for fatalities; I suppose they thought they might fall into the wrong hands. It was like in the song: *We don't live in a house on a street, Our address is the USSR.* So we just spread a tarpaulin over the bodies, a 'communal grave'. War hadn't even been declared; we were fighting a war that did not exist.

A Mother

I sat by Sasha's coffin saying, 'Who is it? Is that you, son?' I just kept repeating over and over, 'Is that you?' They decided I was out of my mind. Later on, I wanted to know how my son had died. I went to the Military Commissariat and the commissar started shouting at me, telling me it was a state secret that my son had died, that I shouldn't run around telling everyone.

My son was in the Vitebsk parachute division. When I went to see him take his oath of allegiance, I didn't recognize him; he stood so tall.

'Hey, how come I've got such a small mum?'

'Because I miss you and I've stopped growing.'

He bent down and kissed me, and somebody took a photograph. It's the only photograph of him as a soldier that I've got.

After the oath he had a few hours free time. We went to the park and sat down on the grass. He took his boots off because his feet were all blistered and bleeding. The previous day his unit had been on a fifty kilometre forced march and there hadn't been any size forty-six boots, so they had given him forty-fours.

'We had to run with rucksacks filled with sand. What do you reckon? Where did I come?'

'Last, probably, with those boots.'

'Wrong, mum. I was first. I took the boots off and ran. And I didn't tip sand out like some of the others.'

That night, they let the parents sleep inside the unit on mats laid out in the sports hall, but we didn't lie down until far into the night, instead we wandered round the barracks where our sons were asleep. I hoped I would get to see him when they went to do their morning gymnastics but they were all running in identical striped vests and I missed him, didn't catch a last glimpse of him. They all went to the toilet in a line, in a line to do their gymnastics, in a line to the canteen. They didn't let them do anything on their own because, when the boys had heard they were being sent to Afghanistan, one hanged himself in the toilet and two others slashed their wrists. They were under guard.

His second letter began, 'Greetings from Kabul . . . ' I screamed so loudly that the neighbours ran in. It was the first time since Sasha was born that I was sorry I had not got married and had no one to look after me.

Sasha used to tease me. 'Why don't you get married, Mum?'

'Because you'd be jealous.'

He'd laugh and say nothing. We were going to live together for a long, long time to come.

I got a few more letters and then there was silence, such a long silence I wrote to the commander of his unit. Straight away Sasha wrote back to me, 'Mum, please don't write to the commander again. I couldn't write to you. I got my hand stung by a wasp. I didn't want to ask someone else to write, because you'd have been worried by the different handwriting.' I knew immediately that he had been wounded, and now if even a day went by without a letter from him my legs would give way under me. One of his letters was very cheerful. 'Hurray, hurray! We escorted a column back to the Union. We went with them as far as the frontier. They wouldn't let us go any further, but at least we got a distant look at our homeland. It's the best country in the world.' In his last letter he wrote, 'If I last the summer, I'll be back.'

On 29 August I decided summer was over. I bought Sasha a new suit and a pair of shoes, which are still in the wardrobe now. The next day, before I went to work I took off my ear-rings and my ring. For some reason I couldn't bear to wear them. That was the day on which he was killed.

When they brought the zinc coffin into the room, I lay on top of it and measured it again and again. One metre, two metres. He was two metres tall. I measured with my hands to make sure the coffin was the right size for him. The coffin was sealed, so I couldn't kiss him one last time, or touch him, I didn't even know what he was wearing, I just talked to the coffin like a madwoman.

I said I wanted to choose the place in the cemetery for him myself. They gave me two injections, and I went there with my brother. There were 'Afghan' graves on the main avenue.

'Lay my son here too. He'll be happier among his friends.'

I can't remember who was there with us. Some official. He shook his head. 'We are not permitted to bury them together. They have to be dispersed throughout the cemetery.'

They say there was a case where they brought a coffin back to a mother, and she buried it, and a year later her son came back alive. He'd only been wounded. I never saw my son's body, or kissed him goodbye. I'm still waiting.

A Nurse

Every day I was there I told myself I was a fool to come. Especially at night, when I had no work to do. All I thought during the day was 'How can I help them all?' I couldn't believe anybody would make the bullets they were using. Whose idea were they? The point of entry was small, but inside, their intestines, their liver, their spleen were all ripped and torn apart. As if it wasn't enough to kill or wound them, they had to be put through that kind of agony as well. They always cried for their mothers when they were in pain, or frightened. I never heard them call for anyone else.

They told us it was a just war. We were helping the Afghan people to put an end to feudalism and build a socialist society. Somehow they didn't get round to mentioning that our men were being killed. For the whole of the first month I was there they just dumped the amputated arms and legs of our soldiers and officers, even their bodies, right next to the tents. It was something I would hardly have believed if I had seen it in films about the Civil War. There were no zinc coffins then: they hadn't got round to manufacturing them.

Twice a week we had political indoctrination. They went on about our sacred duty, and how the border must be inviolable. Our superior ordered us to inform on every wounded soldier, every patient. It was called monitoring the state of morale: the army must be healthy! We weren't to feel compassion. But we did feel compassion: it was the only thing that held everything together.

A Regimental Press Officer

I will begin at the point where everything fell apart.

We were advancing on Jalalabad and a little girl of about seven years old was standing by the roadside. Her arm had been smashed and was held on only by a thread, as if she were a torn rag doll. She had dark eyes like olives, and they were fixed on me. I jumped down from the vehicle to take her in my arms and carry her to our nurses, but she sprang back terrified and screaming like a small animal. Still screaming she ran away, her little arm dangling and looking as though it would come off completely. I ran after her shouting, caught up with her and pressed her to me, stroking her. She was biting and scratching, trembling all over, as if some wild animal had seized her. It was only then that the thought struck me like a thunderbolt: she didn't believe I wanted to help her; she thought I wanted to kill her. The way she ran away, the way she shuddered, how afraid she was of me are things I'll never forget.

I had set out for Afghanistan with idealism blazing in my eyes. I had been told that the Afghans needed me, and I believed it. While I was there I never dreamed about the war, but now every night I am back running after that little girl with her olive eyes, and her little arm dangling as if it's going to fall off any moment.

Out there you felt quite differently about your country. 'The Union', we called it. It seemed there was something great and powerful behind us, something which would always stand up for us. I remember, though, the evening after one battle—there had been losses, men killed and men seriously injured—we plugged in the television to forget about it, to see

342

what was going on in the Union. A mammoth new factory had been built in Siberia; the Queen of England had given a banquet in honour of some VIP; youths in Voronezh had raped two schoolgirls for the hell of it; a prince had been killed in Africa. The country was going about its business and we felt completely useless. Someone had to turn the television off, before we shot it to pieces.

It was a mothers' war. They were in the thick of it. The people at large didn't suffer, they didn't know what was going on. They were told we were fighting bandits. In nine years a regular army of 100,000 troops couldn't beat some ragged bandits? An army with the latest technology. (God help anyone who got in the way of an artillery bombardment with our Hail or Hurricane rocket launchers: the telegraph poles flew like matchsticks.) The 'bandits' had only old Maxim machine-guns we had seen in films, the Stingers and Japanese machine guns came later. We'd bring in prisoners, emaciated people with big, peasant hands. They were no bandits. They were the people of Afghanistan.

The war had its own ghastly rules: if you were photographed or if you shaved before a battle, you were dead. It was always the blue-eyed heroes who were the first to be killed: you'd meet one of those types and before you knew it, he was dead. People mostly got killed either in their first months when they were too curious, or towards the end when they'd lost their sense of caution and become stupid. At night you'd forget where you were, who you were, what you were doing there. No one could sleep during the last six or eight weeks before they went home.

Here in the Union we are like brothers. A young guy going down the street on crutches with a shiny medal can only be one of us. You might only sit down on a bench and smoke a cigarette together, but you feel as if you've been talking to each other the whole day.

The authorities want to use us to clamp down on organized crime. If there is any trouble to be broken up, the police send for 'the Afghans'. As far as they are concerned we are guys with big fists and small brains who nobody likes. But surely if your hand hurts you don't put it in the fire, you look after it until it gets better.

A Mother

I skip along to the cemetery as if I'm on my way to meet someone. I feel I'm going to visit my son. Those first days I stayed there all night. It wasn't frightening. I'm waiting for the spring, for a little flower to burst through to me out of the ground. I planted snowdrops, so I would have a greeting from my son as early as possible. They come to me from down there, from him.

I'll sit with him until evening and far on into the night. Sometimes I don't realize I've started wailing until I scare the birds, a whole squall of crows, circling and flapping above me until I come to my senses and stop. I've gone there every day for four years, in the evening if not in the morning. I missed eleven days when I was in hospital, then I ran away in the hospital gown to see my son.

He called me 'Mother mine', and 'Angel mother mine'.
   'Well, angel mother mine, your son has been accepted by the Smolensk Military Academy. I trust you are pleased.'
He sat down at the piano and sang.

Gentlemen officers, princes indeed!
If I'm not first among them,
I'm one of their breed.

My father was a regular officer who died in the defence of Leningrad. My grandfather was an officer too. My son was made to be a military man—he had the bearing, so tall and strong. He should have been a hussar with white gloves, playing cards.

Everybody wanted to be like him. Even I, his own mother, would imitate him. I would sit down at the piano the way he did, and sometimes start walking the way he did, especially after he was killed. I so much want him always to be present in me.

344

When he first went to Afghanistan, he didn't write for ages. I waited and waited for him to come home on leave. Then one day the telephone rang at work.

'Angel mother mine, I am home.'

I went to meet him off the bus. His hair had gone grey. He didn't admit he wasn't on leave, that he'd asked to be let out of hospital for a couple of days to see his mother. He'd got hepatitis, malaria and everything else rolled into one but he warned his sister not to tell me. I went into his room again before I went off to work, to see him sleeping. He opened his eyes. I asked him why he was not asleep, it was so early. He said he'd had a bad dream.

We went with him as far as Moscow. It was lovely, sunny May weather, and the trees were in bloom. I asked him what it was like over there.

'Mother mine, Afghanistan is something we have no business to be doing.' He looked only at me, not at anyone else. 'I don't want to go back into that hole. I really do not.' He walked away, but turned round, 'It's as simple as that, Mum.' He never said 'Mum'. The woman at the airport desk was in tears watching us.

When I woke up on 7 July I hadn't been crying. I stared glassily at the ceiling. He had woken me, as if he had come to say goodbye. It was eight o'clock. I had to get ready to go to work. I was wandering with my dress from the bathroom to the sitting-room, from one room to another. For some reason I couldn't bear to put that light-coloured dress on. I felt dizzy, and couldn't see people properly. Everything was blurred. I grew calmer towards lunch-time, towards midday.

The seventh day of July. He had seven cigarettes in his pocket, seven matches. He had taken seven pictures with his camera. He had written seven letters to me, and seven to his girlfriend. The book on his bedside table was open at page seven. It was Kobo Abe's *Containers of Death*.

He had three or four seconds in which he could have saved himself. They were hurtling over a precipice in a vehicle. He couldn't be the first to jump out. He never could.

From Deputy Regimental Commander for Political Affairs, Major S. R. Sinelnikov. In fulfilment of my duty as a soldier, I have to inform you that Senior Lieutenant Valerii Gennadievich Volovich was killed today at 1045 hours.

The whole city already knew all about it. In the Officers' Club they'd put up black crêpe and his photograph. The plane bringing his coffin was due at any minute, but nobody had told me a thing. They couldn't bring themselves to speak. At work everybody's faces were tear-stained. I asked, 'What has happened?'

They tried to distract me in various ways. A friend came round, then finally a doctor in a white coat arrived. I told him he was crazy, that boys like my son did not get killed. I started hammering the table. I ran over to the window and started beating the glass. They gave me an injection. I kept on shouting. They gave me another injection, but that had no effect, either; I was screaming, 'I want to see him, take me to my son.' Eventually they had to take me.

There was a long coffin. The wood was unplaned, and written on it in large letters in yellow paint was 'Volovich'. I had to find him a place in the cemetery, somewhere dry, somewhere nice and dry. If that meant a fifty rouble bribe, fine. Here, take it, only make sure it's a good place, nice and dry. Inside I knew how disgusting that was, but I just wanted a nice dry place for him. Those first nights I didn't leave him. I stayed there. They would take me off home, but I would come back.

When I go to see him I bow, and when I leave I bow again. I never get cold even in freezing temperatures; I write my letters there; I am only ever at home when I have visitors. When I walk back to my house at night the streetlamps are lit, the cars have their headlamps on. I feel so strong that I am not afraid of anything.

Only now am I waking from my sorrow which is like waking from sleep. I want to know whose fault this was. Why doesn't anybody say anything? Why aren't we being told who did it? Why aren't they being put on trial?

I greet every flower on his grave, every little root and stem. 'Have you come from there? Do you come from him? You have come from my son.

Translated from the Russian by Arch Tait.

John le Carré
The Unbearable Peace

'I didn't die,' says Jeanmaire proudly. 'They wanted me to, but I wouldn't do them the favour.'

It is evening. We are alone in his tiny flat on the eastern outskirts of Bern. He is cooking cheese fondue for the two of us. On a shelf in the kitchen stand the steel eating bowls he used in prison. Why does he keep them?

'For memory,' he replies.

In the tiny corridor outside hang the dagger and sabre that are the insignia of a Swiss army officer's dress uniform. The drawing-room is decorated with a reproduction medieval halberd and his diploma of architecture dated 1934. A signed photograph from General Westmoreland, commemorating a goodwill visit to Bern, is inscribed 'General, Air Protection Troops', Jeanmaire's last appointment.

'Of course there were some of my colleagues who got nothing,' he says slyly, indicating that he was singled out for this distinction.

He has decided it is time for a drink. He drinks frugally these days, but still with the relish for which he is remembered.

'I permit myself a little water,' he announces. Prussian style, he stiffens his back, raises his elbow, whips the cap off the whisky bottle I have brought him and pours two precise shots. He adds his water; we raise our glasses, drink eye to eye, raise them again, then perch ourselves awkwardly at the table while he rolls the whisky round his mouth and declares it drinkable. Then he is off again, this time to the oven to stir the cheese and—as a trained and tried military instructor as well as judge—lecture me on how to do it on my own next time.

On the desk, and on the floor, and piled high against the wall, papers, files, press cuttings, mounds of them, mustered and flagged for his last campaign.

It is a journalistic conceit to pretend you are unmoved by people. But I am not a journalist and I am not superior to this encounter. Jean-Louis Jeanmaire moves me deeply and humorously and horribly.

Jeanmaire is not cut out to be a mystery, least of all a spy. He is not cut out to be a Swiss, for his feelings are written all over his features, even when he is trying to hide them, and he would be the worst poker player in the world. He is broad-faced and, for a seemingly aggressive man, strangely vulnerable. He has the eyebrows of an angry clown. They lift and scowl and flit and marvel with every stray mood that passes over him. His body too is seldom reconciled. He seems to come at you and retreat at the same time. He is short and was once delicate, but striving has made a bull of him. His brief, passionate gestures are the more massive for being confined in a small room. Wherever you are with him in his life—whether in his childhood, or in the Army, or in his marriage, or in court, or in prison—you feel in him, and sometimes in yourself as well, the need for greater space, more air, more distance.

'I had no *access* to top secret information!' he whispers, with an emotional implosion that his body seems hardly able to contain. 'How could I have betrayed secrets I didn't know? All I ever did was give the Russians harmless bits of proof that Switzerland was a dangerous country to attack!' A wave of anger seizes him. '*C'était la dissuasion*,' he bellows. He is wagging his finger at me. His brows are clamped together above his nose. 'My aim was to deter those mad Bolsheviks at the Kremlin from mounting an assault against my country! I showed them how expensive it would be! What is *dissuasion* if the other side is not *dissuaded*? Denissenko understood that! We were working together against the Bolsheviks!'

His voice drops to make the point more gently: 'I was never a traitor. A fool maybe. A traitor, never!'

He has no time between moods. He has no time. He is pursuing justice every moment that is left to him. He can act and mime. He can camp and scorn and laugh. He has the energy of a man half his eighty years. One minute he is squared at you like a boxer; the next all you have to look at is his soldier's back as, toes and heels together, he bows devotionally to light the candles on the tiny kitchen table. He lights them every day in memory of his dead wife, he says: the same wife whom he never once blamed for sleeping with his Nemesis, the Soviet military attaché and intelligence officer Colonel Vassily Denissenko, Deni for short, who was stationed in Bern in the early sixties and effortlessly recruited Jeanmaire as his source.

He waves out the match. He has the tiny fingers of a watch-maker. 'But Deni was an attractive man!' he protests, as his far-off, pale eyes brim again with love remembered, whether for his wife or for Deni or for both of them. 'If I'd been a woman I'd have slept with him myself!'

The statement does not embarrass him. For all that has been done to him, Jeanmaire is a lover still: of his friends, dead or alive, of his several women and of his erstwhile Russian contacts. The ease with which a man so deceived in his loyalties continues to give his trust is terrifying. It is impossible to listen to him for any time and not wish to take him into your protection. Deni was handsome! he is insisting. Deni was cultivated, charming, honourable, a gentleman! Deni was a hero of Stalingrad, he had medals for gallantry, he admired the Swiss Army! Deni was no Bolshevik: he was a horseman, a czarist, an officer of the old school!

Deni, he might add, was also the acknowledged Resident of the GRU, or Soviet Military Intelligence Service, poor cousin of the KGB. But Jeanmaire doesn't seem to care. The first time he even heard of the KGB, he insists, was when he was cataloguing books for the prison library. The GRU remains even more remote from him. He swears that throughout his entire military career, he never had the least training in these bodies.

And Deni was *faithful to the end*, he repeats, driving his little fist on to the table like a child who fears he is unheard: the end being twelve years in solitary confinement in a cell ten feet by six, after 130 days of intermittent civilian and military interrogation while under arrest, followed by a further six months' detention while awaiting trial and a closed military tribunal that lasted barely four days. Its findings are still secret.

'When they arrested me, Deni wrote a letter from Moscow to the *Soviet Literary Gazette*, describing me as the greatest anti-communist he had ever known. The letter was published in the Swiss press but never referred to at my trial. That was exceptional, such a letter. Deni cared very much about me.'

That is not exactly what Denissenko wrote about him, but never mind. He described Jeanmaire as a nationalist and patriot, which is probably how Denissenko regarded himself also.

And still the anguished eulogy flows on. Deni never pressed him, never tried to squeeze anything out of him he didn't want to give. Ergo—Deni was an honourable man! Not so honourable that Jeanmaire would let Deni pay for drinks or that he could accept an envelope of money from him or even that he could let Deni get a sight of Jeanmaire's signature on a letter, but honourable all the same: 'Deni was a man of heart, a brother officer in the best sense!'

Above all, Deni was *noble*. Jeanmaire awards this word like a medal. Jeanmaire has been pre-judged, reviled and incarcerated. He has come as near to being burned as a witch as modern society allows. But all he asks is that, before he dies, the world will give him back his own nobility. And I hope it will. And so would all of us. For who can disappoint a man of such infectious and vulnerable feeling?

To the suggestion that he might have been jealous of his wife's lover, Jeanmaire expresses only mystification.

'*Jealousy*?' he repeats, as the nimble eyebrows rush together in disapproval. '*Jealousy*? Jealousy is the vice of a limited man, but trust—'

We have struck his vanity again, his tragic, childish, prickly vanity: Jeanmaire is not a limited man, he would have me know! And his wife was a pure, good, beautiful woman and, like Deni, faithful to the end! Even though, in his wife's case, the end came sooner, for she died while he was still in prison. Deni's charm, whatever else it had going for it, did not come cheap.

From the pile of cuttings Jeanmaire extracts a muddy photograph of the great man, and I try hard to imagine his allure. Or was the allure actually all on Jeanmaire's side, and was Jeanmaire the one person who never knew it? Alas, Russian officers are seldom photogenic. All I see in Deni is a grey-suited, doughy-faced military bureaucrat of no expression, looking as if he would prefer not to have been photographed at all. And Jeanmaire, this un-Swiss Swiss, beaming as if he has just won the Derby.

L et me be a journalist for a moment. Jean-Louis Jeanmaire was born in 1910 in the small industrial town of Biel in the canton of Bern, where they do indeed make, among other things, the watches that remind me of his little hands. Biel is bilingual, German and French. So is Jeanmaire, though he regards French as his first language and speaks German with a grating, nasal pseudo-Prussian accent that to my ear is not at all Swiss, but then I was never in the Swiss Army. If there were such a thing as German Canadian, I am thinking as I listen to the rolled *r*s and saw-edged *a*s, that is what Jeanmaire would be speaking. His father was an arch-conservative of chilling rectitude. Like Jean-Louis after him, he was a chartered architect. But by passion he was a Colonel of Cavalry and Commandant of Mobilization for the town of Biel. In a country condemned to peace, the infant Jeanmaire was thus born a soldier's son and longed to be a soldier. He was four when the First World War broke out, and he has a clear memory of his papa standing in uniform beside the Christmas tree and of his great and good godfather Tissot, also in uniform, dropping in to visit.

'*Such a beautiful officer*,' Jeanmaire recalls of his godfather Edouard Tissot, almost as if he were talking about Deni.

Tissot was also beautiful without his uniform, apparently. When Jeanmaire visited him in his spacious apartment, he would likely as not find his godfather wandering around it naked. But no, Tissot was not homosexual! he cries in disgust, and neither was Jeanmaire! This nakedness was Spartan, never sexual.

Yet beside this image of military glory, Jeanmaire has a second and contrasting early memory that reflects more accurately the social upheavals of the times: namely of the Swiss General Strike of 1918, when the 'Bolsheviks of Biel' derailed a train in order to barricade the street, then hoisted the red flag on the capsized engine. Their violence against property and their lack of discipline appalled the young Jeanmaire, and his love of the Army, if possible, increased. Even today, given the chance, Jeanmaire would make an army of the whole world. Without his Army, it seems, he is in his own eyes a man of no parentage.

Jeanmaire is nothing if not the creature of his origins. For those who know Switzerland only for its slopes and valleys, Swiss militarism, if they are aware of it at all, is a harmless joke. They make nothing of the circular steel plates in the winding mountain roads, from which explosive charges will be detonated to seal off the valleys from the aggressor; of the great iron gateways that lead into secret mountain fortresses, some for storing military arsenals, others for sitting out the nuclear holocaust; of the self-regarding young men in officer's uniform who strut the pavements and parade themselves in tea-shops at weekends. They are unaware of the vast annual expenditure on American tanks and fighter aircraft, early-warning-systems, civil defence, deep shelters and (with 625,000 troops from a population of 6,000,000) after Israel the largest proportionate standing army in the world, costing the Swiss taxpayer eighteen per cent of his gross national budget—it has been as high as thirty—or 5.2 billion Swiss francs or 2.1 billion pounds a year. If their alpine holidays are occasionally disturbed by the scream of low-flying jets or bursts of semi-automatic fire from the local shooting-range, they are likely to dismiss such irritations as the charming obsessions of a peaceful Lilliput with the grown-up games of war.

And to a point, the Swiss in their dealings with the benighted foreigner encourage this view, either because as believers in their military ethic they prefer to remain aloof from frivolous explanation, or because as dissenters they are embarrassed to admit that their country lives in a permanent, almost obsessive state of semi-mobilization. For better or worse, Switzerland's military tradition is for many of her inhabitants the essence of Swiss nationhood. And the chain of influence and connection that goes with it is probably the most powerful of the many that comprise the intricate structure of Swiss domestic power.

To its more radical opponents, the Swiss Army is quite baldly an expensive weapon of social suppression, an insane waste of taxpayers' money, which recreates in military form the distinctions of civilian life. But to its defenders, it is the very spirit of national unity, bridging the linguistic and cultural differences between Switzerland's ethnic groups and keeping at bay the swelling numbers of immigrants who threaten to dilute the proud and ancient blood of free Switzerland. Above all, say its defenders, the Army deters the foreign adventurer. Just as apologists of the nuclear deterrent insist that the bomb, by its existence, has ensured that it will never be used, so supporters of Swiss militarism claim that the Army has secured their country's neutrality—and hence survival—through successive European wars.

Jean-Louis Jeanmaire—who still prides himself on having persuaded incarcerated conscientious objectors to change their minds—has subscribed passionately to this gospel since childhood. He had it preached to him by his father and again by his godfather Tissot. In the same breath they taught him the equally fervent gospel of anti-socialism. 'Good,' says Jeanmaire, meant 'patriot and militarist.' 'Bad' meant 'anti-militarist and socialist.'

But the small town of Biel did not at all share the reactionary visions of Tissot, Colonel Jeanmaire and his son. Its inhabitants were mostly workpeople. When the railway workers marched in support of the strike of November 1918—in the same days in which Jeanmaire witnessed the overturning of the train—the Army dealt with them swiftly, tearing into the crowds and shooting one man dead. But the response of Jeanmaire's father and his comrades, he says, was to rally a contingent of technical students to keep the gas and electricity works going, and arm .the bourgeoisie against the rabble. Interestingly, local historical records award no such role to Jeanmaire's father, but say that the strike was broken by imported Italian labour. But whatever his father's contribution to the suppression might have been, his conservative posture did not make life easy for the young Jeanmaire when the time came for him to attend the local school. From his first day, he says, beatings by staff armed with sticks and the inner tubes of car-tyres became his fare. When he was unruly, the diminutive Jeanmaire was strapped to a school bench: 'I was the smallest but I wasn't the most stupid,' he says grimly.

Some boys in this situation might have learned to keep their opinions to themselves, or prudently converted to their oppressors' views. Not Jeanmaire. Always one to speak his mind, he did so more loudly, in defiance of what he regarded as the prevailing cant. Both at school and afterwards, he learned to count on his own judgement and assail mediocrity wherever he found it, whether it was above him or below him on the ladder of beings.

And this attitude stayed with him through his adult life—through the architectural studies on which he hurled himself with impressive result as a prelude to enlistment and into his career as an infantry instruction officer, which he pursued on the orders of his godfather Tissot, who told Jeanmaire that if he joined the Artillery he would never talk to him again.

At first, Jeanmaire's career proceeded well. In 1937, after the usual probationary period, he made instructor, rose to captain three years later and major after another seven. During the Second World War he saw service on the Simplon and in the canton of Wallis, and in 1956 he was made lieutenant-colonel and given his first regiment.

Yet throughout his steady rise, Jeanmaire's reputation as a big-mouth would not go away, as his Army record testifies in its otherwise quite favourable account of him: Jeanmaire was 'intelligent, lively,' but spoke 'too much and too soon.' In his work as an infantry instructor, he 'lacked respect and picked quarrels with his superiors.' He was 'qualified technically but not personally' to command a training school. On one occasion, in 1952, he was even given eight days' punishment arrest 'for insulting officers of a battalion placed under his command' during manoeuvres—though according to Jeanmaire, all he did was tick off a Member of Parliament for not wearing his helmet and call a machine-gunner an arse-hole for nearly mowing down a group of spectators.

True, Jeanmaire had his supporters, even if their admiration of him was played down in the Army's self-serving portrait of his inadequacies. To some of his superiors, he was a capable officer, an inspiration to his men, energetic, good fun. Nevertheless, the abiding impression is of a man impatient of fools, pressing too hard against the limitations of his rank and professional scope.

At best, he comes over as a kind of miniature Swiss Lee Kwan Yew, thrusting to express great visions in a country too small to contain them.

Jeanmaire's accusers, of course, had every reason to present his military career in a poor light, for they were stuck for a motive. They had looked high and low for the thirty pieces of silver, but all they had found was a handful of small change. And not even the most implacable of Jeanmaire's enemies could pin secret communist sympathies on him.

So finally they fixed upon Jeanmaire's transfer to Air Defence in 1956 as the moment of his turning; followed by his being passed over, in 1962, for the appointment as Chief of Air Defence and Territorial Services, obliging him to wait another seven years, by which time the two responsibilities had been separated, and Jeanmaire got Air Defence only. Jeanmaire, it was reasoned, was 'disappointed and traumatized', first to leave the glorious infantry for the unregarded pastures of Air Defence, then to see a lesser man promoted over him. Jeanmaire denies this adamantly: perhaps too adamantly. The Army had always been good to him, he insists; he had status, and he was on the guest list for Bern's diplomatic round of military and service attachés; and in 1969, when he finally made it to brigadier, he got his apartment in Bern as well.

And he had a wife, of whom he still says little, except that she was the soul of loyalty and faithful to the end; and that she was beautiful, which indeed she was; and that he lights a candle to her memory each day.

The Army matters to Jeanmaire above everything. Even today. Even when he lay in the deepest pit of his misfortune, his faith in it burned on. He was in prison awaiting trial when, on 7 October 1976, Kurt Furgler, the Swiss Federal Minister of Justice, rose in Parliament to denounce the 'treasonable activities' of Jeanmaire, his 'disgraceful attitude' and his betrayal of 'most secret documents relating to war mobilization plans.' The next day, Switzerland's most strident tabloid, *Blick*, branded Jeanmaire 'Traitor of the Century' in banner headlines and ran photographs of the villain and his accuser on the front page. Three months later, the Federal President Rudolf Gnägi, addressing a meeting of his own party, confessed his deep disappointment that 'such base actions could be committed by such a high officer,' and demanded 'the full severity of the law.' There are Western countries where such words would have rendered a trial impossible, but Switzerland is not among them. The Swiss may have signed the European Declaration of Human Rights, but they have no law that prevents the public pre-judgement of those awaiting trial. Furgler also denounced Jeanmaire's wife, stating that she had knowledge of her husband's treasonable activities and in the early years had assisted him. (The charges against Frau Jeanmaire were eventually dismissed.) The Swiss insurance company Winterthur, from which the Jeanmaires had rented their apartment, also preferred not to await the verdict of the military court, but gave them notice, forcing his wife on to the street.

Yet among all these calculated humiliations, what hurt him most and hurts him this evening is that *his beloved Army*, also before his trial, caused his pension to be withdrawn 'in eternity'. The reason, according to one reputable paper of the day, was *Volkszorn*, popular fury. 'Our offices were exposed to pressure by angry citizens. A flood of letters demanded that Jeanmaire be paid no further money,' a spokesman for the federal pensions agency explained.

For a moment, it is as if the pale baby eyes are presuming to weep without his permission. They fill, they are about to brim over. But the old soldier talks brusquely on, and the tears dare not fall.

'That was a crime as never before,' he says.

'In prison I was never a slave but I obeyed!' Jeanmaire declares, hastening once more to the defence of old friends: 'No, no, they were good fellows, my fellow prisoners! I never had a bad scene! I was never set upon or insulted for what I was supposed to have done. I never felt threatened by a single one of the prisoners I met! I always made a point of warning the young ones of the perils of prison. I was a father to them.'

Seated at his little table, eating his fondue, we become cell-mates, sharing our hoarded rations by candle-light.

He is talking of the first shock of imprisonment: the terrible first days and nights.

'They took my watch away. They thought I could kill myself with it. It's very bad to be in solitary without a watch. A watch gives rhythm to your day. When you are free, you go to the phone, the lavatory, the kitchen, the book-shelf, the garden, the café, the woman. The watch tells you. In prison, without a watch these instincts become clamorous and confused in your head, even if you can't obey them all the time. They're freedom. A watch is freedom.'

But Jeanmaire's sanity, despite the harrowing assaults on it, seems as pristine as the polished steel bowls he keeps from prison. He has an extraordinary memory for dates and places and conversations. He has been interrogated by a rotating troupe of professional performers for months on end: policemen, lawyers, bit-players from the *demi-monde* of spying. He has been interrogated in prison hospital, on what should have been his deathbed. Since his release, he has given interviews on television, to the printed press and to the growing number of concerned Swiss men and women in public life who begin to share his view that he is the victim of a great injustice.

There are evasions, certainly. You hit them like fog patches along an otherwise clear road: willed unclarities where he is being merciful to himself or to third parties. For example, when you touch upon the delicate matter of his wife's affair with Denissenko—when did it start, please? How long did it last, please? When did he first know of it and what part did it play in his collaboration? For example, the number of encounters he had with his successive Soviet contacts, and exactly what information or documents were passed on this or that occasion? We are talking, you understand, not of the discovery of the H-bomb, but of how the Swiss people would respond to the improbable sight of an invasion force of Soviet tanks rumbling up Zürich's Bahnhofstrasse.

Most difficult of all is to pin down Jeanmaire's own degree of awareness—consciousness, as the spies call it—as he slid further and further down the fatal slope of compliance. There we are dealing not merely with self-deception at the time of the act, but with fifteen years of subsequent self-justification and reconstruction, twelve of them in prison, where men have little to do except relive, and sometimes rewrite, their histories.

Yet the consistency of detail in Jeanmaire's story would be remarkable in any story so frequently retold. Jeanmaire ascribes this to the disciplines of his military training. But the greater likelihood seems to be that he is that rarest of all God's creatures: a spy who, even when he wishes to deceive, has not the smallest talent to do so.

Under interrogation, Jeanmaire was an unmitigated disaster; the tortures of sudden imprisonment worked wonderfully and swiftly on such a thrusting and sociable spirit.

'There were moments when, if I had been accused of stabbing my wife seven times, I would have said, "No, no, *eight* times!" Again and again they promised me my freedom: "Admit this and you are free tonight." So I admitted it. I admitted to more than I had done.

'When you are first locked in a cell you undertake a revolution against yourself. You curse yourself, you call yourself a bloody fool. You're the only person you blame. You protect yourself, then you yield, then you enter a state of guilt. For instance, I felt guilty that I had ever spoken with Russians at all. I believed I was guilty of *meeting* them, even though it was my job. After that came the optimism that the tribunal would deliver the truth, and they encouraged me to believe this. I had been a judge myself, at fifty trials. I believed in military justice. I still do. What I got was a butchery.'

He is no longer alone in this conviction. Today, the witch-burners of fifteen years ago are feeling the heat around their own ankles. The belated sense of fair play which, in Switzerland as in other democracies, occasionally asserts itself in the wake of a perceived judicial excess, is demanding to be appeased. A younger Switzerland is calling for greater openness in its affairs. An increasingly outspoken press, a spate of scandals in banking and government, now lumped together as 'the Kopp affair' after the first woman deputy in the Swiss government and Minister of Justice who fell from grace for warning her lawyer husband that he risked being implicated in a government inquiry into money-laundering—all these have beaten vigorously on the doors of secret government.

The new men and women are impatient with the old-boy networks of informal power, and suddenly public attention is fixing its sights upon the most elusive network of them all: the Swiss intelligence community. It is not Jeanmaire but the 'snoopers of Bern' and the professional espionage agencies who are being accused of betraying their secrets for profit, of spying on harmless citizens, of maintaining dossiers in numbers that would embarrass a country five times Switzerland's size and of fantasizing about non-existent enemies.

And as the decorous streets of Bern echo with youthful protestors demanding greater *glasnost*, it is the unlikely figure of Jeanmaire, the arch-conservative and militarist, the man who for so long hated popular revolt, who now walks with them in spirit, not as 'the traitor of the century' but as some flawed, latter-day Dreyfus, framed by devious secret servants to cover up their own betrayal. In the next few weeks he will hear whether he has won a reassessment of his case.

Yet whatever the final outcome, the story of Jean-Louis Jeanmaire will remain utterly extraordinary: as a tragi-comedy of Swiss military and social attitudes; as an example of almost unbelievable human naïvety; and as a cautionary tale of an innocent at large among professional intelligence-gatherers. For Jeanmaire, by any legal definition, *was* a spy. He *was* seduced, even if he was his own seducer. He *did* pass classified documents to Soviet military diplomats, without the knowledge or approval of his superiors, even if they were documents of little apparent value to an enemy. He *did* receive rewards for his labours, even if they were trivial, and even if the only real satisfactions were to his ego. Immature he certainly was, and credulous to an extraordinary degree. But he was no child. Even by the time of his recruitment, he was a full colonel with thirty years of soldiering in his rucksack.

So what we are talking of is not so much Jeanmaire's guilt in law, as the price he may have paid for crimes he simply could not have committed. And what we are observing is how a combination of chance, innocence and overbearing vanity precipitated the unstoppable machinery of one man's destruction.

'My two great crimes are as follows,' Jeanmaire barks, his delicate fingers outstretched to count them off, while he once more stares past me at the wall. 'One, I had character weaknesses. Two, I had been a military judge. Finish.'

But he has left out his greatest crimes of all: a luminous, fathomless gullibility, and an incurable affection for his fellow man, who could never sufficiently make up to him the love he felt was owed.

To describe Jeanmaire's courtship and marriage is once again to marvel at the cruel skein of coincidence that led to his destruction. For one thing is sure: if Jeanmaire had not, in June 1942, fallen innocently in love with one Marie-Louise Burtscher, born in Theodosia, Russia, on 12 October 1916, and if they had not married the following year, he would now be living out an honourable retirement.

He met her while he was travelling on a train from Bern to Freiburg. She entered his compartment and sat down: 'Lightning struck, I was in love!' They talked, he chattered Army stuff, he could think of nothing better. She was working as a secretary in the Bern bureaucracy, she said; and yes, he could take her out to dinner. So on the next Wednesday, he took her to the Restaurant du Théâtre in Bern, and of course he wore his uniform.

'Thus began the great love. I don't regret it. She was a good, sweet, dear comrade.'

Comrade is the word he uses of her repeatedly. But it was her past, not her comradeship, that became the chance instrument of Jeanmaire's undoing. Marie-Louise Burtscher was the daughter of a Swiss professor of languages who was teaching in Theodosia at the time of the Revolution. So it was from Theodosia, in 1919, that the family fled to Switzerland, penniless, expelled by the Bolsheviks. The Professor's last days were spent working as a translator and he was dead by the time Jeanmaire met Marie-Louise.

But Marie-Louise's mother, Juliette, survived to exert a great and enduring influence on Jeanmaire—greater, one almost feels, than her daughter's. Jeanmaire not only undertook responsibility for her maintenance but spent much time in her company. And Juliette talked—endlessly and glowingly—of the old Russia of the czars. The Bolsheviks were brutes, she said, and they had driven her from her home, all true. But the Bolsheviks were not the real Russians. 'The real Russians are people of the land,' she told Jeanmaire, again and again. 'They're farmers, peasants, intelligent, cultivated, very pious people. My greatest wish is to return to Russia to be buried.'

Thus by the sheerest chance Juliette became another of Jeanmaire's life instructors, taking her place beside his father and his godfather Tissot. And her fatal contribution was to instil in him a burgeoning romantic love for Mother Russia and an even greater hatred, if that were possible, for the rapacious Bolsheviks, whether of Biel or of Theodosia. 'Juliette loved Russia with her soul,' says Jeanmaire devoutly. And it is not hard to imagine that, as ever when he had identified an instructor, he struggled to follow her example.

The marriage began in Lausanne and followed Jeanmaire's postings until the couple returned to Lausanne to settle permanently. In 1947, Marie-Louise bore a son, Jean-Marc, now working for a bank in Geneva. In return for her keep, Juliette kept her daughter company during Jeanmaire's absences and helped look after the child. The couple spent about one third of each year together—Jeanmaire was for the rest of the time with the Army. 'My wife never intrigued, was not vain. One noticed in her that she had begun life from the bottom, as a poor kid. She had no girl-friends. She was a woman who was content with her own company. She read a lot, walked and was a good hostess.' And he uses the word again, this time more clearly: 'She was less a wife than a comrade.'

And that is all he likes to say about her, except to tell you that his lawyer has advised him not to say any more, and that he, Jeanmaire, doesn't know why. It is quite enough, nevertheless, to set the stage for the appearance of Colonel Vassily Denissenko.

John le Carré

I t is April 1959 in beautiful Brissago in the Italian part of
Switzerland, and the Air Protection Troops of the Swiss
Army are giving a demonstration under the able direction of
Colonel Jeanmaire. All Bern's foreign military attachés have been
invited and most have come.

The climax of the demonstration, as is traditional in such
affairs, comes at the end. To achieve it, Jeanmaire has ingeniously
stage-managed the controlled explosion of a house at the lake's
edge. The bomb strikes, the house disintegrates, flames belch out
of it, everyone inside must be dead. But no! In the nick of time,
stretcher parties of medics have arrived to bring out the burned
and bleeding casualties and rush them to the field hospital!

It is all splendidly done. Under cover of the smoke,
Jeanmaire has introduced his 'casualties' from the safety of the
water, in time for them to climb on to their stretchers and be
'rescued' from the other side of the house. The effect is most
realistic. The distinguished guests applaud as Jeanmaire formally
reports to his superior officer that the demonstration is at an end.
When he has done so, Colonel Vassily Denissenko of the Soviet
Embassy in Bern, delivers a short speech of thanks and admiration
on behalf of himself and his colleagues. For Denissenko, though
newly arrived, is today by a whim of protocol, the *doyen* of
Bern's military attachés. His speech over, he turns to Jeanmaire
and, in front of everyone, asks him, in jest or earnest, a very
Russian question: 'Tell me, Colonel, how many dead men were
you allowed for the purposes of this demonstration?'

Jeanmaire's reply, by his own account, was less than
diplomatic: 'We're not living in a dictatorship here, as you are in
Russia. We're in democratic Switzerland and the answer to your
question is "None". I cannot allow myself a single wounded man.'

Denissenko makes no comment, and the party adjourns to
Ponte Brolla for lunch at which Jeanmaire, still flushed with
success, finds himself, thanks to the *placement* required of
protocol, seated at Denissenko's side. Here is Jeanmaire's
account of their opening exchange: 'So that there is no
misunderstanding, Colonel,' Jeanmaire kicks off, 'I don't care for
Soviets. I've nothing against you personally, since you yourself
can't do anything about the mess the Russians have brought

364

upon the world, both in the Second World War and in the Bolshevik Revolution!'

Denissenko asks why Jeanmaire has such a hatred of the Russians.

'Because of my parents-in-law,' Jeanmaire replies, now in full sail. 'They were thrown out of Russia in 1919 and had to flee to Switzerland. They arrived without a penny to their names. As a result, I've had to provide for them.'

And to this, Denissenko replies—spontaneously, says Jeanmaire—'That's a terrible story. I don't hold with that sort of behaviour either. You must never confuse the Bolsheviks with the Russians. The Bolsheviks are bandits.'

Jeanmaire is at once reminded of the stories told him by his late mother-in-law: 'At this moment I recognized in him a czarist officer,' he recalls simply.

As to Denissenko, he may have recognized something in Jeanmaire also, for he soon returns to the subject of the injustice done to Jeanmaire's parents-in-law: 'We ought to put that right,' he says. 'The property should be given back. And you should receive something by way of compensation.'

But Jeanmaire still presses his attack. 'And look here. What about that disgusting business in Budapest three years ago?' he demands, referring to the Soviet repression of the Hungarian uprising.

Once again Denissenko is quick to parade his antipathy to the Bolsheviks: 'I agree with you one hundred per cent. And let me tell you something else. In 1966, a certain Russian officer will be coming to Bern as military attaché with whom you should have no contact at all. He's the man who organized the whole Budapest affair.'

And thus—says Jeanmaire—did Denissenko warn him against one Zapienko, who did indeed come to Bern in 1966, and Jeanmaire avoided him exactly as Deni had advised.

In terms of intelligence tradecraft, the horseman Denissenko had thus far achieved a faultless round. He had presented himself as an anti-communist. He had nimbly touched upon the possibility that Jeanmaire might be eligible to receive Russian money. He had left the door open for further contact. And by warning Jeanmaire against Zapienko, he had planted in him a psychological obligation to grant a favour or a confidence in return. Yet to this day, Jeanmaire seems unable to believe that Denissenko's moves were no more than the classic passes of a capable intelligence officer.

'He didn't prod. He put out no hints,' he insists. 'He was correct in all respects. He had a great admiration for the Swiss Army.'

The meeting over, Jeanmaire hastened home to tell his wife the amazing news. His words, as he repeats them now, are like the headlong declaration of a young lover to his mother: 'He's exactly what Juliette your mother always loved! A real, fine czarist officer! What a shame she's no longer alive to meet him!'

Jeanmaire was so enthusiastic about Denissenko that he insisted that Marie-Louise accompany him the next month to a British diplomatic reception at Bern's Schweizerhof Hotel in order that she could meet Denissenko for herself. So she went, and Jeanmaire hastened to introduce her to his discovery. Denissenko, speaking Russian, asked Marie-Louise whether she spoke Russian also. She understood the question and said no. After that, the two spoke German.

'She saw in him someone who, like herself, had been born in Russia,' says Jeanmaire, explaining his wife's pleasure at this first encounter. And then: 'You can never tell what goes on inside a woman's head. Otherwise nothing happened.'

Speaking this way of his wife, Jeanmaire is once more too dismissive, too much on guard. There is another story here somewhere, but he is not telling it—certainly not to me, but perhaps not to himself either.

Throughout that same year Jeanmaire and Denissenko met at several receptions. Marie-Louise, according to Jeanmaire, came only once. Sometimes Denissenko's wife was present—from Jeanmaire's account of her, a pleasant, tubby, not especially pretty woman, a Russian *babushka* in the making. But the axis was undoubtedly between the men: 'Deni was interesting to talk to and felt bound to me on account of the injustice done to my parents-in-law. Perhaps my wife was somewhere in the background of his mind. I don't know. At that time, nothing had happened.' And this is the second time that Jeanmaire has assured me that nothing has so far happened between Deni and Marie-Louise. How did he know? I wonder —unless he knows better? When *did* something happen?—and did he know then, too?

At one of these occasions, Denissenko suggested a lunch. Jeanmaire says that when he reported this in advance to his brigadier, which he invariably did throughout his liaison with the Russians, the brigadier wished him '*bon appetit*'.

The two men drove in Denissenko's Mercedes to Belp on the outskirts of Bern, to the Hotel Kreuz, Denissenko's choice. Over lunch, Denissenko first talked about the battle of Stalingrad, in which he had served as an air captain. He dwelt on the horrors and the heroism of war. Jeanmaire, the Swiss soldier, was thrilled by this vicarious experience of one of the great sieges of history. The conversation turned to the construction of the new Geneva-Lausanne *autobahn* through Morges and to the uses of *autobahn* underpasses as atomic air-raid shelters. Jeanmaire was impressed by Denissenko's detailed knowledge of the Morges terrain. Denissenko drank no schnapps and little wine—on account, he explained, of his heart. Jeanmaire drank more freely, but not excessively. This is a regular refrain of Jeanmaire's narrative. Other encounters followed through the next year, but it was not until a full two years after the Brissago meeting that the Jeanmaires invited Denissenko to dinner, as usual—says Jeanmaire—with the advance approval of his superiors.

Denissenko arrived by chauffeur-driven car, and he was glowing with excitement. The date was 13 April 1961. On the day before, Gagarin had become the first man to circle the earth in space. Deni's elation was instantly matched by Jeanmaire's. Unlike the Pentagon, which was having kittens at the news, Jeanmaire appears to have been thrilled by Russia's triumph. The party set off for Savigny outside Lausanne for dinner, and the evening was spent discussing the space race. The local police chief walked in and, at Jeanmaire's invitation, joined them for a drink. Jeanmaire on principle always paid his own tab when he was out

John le Carré

with foreign attachés, and he paid it that night. After dinner, the
party repaired to a Bern night-club, the Tabaris, where Jeanmaire
presented Denissenko to the manageress. 'I was proud to be able
to show myself with this man. He was very presentable: always
well dressed—we were in civilian clothes—discreet but well
chosen. He was a Gorbachev. When I think of Denissenko today,
I see Gorbachev. I experienced *glasnost* twenty-five years ahead
of its time.'

Jeanmaire recalls that Denissenko danced with Marie-
Louise. The drinking, in deference to Denissenko's heart, was
again moderate, he insists. All the same, it was a long, late, jolly
evening, and what is significant in retrospect is that Denissenko,
the professional GRU officer, made no attempt in the months
that followed to build on it. If he was setting Jeanmaire up for a
clandestine approach, he was playing a long game.

There are several possible explanations for Denissenko's
apparent reluctance to develop Jeanmaire as a secret
source. The first is that having taken a close look at his
man he had decided, with reason, that Jeanmaire simply didn't
know enough to be worth the candle, either as a present source
or as a future prospect to be directed against a better target.
Jeanmaire was discernibly approaching his professional ceiling,
after all, and it was not, from the point of view of Soviet
intelligence priorities, a sexy one. Other explanations lie in the
still impenetrable marshes of the Soviet espionage mentality. No
potential recruit of the sort Jeanmaire had now become could be
approached without detailed orders from Moscow. Even in the
GRU, which never approached the KGB in professionalism or
sophistication, the choice of restaurant, the allocation of
expenses, topics of conversation for the evening—all would have
been ordained in advance by Denissenko's Moscow masters.

And it is beyond doubt that any effort to shift Jeanmaire
from the status of 'legal' to 'illegal' collaborator would have been
preceded by a ponderous appraisal of the risks and merits. Is he a
plant, they will have asked themselves, in wearying evaluation
sessions? A man so forthcoming might certainly have looked like
one. Is he a provocation to secure Denissenko's expulsion or sour

Soviet–Swiss relations? Does he want money? If so, why does he insist on paying his own way? And if not, how is this passionate anti-communist motivated? The astute Denissenko had not, it seems, detected in Jeanmaire those vengeful feelings against his superiors that became such a feature of the later case against him.

And perhaps—because of the delicacy of the diplomatic situation—the GRU may even have swallowed its pride and called in the KGB, who counselled caution and delay. Or perhaps the KGB gave different advice: perhaps they said, 'Keep Jeanmaire in play, but slowly, slowly. One day we may need to fatten him as a sacrificial lamb.'

All that is certain is that for several months Denissenko made no move towards Jeanmaire. He spent much time in Moscow, allegedly on health grounds, and no doubt when he conferred with his colleagues at headquarters the pace and progress of Jeanmaire's cultivation were discussed: even if he can hardly have rated high on Moscow's shopping list.

Then in March 1963, Denissenko and the Jeanmaires got together again, once more for dinner, and the topic this time turned to a Swiss military exercise which had taken place a few weeks before. A friendly dispute arose between the two men. Denissenko, who appeared excellently informed, insisted that Swiss military planning leaned heavily on NATO support. Jeanmaire, as ever the champion of Swiss neutrality, vigorously denied this, and in order to prove that the Swiss integrity was still intact, he says, he offered to show Denissenko the organization plan of staff and troops at corps and division levels, from which it would be clear that the Army maintained no NATO liaison of the sort Denissenko suspected. The Army, of course, most certainly did maintain such liaison and would have been daft not to, though officially it was denied. And Jeanmaire knew it did, but the organization plan did not reveal this. Ironically, therefore, what Jeanmaire was offering Denissenko in this case was not dissuasion at all but Swiss military disinformation.

But Denissenko in return seems not to have taken Jeanmaire up on his offer. Why not? Too risky? Or simply a warning from Moscow to lay off?

Three months later, however, Jeanmaire bumped into Denissenko at a cocktail party given by the Austrian military attaché and invited him to his apartment in Lausanne. Three days after that, in the company of Marie-Louise, Denissenko and Jeanmaire ate a meal at Lausanne's railway-station buffet, then went on to the Jeanmaire's apartment where Jeanmaire handed over a photocopy he had made of the promised document, or part of it.

The document was graded 'for Service use only' or as the British might say 'confidential'. Whether it should have been so graded is immaterial. Jeanmaire knew it was confidential, knew what he was doing and who for. It may have been a tiny journey, but at that moment he crossed the bridge. In every tale of one man's path to spying, or to crime, or merely to adultery, there is traditionally one crucial moment that stands out above the rest as the moment of decision from which there is no return. This was Jeanmaire's. 'I gave only two pages, not the whole document,' he says. It seems to have made no difference. A Swiss colonel, as he then was, had voluntarily and without authorization handed a classified document to the Soviet military attaché and Resident of the GRU in Bern.

Yet the evening had only begun. Jeanmaire seems to have entered a vortex of reckless generosity. There had been recently a rehearsal of Swiss military mobilization plans. Now Jeanmaire took it into his head to boast to Denissenko that Swiss resistance to a Soviet invasion would be more ferocious than the Kremlin could envisage. He showed Denissenko his personal weapons, including his new semi-automatic rifle. He took him on to the balcony and pointed at the neighbouring houses. He is red-faced and thrilled as he describes this, and that is how I see him on the balcony. 'If your parachutists jump on to that tennis-court, everyone around here will fire at them,' he warned Denissenko. 'Forget orders. They won't wait for them. They'll shoot.'

He produced the *Mobilization Handbook* which is issued to every Swiss company commander. He had it by chance at home, he says, in preparation for a lecture he proposed to give in Geneva. Its classification was 'secret'. The stakes had risen.

Who was pulling now, who pushing? According to

Jeanmaire, Denissenko asked to borrow the handbook, promising to return it the next day, so Jeanmaire gave it to him. As if it mattered who was the instigator! 'Anyway the handbook was common knowledge,' he adds dismissively. 'Everyone knew what was in it.' But that isn't what the official report has him telling his military examining judge on 23 November 1976: 'He [Denissenko] vehemently insisted that I give him these documents. Alas, I was weak enough to yield, and I thus put my hand into a trap that I couldn't get out of. From then on the Russians could blackmail me by threatening to inform my superiors. I told my wife that very day that I had made the blunder of my life.'

But Jeanmaire now denies that he said this.

And Marie-Louise—what did she tell Jeanmaire in return? It seems, almost nothing. Jeanmaire admits that he had an onslaught of guilt after Denissenko left, and confided his anxieties to his wife: 'And *merde*, on Monday I'll go and get the thing back!' he told her. But Marie-Louise, according to Jeanmaire, merely remarked that what was done was done: 'She had no sense that anything bad had happened.'

And still on the same crazy evening, Jeanmaire showed Denissenko parts of another classified document on the requisitioning of Swiss property in the event of war—for example, the seizing of civilian transport for the movement of territorial troops. This time he refused to part with it, but made a list of pages relevant to their discussions on 'dissuasion'. A day or two later, at his office, he made photocopies of these pages under the pretext that they were needed for a study course for air raid troops. A lie, therefore: a constructive, palpable lie, told to his own people in order to favour his people's supposed enemy.

Why?

And on the evening of 9 July, he handed the stolen pages to Denissenko. A criminal act. It was on that occasion also that, in the presence of Denissenko, Marie-Louise proudly displayed to her husband a bracelet which she said Denissenko had given her while Jeanmaire was briefly out of the room.

'When I came back, my wife said, really lovingly, "Look at this beautiful bracelet that Herr Denissenko has given me." I said

"Bravo." I made nothing of it, except that it was a beautiful gesture by Denissenko. If she'd shown it me without his being there, I might have smelt a rat. Today I know he gave it her at a quite different time. It was a gift of love and had nothing whatever to do with betraying one's country.'

Denissenko's gift of love was worth 400 Swiss francs, says Jeanmaire. Referring to it later, he raises its value to 1,200 Swiss francs. Either way, it seems to have been a horribly good bargain in exchange for Jeanmaire's gift of love to him. The evening ended with another trip to Savigny for a celebratory drink. It is hard to imagine what the three of them thought they were celebrating. With Denissenko's bracelet glittering proudly on Marie-Louise's wrist, Jeanmaire had just put a bullet through his muddled soldier's head.

Why? Jeanmaire's prosecutors were not the only ones to hunt for an answer. Jeanmaire himself has had years and years of staring at the wall, asking himself the same question: why? His talk of dissuasion wears thinner the more you listen to it. He speaks of his 'character weaknesses'. Yet what is weak about a lone crusader setting out to deter the Kremlin from its evil purposes against peace-loving Switzerland? He says the information he passed was common knowledge. Then why pass it? Why in secret? Why steal it, why give it and why be merry afterwards? What was there to celebrate that night? Betrayal? Friendship? Love? Fun? Jeanmaire says Denissenko was a czarist, an anti-Bolshevik. Then why not report this to his superiors, who might have passed the tip to people with an interest in recruiting a disaffected Russian colonel? Perhaps the answer was simpler, at least for the landlocked Swiss soldier: perhaps it was just *change*.

For the novelist, as for the counter-intelligence officer, motive concerns the possibilities of character. As big words frequently disguise an absence of conviction, so drastic action can derive from motives which, taken singly, are trivial. I once interrogated a man who had made an heroic escape from East Germany. It turned out that, rather than take his wife with him on his journey, he had shot her dead at point-blank range with a Luger pistol that had belonged to his Nazi father. He was not political; he had no grand notion of escaping to freedom, merely to another life. He had always got on well with his wife. He loved her still. The only explanation he could offer was that his local canoe club had expelled him for anti-social behaviour. In tears, in despair, his life in ruins, a self-confessed murderer, he could find no better excuse.

So again, why?

The more you examine Jeanmaire's relationship with Denissenko, the more it appears to contain something of the compulsive, the ecstatic and the sexual. Again and again it is Jeanmaire himself, not Denissenko, who is forcing the pace. Jeanmaire needed Denissenko a great deal more than Denissenko needed him: which was probably what gave Denissenko and his masters pause.

After Denissenko's departure from Bern, it is true, there came a grey troupe of substitute figures—Issaev, Strelbitzki, Davidov. Each, in the longer narrative, presents himself at the door, uses Denissenko's name, appeals to Jeanmaire's Russian persona, tightens the screws, finds his way to Jeanmaire's heart and receives an offering or two to keep the Kremlin happy—or to dissuade it, whichever way you care to read the story. Jeanmaire's relationship with the GRU is not broken with Denissenko's departure to Moscow, but neither is it advanced. Were *they* anti-Bolsheviks too? The fig leaf seems to have been tossed aside: Jeanmaire barely seems to care. For Deni's sake he gives them scraps; a part of him accepts that he is trapped; another part seems to tell him that his recent translation to the giddy rank of brigadier should somehow exempt him from the unseemly obligation of spying. 'I thought: Now I'm a brigadier, I'll pack in this nonsense.' Yet he continues to enjoy the connection. He dickers like a scared addict, offers them crumbs, warms himself against their fires, fancies himself Switzerland's secret military ambassador, wriggles, warns them off, calls them back, sweats, changes colour a dozen times, allows himself one more treat, swears abstinence and allows himself another. And the grey, cumbersome executioners of the GRU, knowing the limitations of their quarry, and even perhaps of themselves, make up to him, bully him, flatter him, accept what is to be had, which isn't much, and show little effort to force him beyond his limits.

Yet it is the figure of Denissenko that glows brightest to the end: Deni who obtained him; Deni who, if charily, baited the trap; Deni who slept with his wife; who was so fine, so well-dressed, so cultivated; Deni with whom it was a joy to be seen in public. All his successors were measured against the original. Some were found wanting. All were reflections of Deni, who remains the first and true love. Deni was noble, Deni was elegant, Deni was of the old school. And Jeanmaire, on his admission, would have slept with Deni if he had been a woman. Instead, Deni slept with Marie-Louise. The desire to please Deni, to earn his respect and approval, to woo and possess him—with gifts, including, perhaps, if it had to be, the gift of his own wife—seems, in the middle years of Jeanmaire's life, to have seized hold of this affectionate, frustrated, clever, turbulent simpleton like a grand passion, like a fugue.

So it is only natural that Deni, even today in Jeanmaire's recollection, is a great and good man. For who, when he has wrecked his life for love and paid everything he possesses, is willing to turn round and say: 'There was nothing there?'

The love of one man for another has had such a dismal press in recent years—particularly where espionage is in the air—that I venture on the subject with hesitation. There is no evidence anywhere in Jeanmaire's life that he was consciously prey to homosexual feelings, let alone that he indulged them. To the contrary, it is said that after hearing from his defence counsel Jean-Félix Paschoud that his wife had had an affair with Denissenko, Jeanmaire at once wrote her a letter of forgiveness. 'If they had offered me a pretty Slav girl,' he is supposed to have written, 'I don't know what I might have done.' The story certainly accords with his known heterosexuality and his self-vaunted hatred of homosexuals, whom he identifies constantly among his former military comrades: X was one and Y was not; Z went both ways but preferred the boys.

In this respect, Jeanmaire is a product of the Swiss military patriarchy. Women, to this Swiss chauvinist, are a support regiment rather than true warriors. Men, as in all armies, are most comfortable together, and sometimes—though not in Jeanmaire's case—this comfort flowers into physical love. When Jeanmaire speaks of his mother or his wife, he speaks of their loyalty, their good sense, their stoicism, their beauty. He is appalled by the vision of them as victims, for he is their protector. But never once does he speak of them as anything approaching equals.

And when he speaks of his godfather Tissot—the sometimes naked, otherwise superbly uniformed soldier, who, according to Jeanmaire, had to relinquish his command for failing to promote the 'useful' people—he recalls as if it were yesterday the terrible moment when he learned that his idol was about to marry a woman he had kept secret for forty years: 'Tissot had always insisted that soldiering was a celibate vocation. I believed him! I believe him to this day! I was disgusted to observe the two of them embracing. A world collapsed because I had regarded him as absolute. Not that I suspected him of homosexuality, but everyone regarded him as a priest.'

In Denissenko, Jeanmaire seems to have rediscovered the lost dignity of his fallen hero, Tissot, and perhaps in his unconscious mind to have recreated the dashing self-admiring friendship between brothers-at-arms that existed between Tissot and Jeanmaire senior. There is something *accomplished*, something *destined* in the way he still speaks of his bond with Denissenko. There is a sense of elevation, of superior knowledge, of 'I have been there and I *know*.' And something of contempt that adds: 'And you don't.'

Oh, and how the two friends could talk! Between them, the beautiful Russian soldier diplomat and the squat little Swiss brigadier redrew the entire world. They put out their tin soldiers and knocked them down; they fought and played interminably: 'When we talked politics, I represented democracy and Denissenko dictatorship. Each respected the other's position perfectly.'

And here it is necessary to dwell—as a defence witness at the trial is said to have done—on the social poverty of Jeanmaire's life. Good fellowship had been hard to come by until Jeanmaire discovered Bern's diplomatic community. Partners of the sort he craved were scarce in the ranks of his own kind, and his reputation as a big-mouth didn't help. He found solace in the company of foreign nomads. To them, he brought no baggage from his past. In their company he was reborn.

And finally—if love must have so many reasons—there is the agonizing comedy of Denissenko's record of real combat. To the Swiss soldier-dreamer who had never heard a shot fired in anger and never would, who had come from a prolonged military tradition of bellicose passivity, the lustre of Denissenko's armour was irresistible. Not Jeanmaire's father, not even his godfather Tissot, could match the heroic splendour and the vast authority of a man who had fought at Stalingrad, and whose breast, on military feast days, jangled with the medals of real gallantry and real campaigns. No courtship was too extreme; no risk, no sacrifice, no investment too reckless for such an exalted being. If two souls were warring in Jeanmaire's breast on that night of his first betrayal—the one thrilling him with words of caution, the other driving him forward along the path of glory—it was the example of his unblooded cavalry forebears that urged him to drive in the spurs and not look back.

One episode, more than any other, reveals to us Jeanmaire's state of mind during the high-days of his honeymoon with Denissenko: it is the bizarre encounter on 30 November 1963 when Denissenko called on Jeanmaire in his apartment in Lausanne and, in a classic pass, tried to fling the net over him for good. According to Jeanmaire the scene unfolded in this way.

Marie-Louise is in the kitchen. Jeanmaire, with his customary ambiguity when speaking of her, no longer remembers whether she is party to the conversation.

Denissenko to Jeanmaire: 'I told you when we first met that I would like to make reparation to you for the loss suffered by your parents-in-law in Russia.' Producing a large envelope, unsealed, he holds it out to Jeanmaire. There is money in it. Jeanmaire cannot or will not speculate how much. Hundreds, perhaps thousands of Swiss francs. He remembers hundred-franc notes.

'It's a compensation,' Denissenko explains. 'As I promised you. A Christmas present.'

Jeanmaire takes the envelope and flings it on the floor. Money flies everywhere. Denissenko is astonished.

'But it's not for you!' Denissenko protests. 'It's compensation for the damage done to your parents-in-law.'

'Then pick it up for yourself,' Jeanmaire replies. 'I'm not taking your money.'

The first time Jeanmaire told me this story, he was proud of his behaviour. It should prove, he seemed to think, that he was doing nothing underhand—much as introducing Denissenko and his successors to the proprietors of restaurants should prove there was nothing clandestine about the association. But when I pressed him to explain *why* he had refused the money—since Denissenko had offered it for such ostensibly honourable reasons, to repair a loss that Marie-Louise had undoubtedly sustained—he altered his ground: 'I perceived the money at that moment as a bribe. In refusing it, I was admitting inwardly that I had done something impure. I didn't want anyone to be able to say of me, "He can be had for money." I never had the feeling that Denissenko wanted to trap me or pump me, but I didn't want to take his money. It was repellent to me. It had the flavour of a payment for services rendered. I didn't want him ever to be able to say that I had sold my country—although I knew I wasn't selling my country or even giving it away for nothing.'

It would be charming to know what Denissenko and his masters in Moscow afterwards made of this bizarre scene and how much sound planning went to waste at the moment when Jeanmaire refused to swallow such a sweetly baited hook. How on earth could the grey men of the GRU be expected to understand that Jeanmaire wanted love, not money?

'It amazes me that Denissenko could have done it to me,' says Jeanmaire. 'After all, he could have given the money to my wife. But probably he wouldn't do that, because it would have made a whore of her.'

One might suppose that after this uncomfortable scene, the evening would have taken on a sour note. The suitor had made his pitch and been repulsed. Time perhaps to withdraw and fight another day. But not so. True, there were some sticky minutes, but soon the talk brightened and turned to the reorganization of the Swiss Army which had come into effect on 1 January 1962. Jeanmaire produced a copy of the previous order of battle, valid till 31 December 1961 and therefore out of date: 'I reckoned that since he was such a good fellow, I would give him something so that he wouldn't feel useless,' he explains. And adds that he had been told by Swiss military attachés how grateful they were to be slipped the odd 'little bit of paper' to justify their extravagant lifestyle at public expense.

But scarcely is this admission made than he is once more making another: 'I gave him the order of battle because I'd already put it aside for him when the affair with the money got in the way. But then I gave it to him anyway, to show there were no hard feelings.'

But if the path to Jeanmaire's mind appears tortuous and paradoxical, it resembles a Roman road when compared with the devious route that led the Swiss authorities to his arrest and trial.

Here is the Federal Prosecutor Rudolf Gerber speaking before the Parliamentary Jeanmaire Commission, whose task was to examine the affair and whose report, though widely leaked, is still secret:

> On 16 May 1975, we received a warning to the effect that a high-ranking Swiss officer had had significant intelligence contacts with the Russians. The time in question was 1964. It was difficult to work out who it could be. We knew only that the wife of this officer had had relations with Russia during her childhood. Thus we came on Jeanmaire. An investigation was launched in about August 1975.

You don't have to be a counter-intelligence officer to wonder what on earth was 'difficult' about narrowing the field to Jeanmaire on the strength of this information. The number of senior Swiss Army officers whose wives had enjoyed a Russian childhood cannot have been large. Jeanmaire's contacts with Soviet diplomats in 1964 were a matter of Army record. He had been appreciated for them in the military protocol department, where enthusiasts for the official cocktail round were hard to find. He had been deliberately flamboyant in parading them to casual acquaintances.

Where had the tip-off come from? According to the Federal Prosecutor Gerber, only a few initiates know the answer to that question. The intricate game of spy and counter-spy commands his silence, he says: even today, the source is too hot to name. The chief of the Swiss Secret Service at the time, Carl Weidenmann, tells the story differently. From the outset, he says, the only possible suspect was Jeanmaire. He too claims he is not allowed to say why. Apart from such selective nuggets as these, we are obliged to fall back on rumour, and the hardy rumour is that the tip-off came from the CIA.

What did the tip-off say? Did Gerber tell the Parliamentary Jeanmaire Commission the whole or only a part of the information received? Or more than the whole? And if the tip-off did indeed come from the CIA, who tipped off the CIA? Was the source reliable? Was it a plant? Was it Russian? British? French? West German? Swiss? In the grimy market-places where so-called friendly intelligence services do their trading, tip-offs, like money, are laundered in all sorts of ways. They can be slanted, doctored and invented. They can be blown up so as to cause consternation or tempered to encourage complacency. They serve the giver as much as the receiver, and the receiver sometimes not at all. They come without provenance and without instructions on the package. They can wreck lives and careers by design or by accident. And the one thing they have in common is that they are never what they seem.

In Jeanmaire's case, the provenance and content of the original tip-off are of crucial importance. And until today, of crucial obscurity.

After the tip-off—a full three months after it, and fourteen years after Jeanmaire's first meeting with Denissenko —came the grand-slam secret surveillance, like a thunder of cavalry after the battle has been lost. Jeanmaire's telephone was tapped; he was watched round the clock. He was probably also microphoned, but Western surveillance services have a uniform squeamishness about owning up to microphones. A ranking police officer claims to have disguised himself as a waiter at diplomatic receptions attended by Jeanmaire: 'I heard only trivial party gossip,' he told Jeanmaire after his arrest. 'Soldiers' chatter about music, alcohol and women.' Again the police officer speaks as if he was wired.

And after four months of this, the watchers still had nothing against Jeanmaire except the tip-off, and what was vaguely perceived, in Gerber's words, as 'contacts with Russians in excess of the customary level.' But what *was* the normal level, given Jeanmaire's celebrated predeliction for Russian contacts for which the Army's protocol department gave him humble thanks? By December, the watchers were worried that Jeanmaire's imminent retirement would fall due before they had a case against him. Therefore Weidenmann, the Chief of the Secret Service, in collaboration with the Chief of Federal Police and the Federal Prosecutor, decided to offer Jeanmaire employment that would keep him in harness. To this end Weidenmann summoned Jeanmaire to an interview.

'It would be a pity,' he told Jeanmaire, 'to let you leave the Army without first committing to paper your knowledge and experience in the field of civil defence.'

For an extra 1,000 francs a month—later, in a fit of bureaucratic frugality, dropped to 500 francs—Weidenmann proposed that the pensioner Jeanmaire undertake a comparative study of military and civil defence in all countries where the Swiss maintained military attachés. Jeanmaire was flattered, and the investigators had bought themselves more time.

'I suspected nothing,' says Jeanmaire.

On 13 January, Weidenmann summoned Jeanmaire to him again and, in an effort to prod him into a betrayal, arranged for him to have access, through chosen intermediaries, to secret documents in the possession of Switzerland's overseas intelligence service. Weidenmann testified later that his department took care to ensure that Jeanmaire didn't get his hands on anything hot. The intermediaries, of course, were party to the provocation plan.

As a further inducement to Jeanmaire, a small office was set up for him in no less a shrine than the headquarters of Colonel Albert Bachmann, who ran his own special service, known in Swiss circles as the 'Organization Bachmann', and for long the object of much wild rumour and public agonizing, most notably after a ludicrous episode in which one of its agents had been caught spying on Austrian (sic) military manoeuvres. Bachmann was also charged with responsibility for Switzerland's 'Secret Army', which would form the nucleus of an underground resistance group in the event of Switzerland being occupied by hostile forces. No Soviet spy or intelligence officer worth his salt, it was reasoned, could resist such an enticing target as the Organization Bachmann. The office was bugged all ways up, Jeanmaire's phone was tapped and Bachmann was duly added to the team of watchers. But alas the hen still refused to lay.

Chief of the Secret Service Weidenmann before the Parliamentary Jeanmaire Commission: 'He was kept under observation during this period, unfortunately without success.'

After another eight months of frustration, during which Jeanmaire's every word and action were laboriously studied by his watchers, Federal Prosecutor Gerber decided to arrest him anyway, despite the fact that, on Gerber's own admission, he lacked the smallest scrap of hard evidence.

But Gerber and his associates had something on their minds that weighed more heavily than legal niceties and cast a shadow over their professional existence. The American intelligence barons had recently served formal notice on Bern that Washington had no confidence in the ability of the Swiss to protect the military secrets entrusted to them. Vital technical information about American armaments was finding its way from Switzerland to Eastern Europe, they said. The Florida early-warning-system had been compromised. So had state-of-the-art American electronic equipment fitted to Swiss tanks, most notably the 'stabilizor'. It was also rumoured that the Americans were refusing to sell Switzerland their new 109 artillery pieces and, worse still, threatening to relegate Switzerland to the status of a communist country for the purposes of secrets-sharing, a humiliation that rang like a panic bell in the proud back rooms of Switzerland's intelligence and procurement services.

Never mind that Jeanmaire had not been admitted to such secrets. Never mind that he was not qualified in the technology allegedly betrayed, or that the Army had chosen to confine him to a harmless backwater without a secret worth a damn. There was the leak, there was the threat, there was the tip-off, there was the man. What was now needed, and quickly, was to put the four together, silence American apprehensions and re-establish Switzerland's self-image as a responsible and efficient military (and neutral) power.

One of Jeanmaire's principal interrogators, who also arrested him, was Inspector Louis Pilliard, Commissioner of the Federal Police—the same officer who claimed to have dressed as a waiter to spy on Jeanmaire at diplomatic functions. During Jeanmaire's days of 'examination arrest'—that is to say, in the days before he was even brought before a military examining judge—Pilliard, the civilian policeman, questioned him, according to Jeanmaire's secret notes made on scraps of paper, for a total of ninety-two hours. Forget the European Convention on Human Rights, to which Switzerland is a signatory and which requires a prisoner to be brought before a judge in swift order: Jeanmaire had already served 107 days in isolation and had another six months to go before his trial.

'You have betrayed Florida,' Pilliard told him at the end of October.

'You're mad,' Jeanmaire replied. 'I can prove to you that I don't know the first thing about Florida.'

And indeed, on the one occasion in 1972 when Jeanmaire could have attended a demonstration of the Florida early-warning-system, he had sent a letter declining the invitation, which Pilliard to his credit traced. But if the charge of betraying Florida was now struck out, Jeanmaire remained in the eyes of his public accusers—and of Justice Minister Furgler—a spy of monstrous dimensions. Finally, on 10 November, Parliament ruled that all derelictions by Jeanmaire *and his wife* should be tried by military justice.

For Marie-Louise was also charged. While her husband was being bundled into a police car on his way to work, five federal police officers, one a woman, had descended on the Jeanmaire flat in the Avenue du Tribunal-Fédéral in Lausanne at seven in the morning to conduct a house-search which lasted two days. Their finds included Marie-Louise's diary, where she had recorded all meetings with Denissenko, and a television set of unspecified origin, but probably given to the Jeanmaires by Issaev, one of Denissenko's successors. The diary has since disappeared into the vaults of Swiss secrecy, but it is said by Jeanmaire—who helped to decode it—to contain an entry that reads, 'Today Deni and I made love.'

The police also descended on Jeanmaire's friend and neighbour in Bern, Fräulein Vreni Ogg, at her place of work at the Bern office for footpaths. Having seized her, they bundled her too into a car, drove her to a police station and released her half an hour later, having apparently decided she had nothing worthwhile to tell them. The media had another treat and her life was never the same.

Soon Jeanmaire was singing like a bird, but not the song his questioners wished to hear.

Federal Prosecutor Gerber again, before the Parliamentary Jeanmaire Commission, in a lament that should be pasted to the wall of every hall of justice in the free world: 'The nub of the thing is this: in Switzerland we do not have the means to increase Jeanmaire's willingness to testify.' After lightning arrest, solitary confinement, deprivation of exercise, radio, newspapers and outside contacts; exhaustive interrogation; threats and blandishments—what other means was Gerber thinking of, we wonder?

Jeanmaire was interrogated principally by Pilliard, who was sometimes accompanied by another officer, one Lugon, Inspector of the Waadtland Canton Police. Like Pilliard, Lugon had taken part in Jeanmaire's arrest.* But others, including Gerber himself,

*My attempts to obtain the first names of Lugon, formerly Inspector of the Waadtland Canton Police and presently employed by the Federal Police, and Hofer, formerly Commissioner of Federal Police and now in retirement, have met with fastidious rejection. After one and a half days of consultation, the spokesman for the Federal Prosecutor's Office has advised that 'the two gentlemen Lugon and Hofer wish no publication of their first names for commercial purposes.' The spokesman, Herr Hauenstein, valiantly declined further explanation. Rumpelstiltskin himself could not have been better represented.

had their turn at the interrogation—Gerber for four full hours, though the content of their discussion escapes Jeanmaire's recollection: 'He shook my hand. He was decent. I told him I was relieved to be interrogated by someone of authority. My memory is *kaputt* . . .'

It is *kaputt*, perhaps, because it was on this occasion—8 September, according to Gerber's testimony—that Gerber read out to Jeanmaire the list of the confessions he had by now made and which later constituted the bulk of the case against him. It is *kaputt* because a part of Jeanmaire's head knows that, within a month of his arrest and probably less, he had confessed away his life.

Nevertheless, the interrogation seems to have been conducted with a signal lack of skill. Jeanmaire, after all, was an interrogator's dream. He was terrified, disoriented, indignant, friendless and guilty. He was then, and is today, a compulsive, non-stop prattler, a braggart, a child waiting to be enchanted. What was needed in his interrogator was not a bully but a befriender, a confessor, someone who could interpret his dilemma to him and receive his confidences in return. Forget your lynx-eyed intelligence officer, master of five languages: one wise policeman with a good face and patient ear could have had him on a plate in a week. No such figure featured in the cast.

On day two he was visited by Gerber's deputy, Peter Huber, who stayed an hour with him and, according to Jeanmaire, urged him to embellish his confession: 'Herr Jeanmaire, your case is not dangerous, but you should admit to more than you have done, so that we can get the damage out of the way quickly.'

What damage could Huber have meant, if not the damage threatened by the Americans?

Jeanmaire then asked Huber why he was in prison and what had happened.

Huber: 'I'm not allowed to tell you, I can't. But there's been a big leak to the East.'

Jeanmaire: 'But not through me!'

Huber: 'Don't get so excited. Things aren't as bad as they appear. Just own up to more than you did.'

Exactly *when* Jeanmaire confessed to *what* is hard to establish without the help of official records and, presumably, the secret tapes of his interrogations. According to Gerber, before the Parliamentary Jeanmaire Commission, it was not till 6 September that Jeanmaire confessed to handing over documents classified 'secret'. But whenever it happened, Jeanmaire says he was tricked: 'Pilliard promised me I'd be sitting with my pals in the Restaurant du Théâtre that same night if I'd just say this and this and this. They promised I'd be let out, and the whole thing would be buried. They blackmailed me.'

But Gerber's dates for Jeanmaire's confession are precise, whereas Jeanmaire, from the moment of his imprisonment, was living a nightmare, as his own testimony now begins to show, for it becomes fragmentary, surreal and, in several respects, doubtful.

But here it is necessary to pull back from retrospective wisdom and pity the poor intelligence officers saddled with Jeanmaire's case. They too were being blackmailed, if only by the fury of the Swiss—this *Volkszorn*—and by the urgent wish of the administration to heap on to Jeanmaire's shoulders every real or alleged failure of Swiss security in the last decade. The legislature, as well as the executive, was breathing down their necks. Jeanmaire describes a moment when he was telling Pilliard, the Police Commissioner, how Denissenko had remarked over dinner in Belp that *autobahn* underpasses made good atomic shelters. Before the eyes of the astonished Jeanmaire, Pilliard then seized a telephone and related to Minister of Justice Furgler in person that Jeanmaire had talked to Denissenko about shelters and atom bombs: 'I was suddenly a nuclear physicist and a designer of deep shelters. He said nothing of the context in which we had discussed these things.'

Now, of course, Pilliard's call to Furgler—though it is one of several occasions when he paraded a close relationship with his minister—may have been a policeman's bluff. Pilliard may have been talking to the doorman. But Furgler's description of Jeanmaire as a grand traitor was by now a matter of public record, and it is entirely conceivable that, in democratic Switzerland, the Police Commissioner did indeed speak directly to his supremo.

In addition to these pressures from on high, the investigators were weighed down with a mass of case histories of high-ranking spies in other countries who had indeed betrayed their nation's treasured secrets: men such as Wennerström in Sweden, Mitchell and Martin in America, Vassall, Houghton and Gee in England. A sack full of precedents was already raining down on them through the established channels of Western intelligence liaison. It would be remarkable if the CIA and FBI, for instance, had not by now sent out their customary squads of 'experts' and 'advisors', each trumping the other with ingenious theories of conspiracy. In America, James Jesus Angleton had already brought the CIA to a virtual standstill with his theories of moles in high places in the Agency. In Britain, Peter Wright and company were up to the same game.

In such an atmosphere, Jeanmaire was naturally elevated to the upper ranks of the spies' pantheon, and the Swiss were in no mood to be told that *their* spy was not as important as other people's.

Jeanmaire has been watched and listened to for a whole year without success? Then he has been ordered to lie low! Trap him! Smoke him out!

Jeanmaire has no known means of communication with his controllers? Then he's talking to them by secret radio! Strip his television set, tear his flat apart, look for code pads, secret writing equipment, microdot lenses!

Jeanmaire has confessed to handing over trivia? He's giving us chicken-feed! Hold his feet to the fire! Grill his wife!

Jeanmaire has cracked and *still* not confessed to anything of value? He's a hard nut, a professional soldier, work on him some more!

If Jeanmaire is to be believed, even his defence lawyer, Jean-Félix Paschoud, was convinced of his guilt—though no man who collects an eighteen-year prison sentence is likely to think well of his defence lawyer. Entering his cell for the first time, Paschoud, Jeanmaire says, shook his fist in Jeanmaire's face and cursed him to hell and back: 'What you've done is an imbecility! You're a complete idiot! *Nobody* goes around with Russians, shaking hands with them!'

Well, perhaps Paschoud did say that, though it is not proof that he thought Jeanmaire guilty. Paschoud, according to Jeanmaire, was a member of the *Ligue Vaudoise*, an anticommunist group of patriotic cold warriors, and Jeanmaire's flirtation with Russians may indeed have shocked him. At the terribly brief trial, Jeanmaire complains, Paschoud was more exercised to keep his client quiet than to obtain justice for him. But Paschoud may have had professional reasons for wishing to keep Jeanmaire quiet. Jeanmaire was frequently his own worst enemy, and Paschoud was arguing that the charges against his client were out of date, which made defence irrelevant.

Jeanmaire likes to paint Paschoud as some small Lausanne lawyer whom he had known slightly in the Army, but the larger truth is that Jean-Félix Paschoud is one of Lausanne's few lawyers of international reputation, and was, among other things, lawyer to Charles Chaplin and his family.

The trial was from Kafka and beyond. Spread over four days, it lasted some twenty hours—roughly one hour for each year of the sentence. As of today, no official record of it has been released. The detailed charges against the Jeanmaires are still secret, though they have since been pretty thoroughly leaked.

Months before it finally started, both the accused had acquired a smell of death about them. From 21 September to 5 October, Jeanmaire, with severe angina and galloping fever, had been confined to a subterranean hospital. Under drastic medication, he had twice refused the extreme unction offered by the nursing Sisters. The interrogation by Police Commissioner Pilliard had nevertheless continued. Pilliard had thrust documents in his face and challenged him to admit he had betrayed them to the Russians. Jeanmaire believes this was the work of Colonel Bachmann. On Jeanmaire's return to prison, Pilliard, playing the good guy, had brought him a bottle of wine and two glasses. Jeanmaire asked him whether he was mad.

Marie-Louise, partly crippled by a stroke, was deemed too ill to be imprisoned, but not too ill to stand trial. How she had deported herself under arrest is left to Jeanmaire to describe. At first, he says, she had admitted nothing. 'She lied. She wanted to save me. She was braver than I was. If I'd behaved the same way, nothing would have happened.' She also denied having an affair with Denissenko, but her diary betrayed her. Jeanmaire, the transparent liar, off guard: 'I never told them about it either.' And as he hastily corrects himself: 'I never even knew about it.'

The Tribunal was convened in the classical Palais de Montbenon, in a small court-room belonging to the cantonal court of Waadtland. Jeanmaire was brought to a side entrance under heavy guard and allowed to change into his brigadier's uniform, fetched specially from Lausanne. The one painting in the court-room portrayed the judgement of Solomon. The spectators comprised some fifty journalists and the same number of members of the public. Jeanmaire entered and soon after him came Marie-Louise, walking with difficulty and in pain on the arm of a wardress, who led her to a leather armchair. She wore a blue suit. The judges entered; everyone stood. After a warning that the court would shortly be cleared in the interests of military security, the clerk to the Tribunal read a brief extract from the indictment. This accused the Jeanmaires of having maintained 'friendly relationships' with two Soviet military attachés and their successors, and with a colleague of the military attaché at the Soviet Embassy in Bern, presumably the GRU Resident Davidov, their last contact, during the period before he was an attaché. The rest was broad-brush: the result of these relationships, said the indictment, was the deliberate and persistent betrayal of matters or objects which in the interests of national defence were kept secret. The maximum sentence for such offences was twenty years in prison.

There was also a reference to 'passive bribery', though interestingly no such reference appears in the thirty-five leaked charges published in the *Wochenzeitung* in 1988. And this is hardly surprising, since the total haul of Russian gifts received by the Jeanmaires in the fourteen years since their meeting with Denissenko, including Marie-Louise's bracelet, the television set and a pair of 'freebie' cuff-links given to Jeanmaire, amounted to no more than around a thousand pounds—hardly a proper recompense for 'the traitor of the century', particularly when several senior officers of Jeanmaire's acquaintance had happily accepted free shooting holidays in Russia, not to mention such customary diplomatic hand-outs as caviar and vodka.

Still in the presence of the public, Defence Counsel Jean-Félix Paschoud, himself a military judge and lieutenant-colonel of infantry, and his colleague, Maître Courvoisier for Marie-Louise, then read statements declaring that there was no reason to believe that the Jeanmaires had accepted money from the attachés or that ideological motives had played a part in their actions. Paschoud's attempt to invoke Switzerland's statute of limitations in relation to the accuseds' earliest transactions with Denissenko was held over until the Tribunal had decided whether their derelictions were continuous or merely repeated.

The public was then excluded and the detailed charges were read out. While this was happening, Jeanmaire says, he caught sight of his interrogator Pilliard, who was listed as a witness, sitting in the court-room. He drew this to the attention of Paschoud, and the Tribunal's proceedings were suspended.

'Monsieur Pilliard,' said the presiding judge, according to Jeanmaire. 'You are a witness in this case. What are you doing sitting in the court?'

'I am here on the orders of Herr Furgler,' Pilliard replied.

The presiding judge asked his colleagues whether they had any objection to Louis Pilliard's presence. They had none, so the chief witness for the prosecution, according to Jeanmaire, sat through the entire trial.

Marie-Louise was dealt with first. Though no reference was made to her affair with Denissenko, Jeanmaire insists they treated her like dirt, barking statements at her instead of questions. Particular play was made of an incident in which Marie-Louise had wrapped a military handbook in a chocolate box before her husband handed it to Denissenko. In a whisper, Marie-Louise admitted she had done this. Nevertheless, when she was accused of influencing her husband to pass on information, she became extremely animated: 'My husband knew very well what he was allowed to do, and what not!'

At midday, her examination ended and she was led from the court. The examination of Jeanmaire began. 'The tone was malicious and appalling,' says Jeanmaire. 'The Grand Judge Houriet was like a snarling dog.' From the Tribunal, Jeanmaire learned his motive: it was vengeance for being passed over for promotion, and nothing he could say persuaded anybody otherwise. Frequently the presiding judge cut him short. Frequently Paschoud did. Towards the end of the day's hearing, an assistant judge who had not till then spoken made an appeal to him. It seems to have come from the heart. Jeanmaire relates it thus: 'Listen, Brigadier Jeanmaire, you're an honest man, it's known of you. Now tell us in Heaven's name what you have done. Tell us the truth finally.'

'I've told you the truth,' Jeanmaire replied.

So alas, still no confession to betraying the Florida early-warning-system, or any other of the vital American defence secrets whose nature we are only allowed to guess at. The dreadful shadow of communist status had still not been removed.

On the morning of the second day, according to the Tribunal's press officer, witnesses for the prosecution were heard. The first was the doctor who had attended him in hospital. The prisoner, he said, was in good health. The doctor was followed by Commissioner Pilliard, who spoke generally about Jeanmaire's awareness of what he was doing and his admission that the information he was supplying to Denissenko and his successors was probably being sent to Moscow: 'It was after all his job as a military attaché,' Jeanmaire was alleged to have said.

Before Pilliard left the stand, he was asked by the judges where the tip-off had come from that had led to Jeanmaire's arrest. He replied that he could not reveal the source, since Justice Minister Furgler had ordered him to keep it secret.

Defence witnesses—all selected by Paschoud, says Jeanmaire —tended to compound the mystery of the accused's personality, rather than explain it. They testified to Jeanmaire's stalwart character and challenged the suggestion that he had acted out of vengeance. He was 'jovial' but never 'drunken'. He could shock with his outspokenness and disliked pomposity. Under his coarse exterior lurked 'a sensitive, soft centre'. He was a virulent anti-communist. An attempt by Paschoud to submit favourable written testimonials from brother officers was dismissed by the

presiding judge. 'Let's get on with it. They don't interest us,' he is
alleged by Jeanmaire to have said.

For the Prosecution's final address, Marie-Louise was
brought back into court.

Remember, please, that we still have only Jeanmaire's
testimony and the official press release and rumour to tell us
what took place. The Prosecutor emphasized Jeanmaire's high
responsibility as one of the Swiss Army's few brigadiers and the
commander of 30,000 men. He dwelt on Jeanmaire's weakness of
character and described him as a man trapped by Denissenko's
charm and cunning. He dismissed Paschoud's claim that the early
derelictions were outdated under the statute of limitations,
maintaining that they were part of a continuum. He demanded
twelve years in prison, reduction to the ranks, expulsion from the
Army and the obligation to pay court costs. For Marie-Louise he
demanded a year in prison, but would not object to a suspended
sentence.

At this, Jeanmaire's counsel, according to his client, broke
down and wept. 'Paschoud had never expected a bid for twelve
years,' Jeanmaire explains—as if his own emotions were suddenly
of less account than his defence lawyer's. In the midday recess,
Paschoud had come weeping to him in his cell and said, 'They
want to butcher you.' Did Paschoud, a toughened lawyer, really
weep? Did Jeanmaire? Was Jeanmaire, at that devastating
moment, in a position accurately to observe and remember the
reactions of anyone, even of himself? Men facing sentence—
whether of life imprisonment or even death—are known to
experience a whole scale of sensations, from despair to hysterical
elation. As far as Jeanmaire is concerned, Paschoud broke down
and wept, and that is the end of it. What Jeanmaire himself saw,
or thought, or felt, is probably beyond description. Fifteen years
after the event, he seems intent upon turning the description
outward on to his lawyer.

Only once, apparently, has Paschoud broken his silence since
that day and with Jeanmaire's written consent: in an interview to
a Lucerne newspaper published in September 1988 Paschoud
accuses Commissioner Pilliard of extracting signed confessions
from Jeanmaire by inducements and threats. He describes the

circumstances of Jeanmaire's detention under investigation as 'scandalous' and takes exception to Pilliard's presence—as court witness and *de facto* prosecutor—throughout the trial. 'That certain people act wrongly is no excuse to do the same to them,' says Paschoud. Jeanmaire betrayed only trivia, he insists, and did so in order to show the Russians that the Swiss were ready to defend themselves. He was not a traitor, and he was treated like a hunted animal. Oddly enough, reading the interview, one can imagine Paschoud weeping after all.

Marie-Louise's lawyer, Courvoisier, on the other hand, rose superbly to the occasion—thus Jeanmaire, thus the Tribunal's press officer and thus, obediently, the press of the day. He emphasized Marie-Louise's subordinate role, an argument readily acceptable to an all-male Swiss court, and her freedom from greed or ideology. She was today a different woman from the one Denissenko had seduced, he said. He quoted from *Madame Bovary*. She had seen in Denissenko a man she could admire, he said. And at the end of his speech, Marie-Louise—'very sweetly' in Jeanmaire's words—asked the judges to exercise clemency towards her husband.

Still not recovered from his breakdown, according to Jeanmaire, Paschoud now rose to his feet. As he spoke, he choked through his tears, says Jeanmaire. On behalf of his client, he pleaded guilty, a course that had not been previously agreed between them: 'He had never told me how he intended to defend me,' Jeanmaire complains. 'He wanted to minimize me, rather than contest specific charges.' Jeanmaire gives otherwise no account of Paschoud's defence, beyond saying that it ended with these words: 'I demand that Jeanmaire be judged and not condemned.'

But the press of the day accords Paschoud a more impressive role and credits him with attacking the 'poisoning of public opinion, political intervention and certain statements by representatives of the executive which had influenced the general public against his client.' According to the press, Paschoud even mentioned Furgler by name and described his speech of October 1976 before the National Council as 'not in agreement with the Tribunal's understanding of the case.' Paschoud is also credited with saying that Jeanmaire had possessed no proper friends in

Switzerland, and that he wished to prove to Denissenko that Switzerland's defence preparations were strong and effective. This appears to be the only occasion on which the Defence offered Jeanmaire's much rehearsed argument of 'dissuasion', which today is his main self-justification.

Finally, Jeanmaire added his own last plea: 'It was never my intention to betray my country. In so far as I have done harm, I am sorry.' The session was declared closed, and Jeanmaire was taken down to his cell. Press and public were re-admitted for the verdict. Jeanmaire was brought up again. The Tribunal deemed the prosecution's request for twelve years too merciful and awarded him eighteen. The extra six were to be explained by Jeanmaire's high rank, which added 'exceptional gravity' to his crime. Only 'mitigating circumstances' had spared him the full twenty. These were: the services he had performed for Switzerland, the positive feelings he had retained towards his country and the absence of any profit motive. The Tribunal described his true motives as: ambition, self-glorification and resentment. The charges against Marie-Louise were dropped.

If the grounds for the verdict are still secret, the reason for the massive sentence appears less so. The Tribunal had done what was needed of it. It had made a big spy out of a small one. Such a huge sentence must betoken a huge betrayal. The witch was burned, a great leak had been stopped and America need no longer equate Switzerland with a communist country.

It is late, the fondue is long finished and Jeanmaire has tired himself with talking. A leaden prison pallor has descended over his too-expressive features. He is a little tired of me. The old soldier has served his time. But he is my host still. One last schnapps while we wait for the taxi, and soon I will return to my grand hotel, and he perhaps to the lady companion who now cares for him with the same loyalty as her predecessors.

He is preparing an autobiography, he says. Those files stacked against the wall contain just some of the thousands of pages that he wrote in prison.

A pause, then unable to contain himself, he asks me: 'So, how was it?'—meaning, 'How did I do?' As if we who come to him should declare ourselves for the defence or the prosecution, leaving through the 'yes' door or the 'no' door.

For a moment, I am stuck for an answer. His courage and his age alone, these days, make an innocent man of him, and there is a grandeur in Jeanmaire at eighty that is its own virtue. But old age can be a different state. The sweetness of old men need not be the sweetness of their younger days, not by any means. And it occurs to me that catastrophe has made a special case of him, accorded him a separate redemption beyond the reach of human judgement.

'I just want to report what I've seen and heard,' I tell him lamely.

'Do that! Do that!' His eyes, as he wishes me goodbye, are once more brimming with tears, but whether of tiredness, or regret, or merely old age, I cannot tell.

So how was it? as Jeanmaire would say.

Only one thing is certain: he had no way of betraying what they wanted him to have betrayed, and no evidence was ever offered that he had done so.

All he ever gave the Russians was peanuts, not least because peanuts were all he had. And until anyone can prove the opposite, eighteen years was a barbaric sentence.

What he *might* have betrayed, if he had had any real information, is a nightmare that, thank Heaven, need not trouble us. He didn't have it.

And no, he is not dead, not by a million miles. There are men and women a quarter of his age in every small town in Switzerland, or England, who are a great deal more dead than Jean-Louis Jeanmaire ever was. He is a lover and a striver and a dreamer and a frustrated creator. He is a humble braggart and a tender bully. Perhaps he should have stayed with the architecture in which he was trained and briefly excelled. Then he could have enraged clients, insulted city councils, triumphed, failed, triumphed again with impunity. Perhaps he should have been an impresario like the Jeanmaire who staged the burning house in which his own life went up in smoke. Certainly he should have stayed away from any world that had its secrets.

He was never made for the Army, even if he loved it. He was born to it and, like the good soldier he was, he set out to fight the non-combat wars he had inherited. As the Army began to weary him, he started to dream that there was another, larger destiny being prepared for him elsewhere. In Denissenko, he thought he had met it: 'He's come!' he thought—*he*, my destiny; *he*, my rainman; *he*, the door to the lives I have not led.

Was there really a big spy somewhere? Does he or she still walk the corridors of Bern, knowing that Jeanmaire served his twelve years for him? Jeanmaire does not think so, but in the Swiss press, rumours abound and conspiracy theories tumble over one another every week. The Russians engineered the whole thing, goes a favourite story: they had the big spy, they were buying his wares, and when he came under suspicion they planted the tip-off on the CIA and fitted out the little spy Jeanmaire to take the fall.

Accusations and cross-accusations between members of the Swiss intelligence establishment are daily fare: it was Colonel Bachmann himself who was selling the secrets! says one cry—no, no, it was Weidenmann; it was Gerber; it was Santa Claus; it was all of them and none of them.

And certainly, like the spate of espionage scandals that have entertained the British for the last forty-odd years, the revelations about the Swiss intelligence establishment in the sixties and seventies point to a swamp of private armies, private interests, private fantasies and startling incompetence hidden behind walls of secrecy.

But the Swiss, like the British, love their spies even while they hate them. In purging 'the snoopers of Bern' the Swiss are also purging their own age-old practice of mutual surveillance. And the new men and women mean to end all that. They want to give the Swiss back their joy in one another, just as they mean to rescue their country from its perennial fantasy of being a threatened bastion of sanity encircled by mad foreigners.

Somewhere in the soldier and patriot who is Jean-Louis Jeanmaire—though he would be the last man on earth to admit it—there slept a man who had become sick to the heart of being Swiss.

Postscript, 16 January 1991

Revelations about the Jeanmaire case continue. The most notable source of information is, alas, still eagerly awaited as I go to press—namely the second volume of the report of the Parliamentary Commission. Some of its findings are already current, if unofficially and in draft form, and shed more light (or darkness) on the questions I have raised.

Unlike Federal Prosecutor Gerber, the Commission sets the genesis of the affair not in May 1975, which was Gerber's date, but in October 1974, when the 'representative of a foreign intelligence service' was despatched to Bern on a special mission to the Chief of the Swiss Federal Police to inform him that a high Swiss officer was giving information to the USSR and that this officer was married to a Swiss woman born in the Soviet Union.

The source of the intelligence was 'a Soviet officer', but the draft report does not tell us whether he or she was still serving or had defected.

The tip was at once passed to Federal Prosecutor Gerber, says the report. At further meetings on 29 October and 1 November 1974, the same 'representative of a foreign intelligence service' referred to a list of some sixty persons suspected of contact with the GRU in Switzerland and dwelt on the sensitivity of his source, who was not in a position to expand on the information or answer questions. This injunction seems later to have been ignored by both sides.

The foreign intelligence representative's information pointed specifically to 'a married couple living in Lausanne in 1964, who for at least a year had maintained contact with Vassily Denissenko, Soviet attaché and GRU Resident in Bern, and afterwards with his successors.' Their GRU cover-names were 'Mur' and 'Mary'. The wife spoke no Russian despite her origins, said the source, and regarded French as her mother tongue.

Gerber's later date for the start of the affair—16 May 1975—is evidently a reference to the visit of a different emissary from the same intelligence service, which resulted in a 'stock-taking'—thus the report—'at which new spy cases involving Swiss subjects came to light.' It was also on this date that the Swiss officials, in the persons of Pilliard and Hofer, handed the emissary a questionnaire designed to obtain more information about the *still unidentified couple*.

On 2 June another meeting took place between the same players, and the foreign intelligence representative produced a new document containing yet more details about the suspected 'couple'. The husband lived in Lausanne but worked in Bern. He commuted daily, probably by car rather than by train. He was active in 'air defence' and had visited France in 1964 to acquaint himself with 'air raid' installations.

On 24 June the Federal Police received a reply to its questionnaire, confirming that the wife of the couple regarded French as her mother tongue, while the husband at least spoke it well. On the strength of this, the report concludes, the Jeanmaires were positively identified on 24 June 1975, a full eight months after the tip-off.

The draft report also refers to a *second* foreign intelligence service which came forward and confirmed the information given by the first. The British then? We cannot know, any more than we can know whether both services were getting their information from the same service—in that trade, no rarity.

On one point, however, the report is unambiguous: Jean-Louis Jeanmaire 'never had access to top secret files.'

I last saw Jeanmaire on 16 January and mentioned to him that I had succeeded in tracking down Denissenko. He was living in Moscow, I said, but was presently in hospital with a liver ailment. I said I might visit him next time I was there. Jeanmaire seemed not to hear. He looked down; he peered round his kitchen. Finally, like a schoolboy who has been promised a treat, he gave me a radiant smile.

'Oh, you *are* lucky,' he said.

RICHARD RAYNER

LOS ANGELES

I live in a Spanish-style villa in Los Angeles, at the corner of Franklin and Grace, two blocks from Hollywood Boulevard and only one block from Yucca and Wilcox, known as 'crack alley'. One morning my girl-friend walked down into the garage beneath the building and found human excrement on the windscreen of our car. The excrement had not been thrown or carelessly daubed, but somehow painted in a perfect rectangle, thick, four feet by two. Someone had gone to a lot of trouble; from a distance the excrement looked like a nasty modern painting; it also smelled powerfully and took over an hour to wash and scrape off. 'Why didn't they just steal the fucking car?' she said. I did my best to be urbane about another unpleasant reminder of the nature of our neighbourhood. The homeless, I told her, couldn't afford the gas, and the homeboys wouldn't be seen dead in a Volvo; they preferred old Cadillacs and new BMWs, white, loaded with extras.

Several times during the past year I'd watched from my study window as officers of the Los Angeles Police Department staged elaborate busts on the streets. The officers, always white, wore sun-glasses and had Zapata moustaches and carried shotguns or had handguns strapped to their thighs. A car was surrounded and stopped. The suspects, always black, usually young, often well-dressed, were dragged out and made to lie on the ground. They were cuffed with plastic thongs that, from a distance, looked like the tags with which I closed up bags of rubbish. Then they were searched and made to kneel, one on this side of the street, one on the other, while the officers talked among themselves or, swaggering to and fro, conducted an ad hoc interrogation: 'Shut the fuck up and don't move,' I heard on one occasion. 'Feel clever now, black boy?' 'Be careful now, I'm in the mood to hit me a homer.' Every now and then a helicopter would appear, a roaring accompaniment to the scene's edgy surrealism. Sometimes my neighbours came out: an old lady who used to sit in her car, although she never drove it (that was what she did most mornings: she sat there, in her car, not driving it); a long-haired heavy metal musician; a blonde from Texas, pretty, but probably not pretty enough to make it in the movies; a black one-time boxer whose presence was always a comfort. They watched without any sign of animation—it was all fairly routine —and after fifteen minutes or so the suspects were driven away in the back of a black and white police car, known to the officers as 'a black and normal' ever since police chief Daryl Gates said that the reason why so many blacks died from the carotid chokehold —the controversial technique once used to detain suspects—was that 'their veins and arteries do not open up as fast as they do on normal people.'

I was surprised, not by the fact that this was happening in my neighbourhood, but by the fact that the people of my neighbourhood accepted it all with such indifference. There was, it was apparent, nothing remarkable about the behaviour of the LAPD, which was seen less as a police force than an army at war, a perception encouraged by the department's chief. Gates referred to black drug dealers as 'Viet Cong'. He told a Senate Committee that even casual drug users 'ought to be taken out and shot.' And part of his strategy, Gates said on another occasion, 'is to put a lot of police officers on the street and harass people and make arrests for inconsequential kinds of things.' Gates was known to model his police department on the US Marines; its stated aims were to be fast, mobile and extremely aggressive.

'You're *supposed* to be frightened of the LAPD,' a friend told me. 'The question is why you live in the neighbourhood you do.'

My apartment, I explained, was a particularly beautiful piece of history, designed and built in the 1920s by the movie director Cecil B. De Mille.

'Are you insane?' my friend said. 'Move somewhere else, move away from that shit, move to the Westside,' by which he meant a small rectangle within the new 310 area telephone code: west of La Cienega Boulevard and north of the Santa Monica freeway. My friend stressed the borders: these weren't just streets; they were magical divides. By entering this area, I would be safe, secure and white. Hispanics would be the people who didn't speak English; they would clean the house and clip the lawn, then get on the RTD and disappear back to the nether worlds of East and South Los Angeles. And blacks wouldn't exist at all, unless they wore Armani and worked at CAA.

Seeing a black in Los Angeles, I had come to realize, wasn't the same experience as seeing a black in New York. I found myself making categories. There were the smart professional blacks—lawyers, entertainers, film-industry schmoozers. These I greeted with a smiling 'Ciao!' There were middle-class blacks, who ran businesses and owned property in more or less exclusively black and Hispanic areas—Inglewood, Compton, Crenshaw. These I knew about but never met: our worlds didn't intersect. There were the bums on Hollywood Boulevard, asking for a quarter or shouting their rage among the tourists, the runaways, the hustlers and hookers, the followers of L. Ron Hubbard and his Scientology Church. These it was safe to ignore. And then there were the homeboys, the gang-bangers, who pulled up alongside at a stop-light, or ran whooping through the aisles of smart movie theatres in Westwood and Century City, or strutted along that same stretch of Hollywood Boulevard in Nike Air Jordans, baggy shorts, Gucci T-shirts and baseball caps with an X on the front. Perhaps they really were in a gang, perhaps not, but they behaved with an anger, an arrogance, an aura of fearlessness that suggested they might be. With them, I was the one who became non-existent. Staring straight ahead, I would quicken my step, but not enough to attract attention, and was most comfortable if I happened to be wearing sun-glasses, so that no eye contact was possible. I would hold my breath. I would be invisible.

I knew that my fear was out of all proportion to the true nature of the threat, but, like the earthquake that must happen eventually, the black street gangs of South Los Angeles were a part of the city's apocalyptic demonology. They were armed with Uzis and AK-47s and even rocket launchers, killing each other, and sometimes innocent bystanders, not just for money or 'turf', but for wearing the wrong colour of shoelace or baseball cap. There were said to be as many as 100,000 hard core gang members. Their tags were sprayed on the wall of our building and on the sidewalk outside, an indecipherable crossword, a labyrinth of black paint on white concrete that our Mexican gardener washed away with Chlorox and whitewash. A few days later the crossword was always back.

So it was: don't go here, don't go there, lock the car doors, never spend more time than you have to in parking lots, avoid eye contact on the freeway. This wasn't *just* paranoia. One Friday night I happened to glance at an old Cadillac Coupe de Ville cruising alongside us on the Hollywood freeway. I saw a black kid hand a gun to a friend in the back, not even looking, passing the gun over his shoulder as casually as if it were a pack of cigarettes. So it was: don't go south of Wilshire, here's a homeboy, here's a cop car, a black and white, a black and *normal.* Good. The police spoke about perimeters and containment and points of control. They spoke about South-Central as if it were a township.

Los Angeles was a lot like South Africa. The apartheid wasn't enshrined by law, but by economics and geography, and it was just as powerful. In Los Angeles I was afraid of blacks in a way I had never been. I behaved in a way that would have disgusted me in New York or London. I was a racist.

The Taser stun gun was introduced by the LAPD in 1980, and it was used against Rodney King, the black motorist whom LAPD officers Lawrence Powell, Ted Briseno, Timothy Wind and Sergeant Stacey Koon were accused of unlawfully beating shortly after midnight on 3 March 1991. Despite all that had been written about the incident, I had read very little about the operation of the Taser. It was, I discovered, a weird-looking device, a crude, chunky grey pistol which fired darts into people. The darts were attached to wires, which on pushing a button administered a shock of 50,000 volts. 'Seems to cool off most people pretty good,' said a representative of Ray's Guns of Hollywood. It had been used more and more to restrain suspects following the banning of the carotid chokehold in 1984.

Rodney King was stopped after a high speed pursuit, first on the Foothill freeway, and then on the streets of Pacoima, during which he drove at speeds in excess of 100 miles per hour and ignored a number of red lights. The initial pursuit was made by Melanie and Timothy Singer, a husband and wife team of the

California Highway Patrol, but when LAPD cars arrived on the scene it was Sergeant Stacey Koon who took charge. As Koon notes in an as yet unpublished autobiography, he looked at the petite Melanie Singer and then at the six foot three inch, 225-pound Rodney King (who, according to Koon, had dropped his trousers and was waving his buttocks in the air), and decided that this was about to develop into 'a Mandingo type sex encounter,' a reference to a Hollywood movie which involves black slaves raping white women.

Koon used his Taser stun gun, firing two darts into Rodney King and giving him two shocks. One was enough to subdue most suspects and even the Mandingo Rodney King himself was on the ground by now, showing little sign of resistance. Koon and the three other officers then kicked him and hit him fifty-six times with their batons, breaking his ankle, his cheek-bone and causing eleven fractures at the base of his skull, as well as concussion and nerve damage to the face. The force of the blows knocked fillings from his teeth.

The last of the not-guilty verdicts was announced in Simi Valley at three forty-five p.m. on Wednesday, 29 April 1992. As Stacey Koon left the court-house, it was declared that he had hired an entertainment attorney to sell the movie and book rights to his story, which would be titled *The Ides of March*, since he had been indicted on 15 March of the previous year.

After the verdict, I went to the Mayfair Market, to a bookstore, to a bar on Franklin. People were nervous, excited. Something was going to happen in South-Central; the question was how bad it would be. When I got home, the phone was ringing. Crowds had gathered downtown at the Parker Center, LAPD headquarters. A police car had been turned over. Looting was said to have started in other places, though the moment when the riots began in earnest was easy to spot: it was broadcast live on TV.

At six-thirty p.m., Reginald Denny stopped at a traffic-light at the intersection of Florence and Normandie. He was on his way to deliver twenty-seven tons of sand to a cement-mixing plant in Inglewood. Denny, thirty-six, would have been driving through South-Central to avoid the rush-hour traffic on the freeways. It was the territory of the Eight-Trey Gangster Crips, one of the city's most famous gangs. While waiting for the light to change, he was pulled from his rig by five or six black youths. Two news helicopters were overhead, watching the crowd which had been gathering since the verdict was announced, and the incident turned into an uncanny mirror-image of the Rodney King beating, though where the King video had been dim and murky, captured by an onlooker from his balcony with a newly acquired Sony camcorder (a few days earlier, on the same tape, he'd bagged Arnold Schwarzenegger, filming a scene from *Terminator 2* in a nearby bar), what I saw now was shot by professionals—the camera zooming in and out, the images well-defined and horribly colourful.

Denny was kneeling in the middle of the street, now empty. Two blacks entered the frame and beat Denny's head with their fists and then kicked him. Another black raised his arms and hurled the truck's fire-extinguisher, hitting Denny on the side of his head, which lurched from the impact. Denny tried to move and rolled on to his side. The helicopter circled for a better angle. You could now see how Denny's white T-shirt, which had slid up his belly, was saturated with blood. A black appeared briefly, smashing what appeared to be a lamp-base over Denny's head. He collapsed again. Another black appeared: this one was holding a shotgun at arm's length, very casual, and shot Denny in the leg. A black was wheeling a bicycle in the background. A black ran up, leaped athletically in the air and kicked him in the head. Denny tried to stand up. The right side of his face was a mess of red, as if it were melting. A black hit him with a tyre-iron; Denny went down. A black hit him with a beer bottle and then raised his arms in triumph. Another black appeared, went through Denny's left pocket, right pocket, back pocket and then ran away with his wallet. A black in baggy shorts stepped up and kicked Denny in the head and danced away on one leg very slowly.

It happened in silence since the scene was filmed from a helicopter, but later I watched a video shot by an eyewitness —again the uncanny mirror image. In this one there was sound;

you could hear the voices: 'No mercy for the white man, no mercy for the white man.' It seemed to be choreographed and went on for a very long time—thirty minutes. Watching the Rodney King video, I had thought it reasonable for American blacks to hate the police and be suspicious of all whites. This didn't make me suspicious of these particular blacks; it made me want to kill them. If any of them had been in my power in that moment, as Reginald Denny was in theirs, I would have done it gladly. I actually saw myself with a gun in my hand. Pow. Pow. Pow.

A few feet from Reginald Denny's truck was Tom's Liquor and Deli; it was the first store looted. The first fire-call was received thirty minutes later at seven-thirty p.m. Forty-five minutes later was the first fatality, Louis Watson, thirty-two blocks and three miles (a distance which in Manhattan takes you from Greenwich Village to Central Park) from where Denny's truck had been, yet still in the heart of South-Central. Watson, an eighteen-year-old black who had wanted to be an artist, was shot to death at Vernon and Vermont, hit by a stray bullet while waiting for a bus.

The TV showed a fire, then another and still more. Soon there were so many that fires normally requiring ten trucks were dealt with by one. A fire captain was threatened with an AK-47 to the head by a gang-banger called 'Psycho'. Another fireman was shot in the throat, and more people began to die, a lot more people. Dwight Taylor, forty-two, was shot to death at 446 Martin Luther King Boulevard. He had been on his way to buy milk. Arturo Miranda, twenty, was shot to death in his car on the way back from soccer practice. Edward Travens, a fifteen-year-old white youth, was shot to death in a drive-by attack in the San Fernando Valley. Patrick Bettan, a white security guard, was shot to death in a Korean supermarket at 2740 W. Olympic. But the dead were mostly black. Two unnamed blacks were shot to death in a gun battle with the LAPD at the Nickerson Gardens Housing Project. A robber shot to death at Century and Van Ness. *Shot to death*: the phrase itself had a velocity, a connectedness to the violence it described, that even constant repetition couldn't reduce to TV babble. At ten-forty: Anthony Netherly, twenty-one, was shot to death at 78th and San Pedro. At eleven-fifteen: Elbert Wilkins, thirty-three, was shot to death in a drive-by attack at 92nd and Western. Ernest Neal, twenty-seven, was shot to death in the same incident. Time unknown: an unknown black male shot to death at 10720 Buren Street. A man *of unknown race and age* was dead of 'riot-related injuries' at Daniel Freeman Memorial Hospital: what possible state was he found in?

Thirteen dead by the end of the night, 1,600 fire-calls, and in the moments when TV stations had nothing new to show, they always went back to Reginald Denny, a white man, for ever on his knees, being beaten. Outside, the choking, fried-plastic smell of the fires wafted across the city.

On Thursday morning people were wanting the riots to be over, hoping they were, believing that they had been a one-day affair. At nine-thirty the radio weatherman was still trying to be wacky. 'Our weather today calls for hazy sunshine. Let's change that,' he chortled, 'smoky sunshine.' If the riots were going to start again, I wanted to see them for myself, and I wanted to see them with a black, not, I'm afraid, because I thought I'd get a special insight (although that was the way it turned out), but because I knew I'd be safer. I called Jake, a black screenwriter. He had grown up in Los Angeles, in South-Central in fact, where his father had been a preacher, and he had gone to college in New York. He had only recently moved back. 'I've been talking to people, not just the gang-bangers, and they're saying they just ain't gonna take it. They've been resting a couple of hours, but it's all going to start up again.' Today, he predicted, the rioters and looters would march across the city. He said he'd pick me up soon.

Jake arrived by eleven and we drove down Normandie, a helicopter overhead, following us south.

Hispanic families stood in doorways, waiting. A street was taped off where a building had burned the previous night, and twice we were passed by LAPD cars, not moving singly, or even in pairs, but in groups of four and five. 'For safety,' said Jake.

'Those guys are nervous. The LAPD got burned last night.' He exchanged a fisted salute with the black driver of a Chevrolet. 'The way they left that guy there, at the intersection? The *po-lice*,' he said, as if it were the rock group he were talking about. 'The homies think they've got something on them *for ever*.'

A palm tree was on fire. Flames ran up from the base to the leaves above and seconds later the entire tree was ablaze. Five or six young black kids were running. For a moment I thought they were frightened, running away, and then I realized, of course, they'd set it alight. There was the sound of a gunshot, though it wasn't clear who had fired it; it seemed some way off.

But it was my first experience of the riot close at hand. I was afraid and began to babble. I explained to Jake that I hated gunfire. Americans were obsessed with guns. Before New Year the city authorities had found it necessary to place billboards all over Los Angeles, in English and Spanish, warning people not to fire their guns into the air at midnight. So lots of people fired their guns *into the ground*. Sometimes, lying in bed, or finishing dinner in our Cecil B. De Mille dining-room, with its wood beam ceiling and baronial stone fireplace, I heard shots outside the building. 'Car backfiring again,' I'd say, and my girl-friend would roll her eyes.

'I'm the sort of person,' I told Jake, 'who lies awake in bed thinking someone's about to break in and slit my throat.' No doubt I'd be like that if I lived in the Cotswolds or on the Isle of Skye. Unfortunately I lived in a neighbourhood where corpses were found stuffed into our garbage bins or decomposing in closets in nearby apartments. These stories never made it into the *Los Angeles Times*.

'Move to the Westside,' said Jake, and I presumed he was joking, though I remembered the first time he'd visited our apartment when he walked around checking the locks; then he'd gone around the block and advised us not to walk on Yucca.

Jake wasn't joking. 'You can afford to move away. Move the fuck away,' he said. 'What's your problem?' He'd been living down at the ocean in Santa Monica since returning from New York. He said, 'You live in a marginal neighbourhood, so it's real for you, because you know it's there, but at the same time it's not real, it's just this big bad boogie thing you glimpse from time to time.' The 'it' he was talking about was violence. 'But it's never reached out and really hurt you.'

I agreed; I was lucky.

'I was lucky too. I grew up in a bad neighbourhood. Guys I went to school with are in jail now, or long dead, or crippled in wheelchairs, or have had twelve feet of intestine ripped out by a gunshot.'

On Vermont we passed a furniture store, burnt out and still smoking, and then a mini-mall from which people were running with armloads of loot, or calmly wheeling laden checkout trolleys. It seemed extraordinary that traffic was moving about quite normally at these places, and that these events were visible as we cruised about, snug inside Jake's Honda with the radio and air-conditioning on. We drove past a Blockbuster video store—its window already smashed—as two police officers struggled to cuff a black who was kicking out at them from the ground. Three black kids were getting out of a white Toyota that had just driven up. They walked past the black on the ground and the two officers trying to hold him there, entered the shop and started filling up their arms with videos.

I wanted to say, this is it, we're really in the riot now, it's starting up again, but Jake was so casual about it all. He said that these kids had no hope of getting out as he had. Everything about society told them they were worthless, non-people. They had nothing, so they had nothing to lose, something I'd hear a lot of blacks say over the next days.

We drove east on Pico, past blocks that were quiet, then past blocks where crowds had gathered in anticipation of something happening, and then, once again, past blocks where something *was* happening already. There was a mob inside a Payless shoe store and a black kid, very young, emerged running with two boxes, stopped for a moment, then sat down in the parking lot to try the shoes on. There was a Vons supermarket that Jake had passed some hours before, while it was being looted, which was now on fire, flames leaping through the roof, a fire-truck yet to arrive.

Jake said, 'Sometimes they do it at the same time, other

times they clean it out and come back hours later and burn it then. Keeps the cops on their toes.'

I nodded, as if to say, yes, I could see the logic of that. Two Hispanic youths appeared, casually wheeling a piano around a corner. I was beginning to get a sense of the sheer scale of what was going on. It was huge. The radio was announcing a curfew. After sundown tonight people on the streets anywhere in Los Angeles would be stopped and questioned. The National Guard was on its way, and 2,400 federal troops, veterans of the Gulf war, were set to follow.

'Hubba, hubba,' said Jake.

By one o'clock we were looping back to the east. We came up to 3rd and Vermont. There was a big crowd and a fire in the distance, and now another one, closer, but just starting, and to my left, a column of thick black smoke which made my eyes water and got into my throat almost at once. I began to cough. Twenty or so young men of various races, not running and not walking either, but hurrying as if towards a very serious appointment, crossed the street and kicked down the door of a toy shop. The Korean owner stood by, offering no resistance, shaking his head. On the other side of the intersection three black looters were running, away from the Unocal station, lugging cans of oil in either hand. I didn't need a diagram to figure out what they were going to do with the cans. A hydrant was shooting a plume of water high into the air. At the Thrifty Drug Store, there was a line of people waiting to enter through a door, its glass smashed out, while others made their way out with plastic bags or trolleys filled with stolen goods. A man kicked some glass aside and emerged leaning backwards like in a Monty Python silly walk, his cradled arms piled so high with white and brown boxes that I couldn't see his face.

The traffic lights were out at the intersection. Making a left turn, not a simple exercise at the best of times in Los Angeles, was now a game of chicken, with fire trucks speeding up the hill and drivers nosing forward anxiously, or stopping and then making perilous surges across the intersection, windows open. A mouth and a yellow baseball cap in a Ford truck was yelling: 'MOTHERFUCKER.' The TV hadn't prepared me for the deafening noise of the riot—breaking glass, engines, sirens, smashing, shouting. Everyone was shouting. The noise of the riot was a shape, and it approached and receded like a wave, surging this way and that.

There was another thing: a lot of people had guns, in the waistbands of their trousers or even in their hands. They weren't firing the guns, they merely had them, but that was frightening enough. In England people don't carry guns.

Patrol cars must have pulled up, because there was now an LAPD sergeant shouting commands, and a line of officers— perhaps fifteen in all—was forming at the far end of the Thrifty Drug Store parking lot. The sudden phalanx of officers had no effect on the looters, and, as it advanced, they tended merely to drift into the next store. One sprinted straight at the police line, yelling, and then swerved off at the last moment, jumping over the low wall of the parking lot. A looter stopped to say cheese for a cameraman wearing a flak jacket. Another, a bearded black in a long white T-shirt, and with a cigarette in his mouth, was pointing to his penis, inviting the officers to suck it. The phalanx of police advanced a few steps further; they began beating on their riot shields with their batons.

A kid stepped up and hurled a rock into the street. I didn't see if anyone was hit. The kid threw another rock, launching it from low behind his back as if it were a javelin. Suddenly there were lots of kids, all of them throwing rocks, and then more police cars, coming up behind the phalanx. Jake said in his view the situation was about to get nasty.

In my view the situation had gone some way beyond that. This wasn't at all like the quite pleasurable thrill of fear I'd felt at first. I was terrified. A young black, a teenager, stopped in the middle of the street with a bottle of Budweiser which he was getting ready to throw at a car, ours. The bottle was nearly full. He stared at me, saw I was white, glanced at Jake, saw he was black, and made an obvious calculation. He ran on.

It was about two o'clock when Jake dropped me home. I didn't go out again until the early evening. I made a Waldorf salad, thinking: Now I'm making a Waldorf salad. It seemed a startling way to be carrying on. I had to force myself to eat it. The radio said that a fire was being set every three minutes. That night's performance of *The Phantom of the Opera* at the Amundsen Theatre was cancelled; for some reason this piece of information was repeated over and over again. An interview with an analyst from Harvard was cut abruptly short for another repeat of the crucial *Phantom* announcement, and then it was back to the Harvard man, who was interrupted again, but this time for news of yet another fire and looting.

On TV, Tom Bradley, LA's black mayor, appeared, calling for calm. As he spoke, the screen was split, one half showing a respectable black man urging restraint, the other showing the looting of a clothing store. Mayor Bradley urged everyone to stay at home and watch the final episode of *The Cosby Show* that night; perhaps that would help us solve our problems, he suggested. Then Pete Wilson, the Governor of California, quoted Martin Luther King. His face wasn't shown, but King's words, spoken by Wilson in a slow and sanctimonious tone, were used as the soundtrack as hundreds of black youths rampaged through a mini-mall.

A friend called, a little hysterical, having been trapped in a gridlock for over an hour at Century City. It was like a scene from a Godzilla movie, she said, with Westsiders heading for hotels in Santa Barbara and San Diego, leaving the city in droves. She often had trouble because of her very blonde hair; it gave her the appearance of a Nazi, she said, and homeboys sometimes took exception. She explained all this as if it were no more remarkable a fact of her life than having a mole on her cheek. She was from Sweden and nothing about America surprised her. She'd been on Olympic when someone threw a rock through the passenger window of her car with such velocity that it passed directly in front of her face and then shattered the window on the driver's side. She'd held the steering-wheel so tight on the way home that her arms were still trembling.

At six o'clock on the Thursday night, my girl-friend and I drove to the hills above Silver Lake. I wanted the view. A smart Korean gentleman in his early forties was

413

watching as well. He had on a blue silk shirt and blue linen trousers, baggily cut, and his sun-glasses were by Oliver Peoples. He was a *very* smart Korean gentleman and he remarked with a world-weary air that he had a business in the mid-Wilshire district, right next door to the Sears building, which now appeared to be ablaze. He wasn't going to defend it, though he knew some of his countrymen had armed themselves with shotguns and machine-guns in Koreatown. But they were shopkeeepers and he—he shrugged, a little apologetically—was not a shopkeeper. 'Nor am I Clint Eastwood,' he said. 'I pay America lots and lots of taxes so I don't have to be.'

I asked what line of business he was in.

'I have a gallery,' he said. 'You're English?'

'That's right.'

'Two foreigners together,' he said. 'And here we are, watching Los Angeles burn.' He smiled, revealing his teeth, very white and even. Ah me, he seemed to be saying, the wicked, wicked way of the world.

On a clear day I'd seen the ocean from here, but not this evening; the entire Los Angeles basin was covered in a thick grey haze. The twin towers of Century City, a little more than halfway to the sea, were invisible, and looking south and east, the sky was darker still. Black smoke indicated fires that were out of control; white smoke, those that were now contained. The sound of sirens came from all over, and there was a convoy of army vehicles on the Hollywood freeway.

I said, 'Do you think they'll ever feel the same about the city again?'

He asked, 'Who?'

'The rich.'

'The rich?' he said and laughed, a sudden explosion. 'The *rich*?' He found this very amusing. 'Oh my dear, you're so naïve. They might feel guilty for a day or two. Some of them might even be panicked into leaving, for good I mean, for Paris or London or Seattle, not just getting the children into the buggy and high-tailing it for the Sierras. The rest will pull the wagons in even tighter than before. Watch those security bills soar!'

We were on the way back from Silver Lake, driving down Sunset towards a sun that was in fact setting, when I realized that the looting had got very close to my home. I'd been expecting it all day, and I felt a thrill as I saw a pair of homeboys, shouting and jumping, dodging among the cars on Sunset, their arms full of bandannas and Ray-Bans and studded leather jackets, looted, I presumed, from L. A. Roxx, a store which pulled in tourists from the Midwest, relieved them of a couple of hundred dollars and sent them away looking like clones of the whitebread rockers Guns 'n' Roses. I wondered how the homeboys would manage to dispose of all *that* in South-Central.

I didn't know why, but I felt a little proud. The riot had reached my neighbourhood.

This time I was determined not to be such a wuss. I got out of the car at Highland and walked east along Hollywood. There were people running towards me. There was a small boy, he couldn't have been more than seven years old, with two cartons of Marlboro tucked under his arm; a middle-aged white woman was clutching a beat-box still in its box, saying as if she couldn't quite believe it, 'For free.'

A photographer stood beneath the awning of the Ritz Cinema, shooting down the street. 'It's a party now,' he said. 'It's carnival time.'

There was a big crowd between Cherokee and Whitley. They were the type of people I usually saw in the neighbourhood, which is to say tourists, teenagers from the Midwest who still dressed like punks, some kids, a few homeboys, even a few young middle-class types in suits. There was a balding fellow who worked in the Hollywood Book City bookstore. They had all gathered round to watch a very bewildered police officer.

The back of a car was hooked to the steel protective shutter in front of an electronic appliance store. The driver was black, about twenty, with a scrubby beard and a woollen hat. The oblong badge on the officer's chest said: *Barraja*. Officer Barraja wore a helmet with the visor down and sun-glasses behind it. In any other circumstances, we would all have been very frightened of Officer Barraja. But the moment he walked forward and aimed his shotgun at the head of the driver, I knew, and the crowd

knew and the bearded man certainly knew that Officer Barraja
had put himself in an absurd situation; I knew, the crowd knew
and the bearded man certainly knew that Officer Barraja would
not shoot. Officer Barraja did not know this yet; he learned it a
few moments later when the bearded driver turned and grinned
and, gunning his engine, then accelerated until the protective
shutter gave way with a groan. Officer Barraja stepped back and
shouldered his weapon and then: did nothing. People were
hooting and clapping. Someone paused to take his picture.
Outside the electronics store a queue was forming, as the people
in front ducked through the wrecked fence and stepped inside.

The swap-meet was on fire at the corner of Wilcox, making
my eyes smart again, sirens in the distance. I had an exhilarating
sense of chaos. I wondered what was going to happen next, when
up ahead I spotted a black teenager smashing the door of
Frederick's of Hollywood with a hammer. Another pitched a
chair and then climbed through the shattered window into the
display. Alarm bells sounded, and the crowd, my neighbourhood
crowd, responded as though to an invitation, and so I went along
as well, not trying to resist as I was almost lifted off my feet in
the dense mass of bodies that suddenly crushed forward. I had
somehow become part of a mob about to loot and trash what
passed in Hollywood for a landmark: a lingerie store.

Someone found a switch and turned on the lights.
Frederick's was classier than I'd imagined. The floor was slippery
marble tile. The lingerie was red and pink and emerald green, as
well as black and white, and each piece had its own hanger, its
own place in the spacious arrangement of spinners and wall
racks.

No one but me appeared to be admiring it. A girl ran to the
far corner of the store, ahead of the pack, earning herself just
enough time to be a little selective, as she lifted down hangers one
by one. A fat lady in white appeared at the back, pushing,
shouting at a man, 'Let's go, let's go.' She, along with the others
crushing in behind her, were panicking at the prospect of having
arrived too late. The members of this new lot had a strangely
fixed expression, concerned perhaps that everything had gone,
and were determined to make up for lost time. Broken glass

crunched under my feet. Someone had found a ladder and was carefully prising loose an imitation art-deco light fixture. There was no anger or fear; just bedlam. A black teenager in a T-shirt with a big cross around his neck made for the door with a mannequin under his arm. Pieces of other mannequins, stripped and smashed, were lying in the window display. The fat lady in white was on her hands and knees, her broad butt swinging in the air, as she rushed to fill up a suitcase. The suitcase had price-tags; she'd just taken it from somewhere else. She looked at me, a round, chubby face, and smiled, nodding, a gesture that I'm sure was supposed to say to me: *Go on.* I wasn't sure how to behave. I must have looked a little odd, standing there. I fingered some silky stuff.

'Hi!' someone shouted. Not at me, I assumed, but then it came again: 'Hi, Richard.' It was the not-quite-pretty-enough Texan from the building next to mine, on her way from something called the Lingerie Museum at the back of the store. She picked up an intricate lace bra. 'What do you think?' she said, and, without waiting for my reply, folded the bra carefully inside her black leather duffel bag. 'I'm having a ball,' she said, though she was disappointed that the Madonna bustier—the prize exhibit of the Lingerie Museum—had gone before she got to it; there'd been quite a race. She could have got a leather bra belonging to the pop star Belinda Carlisle, but she didn't care for that sort of music and, in any case, 'Definitely a D-cup.' She had the same pouty expression I'd seen on her face once before, when a producer of violent action films had brought her home one morning and ridden off on his Harley-Davidson, leaving her without so much as a kiss.

Frederick's, five minutes after being broken into, was picked bare.

A block and a half away, back up on Grace Avenue, a man was wetting the roof of our building with a hose in case somebody set fire to it. Some of our other neighbours were out on the street. They'd formed a vigilante committee, they said.

But of course, I replied, a little dazed, why not? I felt like

Bertie Wooster. A fat man I'd never seen before wore a baseball cap that said FUCK EVERYBODY.

The black ex-boxer said, 'This town is lost, man. This town is so *lost*.'

The heavy metal musician, standing nearby, opened his jacket to reveal an Ozzie Osbourne T-shirt and, stuffed inside the waistband of his jeans, a gun. 'Browning automatic,' he said proudly. It turned out he was English too.

'Oh, my God,' said my girl-friend. This fellow didn't look like he should be let loose with a water-pistol. Was I the only person in Los Angeles who *didn't* have a gun?

'I was in the Falklands, man,' said the heavy metal musician. 'I've seen this kind of stuff before. Let 'em come.'

'Let them not,' said the ex-boxer. 'I can't afford to move again. I've been moved too many times.'

I wondered what he meant by 'been moved', but then it was the heavy metal musician again, saying, 'The curfew's in force already so you folks had better go home now, OK?' It struck me that he was a strange authority figure. Had he really been in the Falklands? Everything was so extraordinary now I could almost believe he was for real. He walked towards the corner, not without a certain John Wayne swagger. 'You all take care now. OK?'

Nine-thirty, Thursday night, and the death toll was up to thirty. Howard Epstein shot to death at 7th and Slauson. Jose L. Garcia shot to death at Fresno and Atlantic. Matthew Haines pulled off his motorcycle and shot to death in Long Beach. Eduardo Vela shot to death at 5142 W. Slauson. Some of the dead were very young. Fourteen, fifteen. Keven Evanahen died while trying to put out a fire in a cheque-cashing store at Braddock and Inglewood. At least that made for variety. I blinked and shook my head as soon as that thought popped out. I'd been amazed by the riot, thrilled by it, swept along by it, terrified by it. It wasn't just that events had moved at such speed; the actual nature of what had occurred seemed to be shifting all the time. The riot had started with a particular angry focus: race. It had turned quickly into a poverty riot and then, diffused, became interracial anarchy. I wasn't sure what I'd seen, but I felt

changed. Los Angeles itself seemed more tangible, now that
everyone, even the players themselves, would have to
acknowledge that there was more to the city than the make-
believe Medici court of the movie business.

The Gap was being looted on Melrose.

The TV news was replaying a bulletin from earlier in the
day. At 3rd and Vermont an unknown Latino had been shot with
his own gun and was lying dead in the back of his car. No
ambulance had been able to get there. This was the very
intersection where I'd been with Jake. The reporter, talking to
camera, was trying to describe the situation, while black
teenagers milled around behind him, clowning it up. At last the
reporter gave up. 'There's a dead person here and it's a big joke.
Back to you at the studio.'

At midnight we went for a drive. Hollywood Boulevard was
blocked off by National Guardsmen in combat fatigues—they
were on every corner—so we got on to the Hollywood freeway.
Even at his hour, the freeway was normally crowded; now it was
deserted. Los Angeles had become another city. We headed south
and just as we were passing L. Ron Hubbard's Church of
Scientology Celebrity Center, a police car came up alongside. A
voice came through the patrol car's loudspeaker. '*A curfew is in
force. You are breaking the law. Go home. Get off the streets. You
are breaking the law.*'

In the middle of the afternoon on Friday, it became clear that
it was probably over, and, curiously, there was a sense not of
relief but of disappointed expectation: people wanted more.
The rioting had become an entertainment. Announcers at KWIB
—news twenty-four hours a day, all day, give us twenty minutes
and we give you the world—actually apologized for the fact that
the station was now returning to its true obsession, sport, and it
occurred to me that during the time of the riot the city had
gathered round a spectacle, as it might during the Super Bowl.

I wanted to see the damage where it had been worst, in
South-Central, so I went to see Beverley, a black school-teacher I
had recently been introduced to. I was cadging a ride with blacks
again, this time so that I wouldn't feel threatened while I looked

at their burnt-out neighbourhoods.

We started off on Vermont, heading towards South-Central. Straight away Beverley's eleven-year-old daughter Maya declared that she was thirsty, so I said I'd keep my eyes peeled for a store still standing to buy her a soda. The task turned out not to be so easy.

'Burned,' said Beverley, pointing to one store, and then to another. 'Razed . . . Looted and burned. See that cheque store over there? Korean-owned, looted and burned.' Above it was a bright green sign, still intact: INSTANT CASH. On top of the sign stood a National Guardsman with his assault rifle.

'Burned,' she said, as we continued on our quest. 'Levelled to the ground.' Delicatessens, liquor stores, furniture stores, a Fedco warehouse where six hundred workers had turned up and found, literally, no job to go to—building after building was burned. Before the riots, there was one store for every 415 residents, less than half the Los Angeles average. That ratio looked pretty good now. On some stores metal cutters had been used. Solid steel shutters had perfect triangles cut into them, like cans popped with an opener. At the intersection of Vernon and Central all four corners had been wiped out.

'Burned, burned, burned, burned. That's the deli where Latasha Harlins was killed,' Beverley said, pointing to the store whose Korean owner Soon Ja Du had been fined $500 for shooting dead a fifteen-year-old black girl in a dispute over a $1.79 bottle of orange juice. It was one of the first stores attacked (nearly 1,000 Korean businesses were destroyed, I would learn later). 'Homies,' Beverley continued, 'tried to burn that deli three times, but they were ready. Not open now, of course.' In the Watts riots of 1965 many Jewish businesses had been burned in South Los Angeles, and the Jews had left the neighbourhood for good; this time the Koreans had been a target. Yet here, ironically, a BLACK OWNED sign had been a less effective guarantee of safety than in other areas of the city, because the destruction had been so general. 'See that furniture store over there? A black family ran that for twenty-five years. Razed. Look at the job they did there, that was a liquor store, burned to the ground, Korean owned.'

Beverley had been ten in 1965. 'This was much worse,' she said. 'Spread further and faster. More people died. The abuses that people reacted to in 'sixty-five were just the same—police abuse, economic discrimination, lack of jobs, but those riots were about hope. We had hope then. Gone now.' It had taken twenty years to get a shopping centre built in Watts after 1965. How long would it take to recover from this?

There was graffiti everywhere, on the remains of the buildings that had been burned, on the walls of every one that was still standing:

FUCK THE POLICE
FUCK WHITE PEOPLE
FUCK LAPD
FUCK GATES
FUCK THE LAW
POLICE KILLA
FUCK WHITIES
FUCK THE LAW
FUCK WHITEBOYS
NO JUSTICE, NO PEACE
GATES KILLA
BLOODS 'N' CRIPS TOGETHER FOR EVER
POLICE 187

And then: THIS IS SOUTH-CENTRAL.

When I'd first spent time in Los Angeles in the mid-1980s, I'd had no more thought of coming here than to the moon, though I did go with friends to the Los Angeles Coliseum or the Forum, sports arenas close enough to make us very careful about planning the way back to the freeway. Turn a corner, I'd thought, and there I'd be, with bad street lighting and people dreaming of doing me damage. For me South-Central hadn't been just a small, bad neighbourhood of the sort that existed in any city; it had been a very big bad neighbourhood the size of a small city, and it had existed in my mind not as a real place—with stop-lights and movie theatres and stores on the corner—but as a black hole stretching from downtown to Long Beach. I was ashamed of that. It seemed quite possible, now that South-Central had had the effrontery to impose itself on the rest of the city, that the rest of the city would respond by turning it into an even grimmer ghetto.

'Security Pacific Bank, burned, razed to the ground,' said Beverley. 'Burning a corner store, that's one thing. But to get into a bank and leave nothing except the empty safe still standing at the back. That takes dedication.'

Beverley's daughter Maya reminded me that she was still thirsty, and Beverley said there was a 7-Eleven over on the edge of Inglewood. The rioting hadn't been so bad there, and we drove for another ten minutes only to find another destroyed building. 'Looted,' said Beverley. 'Burned *to the ground*.' She began to laugh, and it did seem funny all of a sudden; we'd spent forty-five minutes driving through the geographical centre of America's second largest city, and we'd been unable to buy a Coca-Cola.

I had never seen Simi Valley, the town where the four officers had been found not guilty of beating Rodney King and from where, every morning, more than 2,000 LAPD officers, county sheriffs and other law-enforcement personnel commuted to their jobs in distant Los Angeles. I wanted to make the journey myself. My girl-friend and I drove there from South-Central.

The journey took us about an hour; in traffic, it could take two hours: the Harbour freeway to the Hollywood freeway, short stretches of the Ventura and San Diego freeways and the bland sprawl of the San Fernando Valley. It was on our last freeway, the Simi Valley, that the landscape changed. This had all been part of Southern California's ranch country; its nineteenth-century history concerned trails and horses and men who did what men had to do. But now housing estates could be seen on most hillsides, and freeway exit ramps were marked CONSTRUCTION VEHICLES ONLY, where new dormitory suburbs were being built. It was like a passage between continents.

At the far end of Los Angeles Avenue, there was a sale of 'recreational vehicles', where a short man called Ted said that, while he had been shocked by the verdicts, and horrified by the riots, this was all good news for him. He was a real estate agent. He predicted a boom in Simi Valley, and indeed throughout the whole of Ventura County, as more and more fled black street crime and the Dickensian hell of Los Angeles. 'You know the worst thing about the looting all those niggers did down there?' he asked. '*They couldn't afford it.*' Ted paused. 'Just kidding,' he said.

We drove through the city. Los Angeles Avenue itself consisted of shopping malls: Simi Valley Plaza, Mountain Gate Plaza, Madre Plaza, the Westgate Center. In these plazas huge parking lots were surrounded by stores of all kinds. A cavernous home improvement centre issued the smell of wood. Everything else issued the smell of air-conditioning. You could buy things here: a new Ford, a taco, a garden hose, and ice-cream, an airline ticket to Lake Tahoe, a pair of jeans, a carton of frozen yoghurt, a CD player, a hair-cut, a chilli burger, a spade, a doughnut, a bag of enriched soil fertilizer, a vegetarian health sandwich, the *Simi Valley Advertiser*, a novel by Stephen King, a new tie, a bathing suit that dries in minutes, spark plugs, a suit for $250, a non-stick frying pan, a small plastic container of Anacin, the *New York Times*, a set of plastic poker chips. You could collect interest on your savings, wash your car or go bowling. You could buy beer, Gatorade and many different kinds of California Chardonnay. You could buy a Coca-Cola. I bought a Coca-Cola.

You could tell who lived in Simi Valley (they were white) and who worked there but lived elsewhere (they were Hispanic). We didn't see any blacks but we may not have stayed long enough. I'm sure there were blacks in Simi Valley.

At the East County court-house, where the King verdicts had been reached, I was confronted by a local resident, a middle-aged woman in a beige suit made of an indeterminate fabric. She smiled at me coldly.

'You're not from here, are you?'

'No,' I replied, a little surprised. Was I really so obvious? Perhaps I looked a little thin. Simi Valley seemed to be a place where fat people got fatter.

'I thought so,' she said. 'And you've come because of that Rodney King thing.'

I said yes.

'I don't feel guilty,' she said, answering a question I hadn't asked. 'I refuse to feel guilty. I did everything I could back in the sixties for those people. They just refused to make the most of their opportunities.'

'Why was that?'

'Oh, they're lazy,' she said. 'Those people are just plain lazy. 'Go back to Los Angeles,' she said, 'and take your issue with you. It has nothing to do with Simi Valley. Those people on the jury did the best job they could, and for you to assume that twelve white people can't hand down a fair verdict in a case like that, well, that's racist in itself, isn't it?'

She was right: if thinking that twelve people like her couldn't be relied upon to hand down a fair verdict was racist, then I was a racist. I hated her. I wanted to hurt her. I didn't want to argue or protest. I wanted her injured. I saw myself doing it. Pow. Pow. Pow.

We returned to Los Angeles.

The riots began on Wednesday, 29 April 1992. Monday, 4 May, was the first day—the first of many—that gun sales topped 2,000 in Southern California, twice the normal figure, a gun sale every forty seconds. By that Monday, this was the riot toll: 228 people had suffered critical injuries (second and third degree skin burns; blindness; gunshot wounds to the lung, stomach, neck, shoulder and limbs; knife wounds; life-threatening injuries from broken glass), and 2,383 people had suffered non-critical injuries (requiring hospital treatment); there were more than 7,000 fire emergency calls; 3,100 businesses were affected by burning or looting; 12,111 arrests. As this goes to press there are reports of 18,000 arrests. Fifty-eight people are dead.